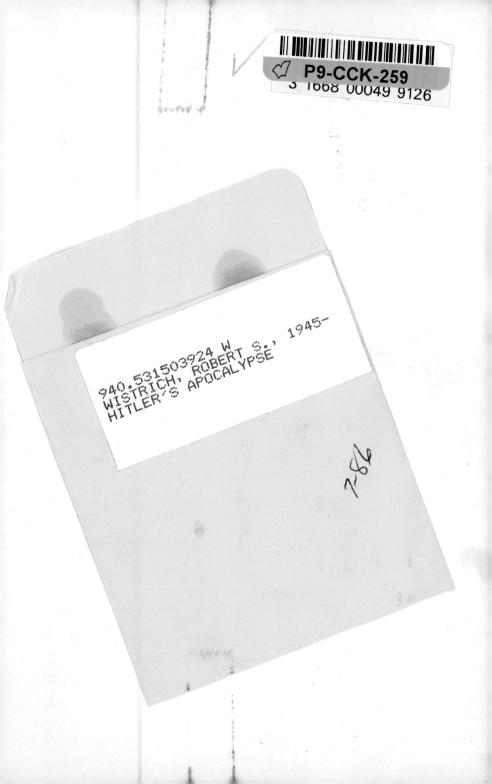

# HITLER'S
# APOCALYPSE

# HITLER'S APOCALYPSE

## JEWS AND
## THE NAZI LEGACY

## Robert Wistrich

St. Martin's Press
New York

Library of Congress Cataloging in Publication Data

Wistrich, Robert S., 1945–
  Hitler's apocalypse.

  1. Antisemitism—History—20th century.  2. Holocaust, Jewish (1939-1945)—Causes.  3. Hitler, Adolf, 1889-1945—Views on Jews.  4. Antisemitism—Arab countries.
5. Antisemitism—Soviet Union.  I. Title.
DS145.W55   1986        940.53′15′03924        85-27816
ISBN 0-312-38819-5

First published in Great Britain by George Weidenfeld & Nicolson Limited.

First U.S. Edition

10 9 8 7 6 5 4 3 2 1

# Contents

# Preface

'Every true history is contemporary history,' wrote the Italian neo-Hegelian philosopher, Benedetto Croce, over seventy years ago. The historian can only fully understand his material when he has relived or re-experienced the facts with which he must deal and integrated them in his consciousness. But that consciousness, as I understand Croce, is itself a reflection of the parameters of time and place in which the historian operates. It is our present which gives new meaning to the past even as we imaginatively seek to reconstruct it in its own terms. These methodological considerations seemed particularly applicable as I sat down in the summer of 1984 to complete this book. The year *Tashmad*, signifying 'Destruction' in the Hebrew language, had not yet drawn to its close, adding a further apocalyptic dimension to the nightmare vision of the English novelist George Orwell; the setting, Jerusalem, provided its own incomparable messianic hopes and prophetic warnings of doom. The country, Israel, ravaged by an inflation gradually approaching Weimar proportions, by internal political tensions, nagging anxieties and interminable disputes, rent by the maddening confusion and increasing futility of its involvement in Lebanon, supplied a different kind of stimulus. One could scarcely hope to isolate oneself completely from such external stimuli and pressures; yet the effort had to be made to somehow rise above the general mood of crisis and even despair, and to attempt a global analysis of the recent past which would place the last fifty years in a wholly new light.

The original idea out of which this book had arisen went back almost ten years to the time when I began working at the Institute of Contemporary History and the Wiener Library in London. Since 1975 I had become increasingly concerned by certain trends in Western Europe towards denying the Holocaust, by the resurgence of racism, and the increasingly hostile climate towards young Jews at British universities engendered by fashionable left-wing anti-Zionism. Having grown up in England, I was acutely aware from personal experience that anti-Jewish feeling, though generally of a mild and genteel variety, was far more widespread even in that liberal country than is often realized abroad. I also knew from my own studies and my parents' continental background (they had emigrated from Poland to France and then to England in 1948) that antisemitism had been an endemic feature of twentieth-century European history. During my post-graduate work, which led me to specialize in aspects of the 'Jewish' question in late nineteenth-century Germany and Austria and in subsequent research on the Holocaust, the nagging question of Nazism, its causes and consequences, was never far from my mind. Through the 1970s, moreover, my intuitive feeling that there was a historical connection which had never been seriously investigated between the Nazi legacy and the more sophisticated contemporary forms of anti-Zionist antisemitism with which I was immediately concerned began to crystallize into a firm conviction.

Following my arrival in Israel in October 1980 such questions became even more acute in my mind, while my own outlook gradually underwent a shift under the impact of a new environment and its challenges. This book is an attempt to resolve many of the unanswered questions arising out of my earlier research, concerning the nature of twentieth-century antisemitism, the causes and consequences of the Holocaust and the impact of the Nazi legacy on the post-war world.

The personality and politics of Adolf Hitler inevitably take up a major part of the first section of the book, not only because he was the most powerful antisemite in history and the architect of the Holocaust, but because the existing literature has in my view consistently misinterpreted and with a few honourable exceptions failed to understand the central importance of the 'Jewish question' in Hitler's ideology and in Nazi political behaviour. In the chapters that cover post-war developments I have largely had to plough virgin territory and hazard interpretations whose correctness perhaps only time can prove. But the evidence I have been able to marshal concerning the continuity of a radical and murderous antisemitism into the post-war era convinced me that we are dealing with a highly dangerous and fateful phenomenon which may possibly determine the future of our planet. Therefore it seemed to me a particularly urgent and important task to attempt the kind of bold synthesis of historical and contemporary materials set forth in this book.

I am grateful to my publisher Lord Weidenfeld for his confidence in my work, to my editor Robert Baldock for his patience and to Janet Lieber for typing the manuscript. My intellectual debts are amply indicated in the footnotes. I dedicate this work to my wife Danielle and my three children, Anna, Dov and Sonia, for their love, warmth and understanding during a difficult period which gave me the courage to complete this challenging task!

ROBERT WISTRICH
*Jerusalem*
*October 1984*

# HITLER'S APOCALYPSE

# Introduction

' "We were chosen to be the conscience of man," said the Jew. And I answered him, yes, I gentlemen, who now stand before you: "You are not man's conscience, Jew. You are only his bad conscience. And we shall vomit you so we may live and have peace. A final solution. How could there be any other?" '

These words of an aged but unrepentant Adolf Hitler, spoken on a London stage in February 1982 to his Israeli captors, form a kind of imaginary backdrop to the subject of this book. The perversely powerful, growling final speech of Hitler, dramatized from George Steiner's parodistic fantasy, *The Portage to San Cristobal of A.H.*, probably shocked many theatre-goers and upset others with its deliberately provocative, rhetorical questions. 'Perhaps I am the Messiah, the true Messiah whose infamous deeds were allowed by God in order to bring his family home. The Reich begat Israel – these are my last words.'

Dragged out of the bowels of the South American jungle, standing trial for his life, the old man in the stained trousers and torn coat turns into a defiant and angry accuser. The fictional Hitler raises embarrassing points which most historians generally prefer to avoid. For example, did the ancient Hebrew idea of the 'Chosen People' not contain within it the seeds of the Nazi doctrine of a *Herrenvolk*? Was the transcendent, imageless God of Judaism not a permanent thorn in the flesh of the Gentiles, who could only dream of destroying its standard-bearers? And most scandalously topical of all for a 1980s audience, was not Hitler himself the *godfather* of the Jewish state, the architect of a Holocaust which had given Israel 'the courage of injustice' to drive the Arabs from their homes and fields because they stood in Israel's 'divinely ordered way'.[1]

Unhistorical sophistry, no doubt. Certainly, by any objective standard, a caricature of Zionism and a cynical insult to the murdered six millions who might have contributed so much to the future Jewish state.[2] But the issues raised by Steiner's drama and, no less important, the intellectual climate out of which it arose, require much deeper analysis and need to be addressed on another level of argument. Hitler's last speech in his own defence distils in some respects the essence of Nazism and the antisemitic mythology it both

1

inherited and bequeathed to the post-war era. The aging Führer is obsessed by the 'secret power' of chosenness, by the singularity of the Jews, by the idea of setting apart the races under an iron law, until the end of time. Like the antisemites of every generation, he seeks to appropriate the 'chosenness' of the Jewish people and turns with ferocity against its original representatives. It is from the biblical Israelites that he claims to have learned his racist credo: 'That a people must be chosen to fulfil its destiny, that there can be no other thus made glorious. That a true nation is a mystery, a single body willed by God, by history, by the unmingled burning of its blood.'[3] Nazifying the Bible, Hitler turns the book of Joshua into a tractate on extermination and adds his own blasphemous gloss on Mosaic teaching: 'One Israel, One *Volk*, one leader.'[4] For this fictional Hitler is a humble pupil of the Jews. 'My racism was a parody of yours, a hungry imitation. What is a thousand-year *Reich* compared to the eternity of Zion? Perhaps I was the false Messiah sent before. Judge me and you must judge yourselves.'[5]

Why, then, a *final* solution? What did the Germans have to fear from the powerless, stateless, dispersed Jewish people? How many divisions did the Jews possess? Clearly it was their very existence, not by power but by the spirit alone, that presented a threat. This uncanny Diasporic nation undermined Hitler's belief in military and political power as the epitome of chosenness. The 'Final Solution' was necessary to prove to the world the falseness of the Jewish claim. Hitler's 'struggle' emerges, then, as an apocalyptic war, not on the Christ-killers but on the *Godmakers* – the Jew is guilty of having discovered an imageless, abstract God, of inventing the very notion of a moral conscience. The Christianity of 'the white-faced Nazarene' is, for the stage Hitler, a Judaic creation. So too is Marxism, the promise of the classless society, the brotherhood of man, the messianic era. Moses, Jesus and Marx have infected Gentile blood 'with the bacillus of perfection'. Hitler's revolution of nihilism would propose to liberate mankind from this 'Jewish' addiction to the *ideal*. By destroying Judaism, and its offshoots (Christianity and Communism), Hitler promises at one blow to return humanity to its natural condition. The state of Israel, on the other hand, has preferred to rely on the truth of Hitler's harsh lesson in survival – in Steiner's drama the Führer proudly points to it as a creation in his own image, a paradigm of elitism, racial purity and the soldierly virtues. 'Should you not honour me who have made you into men of war, who have made of the long, vacuous day-dream of Zion a reality?' Hitler asks of his stunned Israeli captors. 'Should you not be a comfort to my old age?'[6]

The twisted notion that Hitler might be given pride of place in the Zionist pantheon did not, however, simply spring out of Steiner's imagination, any more than did the view of Nazi racism as a parody of the Old Testament. The idea had indeed been a favourite fantasy of the Nazis themselves. Hitler's comrade-in-arms, the fanatical antisemite, Julius Streicher, had stated as much in his last testament composed in the summer of 1945, before he was hanged in Nuremberg.[7] Repeatedly, Streicher quoted from the books of Moses to justify racial purity, the ideal of the *Herrenvolk* and the Nazi policy of genocide.[8] Theodor Herzl's *Judenstaat*, too, was introduced to prove the existence of a global 'Jewish question', the inevitability of antisemitism and the need for strict racial separation.[9] The Nuremberg Laws were merely a modern Germanic version of Moses' instructions to the Israelites before the conquest of Canaan and of the 'Zionist' legislation described in the Book of Ezra.[10] Streicher even closed his testimony with a quotation from Theodor Herzl, the founder of modern political Zionism, to the effect that world peace would only be achieved when world Jewry was settled in a national home. Until then, antisemitism would persist, for the Jews represented the 'principle of unrest' among the nations of the world.[11]

Even before the final collapse of the Third Reich, Hitler, Streicher and other leading Nazis had prepared their excuses for perpetrating the Holocaust and in some cases their prophecies for the post-war world. In his own political testament of 13 February 1945, Hitler had strongly denied that his racism was aggressive 'as far as the Jewish race is concerned'. The persecutions of the Jews had been provoked by their own activities throughout the centuries. It was 'the Jews' who had declared war on Nazi Germany in 1939 and thereby forced his hand. Even if the 'Final Solution' had not been fully completed, Hitler was confident that it would only be 'a temporary failure'. There was no danger that antisemitism would fade, 'for it is the Jews themselves who add fuel to its flames and see that it is kept well stoked'. Like Streicher, Hitler was convinced that he could always rely on the Jews – 'as long as they survive, antisemitism will never fade'.

In the post-war years neo-Nazis continued to cultivate Hitler's fiction of the Jews' war, in the hope of rehabilitating Nazism from the ashes of Europe's death camps. But their paranoid efforts to turn the murdered Jews into warmongering tyrants and the Nazi executioners into innocent victims understandably aroused little response in the first twenty-five years after the Second World War. The extreme Right remained by and large a marginal phenomenon in European politics at that time and Jew-baiting had ceased to be a popular feature of its agitation.[12] In the aftermath of the Holocaust, political antisemitism was simply no longer in vogue and in any case tended to be superseded by the xenophobic backlash against non-white immigration from Europe's former colonies and the mounting influx of guest-workers.[13] Nevertheless, it remained embedded in a latent state not far beneath the surface of Western society and has continued to form the central thrust of hard-core neo-Nazism. In the Radical Right rhetoric of the 1970s and 1980s antisemitism has once again raised its ugly head, whether in the guise of historical 'revisionism', 'anti-Zionism', or the elitist doctrines of the French New Right, or as part of a modest neo-Nazi revival.[14] Admittedly, the postwar politics of the extreme Right has remained too fragmented and poorly organized, too lacking in mass support to make it an effective vehicle for the dissemination of antisemitism. But the climate of international opinion has gradually become ripe for a revival of latent anti-Jewish feelings and the sophisticated representation of 'fascism with a human face'.

During the 1970s an outpouring of films and literature in Europe and America, revising earlier images of Nazism and fascism, unconsciously prepared the ground for this shift in attitudes.[15] *Le mode rétro* in films like *Lacombe Lucien, Night Porter* or *Pasqualino Settebelleze* not only subverted the historical relationship between executioners and victims but eroticized the nature of Nazism and fascism, suggesting it was the collective expression of a sado-masochistic charade.[16] In this cinematic hall of mirrors, Nazism was not dead because it latently existed in all of us as a fact of human nature;[17] it supposedly derived from the ineradicable will to dominate the *other*, from the basic drives for sex and power which had found their repressed and perverted expression in the concentration camps. Thus the Holocaust and the reality of Nazi racism gradually dissolved in the 1970s into a metaphor for morbidly privatized power-games, the gas chambers serving merely as the lurid backdrop for an erotic dance of death.[18] The real political context of Nazi oppression was blurred and trivialized while the deeply puritanical character of fascist aesthetics became, of all things, an inspiration for mass pornography.[19] Nazism, which had repressed normal heterosexual expressions of sexuality and ruthlessly persecuted homosexuals, became in the mass culture of the 1970s a symbol of erotic adventurism and kinky fantasy.

During this same decade, the personage of the Führer, too, became an object of renewed fascination; both at the level of popular culture and in the flood of films, books and articles that journalists were subsequently to christen the *Hitlerwelle*. Hans-Jürgen Syberberg's monumental *Hitler – ein Film aus Deutschland* was one of the more serious of these efforts, at the end of the 1970s, to come to grips with the Nazi phenomenon; his cinematic Hitler, a bizarre mixture of grandeur, kitsch and nothingness, emerges as a grotesque Wagnerian consummation of the dreams of German romanticism. Syberberg could not, however, resist the temptation to jump from the monstrous crimes of the historical Führer to a wholly unconvincing allegorization of Hitler as godfather of the soulless, materialistic culture of post-war West German society.[20] In Syberberg's epic exercise in exorcism, the distinction between victims and murderers is ultimately subordinated to aesthetic effects, and Hitler's death-dealing on a massive European scale serves as little more than the starting-point for a neo-romantic cinematic critique of modernity. In fact, industrial capitalism and its consumer culture had, of course, existed well before Hitler and was neither advanced nor retarded by Nazi rule. What *was* fundamentally changed by Hitler's defeat was precisely that acquired German taste for the millenarian politics of redemption, which lay at the root of the Nazi catastrophe.

Hitler was in that special sense perhaps the last representative of 'the salvationist logic in Romantic culture', the last of the false Messiahs whom Germany had for so long anticipated and who ultimately failed to deliver.[21] In this context it is revealing that it was not Hitler's murder of the Jews which concerned the young West German director but rather the irreversible aesthetic wound he had inflicted on Europe, on civilization as a whole and on all those who followed him. In the fourth part of Syberberg's film, entitled *We, Children of Hell*, a weary studio actor bitterly reproaches the puppet who represents Hitler, for having killed all his joy in life. 'You took away our sunsets. . . . You are to blame that we can no longer look at a field of grain without thinking of you. . . . You occupied everything and corrupted it with your deeds, everything – honour, loyalty, country life, hard work, movies, dignity, fatherland, pride, faith. You are the executioner of Western civilization . . . the plague of our century. . . . We are snuffed out. Nothing more will grow here. . . . Congratulations!'[22]

Syberberg's Hitler remains a nihilistic, aesthetic symbol in whom all and none are guilty. He is ultimately a figure of mythology, not of history, whose fascination for the Germans is shown to have derived from his ability to somehow express their deepest dreams and unconscious aspirations.[23] His greatest abomination – the destruction of the Jews – is never seriously confronted and is even implicitly compared at one point with the Hollywoodian perversion of the cinema into an instrument of mass culture, which in Syberberg's eyes would appear to be the ultimate 'crime against humanity'. Such escapism has, unfortunately, been characteristic of much of the Hitler Boom in the 1970s;[24] the more recent historical literature has tended either to overpersonalize and trivialize the Nazi regime in a dangerously misleading way or else to fall into the opposite trap of describing it as a polycratic chaos of conflicting authorities with no dominant figure or clear direction at the centre. The problem of Nazism has frequently been reduced by recent biographers to idiosyncrasies and quirks in Hitler's 'charismatic' personality, and its legacy is thereby assumed to have vanished with his suicide in the Berlin bunker; or, going to the other extreme, the Führer has been presented as a shadowy, weak ruler, incapable of making decisions and uninvolved even in such core-issues of the Third Reich as the making of Jewish policy. Neither the myth of the super-Hitler or that of the mini-Hitler, of the man of destiny or the banal petty-bourgeois who loved sweets, cream cakes and Hollywood musicals, has, however, resolved the enigma; the Führer remains both a kind of folk-hero at the lowest levels of mass culture and a source of endless fascination to serious historians, psychologists and artists.[25]

Alongside Hitler's remarkable rise to 'superstar' status in the mass media, the trend in 1970s historiography was to normalize and de-demonize, in a sense even to 'de-Nazify' the Führer. The most obviously eccentric and sensation-mongering example of this tendency was British historian David Irving's effort in *Hitler's War* (1977) to claim that the Führer neither desired nor even knew of the 'Final Solution' until long after its implementation had begun.[26] Like countless neo-Nazi apologists since 1945, Irving insisted, contrary to all the known facts, that Hitler had always desired only the emigration and not the extermination of the Jews. Since no formal written Führer-order for the mass murder of European Jewry has ever been found, it was not too difficult for Irving to give a superficially scholarly coating to his thesis of an innocent Hitler.[27] Unlike the neo-Nazi 'revisionists', he did not, admittedly, deny that the Holocaust had actually happened, blaming it instead on the 'over-zealous' Himmler and other subordinates who had supposedly 'pulled the wool over the Führer's eyes'.

Against such pernicious nonsense I have tried to show in this book that there is overwhelming evidence that Hitler ordered the genocide of European Jewry, that he pursued this goal with brutal, undeviating consistency and that it formed the mainspring of his entire political career. In contrast to a number of leading contemporary historians who more plausibly argue that the 'Final Solution' was a mere *ad hoc* affair into which Hitler and the Nazis stumbled or blundered as a result of chance and their own mistakes, I suggest that it was on the contrary the logical and desired outcome of Hitler's eschatological politics. Antisemitism was never a secondary issue to Adolf Hitler but the very core of his creed, his deepest existential conviction and the *raison d'être* of his activity both as Nazi Party leader and as an international statesman. Only by following through *all* the ramifications of his antisemitic *Weltanschauung* in German domestic and international politics can one properly understand, not only the fate of the Jews, but also that of Europe and the world in the inter-war period. There would, I suggest, have been no Second World War at all, had it not been for Hitler's radical antisemitism and its far-reaching political repercussions. This cannot be understood solely in conventional instrumentalist or rational terms. Antisemitism in Hitler's mind meant the *inevitability* of a cosmic war against the Jews, as the earthly representatives of the powers of Darkness and as the 'Chosen People' of an alien God, whom Hitler sought to finally eradicate from the surface of the earth. In that sense Hitler was closer in outlook to the Gnostic heresies of early Christianity than to the European statesmen of his own era;[28] he was closer in temperament to Martin Luther and his early sixteenth-century visions of the *Endzeit* than to the aristocratic or bourgeois antisemites of the late nineteenth and early twentieth centuries.[29]

Hitler always spoke of the destruction of Jewry in the tones of apocalyptic fervour characteristic of the popular Christianity of the Middle Ages and of the millenarian sects who believed they had a divine mission to purify the world by wiping out the 'sons of Satan'.[30] In the 'anti-Christian' Catholicism of Hitler, Goebbels and Himmler something of this medieval chiliast tradition had survived. Dieter Wisliceny, SS Major and Eichmann's deputy, responsible with others for the mass deportation and murder of Jews from Slovakia, Greece and Hungary, revealingly described Nazi antisemitism, on 18 November 1946, in the following terms: it was based, so he claimed, on a mystical view 'which sees the world as ruled by good and bad powers', where Jews represented the 'evil principle', with the churches, freemasonry and Bolshevism as auxiliaries. It was absolutely impossible to make any impression on this outlook through logic or reason; it was rooted in 'a sort of religiosity, and it impels people to form themselves into a sect'. Under the impact of the literature of the *Protocols of the Elders of Zion* and the theories of Rosenberg, Hitler, Hans Günther and other ideologues, 'millions of people believed these things – an event that can only be compared with similar phenomena in the Middle Ages, such as the witch-mania'.[31] Wisliceny went on to argue what is in its bare essence the thesis of the first half of this book, though one which in the circumstances he obviously could not work out and prove in all its historical intricacy and detail: 'Against this world of evil the race-mystics set the world of good, of light, incarnated in blond, blue-eyed people, who were supposed to be the source of all capacity for creating civilization or building a state. Now these two worlds were alleged to be locked in a perpetual struggle, and the war of 1939, which Hitler unleashed, represented only the final battle between these two powers.'[32]

I have argued in the opening chapter that Hitler picked up this apocalyptic, sectarian fanaticism in pre-1914 Vienna and that the specificity of his militant antisemitism can only be fully understood against the Austrian background. To my mind, a great deal of the existing literature on Hitler and Nazism which mechanically traces its roots to the Second Reich or even further back to the

7

earliest traditions of Prusso-German history is fundamentally flawed and misleading. Hitler was not born a citizen of the Hohenzollern Reich but of the multi-national Habsburg Empire; his racism had all the *Angst*-ridden hysteria of Austro-German border nationalism. The fact that this Austrian *Grenz-nationalismus* was eventually to conquer the German heartland was of fateful significance; it cannot be explained if one is fixated on seeking the seeds of Nazism solely in Germany's flawed historical development without reference to the burgeoning race war in the Dual Monarchy. As Karl Kraus once pointed out, Austria-Hungary was a 'proving ground of world destruction'. This background did not, however, make Hitler the inevitable product of Austrian any more than of German history. It provided a necessary rather than a sufficient condition for his emergence.

Nor is the long history of European antisemitism all that helpful in understanding the *unprecedented* nature of the Holocaust. The Nazis were of course fully aware of the uninterrupted continuity of Judeophobia in the Christian era, and used this fact to their advantage on every possible occasion. They also eagerly seized on all available predecessors, especially among the racist antisemites of the nineteenth and early twentieth centuries, to give a greater intellectual legitimacy to their own movement.[33] But even where Hitler and the Nazis were most obviously repeating the standard charges both of traditional Christian and of anti-Christian racial antisemites, the dynamic thrust of their ideology and *praxis* was quite different. Not only had antisemitism never before been used with such devastating efficacy and skill as a weapon of political mobilization, but never had it been posited in so totalistic and absolute a manner as a self-contained *Weltanschauung*. It was this fusion of an essentially modern, totalitarian political *praxis* with a gnostic-racist Manichean ideology of war against the forces of Darkness that provided the radical novelty in Hitler's movement. He took the existing ideologies of nineteenth-century antisemitism to their ultimate limits, using the Tsarist Russian idea of an international Jewish conspiracy as his inspiration for a radical restructuring of the modern political world.

This book attempts, however, to provide something more than a new interpretation of Hitler's apocalyptic antisemitism and its lethal genocidal content. For essentially it argues that, ever since 1933, the war on the Jews which was inaugurated by Nazism has never really stopped. The *Protocols of the Elders of Zion* were reborn almost immediately after the end of the Second World War and have provided the inspiration for continuing further efforts at completing in the Middle East what the Nazis narrowly failed to accomplish in Europe. The Soviet, Arab and Islamic antisemitic campaigns described in the second half of this book are, to my mind, part of a multi-layered *continuum* of

8

bloodcurdling rhetoric which has been going on uninterruptedly for almost forty years; it is in fact no less intense in its scope than that initiated by Hitler and the Nazis before the Second World War, for today antisemitism is no longer limited to one political centre. Though more widely diffused, it is potentially no less dangerous with a mighty superpower, the Soviet Union, and a major and rising force in international politics, the Islamic world, as its chief sponsors. Soviet, Islamic and Arab propaganda is essentially built on the Nazi *Protocols* pattern which postulates the existence of an international, shadowy occult conspiracy with its Jewish political centre in Israel and its hinterland in the Diaspora.

This crusade goes today under the name of 'anti-Zionism', but the lexicographical innovation should not deceive anyone as to its true content. The reason for the disguise is self-evident. Hitler's Holocaust made the direct expression of hostility to Jews as a racial, religious or ethnic group unacceptable to most of *Western* public opinion, though this was much less the case in other parts of the world. As a result, an alternative intellectual framework and mode of expression had to be found by Communist, Arab, Islamic and even fascist antisemites for justifying their new goal – the extinction of a sovereign Jewish collectivity. 'Anti-Zionism' has provided this post-war substitute, just as a hundred years ago 'antisemitism' itself replaced Jew-hatred (or anti-Judaism) in the European political vocabulary. Because of Hitler's genocide, uninhibited *racist* antisemitism still remains virtually taboo in the West, except for the incorrigible nostalgics and unreconstructed worshippers of the Nazi era. Contemporary antisemitism had therefore to be transmuted and masked under its ideological antithesis – the struggle *against* fascism and antisemitism – if it was ever to be effective. Today it invariably sails under the fashionable 'anti-Zionist' colours of destroying Israel. Hence the paradox of an anti-Zionism which, in the West no less than in the Soviet and Islamic world, insists that it has nothing against Jews yet has increasingly staked its claim to be the *historical heir* of Hitler and Nazi antisemitism.

It is naive to assume that under certain circumstances the forces ranged against Israel and the Jewish people today could not repeat the performance of the German Nazis. The wars of 1948, 1967 and 1973 in which Israel was fighting for its life and its very survival are proof enough of this possibility. The obstinate refusal of the Arab states and the Islamic fundamentalists after thirty-seven years to renounce their strategy of Holy War (*Jihad*) and annihilation against Israel, as well as the intransigent National Covenant of the PLO, underline the intensity and persistence of the threat.[34] Even the Egyptian–Israeli Peace Treaty, the one ray of light in the Arab wall of hate, has not significantly diminished the virulence of Egyptian antisemitism. Here, as elsewhere in Muslim and Arab countries, Nazi and Western notions of the 'world Jewish conspiracy' have been easily integrated into traditional Islamic thought about the Jews.[35] Indeed, the more that militant Islam reaffirms itself, as in contemporary Khomeinist Iran, the greater the antagonism to Israel, Zionism and Jewry. As with Nazi radicalism, there is the same fanatical anti-Western orientation and hostility to liberal democratic values which frequently goes hand in hand with extreme antisemitism.

In their search for authenticity and in their return to pristine Muslim values, both the conservative Islamic fundamentalists and the 'radicals' have turned their backs not only on the West but also on all attempts at dialogue with Christianity and Judaism. Moreover, exploiting Koranic anti-Jewish lore and the more contemporary hatred of Israel to demonstrate the impotence of secular Arab nationalist rulers, the Islamic radicals have turned the duty of *Jihad* into a weapon for revolutionary purification from *within* – the necessary prelude to future expansion abroad.[36]

At the same time, in Soviet 'anti-Zionism' there has been a bizarre fusion of the *Protocols* mythology derived from the old Tsarist Russian Radical Right with the Marxist-Leninist vocabulary of Communist tradition. From this hybrid monster of Russian National Socialism, Judeophobia has emerged as one of the most potent single elements in Soviet domestic and foreign policy. Holy Russia, the classic land of nineteenth-century Jew-baiting, which gave to the world the ugly word *pogrom* and whose secret police originally invented the myth of the international Jewish conspiracy, has in the late twentieth century become the centre of the so-called struggle against 'world Zionism'.[37] Now well advanced into its imperial phase of expansion, the Soviet Union of the 1980s presents a no less powerful source of antisemitism than Hitler's Third Reich in the 1930s and 1940s. In both cases the assault on Jewry appears both as the expression of a messianic great-power nationalism and as a central part of a broader thrust to destabilize, undermine and ultimately destroy Western democracy itself.[38]

In the face of these threats, Israel exists as an essential lifeboat for the survival of the Jewish nation in a cruel world. Stateless peoples and minority groups have been rather ruthlessly treated in the twentieth century. As a consequence, lack of territorial concentration became, in the age of Nazism, a luxury that not even the world's oldest Diaspora people could afford. In the post-Holocaust age, without the protection of an independent national state and a modicum of political and military power, how much hope would there really have been for the continuity of three-thousand-year-old Jewish civilization into the next century? Furthermore, was it not the existence of Israel and the Zionist spirit of national renaissance that saved many of the persecuted Jews of Arab lands after 1948 and inspired new hope in Soviet Jewry, leading to the unprecedented exodus movement in the 1970s? Did not the resurrection of Jewish nationhood give new meaning to the existence of a Diaspora which would otherwise have been psychically shattered by the numbing catastrophe of the Nazi Holocaust?

But the extraordinary achievements of Zionism have obviously been won at a high price. Israel, as a society which is still confronted with staggering internal and external pressures, has had to sacrifice something of the moral and spiritual uniqueness which accompanied its long march through the Diaspora. Its democratic spirit is obviously far from immune to the dangers of a right-wing ultra-nationalism which has thrived in other parts of the world on virtually identical obsessions of territorial security, the temptations of a witch-hunt for the 'enemy within' and the mystical cult of manifest destiny. Furthermore, it must be admitted that the growth of isolationist and Arabophobic tendencies in Israeli society could yet turn diabolic fantasy-images of Zionism concocted abroad into nightmarish reality, unless they are uprooted in time.

These dangers ostensibly stem from current political dilemmas and the unresolved regional problems of the Middle East and might be thought by some to have no connection at all with the tragedy of the Holocaust. Such an impression would, however, be superficial, as this study seeks to illustrate in many different ways. The memory of Hitler continues to cast a dark menacing shadow not only over Israel and its neighbours but over the whole of humanity in the closing years of this century. Only through a piercing diagnosis of the meaning of this legacy and its contemporary uses and abuses, may we perhaps finally free ourselves from its posthumous vengeance.

CHAPTER ONE

# Laboratory of World Destruction

In a speech in the Upper Austrian city of Linz on 7 April 1938, Adolf Hitler, already *Führer* of 'Greater Germany', declared: '. . . probably it was only a South German who could effect the second unification, for he must want to lead back into the great Reich that part which in the course of our history had lost its connection with the Reich'.[1] The *Anschluss* with Austria, which returned his homeland to the bosom of *Mutter Germania*, had a deep psychological and political meaning for Hitler – it was 'the fulfilment of my most ardent and heart-felt wish'.[2] The German Reich, as he told his audience in Linz, had always represented 'the land of my dreams and of my longing'; indeed, since his youth in Habsburg Austria, Hitler had in a sense already been a citizen of this coming *Grossdeutschland*. By upbringing and outlook he had long been convinced that the separation of Austria from Germany was a freak of history and that it was his mission to reunify all the Germanic tribes. By bringing his homeland *heim ins Reich* he was in his own mind completing the unfinished work of Bismarck, who in 1866 had opted for a *Kleindeutsch* solution to German unity, by excluding Austria. Like other Austrian Pan-Germans, Hitler had always despised the Habsburgs and Austria, admiring Bismarck's Prusso-German Reich as the true arbiter of German destiny. But the Austrian-born Hitler altogether lacked the Prussian Junker's sense of measure and restraint.

By a curious twist of fate, Hitler had been born at Braunau-am-Inn by the Austro-German border on 20 April 1889, almost exactly equidistant in time from the battle of Königgratz and the death of the Emperor Francis Joseph I – which heralded the collapse of the Habsburg Empire. Since his early teens in Linz he had espoused, like many of his generation, the secessionist ideology of the Austrian Pan-Germans, which demanded the break-up of the Habsburg state and its replacement by union with the Hohenzollern German Reich.[3] The morbid suspicion of Slavs and Jews which Hitler was later to develop into the devouring hatred that led to their extermination was born out of this same cultural matrix. At the turn of the century, extreme nationalism was already rife in Linz, a stronghold of the *deutschnational* movement led by Georg Ritter

12

von Schoenerer, who had a special following among the provincial German middle classes, intelligentsia and student youth.[4] There is little doubt that the adolescent Hitler was first exposed to sectarian racism among schoolmasters and fellow pupils at the Linz *Realschule* which he attended until 1904. This xenophobic sentiment was primarily directed against Slavs, probably as a result of the proximity of Bohemia and the fears of a considerable Czech immigration. There were, on the other hand, relatively few Jews in Linz, most of them assimilated to German culture and outwardly indistinguishable from Christians.[5] Hence, not surprisingly, there was no 'Jewish question' in Linz to compare with the rampant agitation then prevalent in Vienna; nonetheless Pan-German newspapers and journals which were available to the young Hitler, such as *Linzer Fliegenden Blätter*, were axiomatically antisemitic as part of their anticlerical, racist nationalism. Moreover, it is likely that Hitler had already inherited from his father Alois – a petty-bourgeois Austrian customs official, who sympathized with von Schoenerer's movement – some of the classic prejudices of his milieu and period.[6]

By the time the by now orphaned Hitler arrived in Vienna in 1907 he was almost certainly a convinced Pan-German. His *grossdeutsch* aspirations were already incompatible with the continued existence of the multi-national Habsburg state, for which he came to feel an abiding and all-consuming revulsion. In *Mein Kampf* he referred retrospectively to the Habsburgs with loathing and contempt for having betrayed the Germans of the *Ostmark*.[7] Wherever possible the Royal House had, so he claimed, tried to institute 'Slavization' from above 'and it was the hand of the goddess of eternal justice and inexorable retribution, which caused Archduke Francis Ferdinand, the most mortal enemy of Austrian Germanism, to fall by the bullets which he himself helped to mould'.[8] Hitler regarded Habsburg nationality policy as designed 'slowly but inexorably to exterminate the dangerous German element in the dual monarchy'. The Reich Germans, too, were not entirely blameless, for they had 'lived by the side of a corpse, and in the symptoms of rottenness saw only the signs of a 'new' life. The unholy alliance of the young Reich and the Austrian sham state contained the germ of the subsequent World War and of the collapse as well'.[9] Hitler's vocabularly in speaking of the supra-national Habsburgs, like that of many contemporaries, was replete with images of death and destruction. The decaying dynasty was a 'living corpse' (*Leichnam*), an 'impossible State', a linguistic and ethnic Babel (*Völkerbabylon*). In his eyes Austria was already doomed by virtue of its hybrid character as a multi-national state.

From the perspective of turn-of-the century cosmopolitan Vienna, German nationalists like Hitler could the more readily ruminate on the ruinous effects of miscegenation in bringing about the decadence and fall of empires. Indeed he was not alone in recalling with disgust 'this Babel of races' which he first encountered in the Habsburg metropolis; Houston S. Chamberlain, the ideological godfather of Nazism, who composed his epoch-making *Foundations of the Nineteenth Century* (1899) in Vienna, was no less scathing. Austria-Hungary was, for the *völkisch* prophet of the Reich, the final metamorphosis of Roman decadence, of the *Völkerchaos* which had destroyed the imperial structure of Antiquity. A racially degenerate state without national cohesion and 'held together only by dynastic interests', it represented the German nemesis.[10] Both the ex-Englishman Chamberlain and the provincial Austrian Hitler constructed their *Angst*-ridden racist philosophies as the conscious antithesis to the Habsburg melting-pot of cultures, languages and nationalities. They both looked to the streamlined, relatively homogeneous, virile Prusso-German Reich as the herald of a radiant Teutonic future, provided that it would strictly observe the laws of race. Indeed the origins of Nazism would be incomprehensible without taking into account the youthful experiences of its founder in early twentieth-century Vienna, sickened as he was 'by the conglomeration of races which the capital showed me, repelled by the whole mixture of Czechs, Poles, Hungarians, Ruthenians, Serbs and Croats, and everywhere, the eternal mushroom [*Spaltpilz*] of humanity – Jews and more Jews'.[11]

Hitler's nightmarish vision of 'the poison of foreign nations' gnawing away 'at the body of our nationality';[12] his horror and hatred for the 'foreign mixture of peoples' corroding Vienna, 'this ancient site of German culture', were lasting impressions that conditioned his future political behaviour as *Führer* of the Third Reich. In the 1930s he confided in Hermann Rauschning that 'Slav mestizos' had overrun Vienna, which was 'no longer a German city'; the priests and Jews who ruled the country would have to be thrown out; it would be his special task to train the lazy, easy-going Austrians to *German* ways and above all to remove the Jews.[13] When speaking of Vienna, Hitler was still seized by a flaming contempt, hatred and the desire to revenge himself 'for early years of poverty, for disappointed hopes, for a life of deprivation and humiliation'.[14] His crude, indigestible racialism, the primitive, irrational Darwinism and boundless capacity for hatred which were later crystallized into his Nazi *Weltanschauung*, had their origins in the dismal hopelessness of those early years spent in the lower depths of Viennese society. The witches' brew of National Socialism with its morbid fixation on blood and race was the perverse product of that strange amalgam of personal traumas and collective anxieties born out of the unique ethnic situation in *fin de siècle* Habsburg Austria.[15]

In no area was the prevailing atmosphere of hysterical overheated nationalism and racial conflict to have more fateful consequences than in Hitler's encounter with the 'Jewish question' in Vienna. The city in which he learned his first important political lessons also opened his eyes to the presence of a large Jewish community (175,318 in 1910: 8.6 per cent of the total population) which played a dynamic innovative role in commerce, industry, journalism, the arts and sciences. Many of Vienna's Jews were already thoroughly acculturated and identified fully with German cultural values, with the Habsburg Austrian state and liberal politics. Some of the more assimilated German Jews had even been among the founders of the Pan-German movement in Austria, before Hitler was born.[16] On the other hand, there was a significant immigrant population of traditionalist, Yiddish-speaking *Ostjuden* from Hungary and Galicia who were concentrated in Vienna's Leopoldstadt ghetto. They still dressed, talked and behaved like *shtetl* Jews; many of them were Orthodox and quite impervious to the seductions of German *Kultur*. It was these exotic-looking *Ostjuden* that Hitler presumably first encountered around 1908, at a time of massive Galician influx into Vienna.[17] Lacking any insight into their distinctive culture, the young Hitler simply seized on outward signs of difference, of alienness and unGerman appearance.[18] The sight and smell of the *Ostjude*, this 'apparition in a black caftan and black hair locks', seemed to confirm his worst fears and anxieties concerning the future of the German nation.[19] 'Wherever I went, I began to see Jews, and the more I saw, the more sharply they became distinguished in my eyes from the rest of humanity. Particularly the inner city and the districts north of the Danube Canal swarmed with a people which even outwardly had lost all resemblance to Germans.'[20]

The 'visual instruction' of the Vienna streets also brought the lonely, puritanical Hitler into contact with social evils such as the white slave trade (*Mädchenhandel*) which 'could be studied in Vienna, as perhaps in no other city of Western Europe, with the possible exception of the southern French ports'.[21] No doubt an element of Hitler's own repressed sexuality can be felt behind his rage at the Jew 'as the cold-hearted, shameless and calculating director of this revolting vice traffic in the scum of the big city. . . .'[22] Probably recalling his own fairly frequent forays into the Jewish quarter where prostitution was rife, Hitler observed in *Mein Kampf*: 'If you walked the streets and alleys of Leopoldstadt, at every step you witnessed proceedings which remained concealed from the majority of the German people until the war gave the soldiers on the eastern front occasion to see similar things.'[23]

The relation of *Ostjuden* to the white slave traffic in Vienna was not simply an invention of Hitler but a serious social problem which attracted the attention of Jewish and non-Jewish reformers alike.[24] At the same time the moral crusade against white slavery, especially in Austria-Hungary, had from the outset been strongly tainted by antisemitism. The Jewish procurers preyed in fact mostly on immigrant Jewesses from Galicia rather than on the young, 'defenceless' Christian girls who in Hitler's feverishly racist imagination were being 'stolen forever' from their people. The image of the dark-haired Jewish youth 'with satanic joy in his face' lying in wait for the opportunity to seduce and 'defile with his blood' the flower of Aryan womanhood was of course a pure figment of antisemitic fantasy, though one especially prevalent in pre-1914 Vienna. In the Weimar Republic, too, the Nazis would capitalize on this strand of popular sexual antisemitism, linking it to the theme of a Jewish conspiracy to destroy the racial foundations of the 'Aryan' peoples. Veteran German antisemites like Theodor Fritsch, whose popular *Handbuch der Judenfrage* Hitler had studied 'intensively during my youth in Vienna', had already singled out for comment at the end of the nineteenth century[25] the lust of Jews for 'Aryan' women and their allegedly magnetic sexual powers. For Fritsch, as for Hitler, eroticism was a weapon of racial bastardization and for 'pulling down the blood barriers' which would prove fatal to a people like the Germans who lacked the imagined unity and homogeneity of the Jews. Hence, the most important of Fritsch's racist commandments which was to become one of the foundations of the Nazi creed: 'Thou shalt keep they blood pure. Consider it a crime to soil the noble Aryan breed of thy people by mingling it with the Jewish breed. . . .'[26]

The young Hitler, influenced by such writings and the semi-pornographic tone of much Viennese *fin de siècle* antisemitism, tended to link or even identify the related social evils of prostitution, white slavery, syphilis and (racial) degeneration with Jewry – especially with its East European branch. Moreover, it must be remembered that for Hitler the 'lost purity of the blood' had an almost mystical significance in addition to its national-political implications. It alone destroyed 'inner happiness forever', plunging the individual into an external abyss while those peoples whose blood has been tainted 'renounce with it the unity of their soul in all its expressions'.[27] In *Mein Kampf* Hitler evoked in ugly, hysterical tones 'the seduction of hundreds of thousands of girls by bowlegged, repulsive Jewish bastards' as nothing short of a 'desecration' of the noble Aryan race. The stereotypes of the Jew and the Negro blend in his turgid prose into a hybrid menace to the virginal purity of Germanic womanhood. 'Systematically these black parasites defile our inexperienced young blond girls and thereby destroy something which can no longer be replaced in this world.'[28] The theme probably originated out of the sexual melting-pot of 'gay Vienna' but it was no less usable in the context of 'decadent' Weimar, as Hitler proved in one of his many Munich beer-cellar orations: '. . . I would like to take you . . . only for a moment to Berlin', he told his rapt audience, 'for a glance into the Friedrichstrasse.' With mounting excitement, Hitler visualized to his listeners 'Jew-boy after Jew-boy with a German girl on his arm'. The message of sexual defilement (*Rassenschande*) rang through loud and clear, for 'on that very night, thousands and thousands of our blood are annihilated forever in an instant and that child and grandchildren are lost to us'.[29]

Sexuality was no marginal issue in Hitler's antisemitism but at the very heart of his diagnosis of the social and national sickness from which the German-speaking world was allegedly suffering. If its body and soul were not to be irredeemably poisoned then the whole of German public life and morality would have to be cleansed 'from the stifling perfume of our modern eroticism'. Hence the morbid fixation on syphilis in *Mein Kampf*, the call for focusing the national effort on this question as if 'life and death actually depended on its solution'. In Hitler's mind, 'the struggle against syphilis and the prostitution which prepared the way for it is one of the most gigantic tasks of humanity, gigantic because we are facing, not the solution of a single question, but the elimination of a large number of evils which bring about this plague. . . .'[30] Syphilis not only represented a 'terrible poisoning of the health of the national body' whose consequences were apparent in the spread of mental illness and defective children; the prostitution of love symbolized what Hitler called the 'Jewification [*Verjüdung*] of our spiritual life and mammonization of our mating instinct'.

The sexual and racial obsessions which Hitler picked up as a young man in Vienna and which were to become an integral part of his antisemitic *Weltanschauung* derived from a bizzare mixture of pseudo-scientific race theory and mystical occultism.[31] Much of this antisemitic literature was extremely primitive and unsophisticated so that the young Hitler's self-proclaimed disappointment at the 'dull and amazingly unscientific arguments' he encountered is not perhaps surprising. Nevertheless it appears likely that he was a regular reader of his fellow Austrian Adolf Lanz von Liebenfels, a self-appointed aristocrat whose *Ostara Bände* were sold at tobacco kiosks in Vienna during the crucial years after 1908 when Hitler became a fully-fledged antisemite. Von Liebenfels, a renegade Cistercian monk turned race mystic and Ariosophist, had founded the 'Order of the New Templars' in 1900 and flown the swastika a few years later from his Danubian castle, Burg Werfenstein, as a symbol of the Aryan movement for race purity. Hitler's own views on miscegenation as a sin 'against the iron logic of nature' were remarkably close to those of von Liebenfels. Both Austrians believed in the

God-given right of the Aryan-Germanic people to dominate the world. They shared the belief first put forward by the founder of modern race theory, the Comte Arthur de Gobineau, that the race-mixing of the superior culture-bearing 'Aryans' with inferior breeds would lead to mongrelization and had throughout his history caused the decline and fall of civilization.[32] In *Mein Kampf*, Hitler had even given a new racialist interpretation to the traditional Christian doctrine of 'original sin' (*Erbsünde*); it was not so much human nature *per se* which was corrupt but rather it was 'blood sin and desecration of the race' which were the supreme transgressions and 'the end of a humanity which surrenders to it'. Miscegenation had caused the Fall from Paradise.

Von Liebenfels put forward similar notions in the context of a Manichean secular cosmology, in which the 'Aryans' – the blond, blue-eyed, divinely conceived People of Light – were threatened by a demonic animal-like race of Darkness.[33] The susceptibility of 'Aryan' womanhood to the sexual charms of the Apemen and the incitement of this underworld to revolt against the heroic race of supermen, encouraged by Jews, freemasons and socialists, was sapping the foundations of civilization. Precious 'Aryan' blood was in danger of being washed away by subhuman fluids.[34] The solution to this race-defilement would have to be sterilization and the enslaving of the lower races as well as a state-controlled programme of racial hygiene for the regeneration of Teutonic blood. The 'Jewish question' would be dealt with by deportation or the 'castration knife'. Von Liebenfels' aim, which anticipated at some points the future breeding and extermination policies of the SS, was to ensure the restoration of the blond, Teutonic race to its rightful place of supremacy. In a world threatened by class-struggle, socialism, feminism, democracy and the revolt of dark-haired *Untermenschen*, drastic measures would be called for if the Aryan-Germanic counter-revolution were to succeed.

Whether Hitler was ever a secret devotee of Von Liebenfels' mystical anthropology and plagiarized his crackpot racial theories without acknowledging the debt, will probably never be definitively established.[35] There were, however, some significant differences in outlook which make it implausible to regard Hitler as a mere disciple of Lanz. The Austrian ariosophist remained a Christian of sorts and the religious colouring to his biological racism was stronger than that of Hitler, who officially eschewed all forms of metaphysics. Lanz continued to idealize the Habsburg Empire which Hitler passionately hated. Moreover, Lanz focused on the 'Aryan' group of races as a whole where Hitler tended to be more Germanocentric and to emphasize the centrality of the 'Jewish question' rather than the threat posed by the non-white races. Nevertheless something of the irrational racial sectarianism of this occult Viennese subculture, symbolized by Lanz and reinforced by Hitler's subsequent encounter with the Thule Society in Munich, did undoubtedly contribute to shaping his Manichean world-view.[36] Not only the vision of an Aryan Prometheus restored, but the malignant fear of Jews and Social Democrats, were common ground to the rootless, embittered young artist and the occult *völkisch* seers of turn-of-the-century Vienna and Munich.

Hitler's own account in *Mein Kampf* of his metamorphosis from a 'weak-kneed cosmopolitan' to fanatical antisemite does not mention Lanz von Liebenfels and is perhaps too self-serving to be taken as literal truth. There is, however, no solid reason to doubt that Vienna was indeed the scene of the conversion-experience which was to have such catastrophic consequences for European Jewry. Hitler presented this self-transformation in high-flown religious language – for him 'this was the time of the greatest spiritual upheaval I have ever had to go through';[37] he writes of 'the greatest inner soul struggles', of months of battle 'between my reason and my sentiments' before all doubt and ambiguity were stilled and he emerged as a sworn enemy of the Jews.[38] This self-dramatization was characteristic of Hitler's histrionic style. Several years before he composed *Mein Kampf*, he had in fact written in his curriculum vitae (to an unknown recipient): 'Though I came from a fairly cosmopolitan family, the school of harsh reality turned me into an antisemite within a year.'[39] What was this 'harsh reality' which confronted the bohemian dropout from the provinces upon his arrival in Vienna? Did it refer to something more than his uprooted, *déclassé* status of a postcard painter consorting with tramps in the Männerheim men's home in Vienna's Meldemannstrasse?[40] Was it the hunger which had become his 'faithful bodyguard', forcing him to remove his petty-bourgeois blinkers and confront the struggle for existence in all its naked reality?

Hitler's own narration of the dark years between 1908 and 1913 suggests part of the answer. Superimposed on the nationalist vision of a *Rassenbabylon* swarming with Jews, we also find the nightmarish image of a proletarian metropolis whose miserable hovels and scenes of deprivation fill him with loathing and horror. The young Hitler's encounter with the poverty of the Viennese lower depths did not, however, inspire him with any feelings of compassion for the working classes. On the contrary, his contact with the Viennese proletariat initially provoked in him a feeling of impotent rage at their dismissal of patriotism, religion and morality as so many outmoded bourgeois prejudices. Similarly he came to regard the trade unions and Social Democratic organizations as mortal enemies of the German nationality and its struggle to avoid extinction in the *Ostmark*. Their courting of 'Slav comrades', their internationalism and preaching of class-struggle doctrines aroused in him emotions of anger, fear and despair. Not only did there seem to be an irremediable cleavage between the nationalism of the bourgeois world and the Marxist internationalism of the workers; the content of Social Democratic ideology appeared to cut the ground from under the feet of Hitler's own Pan-German assumptions concerning the unity of the *Volk*.

It was only the revelation of the 'Jewish question' in Vienna and its connection with 'the inner, and consequently real aims of Social Democracy' which, according to Hitler, enabled him to resolve this personal crisis. 'When I recognized the Jew as the leader of the Social Democracy the scales dropped from my eyes', he recounts in *Mein Kampf*. 'A long soul struggle had reached its conclusion.'[41] Marxism and Jewry were henceforth inextricably linked in his mind as twin evils threatening the existence of the German nation.[42] Without first grasping the phenomenon of Jewry one could not penetrate to 'the inner core' of Marxian doctrine; equally, only by studying the methods of the Social Democrats could one understand the hidden essence of the Jewish people.[43] Hitler naturally did not fail to notice the predominant role that Jewish intellectuals actually played in the Austrian Social Democratic Party. This was true not only in the realm of theory and professional journalism (Austro-Marxism was largely a 'Jewish' creation) but in the Reichsrat representation as well as the party and socialist youth organizations. 'The names of the Austerlitzes, Davids, Adlers, Ellenbogens, etc.', Hitler bitterly recalled, 'will remain forever engraven in my memory.' In these Jewish Marxists, he perceived the commanding officers of a diabolical conspiracy to destroy 'Aryan' civilization by seducing the working classes and instigating them to revolt. The labouring masses were luckless victims of infinitely cunning leaders whose real goal was to ruin the national economy and prepare their own route to world power. The workers' struggle for existence was being harnessed in the interests of the stock exchange and the future hegemony of the Jewish race. The ultimate aim of Social Democracy was to plan 'the enslavement and with it the destruction of all non-Jewish peoples'.[44]

Hitler's assumptions which ultimately led to the mass murder of European Jewry were of course utterly remote from the theory and practice of European Socialism. They also ignored completely the attitudes and outlook of those Jewish intellectuals who came to play leading roles in the labour movements of Central Europe. Ironically enough, Victor Adler, the founder and leader of the Austrian Social Democrats before 1918, had in his youth developed strong Pan-German sympathies which continued to influence his socialist policies.[45] This was equally true of other 'Jewish' Social Democrats like Friedrich Austerlitz, Otto Bauer and Ludo Hartmann who were thoroughly assimilated German-Austrians, far removed from any identification with Jewish religion, culture or political interests. Indeed the Austro-Marxist Jews made extraordinary efforts to avoid any suspicion of being a *Judenschutztruppe* ('Jewish protective guard') to the point of actually muting their opposition to antisemitism and even flirting with the populist agitation against Jews.[46] Their negative attitude to Jewry failed, however, to diminish in the slightest the antisemitic conspiracy theory promoted by the Austrian Pan-Germans and the Christian-Social Party in Vienna, which Hitler later adapted to suit his own needs. By focusing attention on the so-called 'Jewish' leadership of Social Democracy and its subversive role in a traditional Catholic society, the conservative and Radical Right in Austria, Germany and elsewhere hoped to discredit and weaken the labour movement. The Nazis themselves were to employ this tactic with considerable success against the Socialist and Communist parties under the ill-fated Weimar Republic.

In Hitler's own *Weltanschauung*, the identification of Jewry and Marxism assumed an apocalyptic significance that ultimately transcended questions of political expediency. 'Jewish Marxism', by rejecting the 'aristocratic' principle that might is right and replacing 'the eternal privilege of power and strength by the mass of numbers and their dead weight' (i.e. by advocating democracy!), had unforgivably infringed the commands of 'eternal Nature'. Its doctrine of brotherhood and equality was in conflict with the will of the 'Almighty Creator' and if the Jew was victorious over the nations 'with the help of his Marxist creed', then his crown would become 'the funeral wreath of humanity. . . .'[47] Marxism was for Hitler a deliberate effort to sap the principles of personality and race, hierarchical command and authority, on which all powerful states in history had been constructed.[48] Its 'persistent corrosive acid' of majority rule and seventy years of annihilating, destructive criticism had undermined the traditional monarchies of Europe. With the 'sure eye of the prophet', Karl Marx, the Jewish-born founder of Communism, had 'recognized in the morass of a slowly decomposing world the most essential poisons, extracted them, and, like a wizard, prepared them into a concentrated solution for the swifter annihilation of the independent existence of free nations on this earth. And all this in the service of his race.'[49]

In the specific contribution of 'the Jew Karl Marx', Hitler saw the culmination of all the fallacious and corrosive doctrines of the bourgeois world which had fathered Marxism and were now unable to combat it. Only a movement, such as National Socialism, which was no less brutal in its methods of propaganda, organization and terror could hope to conquer this plague. Hitler openly admitted that he had learned from Marxist Social Democracy many of his techniques of agitation and mass mobilization, even as he denounced it for encouraging subversion, terror and sabotage. In pre-war Austria he had already been deeply impressed by the discipline and mass appeal of the Social-Democratic labour movement; the victory of the Bolsheviks in Russia was to add a further dimension of revolutionary violence and to demonstrate the uses of elitist shock-troops – methods which Hitler and the Nazis eagerly adapted in the 1920s.

The abortive November 1918 revolution in Germany, like the successful Bolshevik uprising a year earlier, was to reinforce Hitler's earlier identification in Vienna of the Jews with Marxism, as the supreme ideological enemy. It was an amalgam which he had most probably first picked up from the propaganda of Karl Lueger's Christian-Social party in Austria, which had made the 'Red Menace' a focal-point of its agitation ever since the turn of the century.[50] By the time the young Hitler arrived in Vienna, the Christian-Social movement stood at the peak of its success, having emerged as the largest single group in the first democratically elected Austrian Parliament. Although he had once been a fanatical adversary of Lueger[51] and his 'sympathies lay at first on the side of the Pan-German Schoenerer', Hitler soon modified his political assessment. The Christian Socialists, he concluded, had shown shrewder judgement concerning 'the worth of the popular masses' than their Pan-German rivals. Their attitude toward socialism was also far superior to that of the *Deutschnationale*, since they had skilfully learned how to tap and mobilize the socio-economic anxieties of the Viennese *Bürgertum* against the rising proletarian movement. Admittedly, the Lueger movement was not truly nationalist, lacking any correct appreciation of 'the importance of the racial problem' and the centrality of the Jewish question in German politics.

National Socialism, on the other hand, was, in Hitler's concept, a fusion of the strengths of the two Austrian movements he had observed in pre-1914 Vienna. As a higher synthesis of the opposition between the 'two great Germans', Lueger and von Schoenerer, it sought to combine the national idea of the *Alldeutsche* with the social praxis of the *Christlich-soziale Partei*. The Pan-German ideology was inextricably bound up with a racial struggle against Jewry and secession from the Habsburg Empire. This was the revolutionary kernel of the German nationalist movement in Austria. The social concept had, however, to be based on the successful use of mass politics as exemplified by Lueger's struggle against Social Democracy.

Clearly Hitler's critique of the strengths and weaknesses of the two pre-1914 Austrian parties owed something to his post-war experience of Weimar politics and his search for ways to mobilize the masses and in particular the threatened German *Mittelstand* which was fighting for its very existence. Hence the sharpness of his criticism of Austrian Pan-Germanism as insufficiently 'social' and therefore incapable of destroying the hold of Marxism on the working masses. No doubt, in his scathing dissection of von Schoenerer's mistakes, Hitler was also settling accounts with post-1918 *völkisch* and right-wing conservatives in the Weimar Republic who were still encrusted in antiquated elitist notions and had failed to grasp the need to appeal to the broad masses and inspire them with the positive ideal of a classless *Volksgemeinschaft* (people's community). Nevertheless Hitler did not dispute the fact that it was the *Alldeutsche* who had first developed a correct vision of the 'principles' of German renewal. Nor did he deny that von Schoenerer had foreseen 'the inevitable end of the Austrian state more correctly than anyone else' and had grasped problems in their innermost essence, though he lacked the astuteness 'to transmit his theoretical knowledge to the masses'.[52] In his 'visionary wisdom', the Pan-German leader had seen the goal but paid no attention to the *means*. His movement had lost impetus by engaging in a parliamentary struggle (Hitler was utterly contemptuous of the Austrian *Reichsrat* which he described as 'the greatest babblers' club of all time') instead of relying on great public meetings and seeking to capture the soul of the masses in the workshops and streets.

This inner driving-force of great revolutions was better understood by the more conservative Lueger than by the would-be revolutionary von Schoenerer. By going into parliament, the Pan-Germans had not only lost their soul but also their credibility as a party of struggle. Henceforth they attracted naive parliamentarians, professors, schoolmasters, lawyers and pacifists instead of leaders and fighters. Hitler emphatically did not believe in a nationalist movement led by a 'bourgeois, idealistic and refined class' which lacked the spirit of sacrifice, the fanatical ardour and 'brutal will' which in his view was indispensable to political success. On this score, Nazism was definitely a departure from the norms of conventional bourgeois politics.

Von Schoenerer, like the post-war leaders of the German *völkisch* movement, not only lacked a broad mass base outside of respectable bourgeois circles but had failed to grasp the significance of the *social question*. He lacked *Menschenkenntnis* (understanding of men), practical wisdom and a 'socialistic' appeal – qualities that his great rival, Karl Lueger, with his acute tactical sense, possessed in abundance. Moreover, Hitler intuitively grasped the Don Quixote component in von Schoenerer's political strategy, which was revealed in his misjudgement of old-established institutions and his 'insufficient understanding of the spiritual nature of the people'.[53] His *Los-von-Rom* movement which sought to convert ten million Austro-Germans to Protestantism, thereby hoping to heal the tragic German church schism and to facilitate the unification of the *Ostmark* Germans with the Reich, was rightly regarded by Hitler as a disastrous blunder. Von Schoenerer had failed to see that lack of national consciousness, not membership of a particular religious denomination, was the central German problem. He had confused politics with religion. A fight against the Catholic Church was not only doomed to failure in the Austrian context, it was utterly wrong on principle, robbing Pan-Germanism of some of the best elements in the nation and making it 'impossible in numerous small and middle circles'. Furthermore it had fragmented the forces of opposition to the dynasty, confusing the masses with two enemies instead of one (*Ohne Juda, ohne Rom wird gebaut Germaniens Dom* was the slogan of the *Alldeutsche*), thereby weakening the impetus, drive and fighting-power of the movement.[54]

On the other hand, Hitler did acknowledge some merits to Pan-Germanism, the core ideology of his boyhood in Linz, whose emotional appeal remained basic to his entire outlook. First and foremost it was a movement which had arisen to defend the very existence of the threatened German *Volk*. It had ruthlessly exposed the rotten façade of the Habsburg dynasty and the swindle of Austrian dynastic patriotism. Hitler, as late as December 1941, reminiscing in the presence of Goebbels and Himmler, recalled that von Schoenerer had been the first 'to oppose the Germanic racial community to the monarchy'. Hence he had initially preferred von Schoenerer to Lueger as 'the most logical of the two for he was determined to blow up the Austrian State'.[55] Precisely because it was in opposition to the State as such and stressed the priority of the *Volk*, Pan-Germanism had always appealed to the subversive revolutionary impulse in Hitler. Its treasonable quality did not in the least disturb him, for the downfall of Austria 'could only seem to me the beginning of the redemption of the German nation'.[56] Indeed, Hitler shared von Schoenerer's idealization of the Hohenzollern Reich and his belief that salvation lay in reunion with Germany.

For personal as well as political reasons, Hitler also fully vindicated von Schoenerer's radical, uncompromising antisemitism, which his mentor had proclaimed as 'the mainstay of our national ideology, as the most essential expression of genuine popular conviction and thus as the major national achievement of the century'.[57] Like the Austrian Pan-German leader, Hitler directed his antisemitism not against the Jewish religion but against the allegedly unchanging racial peculiarities of Jewry.[58] To the Pan-Germans, the Jew, unlike the Slav, was the eternal enemy of the *Volk*, the symbolic representative of urban mobility and supra-national money-powers, responsible for uprooting Germanic peasants from home and hearth. Unlike Czechs or Slovenes, who at least shared a common 'Aryan' descent and Christian culture with the German people, the Jews were depicted as biologically unassimilable aliens and subverters of the *Volk*. Hitler may have scoffed at the backward-looking, romantic, neo-pagan Teutonic cult of the Schoenerite movement, but on its premise of an unbridgeable, absolute cleavage between 'Aryan' and 'Semite', he never wavered.[59]

Only an antisemitism based on the race principles espoused by von Schoenerer and his followers could be serious, to Hitler's mind. This indeed was his major reproach against Karl Lueger's Christian-Social party, which had come to power in Vienna at the end of the 1890s on an anti-Jewish platform, yet was already notorious for its cynical *Geschäftsantisemitismus*.[60] Lueger had laconically warned his more fanatic Austrian followers after assuming office as Mayor of Vienna that he would determine who was to be defined as a 'Jew' (*'Wer a Jud ist, das bestimme ich'*). For pragmatic reasons he resolved to maintain amicable relations with the wealthy Jewish business community of Vienna whose financial assistance was indeed indispensable to his ambitious municipal projects. As he once pointed out to Sigmund Mayer, a prominent Jewish communal leader in Vienna, antisemitism was 'an excellent means of propaganda and getting ahead in politics' but it was 'the sport of the rabble', useless once in office.[61] Such *Scheinantisemitismus* (sham antisemitism) on the 'Jewish question' seemed 'almost worse than none at all' to Hitler, who found it both immoral and reprehensible. Not only was it superficial and 'unscientific', exploiting emotional feeling rather than being based on true knowledge, but 'it lulled people into security; they thought they had the foe by the ears, while in reality they themselves were being led by the nose'.[62]

Christian-Social antisemitism was really no inconvenience at all to the Jews. 'If the worst came to the worst, a splash of baptismal water could always save the business and the Jew at the same time.'[63] Its underlying cynicism lacked the conviction that drove Hitler – namely that 'this was a vital question for all humanity, with the fate of all non-Jewish peoples depending on its solution'.[64] The Lueger movement had reduced what should have been the outcome of an 'inner' or 'higher' consecration to an expression of competitive envy or, worse still, to the attempt at a new conversion of the Jews. Hitler had no sympathy at all for this type of clerical antisemitism which he considered to be based on fallacious and outworn religious notions. But he could see its political expediency for the Christian-Social Party which sought, not unsuccessfully, to win over the large Czech element in Vienna (over 100,000 immigrants), especially the small artisans, by an appeal to traditional religious and economic antisemitism.[65] Any reliance on Pan-German racial principles would not only have diminished Christian-Social support among Viennese Czechs but have undermined the Habsburg monarchy which Lueger desired at all costs to save. Hence, both the half-hearted character of Christian-Social antisemitism and its desire to reconcile the Slavs were linked to the essentially *staatserhaltend* and supra-national orientation of Lueger's party – all negative attributes, in Hitler's mind.

The Catholic Mayor had erred in his struggle against the Jews, in his tolerance of the Czechs, in his respect for the existing *Rechtsstaat* and above all in his desire to try and bolster an 'impossible state'; nonetheless, although his constructive work was doomed by the decaying structure within which he worked, Hitler still regarded him as 'the greatest German mayor of all times' and as 'the last great German to be born in the ranks of the people who had colonized the *Ostmark*'.[66] Even if it was too late to save the monarchy, Lueger had given imperial Vienna a new lease of life and brought off a string of remarkable achievements as a social reformer with his beautification projects and communalization of utilities.[67] Though his party had no clear conception of the 'German reawakening' and the centrality of race, Lueger by his practicality and mastery of the art of leadership had shown what could be accomplished in the field of municipal politics. Hitler, the Pan-German ideologue who had arrived in Vienna convinced that the Christian-Socials were a reactionary party, was persuaded by the pragmatic Lueger's charisma, his political skills and oratorical ability that had the Viennese Mayor lived in Germany 'he would have ranked among the great minds of our people'. He could not refrain from admiring a popular leader who was such a virtuoso in the arts of mass persuasion, even if he felt no sympathy for his 'ideology' or for the programme of the Christian-Social Party.[68]

In particular, Hitler singled out for praise 'the infinite shrewdness' of Lueger's policy towards the Catholic Church, his winning over the younger clergy and his clever method of drawing on old sources of power to consolidate his position.[69] At the same time Lueger had grasped the crucial importance of the lower middle classes and the need to mobilize them for his cause. He understood only too well 'that the political fighting power of the upper bourgeoisie at the present time was but slight and inadequate for achieving the victory of a great movement. Therefore he laid the greatest stress in his political activity on winning over the classes whose existence was threatened and therefore tended to spur rather than paralyse the will to fight'.[70] Thus Lueger became in some respects a role-model for the young Hitler in spite of the gulf in ideology and temperament. Both leaders grew out of the same soil of Austrian Catholicism and the crisis of the decaying *Mittelstand*. One difference, however, remained central. Lueger represented the last flowering of the pre-war *Bürger* political culture based on social deference, economic security and the rule of law. Adolf Hitler and his band of *déclassé* desperadoes were destined to be its destroyers.

# CHAPTER TWO

# The Politics of Either-Or

In a letter from the front to a Munich acquaintance, written on 5 February 1915, Hitler expressed the hope that 'the daily sacrifices and sufferings of hundreds of thousands of us and the torrent of blood that keeps flowing here day after day against an international world of enemies will not only help smash Germany's foes outside but that our inner internationalism will collapse [*unser innere Internationalismus zerbricht*]. This would be worth much more than any gain in territory.'[1] For Hitler, as for many of his generation, the great conflagration that began in August 1914 was to be the decisive existential experience in his life. Compared to 'this gigantic struggle, everything past receded to shallow nothingness. . . .'[2] Vanished were the feelings of impotence and bitterness for 'having been born at a time which erected its Halls of Fame only to shopkeepers and government officials. . . .' Gone, too, was the sense of boredom, alienation and feckless bohemian drift which had characterized Hitler's pre-war years in Vienna and led him to evade military service in the Habsburg colours.[3] Now began what he somewhat pathetically called 'the greatest and most unforgettable time of my earthly existence' as a soldier in the German Imperial Army.

From Hitler's standpoint, the World War had been fought to safeguard the very existence of the entire German nation, whose survival was threatened by 'foreign influences' (*Fremdländerei*) within, as much as by the ring of enemies encircling its borders. Furthermore his long-standing suspicions of the hinterland, of the machinations of Marxists and Jews, were to be hardened into an irreconcilable hatred by a series of shocks, personal and collective, which occurred in November 1918; as he lay in Pasewalk military infirmary in Pomerania, recuperating from the blindness inflicted by mustard gassing at the front, he learned in rapid succession of the Kiel naval mutiny, the councils' revolution in Munich, the Emperor Wilhelm's abdication and Germany's military surrender. According to Hitler, it was this shattering series of events which determined his future course of action and decision to enter politics. Many times in the future he was to recall the trauma of that period and to vow that 'there will never again be another November 1918 in German history'.

Hitler's pre-war involvement in politics had at best been passive – 'not so much through meetings as through a thorough study of practical economics and also in the available antisemitic literature'.[4] In Vienna he had not formally joined any political party and in Munich his activities before 1914 had been restricted to informally haranguing small groups of *völkisch* proto-Nazis in local beer-cellars and taverns. But now in the aftermath of the German defeat and the ill-fated Bavarian Soviet Republic headed by the Jewish-born pacifist Kurt Eisner, Munich provided an ideal terrain for counter-revolutionary agitation. In particular, militant racist groups like the Thule Gesellschaft, a secret society established in January 1918 by the occultist Rudolf von Sebottendorf, offered a framework for promoting Pan-German, *völkisch* and antisemitic causes.[5] Among its members and guests were a number of leading figures in the early Nazi movement such as Dietrich Eckart, Alfred Rosenberg, Gottfried Feder, Rudolf Hess and Hans Frank. The Thule Society had close links with the Free Corps, Grassinger's German Socialist Party, Karl Harrer's *Arbeiterzirkel* and national socialist groups like Anton Drexler's *Deutsche Arbeiterpartei* to which Hitler would shortly gravitate as part of his post-war intelligence work for the Bavarian Reichswehr.[6] Hitler accepted many of the ideological premises of the *völkisch*, antisemitic circles as self-evident, especially the emphasis on race, the negative stereotypes of Jews and the fight against Marxist internationalism.[7] On the other hand, theosophical, mystical and spiritualist aspects of the *völkisch* movement left him cold.

He came to despise the sectarianism, impracticality and lack of political discipline of the German Radical Right who reminded him all too vividly of all the failings of the pre-war Austrian Pan-German movement. Even the term *völkisch* struck him as 'extremely vague' and imprecise, smacking of doctrinaire elitism.[8] Increasingly, Hitler rejected the conventional bourgeois nationalism of these circles and their remoteness from the masses.[9] To buttress his own claims to be the leader of a classless popular party, he could draw very effectively on his own experiences as an ordinary front-line soldier who had emerged from the ranks of the people. His *Fronterlebnis* had inculcated in him one of the central beliefs shared by all the leaders of the Nazi movement, that war and struggle represented the highest of all values. It was not only *the* authentic life-experience but also the ultimate test of the individual and the nation.[10] The 'socialism' of the Nazis also grew out of precisely this spirit of self-sacrifice for the interests of the national community. National Socialism, after all, was to many of his early followers an extension of the camaraderie of the trenches to civilian life and an attempt to counter the endemic class divisions of German society with the myth of a *Volksgemeinschaft* drawn from wartime experience.

Hitler's conception of politics as a 'reckoning' (*Abrechnung*) also drew heavily on his wartime service and the trauma of collapse and national humiliation in November 1918, besides being peculiarly suited to his vengeful, absolutist temperament. Unlike the professional politicians of Weimar Germany, Hitler the Austrian Catholic outsider looked on politics in *salvationist* terms as a series of either-or choices which would lead to deliverance or catastrophe. Political problems had therefore to be simplified and reduced to their existential core of being and non-being, the freedom and fate of the nation, its survival or destruction. For Hitler and many of those who joined the ranks of the National Socialist movement in the early 1920s were convinced that Germany had succumbed not only to economic and political chaos but to something approaching an ontological disaster.[11] The nation, it was endlessly repeated, lay in the grip of alien, demonic forces who were seeking its perpetual enslavement as a step on the road to their world domination. Germany in the early 1920s was already tottering on the edge of an abyss, threatened with extinction by the crushing burdens of reparations, rampant inflation, the iniquitous provisions of the Versailles Treaty, the imminence of Communist revolution and a chronic absence of national will and authority. This Nazi perception of the internal and external threats confronting the nation was in fact shared by many conservatives, by sections of the middle classes and also those social groups most directly threatened with loss of status, income and position. What provided Nazism and especially Hitler's own oratory with its dynamic edge was, however, not so much the objective situation as the intensity of the eschatological vision of impending doom and the promise of ultimate redemption. Since the 'catastrophe' of November 1918 Hitler had become convinced that the resurgence of Germany and the destruction of the Jews were organically related processes. 'There is no making pacts with Jews,' he declared in *Mein Kampf*, 'there can only be the hard either-or.'[12]

This either-or, which formed the central core of Hitler's ideology and sense of mission, was built on an essentially religious perception of the world – one that resembled ancient Manichean and Gnostic heresies within Christianity. Hitler's struggle against the Jews was in fact conceived as an eschatological war of the Forces of Light against a fiendish enemy whose agents were everywhere hell-bent on the destruction of Germany and of the 'Aryan' races. 'The goal then was clear and simple', as he told an audience in the Munich beer-cellars on 27 February 1925: 'Fight the devil power that has hurled Germany into this misery. Fight Marxism as well as the spiritual supporter of this world pest and epidemic disease, the Jew. . . .' There were only two possible outcomes in this life-and-death struggle. 'Either the enemy will walk over our corpses, or we will walk over his.'[13] In his fight against the Devil,

Hitler saw himself as the chosen Redeemer of his people and of the entire non-Jewish world, called upon to frustrate a truly satanic design. All methods were therefore justified in conducting this millenarian war for the salvation of the *Volk*. 'We want to prevent our Germany from being crucified too! Let us be inhuman! But if we save Germany haven't we accomplished the greatest deed in the world? Let us be unjust! But if we save Germany, we have eliminated the greatest injustice in the world. Let us be unethical! But if we save our *Volk*, we have broken a path for morality again!'[14] In these and similar passages, Hitler fused traditional Christian images of crucifixion and deicide with the language of radical secular nationalism and the inversion of all humanitarian values. But what did the rescue of Germany from 'crucifixion' and its salvation from the diabolical world-tyranny of Judah really entail? Did Hitler's either-or approach to the 'Jewish question' in those early years in post-war Munich refer to emigration, expulsion or mass murder? Was he merely a conventional antisemite repeating 'the empty claptrap of every Right-wing rabble-rouser' or did his rhetoric already presage something unprecedented and radically new?[15]

Part of the answer may be contained in Hitler's first written political statement, dated 16 September 1919. This already revealed his opposition to the 'purely emotional' antisemitism that would 'ultimately express itself in pogroms'; he favoured, on the contrary, a 'rational', scientific antisemitism (*der Antisemitismus der Vernunft*) which must lead 'to a systematic and legal struggle for the removal [*Beseitigung*] of those privileges which the Jew enjoys – unlike other foreigners living in our midst, who are subject to Alien Laws. The final aim of such antisemitism must unquestionably be the removal [*Entfernung*] of the Jews altogether.'[16] The elimination of the Jews from the midst of the German people was, therefore, from the outset the self-proclaimed goal of Hitler, one that went considerably beyond the pre-1914 *völkisch* objective of repealing their civil emancipation. Did this call for 'removal' mean something more than expulsion? If not, why did Hitler repeatedly reaffirm his 'inexorable determination to attack the evil at its roots and to eradicate it root and branch' (*das Übel an der Wurzel zu packen und mit Stumpf und Stiel auszurotten*)?[17] Why then did he insist in his first political speech devoted exclusively to the 'Jewish question' (13 August 1920) that 'our task must be to arouse the mass instinct against the Jew, to stir it up and keep it on the boil until it decides to support the movement which is prepared to take the consequences'?[18] In the same speech Hitler had again stressed that only 'scientific antisemitism had clearly recognized the frightful danger which that race represents to every people' and warned against judging Jews 'on the basis of sentiments' by differentiating between 'good and bad individuals'.[19] In an earlier letter to Konstantin Hierl (3 July 1920) Hitler had also distinguished between emotional reactions and 'sober recognition of the facts' – which meant grasping that 'over the centuries the Jew in his effects had become the racial tuberculosis of the nations'.[20] Further, in a Salzburg speech of 7 August 1920 he stressed that one could no more blame the Jews for their destructive role in history than one could reproach 'tubercular germs', though the fight against their influence necessitated the ruthless 'removal' of the source of infection. Clearly, if, as Hitler made plain in a speech of May 1923, the Jews were not human 'in the sense of being an image of God'[2] but rather were 'an image of the devil' and a universal form of 'racial tuberculosis', expulsion could scarcely represent a *final* solution. It could at best be a stage towards the ultimate fate reserved for a subhuman species of vermin – namely, physical liquidation.

Many passages from Hitler's early public speeches and writings suggest the fanatical murderous character of his antisemitic obsession and its likely results. Thus the notorious remark in *Mein Kampf* which seemed to presage the gas-chambers of the Second World War, even as it held the Jews responsible for the mass carnage of the First World War: 'If at the beginning of the war and during the war, twelve or fifteen thousand of these Hebrew defilers had been put under poison gas as hundreds of thousands of our very best workers from all walks of life had to endure at the front, then the sacrifice of millions at the front would not have been in vain. On the contrary: twelve thousand scoundrels eliminated in time might perhaps have saved the lives of a million decent valuable Germans.'[22] In recalling the slaughter of the trenches, Hitler seemed to openly advocate a preventive war against the Jews in order 'to exterminate mercilessly the agitators who were misleading the nation'. Such drastic action might in his view have prevented the German defeat in 1918 and its disastrous consequences. It might have stopped the forces of disintegration – the Jews, the Marxists and liberal democrats – before they began to decompose the body politic and eat away the living substance of the nation. In this battle of destiny against the 'world poisoner of the peoples' the most ruthless methods were admissible and indeed essential.

The early Hitler speeches, with their violence, uninhibited language and imagery of extermination, are in this respect a much better guide to his real intentions than the more muted subliminal hints of the party leader and international statesman in the 1930s. To rapturous applause, Hitler would tell his Munich audiences that antisemitism was worthless unless it was implemented in bloody earnest, that 'the Jew's skull will be smashed by Germanic will' and that the enemy could only be neutralized by 'brachial violence'.[23] In a private declaration to Major Josef Hell in 1922 he affirmed that if he gained power, 'the annihilation of the Jews will be my first and foremost task' (*dann wird die Vernichtung der Juden meine erste und wichtigste Aufgabe sein*).[24] Gripped by a paroxysm of hatred, Hitler began to rant: 'As soon as I take power, I shall have gallows erected, in Munich, for example, in the Marienplatz, and as many as traffic permits. Then the Jews will be hanged one after another, and they will stay hanging until they stink. They will be left hanging as long as public health makes possible. As soon as one is untied, the next will take his place and that will go on until the last Jew in Munich is obliterated [*ausgetilgt*]. Exactly the same thing will happen in the other cities until Germany is cleansed of its last Jew' (*bis Deutschland vom letzten Juden gereinigt ist*).[25] When questioned as to why he should desire to murder such talented and intelligent people, Hitler answered in a surprisingly sober and almost dispassionate way. In all revolutions it had been necessary to struggle against some social class or caste – whether the target was the princely houses, the nobility, the clergy or even the peasantry – in order to channel 'the feelings of hatred of the broad masses'. Having carefully calculated which social group in Germany was currently the most vulnerable to such a campaign, Hitler had decided to focus his attack on the Jews. 'I can assure you', he told Major Hell, 'that I have analysed all imaginable and possible solutions to this problem and, on the basis of all the relevant factors, I have come to the conclusion that a battle against the Jews will be as popular as it will be successful. There are few Germans who haven't been angered or injured in their dealings with Jews. With relatively small numbers, the Jews control a massive portion of Germany's wealth, which could be made just as useful to the state and to the community as the possessions of the monastic orders, the bishops and the nobles. Once the hatred and the battle against the Jews are really stirred up, their resistance will inevitably break down in short order. They cannot protect themselves and nobody will stand forth as their defenders.'[26]

The sadistic cynicism, the 'ice-cold calculation' and the hatred in Hitler's attitude to the Jews are revealed in these off-the-record remarks with the clarity of an X-ray photograph. 'To break the power of the Jews' and to free the Germans from the clutches of an alien race was a programme which promised to rally support from across the political spectrum.[27] The Jews could be readily depicted as the symbol of the vengeful Entente powers responsible for the crushing reparations, as representatives of big capital, the banks and international Communism; did they not also control the bourgeois parties, the strings of parliamentary democracy, the decision for war and peace?[28] In Germany they had been made responsible by radical Nationalists for sabotaging victory at the front, for smashing the national economy by strikes, for organizing the workers' councils and the Spartacist uprising, for sowing discord between Prussians and Bavarians and paving the way for the

Dictatorship of International Finance Capital![29] For the Radical Right, there was no essential difference between the interests of the Stock Exchange Jews and 'their' press (the Jewish-owned *Frankfurter Zeitung* or *Berliner Tageblatt*) or the workers' leadership.[30] Thus for Hitler and the Nazis, November 1918 did not represent a socialist but a 'stock-exchange' revolution which served Jewish financial interests and not those of ordinary German workers.[31] Marxism was simply an instrument to undermine the authority of the State and national independence, so that the masses could more easily succumb to the 'interest-slavery' of the Jewish international bankers.[32]

In a speech on 12 April 1922, Hitler explained: 'The guilt of the Jews lies in the fact that they have agitated the masses into this November madness. When we look at the parties we see on the Left lying and deceit on the part of the leaders, blind faith on the part of the led and all alike in the service of a single aim: To destroy this State, to rob this people of its freedom, to enslave its labour-strength. . . .' It was 'the same Jew' who led the masses in 1918 who still championed them four years later whether as majority Socialist, Independent or Communist, but always in the name of his own racial interests.[33] In order to accelerate the disintegration of the 'Aryan' peoples he had whipped up the propertyless proletariat against the industrial bourgeoisie.[34] National Socialism, on the other hand, postulated the unity of the nation and an uncompromising racial and ideological struggle between Germans and Jews, between the *völkisch* and internationalist world-views.[35] Race and not class was the primary datum at the centre of history.[36] In this confrontation, no compromise was possible and heads would inevitably roll, whichever side was victorious.

Within the Nazi *Weltanschauung* racial warfare came to assume the same centrality as class conflict within Marxism. It was not an interchangeable element or a question of tactics but an encounter of cosmic significance between two antagonistic races fighting a life-and-death struggle for world domination. No neutrality was possible and no quarter could be given, for Jewry did not represent a partial defect in society that could be corrected but a *totality* of evils which spelled the doom of 'Aryan' man and his culture unless the Jew was eradicated. Only by annihilating this 'eternal' race could the survival and immortality of the German *Volk* be guaranteed.

The harsh Either-Or that underlay Hitler's Manichean vision had a 'positive' as well as a negative dimension, for to achieve the ultimate objective of transforming the Germans into a new *Herrenvolk* who would dominate the world necessarily meant to the Nazis creating a racially homogeneous, purified and healthy people. This nation of soldier-peasants who were destined to fulfil the German mission of forging a new era of 'Aryan' civilization would first have to acquire the undiluted herd instinct that characterized all conquering peoples. They would have to observe the strictest laws to ensure against racial defilement and weakening the 'unity of the blood'.

Since Hitler, like the *völkisch* ideologues of the nineteenth century, was obsessed by the lack of German racial homogeneity, the purification measures he envisaged were all the more draconian. Though the Prussian state and the discipline of its army admittedly provided one important nucleus for the crystallization of a new Reich, the National Socialist revolution would have to operate at a much deeper level by accomplishing the complete racial purification of the *Volk*. Once Germany was in a position to exercise global hegemony, the 'Aryan' millennium would dawn. The *Pax Germanica* would usher in an era of unprecedented cultural development, for it would blaze the trail for Aryan man to realize 'the divine spark of genius' which had stamped him historically as 'the Prometheus of mankind'.[37] The condition for this golden age was the creation of a sharp barrier between masters and slaves. The mixing of *Herrenvolk* blood with the lower races would be the doom of the Reich.

For Hitler the only serious antagonists to this dream of a new world-order were the Jews, for they too were preparing their bid for global domination.[38] On the one hand there was the 'Jewish world financial power' allegedly centred in Wall Street and the City of London; then there was Marxism, a 'Jewish' invention which destroyed national cohesion through class struggle and led to Russian Bolshevism, which represented the naked thrust of the Jews for political power on a *global* scale. Moreover, *laissez faire*, freedom of the press, religious toleration, freemasonry and liberal democracy were ultimately all weapons of the Jew in his fight to destroy the race consciousness of the Aryan peoples, while safeguarding his own.[39] Thus the Jew was the main enemy of 'Aryanism' and the greatest threat to the racial purity of the European nations. Moreover, possessing no culture-creating capacity of his own, the Jew could only disintegrate and destroy the culture of others.[40] The sovereignty of his 'eternal' Jewish empire would only be erected on the ruins of the individual nation-states. Hitler and other leading Nazis were genuinely convinced that the Jews had continuously schemed and plotted through history to achieve this ultimate messianic goal which was prophesied in their Holy Scriptures.[41]

With the liberation from the ghetto in the early nineteenth century, the acquisition of 'civil rights' and the extension of his economic empire, the Jew had been able to consolidate his social position. Using the fashionable terminology of 'progress', 'freedom', 'humanity', he had managed to undermine the national solidarity of his host-peoples and poison their blood while keeping his male line pure. He had corrupted the princes, then the upper classes and finally the bourgeoisie, which he had previously used as 'a battering ram against the feudal world'; once the victory of democracy and his own civic emancipation had been assured by the bourgeois revolutions in the West, he turned to the new proletarian class to further promote his drive for power. Appealing to the grievances and sense of social justice of the 'Aryan' proletariat, he became the theorist, leader and organizer of the labour movement while at the same time supervising the capitalist exploitation of the workers. 'From now on the worker only has the task of working for the future of the Jewish people. He is unconsciously put into the service of that power which he believes he is fighting.' The result was the destruction of the national economy and 'the triumph of the international stock-exchange'. This opened the way for stock-exchange Jewry to dominate the economies and national life of the individual states. In each nation the Jew adapted to the prevailing mentality and ideological tendencies – for example, in France to 'the well-known and well-understood chauvinism' and in England to 'economic and imperial conceptions'. In every case the objective was identical, namely to subordinate the true national interest of the *Volk* to the needs of Jewish international finance.[42]

Towards the end of the First World War, the Jewish conspiracy had achieved its greatest breakthrough with the Bolshevik Revolution. In *Mein Kampf*, Hitler portrayed Russian Bolshevism as Jewry's twentieth-century effort to achieve world dominion; the Jews had succeeded through the revolution in uprooting the 'Germanic nucleus' which had been responsible for the organization of the Russian state-structure and the development of the Tsarist empire. Bolshevism had thereby robbed the Russian people of its intelligentsia and constructive, state-building element, replacing this with the rule of a race whose genius lay solely in destruction. The Jewish rulers would not be able to maintain their domination for long, since in the nature of things they were incapable of building spatially limited states. 'Impossible as it is for the Russians alone to shake off the yoke of the Jews through their own strength, it is equally impossible in the long run for the Jews to maintain the mighty Empire. Jewry itself is not an organizing element, but a ferment of decomposition. The giant Empire in the East is ripe for collapse; and the end of Jewish rule in Russia will also be the end of Russia as a State. We have been chosen by Fate as witnesses of a catastrophe which will be the mightiest confirmation of the soundness of the folkist theory.'[43]

The next target of 'Jewish bolshevism' would be Germany, which, Hitler and the Nazis claimed, was now the central battle-ground of the global struggle between the Aryan world and Jewry. The ultimate objective of the enemy was the internationalization of the economy and the enslavement of

German labour power to Jewish finance. The methods, as in Soviet Russia, would involve the ruthless extermination of the national (folkish) intelligentsia and the reduction of the masses to a state of helotry. It was the mission of National Socialism to halt the planned 'bolshevization' of Germany which was now imminent, as part of the Jewish strategy of world-conquest. The mighty struggle in Germany would be the fateful turning-point in world history. 'If our people and our State', Hitler wrote in *Mein Kampf*, 'become the victims of these bloodthirsty and avaricious Jewish tyrants of nations, the whole earth will sink into the snares of this octopus; if Germany frees herself from this embrace, the greatest of dangers to the nations may be regarded as broken for the whole world.'[44]

From the early 1920s to the macabre end of his career in the Berlin *Führerbunker*, Hitler regarded this fight against Jewish world power, represented by the twin poles of Bolshevism and international finance, as his sacred mission and the foremost historic task of National Socialism.[45] From an ideological standpoint it was to remain his central war-aim and his *raison d'être* for plunging Germany into a second global conflagration. For not only Bolshevism and international finance, but also the entire system of nation-states and the world economy were decisively shaped, so he believed, by Jewish machinations. Germany could not, therefore, achieve its own mission and bring about the new millennium of Aryan culture without breaking up the old order dominated by Jewish interests. As he told Hermann Rauschning, shortly after the Nazi seizure of power: 'The struggle for world domination will be fought entirely between us, between Germans and Jews. All else is façade and illusion. Behind England stands Israel, and behind France, and behind the United States. Even when we have driven the Jew out of Germany, he remains our world enemy.'[46] In this titanic struggle, the Jews were not only economic and political antagonists but rivals in a deeper metaphysical sense. 'There cannot be two Chosen Peoples. We are God's people', Hitler insisted, whereas the Jews were 'the men of Satan'.[47]

Two irreconcilable worlds and two different species faced one another. 'The Jew is the anti-man, the creature of another god', he told Rauschning. 'He must have come from another root of the human race. I set the Aryan and the Jew over against each other; if I call one of them a human being I must call the other something else. The two are as widely separated as man and beast. . . . He is a creature outside nature and alien to nature.'[48] Yet in spite of this abyss, Hitler could still remark: 'Has it not struck you how the Jew is the exact opposite of the German in every single respect, yet is as closely akin to him as a blood brother?'[49] The Führer of the Third Reich insisted on the paradox of 'two groups so closely allied and yet so utterly dissimilar'; moreover, he added that it was 'impossible to exaggerate the formidable quality of the Jew as an enemy'. Hence this struggle would necessarily be 'the critical battle for the fate of the world!'[50]

Rauschning, correctly in my view, grasped the underlying dimension of meta-historical rivalry in Hitler's antisemitism, perceived as 'an actual war of the gods'. One god inevitably excluded the other. 'Israel, the historic people of the spiritual God', as Rauschning put it, 'cannot but be the irreconcilable enemy of the new, the German, Chosen People.'[51] Precisely because the Jews were historically the protagonists, of the 'independence of the spirit', 'eminent in science', in analysis and criticism, they were pre-ordained to be the object of Hitler's loathing. Were they not the inventors of the moral code, of the conceptions of sin, conscience and faith in divine redemption which Christianity had absorbed from Judaism? This alone would have sufficed to make them the mortal enemy of the Nazi creed with its eulogizing of power, hierarchy, militarism and the natural order. Thus Hitler was perfectly logical in inflating the Jew into a mythical abstract prototype of all those humanist and moral values which his National Socialist revolution wished to sweep away. At the same time the Jew was not just an invisible daemon but a *visible* enemy to be combated in the flesh, one against whom the struggle could never be relaxed. Partly this was the manifestation of what Rauschning perceived as a 'genuine personal feeling of primitive hatred and vengefulness'. Hitler actually believed in the 'natural wickedness of the Jew', who symbolized for him the very principle of evil. On the other hand, he also knew that antisemitism was not all that deeply rooted among the mass of Germans and that many in the rank-and-file of his own party did not take it so seriously.[52]

Even in the top-flight Nazi leadership where racialism was rampant, it is doubtful if the most radical antisemites like Goebbels and Streicher shared the fantastic perspectives in which Hitler envisaged the concrete struggle. For most of the leading Nazis, antisemitism was an exceedingly useful revolution-ary expedient; a way of challenging the middle classes at home and the liberal democracies abroad, while carrying out a displaced revolution which did not actually destroy the bourgeois order.[53] Hitler, too, affirmed that antisemitism was 'beyond question the most important weapon in his propagandist arsenal, and almost everywhere it was of deadly efficiency'.[54] As a weapon of foreign subversion it was almost 'indispensable', unhinging the social system and leading to a radical re-ordering of international relations: 'You will see how little time we shall need', Hitler declared, 'in order to upset the ideas and the criteria of the whole world, simply and purely by attacking Judaism.'[55] But the antisemitic campaign was for him part of an even more far-reaching concept of biological politics through which he aimed at overthrowing the existing

international political and economic order. Antisemitism was the popular
spearhead of a broader conception of race with which 'National Socialism will
carry its revolution abroad and recast the world'. The traditional borders of
the European nation-states would be torn up in a vast re-ordering and
repartition of the globe based on the recognition of biological values. New
elites, based on the most militant, Nordic elements within the nations, would
rise to the fore in countries like Britain, America and France, and with these
'Aryan' rulers the new German Reich might in the future be able to make pacts
and alliances. With the elimination of the disruptive Jewish influence, the
world would return to a state of normal conflicts based on territorial
imperatives and the Darwinian struggle for living space.

Far from being narrowly nationalist or purely opportunist, Hitler's
antisemitism was therefore part of an apocalyptic, universalist vision of the
future. It was his destiny to save the 'Aryan' nations from what he perceived as
a catastrophic danger. Bolshevism, international capitalism and democracy
were only the outward expressions of this danger whose roots lay in Jewish
messianism, which was ultimately responsible for the alienation of humanity
from the natural order. It was the Judeo-Christian ethic and its secularization
in contemporary teachings of pacifism, human equality before the law and the
brotherhood of man, which had corrupted and deformed man and society.
Judaism epitomized the revolt of the weak against the strong, of quantity
against quality, of the mass against the elite. In a word, it destroyed the
natural hierarchy within the nation and between the races. Both Christianity
and Bolshevism, 'inventions of the Jew', had universalized this pernicious
egalitarian teaching; the former had destroyed the power of Rome in
Antiquity, while Communism threatened all nation-states in the twentieth
century.[56] From St Paul to Karl Marx, the seed of revolt against the natural
order lay in the same 'ferment of decomposition' – the Jew and his promise of a
transcendent God.

Hitler's revolt against Judeo-Christian messianism did not preclude but in
fact sharpened the salvationist character of his own movement. Nazism was
from the outset essentially a political religion or eschatology which used sacral
structures patterned on Christian forms even as it undermined and inverted
their spritual content.[57] The role of the Führer as Redeemer of the *Volk* recalled
in caricatural form that of the Christian Saviour. In earlier speeches made
during the *Kampfzeit*, especially in Catholic Bavaria, Hitler actually compared
his own salvationist doctrine to that of Jesus. Like his predecessor, he, too,
lived in a 'materialistic world contaminated by Jews', where state power was
corrupt and incompetent. Christ in Hitler's self-projection had created a great
world-movement by preaching a popular anti-Jewish faith with patriotic

idealism. Hitler wished to bring about the same result in the political sphere.[58] Even when it turned inwardly against Christianity and called for a total revaluation of all values, Nazism inherited from its dogmatic theology the deep-rooted belief that the Jew was the main obstacle to human redemption, the eternal thorn in the flesh of the elect. This continuity was more evident during the early years, when the Nazis sought to present their doctrines as compatible with 'positive' Christianity and were eager to tap the centuries-old tradition of Christian antisemitism for electoral purposes. Hitler, for example, readily found sustenance in New Testament texts for his own public stance toward the Jews, recalling in his earlier speeches and in *Mein Kampf* that Christ 'took to the whip to drive from the temple of the Lord this adversary of all humanity'.[59] Even for his own fanaticism a precedent could be found in one of Jesus' best-known sayings: 'That which is neither hot nor cold will I spew out of my mouth.' Hitler was fond of quoting this 'utterance of the great Nazarene' against those adversaries who believed in the golden mean, whether in politics or in life. 'Until the present day the half-hearted and the lukewarm have remained the curse of Germany.'[60]

Nevertheless, Hitler's radicalism, while it could clothe itself in such traditional Christian pieties, belonged fundamentally to the ideological politics of the twentieth century and revealed the same historical determinism which has invariably been its accompaniment. Nor, in waging war on rival ideologies such as Marxism, did he hesitate to adopt their weapons and stand familiar slogans upside down. In a speech in Munich on 31 May 1920 he countered the Communist rallying-cry, 'Proletarians of all countries, unite!', with his own internationalist call: 'Antisemites of all lands, unite! Peoples of Europe, liberate yourselves!'[61] The 'Jewish question' conceived as a struggle of all 'Aryans' against non-Aryans was Hitler's answer to the Marxian dogma of class conflict.

Marx and the Communists had distorted the true meaning of socialism which was in its essence both national and antisemitic. 'Aryan' Socialism did not repudiate private property, or negate the fatherland or the importance of individuality; it opposed this false internationalist teaching of an alien race which was destructive by nature. Rather it promised to eradicate for ever the taint of Marxism from the German working-class.[62] National Socialism would instead restore national consciousness and a place of honour to the German proletariat which had made the heaviest sacrifices during the First World War for the sake of the fatherland.[63] In contrast to Communism, which in Soviet Russia had merely instituted new forms of class rule, bureaucracy and capitalistic exploitation under 'Jewish' rule, the Nazis offered the workers the prospect of full national integration.[64] The German proletariat, in return for abandoning the illusions of world revolution and international solidarity, would finally take its place as an estate of fully equal *Volksgenossen* (racial comrades) in the ranks of the nation. Only then could the *Volk* come together and act as a single unit, with one outlook, one will and a common commitment to the 'Aryan' struggle for existence. 'For Socialism', Hitler insisted, was 'anything but an international creation . . . it has indeed grown up exclusively in Aryan hearts; it owes its intellectual glories only to Aryan brains. It is entirely alien to the Jew.'[65]

Hitler's early speeches constantly repeat the call for manual and intellectual workers to close ranks and fight for the national liberation of the German people from 'Jewish' tyranny.[66] Only a united Germany could break the power of international capital and its agents – the liberals, the Social Democrats and the Communists. There could be no room for either 'class conscious' proletarians or bourgeois in the Nazi ranks. All Germans had instead to weld themselves into a national front of the productive classes against the Jews, who were responsible for all the internal divisions, the racial degeneration and the enslavement of the *Volk*.[67] His compatriots would also have to overcome not only the class but the religious and regional particularism fomented by Jewry which created dissension and disunity in German Society.[68] It was the great achievement of National Socialism in Hitler's eyes that it had located the origin of all these weaknesses at their source; that it had succeeded by 1919 in transforming antisemitism from a narrow petty-bourgeois ideology 'into the driving impulse of a great people's movement'.[69] Moreover, in contrast to the conservative parties of the Right who identified nationalism with the defunct monarchy or with their narrow class interests and had failed to grasp the centrality of 'the fight against the common hereditary foe of all Aryans', the Nazis stressed the harmony of 'national' and 'social' objectives.[70] The old Right had not freed itself from a traditional class standpoint and it had forgotten that democracy is 'fundamentally not German; it is Jewish';[71] it failed, moreover, to understand that majority rule meant the destruction of 'Aryan' leadership. Similarly, it failed to perceive that the *Socialist* idea of honest labour and the building of a community of people through sacrifice in war was the essential foundation of any State. ' "National" and "social" are two identical conceptions', Hitler declared. 'It was only the Jew who succeeded, through falsifying the social idea and forming it into Marxism, not only in divorcing the social idea from the national, but in actually presenting them as utterly contradictory.'[72]

As early as 1922 Hitler insisted that in this clash of ideologies there were only two possibilities: 'either the victory of the Aryan or the annihilation of the Aryan and the victory of the Jew'.[73] The victory of 'Jewish Bolshevism' would mean nothing less than the complete destruction of 'Aryan' humanity and the ruin of civilization. Again and again, throughout his political career, Hitler would return to this simple formula which for him encapsulated the stark choice that was eventually to justify the Holocaust. In a speech on 30 January 1942, six months after the programme of systematic mass murder had begun, he declared that 'the war can end only in that either the Aryan peoples are annihilated or Jewry will disappear from Europe. . . .'[74] The Second World War would not end 'as the Jews imagine, namely, that the European-Aryan peoples will be annihilated, but on the contrary. . . . The consequences of this war will be the destruction of Jewry'. Once more on 30 September 1942 Hitler returned to the same theme, warning his listeners in anachronistic terms – since the decision for genocide had long since been made – that 'if Jewry would plot an international world war for the annihilation of the Aryan peoples of Europe, then not the Aryan peoples would be annihilated, but on the contrary Jewry. . . .'[75] On 8 November 1942 he obsessively repeated his earlier 'prophecies', to the effect that the consequence of the world war 'will not be the annihilation of the European races, but will be the annihilation of Jewry in Europe'. In Hitler's utterances one can indeed trace an extraordinary consistency of will and purpose from the early 1920s, in which the threat of destruction posed by 'Jewish Bolshevism' would inexorably, in the event of war, bring about the annihilation of Jewry. Here was both promise and totalitarian 'prophecy' presented in the manner of the historical determinist and fanatical ideologue, for whom the apocalyptic clash between Aryan and Jew was *inevitable* and must lead to victory or the total destruction of one of the parties.[76]

Hitler's chiliastic perception of this future Armageddon derived some of its macabre intensity from his view of the Bolshevik Revolution as a Jewish-inspired act of mass murder against the Russian people. In Russia the 'international Jew' had finally cast off his humanitarian mask and 'killed or starved about thirty million people with positively fanatical savagery . . . in order to give a gang of Jewish journalists and stock exchange bandits domination over a great people'.[77] Hitler wrote these lines several years before Stalin actually embarked on his mass liquidation of resistant elements in the Russian peasantry who opposed forced collectivization. His view of Bolshevism was in fact fixed sometime before the Stalinist terror and derived from the antisemitic mythology of the White Russian and German Right rather than from any intimate knowledge of Soviet reality. In particular he was influenced by the Baltic German émigré, Alfred Rosenberg, who had left Russia in the wake of the revolution and arrived in Munich in 1918. Rosenberg convinced Hitler that the Bolshevik upheaval was part of a vast subterranean conspiracy organized by Jews.[78] Soviet Russia was now the centre of world danger and Germany would be the pivot of the coming global confrontation with 'Jewish world bolshevization'.[79] The Russian Revolution represented the uprising of the Asiatic 'spirit' and a racially inferior underworld against Europe, with the objective of establishing Jewish world rule. Communism was the spearhead of this conspiracy of the 'Elders of Zion' carried out in conjunction with Jewish capitalists in the West. It was Rosenberg and the other Russian émigrés like Scheubner-Richter who now reinforced Hitler's long-standing suspicion that all Jews were revolutionaries and all revolutionaries were Jews – adding the anti-Bolshevist and Russophobic dimension to his rabid Judeophobia.[80]

The turning-point in Hitler's attitude to the question of Soviet Russia was to occur around 1923. Until this time he shared the view of many on the conservative Right and also on the Left of his own party that an alliance with Russia against the Entente powers – responsible for the iniquitous Versailles Treaty – was not only feasible but desirable. The Russo-German antagonism had in his view been artificially whipped up before the First World War by Jews whose overriding interest had been the overthrow of the 'antisemitic' Tsarist and Hohenzollern monarchies and their replacement by Jewish revolutionary regimes.[81] The so-called leaders of the proletariat who finally came to power in Russia were millionaire Jews living on the backs of the working masses and driving them to hunger and despair.[82] While the mass of 'liberated' proletarians starved, Soviet Foreign Minister Chicherin rolled across Europe in an express train loaded with four hundred Soviet Jews – staying at the finest hotels, visiting cabarets and watching naked dancers.[83] Thus the conflict between capitalism and Marxism was pure illusion. The first workers' state was in fact nothing but an imposture, for the star of the Soviet was 'the star of David, the sign of the synagogue. The symbol of its race high over the world, of a Lordship which stretches from Vladivostock to the West – the lordship of Jewry. The golden star which for the Jew means the glittering gold.'[84]

In his earliest speeches, Hitler had still anticipated the possibility of an alliance between Russia and Germany 'when Jewry is deposed'.[85] Even a Pan-Slavist Russia driven by territorial aggrandisement and traditional imperialism, though dangerous, was nonetheless a potential partner for Germany against the West. Moreover, it was perfectly possible that the Russian people would one day shake off their Communist Jewish oppressors.[86] But by the beginning of 1923 Russia had been ruled out as an ally and Hitler's attitude had irrevocably hardened.[87] This view was crystallized with brutal clarity in *Mein Kampf*, where the issue was for the first time related to the politics of *Lebensraum* as well as to the global confrontation between 'Aryanism' and world Jewry. 'The present rulers of Russia', Hitler wrote, 'have no idea of honorably entering an alliance, let alone observing one.'[88] They were 'common bloodstained criminals', the 'scum of humanity', who had overrun a great state in a tragic hour, 'wiped out thousands of her intelligentsia in wild blood lust' and for almost ten years 'have been carrying on the most cruel and tyrannical regime of all time'.[89] These Bolshevik rulers, Hitler claimed, belonged to a race which combined 'bestial cruelty and an inconceivable gift for lying, and which today more than ever is conscious of a mission to impose its oppression on the whole world'.[90] Bolshevism had become a world issue because the Soviet Union was viewed by its Jewish internationalist rulers primarily as a 'base of operations' and bridgehead to further conquests.[91]

What had taken place in Soviet Russia was therefore a warning-signal for what was in store, not only in Germany, but wherever the Jews had succeeded in taking root and striving for power. In his *Secret Book*, composed in 1928, Hitler spelled out the consequences. After the overthrow of Tsarism, the Russian upper classes (*Oberschichte*) and national intelligentsia were 'completely extirpated' (*restlos ausgerottet*) amid 'inhuman agonies and atrocities'. According to Hitler's absurdly inflated figures, the total number of victims of 'this Jewish struggle for hegemony in Russia amounted to 28–30 million' – fifteen times the number of German casualties during the First World War: Bolshevism had, moreover, torn down the bonds of order and morality, destroying, for example, the institution of marriage. The result was 'general copulation with the aim of breeding a general inferior mishmash [*Menschbrei*], by way of a chaotic bastardization' (*auf dem Wege eine regelosen Verbastardierung*) – leaving the Jews as the only intellectual element. 'This most terrible crime of all times against mankind' was, however, merely the prelude to the coming power-struggle in Germany and the leading Western states.[92] The eventual 'bolshevization' of the peoples would inexorably entail the butchery of the entire intellectual leadership of the Aryan nations and the establishment of a universal blood-stained 'Jewish' dictatorship.[93] Bolshevism therefore meant nothing less than the slaughter of the old elites, the eventual wrecking of the whole economy and universal race-poisoning.

In Soviet Russia the process had been particularly rapid since Slavdom, historically and genetically, lacked any organizational, state-building ability and therefore the road was wide open for the Jews to seize state-power.[94] However, in his *Secret Book* Hitler foresaw in the near future 'the struggle of the inwardly anti-State Pan-Slav idea against the Bolshevist-Jewish state idea', a conflict which 'will end with the destruction of Jewry'.[95] He thus anticipated the theoretical possibility that a nationalist, anti-capitalist Russia might arise in which the Jewish element would be defeated.[96] In an interview in 1931 he touched, in passing, on the recent power struggle between Stalin and Trotsky, which he regarded as a racial rather than an ideological quarrel. It was 'a battle between the Jewish intelligentsia, which played an important part at the time of the revolution, and the other peoples of the Soviet Union. This quarrel will not be settled for a long time.'[97] Hitler even speculated that the Jews might already have 'let the building of socialism slip through their fingers'. At the same time he sharply rejected the continued advocacy of a pro-Russian orientation by some *völkisch* circles, by the National Bolsheviks and the left wing of his own movement, including Goebbels, the Strasser brothers and Count Reventlow. Russia remained the natural enemy of Germany in the East. On the one hand it was still militarily weak and therefore useless as an ally in the event of war with the West; on the other it stood athwart the path to Germany's *Lebensraum* in the eastern territories. In *Mein Kampf*, Hitler had written: 'If we speak of soil in Europe today, we can primarily have in mind only *Russia* and her vassal border states. Here Fate itself seems desirous of giving us a sign. By handing Russia to Bolshevism, it robbed the Russian nation of that intelligentsia which previously brought about and guaranteed its existence as a state.'[98]

The Soviet Union could not in the long run survive as an independent entity once its Nordic-Germanic nucleus had been eliminated. Thus the new German Reich, when it arose, would be able to follow in the footsteps of the Teutonic Knights of the Middle Ages and win soil for the land-hungry Germanic peasants. Neither a Pan-Slavic nor a 'Jewish' Bolshevik Russia would be strong enough to prevent this *Drang nach Osten*, provided Germany struck first. As Hitler put it in his *Secret Book*, it was a stroke of fortune that Russia would continue to be plagued by Jewish-Bolshevik unrest and instability and therefore, however deeply rooted its anti-German attitudes, it would be powerless to stave off dissolution. Germany's need for *Raum im Osten* should therefore be solved by conquest rather than an alliance with Russia.[99]

In his *Secret Book* Hitler still dismissed the future danger of Russian world hegemony in spite of the huge size of the country, its population and vast natural resources. According to the 'racial' criteria which to the Nazis were far more important than mere head-counting, the Russians lacked the intrinsic worth necessary to become a global power.[100] Subsequently Hitler was forced to modify this contemptuous Slavophobic view, though he never ceased to underestimate Russian qualities of resistance and fighting-power.

In spite of his *rapprochement* with Stalin in 1939 based on temporary tactical considerations of power policy, Hitler never really abandoned his ideological perception of Russia as the major enemy of the Germanic Reich, nor did he modify the racial principles which underlay his political strategy. Not only was

Russian Slavdom inherently inferior and therefore could ultimately play no equal or even secondary role as a partner in the Nazi New Order, but no compromise was in the long run possible with the Jewish-Bolshevik enemies of Aryan civilization. In *Mein Kampf* Hitler had warned his own followers: 'The struggle against the Jewish bolshevization of the world requires a clear attitude toward Soviet Russia. You cannot drive out the Devil with Beelzebub.'[101] No treaty was possible with an ally 'whose sole interest is the destruction of his partner'. Hitler reminded his readers that 'the international Jew, who today rules Russia absolutely, sees in Germany, not an ally, but a State marked for the same destiny'.

Throughout the 1930s Hitler was to fill his speeches with general attacks of a similar nature on Jewish Bolshevism and its world-revolutionary aims. Domestically the Nazi movement would effectively use the theme to neutralize its Communist and Socialist rivals, while attracting support from traditional conservative elites, industrialists, Army circles, the middle classes and sections of the peasantry. Hitler constantly projected himself as the saviour of Germany from Russia and Bolshevism, especially when addressing the influential captains of industry and Prussian Junkers, whose financial and political support he needed in the campaign that preceded the Nazi seizure of power. Similarly, in his foreign policy after 1933, Hitler sought to present National Socialism as the major bulwark of Western civilization against the Russian colossus to the east, in order to win British and French support for his rearmament policy. In both cases he played down the 'Jewish' factor while keeping the structure of his argument intact. The Spanish Civil War provided a further incentive to step up the anti-Bolshevik campaign after 1936. The Nazi propaganda campaign which depicted Bolshevism as the 'incarnation of humanity's destructive elements' thereby distracted attention from short-comings at home, established a cover for the aggressive intervention abroad and gave some credibility to Hitler's pose as the Saviour of Europe. The campaign climaxed in 1937 at the very moment when most of the 'Jewish' Bolsheviks in the revolutionary Old Guard were being liquidated in Stalin's purges! At the Nuremberg Party rally on 13 September 1937, Hitler, basing himself on Alfred Rosenberg's 'researches', made the preposterous claim that 'in Soviet Russia today . . . over eighty per cent of the leading positions are held by Jews'.[102] In his closing speech he spoke of the 'new racial core' which had succeeded in disguising itself as the leadership of the Soviet Union – 'the Jewish minority appropriated to itself the leadership of the national Russian proletariat and thus ousted from their position those who had previously led both society and the state. . . . A brutal dictatorship of a foreign race has seized and exercises undisputed rule over the Russian people.'[103]

In a speech at a Reichstag meeting on 20 February 1938, Hitler stressed that the Russian people were not responsible for the 'ghastly theology of annihilation' by which a 'small upper class of Jewish intellectuals plunged a great nation into a state bordering on insanity'.[104] The Führer contrasted the bloody excesses of the Bolshevik Revolution 'which slaughtered millions upon millions of people' and 'the carnage of the Marxist mob in Spain' with five years of peaceful construction, public order and material prosperity in Nazi Germany.[105] Communism was a world menace because it did not confine itself within the borders of Russia: instead 'the Bolshevism of international Jewry attempts from its central point in Soviet Russia to rot away the very core of the nations of the world, to overthrow the existing social order and to substitute chaos for civilization'.[106] It sought 'to plunge the world into a disaster of unprecedented magnitude' which would mean the end of all independent, national existence. Hence Nazi Germany had signed the anti-Comintern pact in order to oppose with the help of fascist Italy and imperial Japan the spread of Bolshevism wherever it appeared. On 1 April 1939 in front of the Rathaus in Wilhelmshafen, Hitler warned that state after state would either fall victim to the Jewish-Bolshevist plague – 'the gravest menace imaginable' – or have to take drastic measures for self-protection. 'Only when this Jewish bacillus infecting the life of peoples [*dieser jüdische Völkerspaltpilz*] is destroyed can one hope to bring about a co-operation of the nations founded on a permanent understanding.'[107]

The Nazi–Soviet pact did not in fact imply that Hitler's assessment of 'Jewish Bolshevism', or of the future battle of destiny to be waged in the East, had fundamentally changed. It was primarily a tactical manoeuvre which did not affect his guiding foreign policy goals or ideological conceptions. A secret memorandum of Hitler on the tasks of the Four Year Plan, dating from August 1936, had set out these ideas in broad historical perspective. In this document, which had no ostensible propaganda purpose, Hitler observed that since the French Revolution 'the world had been moving with ever increasing speed towards a new conflict, the most extreme solution of which is called Bolshevism, whose essence and aim, however, is solely the elimination of those strata of mankind which have hitherto provided the leadership and their replacement by world-wide Jewry'. No state would be able to remain neutral in this conflict. Ever since Marxism 'through its victory in Russia, has established one of the greatest empires in the world as a forward base for its future operations, this question has become a menacing one. Against a democratic world ideologically rent within itself stands a unified aggressive will founded upon an authoritarian ideology.'[108] Hitler depicted the Bolshevik challenge as comparable to earlier ideological or religious conflicts generated by the rise of Christianity, Islam or the Reformation, events which convulsed the world and determined the historical content of centuries. Because of its geographical position in Europe and its history, Germany stood at the focal point of the West in face of the Bolshevik onslaught. Hitler predicted that Europe would inevitably move towards open crisis and Germany would have to secure its existence against a coming catastrophe, especially with the significant increase in military power of the Red Army. Hitler was in no doubt that 'a victory of Bolshevism over Germany would not lead to a Versailles Treaty but to the final destruction, indeed to the annihilation of the German people'.[109] This would constitute 'the most gruesome catastrophe for the peoples which has been visited upon mankind since the downfall of the States of Antiquity'.[110] In the face of this danger all other considerations were unimportant; hence Hitler's insistence that the German army and economy be fully operational and fit for war within four years.

The ideological consistency between this document and Hitler's public statements over many years suggests that he regarded the coming world war as an inevitable showdown and reckoning with his supreme enemy, Jewry, and its most extreme manifestation, Bolshevism. There might be temporary detours and strategic delays in this confrontation – such as his pact with Stalin – but the central belief that the Aryan world was approaching the last phase in an apocalyptic struggle with Jewry for global hegemony remained constant. Hesitancy, vacillation, factors of expediency and *Realpolitik* influenced the timing of the battle; Hitler even briefly convinced himself (in 1939–40) that Stalinist Russia might have abandoned her world-revolutionary goals for a policy based on Slav Muscovite nationalism with which the Third Reich could co-exist;[111] but the manic dynamism of Hitler's radical eschatology quickly regained the upper hand. The war in the East which he began to plan shortly after the fall of France in June 1940 would not be just another colonial war of conquest and annexation but a racial-ideological struggle of cosmic dimensions against the Jewish spectre which had haunted him ever since November 1918. In a psychological sense, for Hitler the First World War had never stopped. As he told the Czech Foreign Minister Chvalkovsky on 21 January 1939, 'We are going to destroy the Jews. They are not going to get away with what they did on 9 November 1918. The day of reckoning has come.'[112] Hitler's self-appointed mission was to erase the humiliation and shame of that first German defeat and the trauma of Marxist revolution by slaughtering those whom he held responsible for the disaster. It was for the sake of this reckoning that he had entered politics and for which he now plunged his own people, his allies, accomplices, enemies and victims alike into a genocidal war.

# CHAPTER THREE

# A New Order

From the beginning of his public career, Adolf Hitler had been driven by a wide-ranging concept of world history and belief in his own mission to restructure the existing international order in accordance with this vision. Equipped with a brutally simplistic ideology based on the dogmatic premise of race-war and a histrionic talent for his own self-dramatization as a messianic figure, he saw himself as the inaugurator of a new era of humanity. He was the chosen agent of 'Providence', of cosmic forces, of the impersonal laws of history or the iron logic of nature – sent to rescue a sick world that was out of joint and threatened with total annihilation. But in the first instance his message was aimed at the German people. As he told the Nuremberg Party rally on 14 September 1936: 'National Socialism is our most valuable German patent.'[1] It was indeed not intended for universal export as a world-view, but rather as an ideological vehicle for German imperial expansion. The Nazi doctrine was directed first and foremost at the preservation and self-assertion of the German *Volkstum*. It did not advocate the amalgamation of one people with another, rejecting a policy of national 'assimilation' or the Germanization of aliens – which was likely to weaken still further the insecure racial homogeneity and unity of the German nation.[2] National Socialism opposed such policies as anachronistic bourgeois jingoism which belonged to the pre-war conceptions of Hohenzollern Germany and Imperial Austria. Hitler did, however, argue in the 1930s that his *völkisch* conception would provide the basis for a new understanding among the European states. For Western consumption, he even stressed that National Socialism recognized the impossibility of fundamentally altering the character of the European nation-states.

However, at no point did he renounce his plans for German expansion into Eastern Europe, which had been outlined with crystalline clarity in *Mein Kampf*: 'And so we National Socialists consciously draw a line beneath the foreign policy tendency of our pre-War period. We take up where we broke off six hundred years ago. We stop the endless German movement to the south and west, and turn our gaze toward the land in the east. At long last we break off the colonial and commercial policy of the pre-war period and shift to the soil policy of the future.'[3] While hypocritically preaching the merits of a new European system of co-operation based on the *völkisch* ideal, Hitler always envisaged his future world-empire anchored in the vast spaces of the East. The great experimental field for Nazism and the creation of a New Order dominated by the Germanic master-race would be Russia and parts of Eastern Europe. Not only would Germany achieve her natural living-space and continental land-base for future world-mastery to the East, the conquest of these lands was a central feature of Hitler's long-term plans to create a new type of Germanic *Volk*. Only through a war of racial annihilation in the East could he consummate the Nazi revolution at home and sweep away all inherited values and traditional institutions. The destruction of the old society at home and the steeling of German youth to carry out their 'manifest destiny' as a *Herrenvolk* depended therefore on expansion to the East and total war to decimate or wipe out the inferior Slavic, Jewish and gypsy breeds.[4] This pitiless elimination of racial enemies was necessary both to consolidate Nazism at home and in order to forge the new *völkisch* man of the future. In that sense it had a wider universal meaning, for, in Hitler's millenarian political religion, salvation for the reborn Aryan species could only come from this cathartic act of murderous cleansing. Hence *Lebensraum* and the Empire in the East were never conceived in terms of conventional war at all, but represented revolutionary objectives of a far-reaching utopian character which necessitated a *Vernichtungskrieg* (War of Destruction). The living-space obtained in such a victorious war would be the key to the Germanic future.[5] The Asiatic steppes would be Europeanized, the immense spaces populated by 2–3 million German colonists and by 'Nordic' immigrants from the West, especially Scandinavians, Dutch and Americans. The task in Russia, as Hitler was to define it during the war, was 'to Germanize this country by the immigration of Germans, and to look upon the natives as Redskins'.[6] The Russian masses would be allowed to fall back into a state of primitive barbarism while the Jews would be physically eliminated. Significantly, at no time did Hitler envisage the installation of a Russian national government or 'quisling' regime in the Soviet Union. There could be no place for Slav *Untermenschen*, let alone an independent Russian entity in the Nazi New Order.[7] Russian émigré fascists were ruled out from the outset as allies both on racial and general policy grounds.

From 1924 until 1939 Hitler looked to Western support for his pursuit of *Lebensraum* in the East.[8] He believed in particular that the British could approve of an assault on the Soviet Union and the general eastern orientation of German policy, away from the Wilhelminian insistence on confrontation with British commercial and imperial interests. Both Britain and Germany had, moreover, a common interest in resisting French hegemony on the Continent. These assumptions were predicated, as it turned out, on a profoundly mistaken assessment of British policy. Its origins owed not a little, however, to the peculiar 'racial' internationalism of Hitler, in which alliance with England was seen as a necessary act of Nordic solidarity. For a long time Hitler had admired the British Empire, both for the sharp political instincts of its rulers and their ability to control vast spaces of the world with relatively tiny forces. The Russian territories would become a colony for the Germanic Reich, so he hoped, similar to what India represented for the British Raj.[9] While his own millenarian dream of a thousand-year Reich had its roots deep in German history, the most obvious contemporary model of imperial overlordship on which he could draw was that of the British. Only a super-race could in his view have maintained for nearly 300 years such a degree of global domination.[10] Hence on racial as well as strategic grounds, Hitler regarded England as his most natural partner.[11] Until 1941 he remained hopeful that the British might ultimately acquiesce in his pursuit of German hegemony in Europe, provided that he did not frontally challenge their colonial maritime Empire. In his long-range strategy, however, Britain would finally have to accept the role of a junior partner in any future showdown between the more dynamic Greater German Reich and the American colossus. Thus during the Second World War Hitler proposed that if the British accepted his peace terms, Nazi Germany would guarantee the security of their Empire but if England foolishly resisted, she would be rapidly reduced to vassal status. From the early 1920s Hitler had hoped to secure his dream of German hegemony in Europe and a free hand in the East with British consent, but was also ready to do so against her active opposition. In the event of war against England, the objective would be the elimination of the British presence from the Continent rather than the destruction of the Empire. There could be no question of waging a 'war of extermination' against a nation of equal racial value like Britain, such as the Nazis were in fact to unleash in 1941 against the Soviet Union.[12]

In spite of Hitler's almost irrational attraction to the British as fellow-Nordic nation, his admiration for their colonial power and his respect for the bravery of their soldiers, it became increasingly possible by the late 1930s that his hopes for an Anglo-German alliance might be misplaced. Hitler's belief that London would eventually agree to a repartition of the globe and support German efforts to destroy 'Jewish Bolshevism' did not in fact materialize. England seemed determined to thwart his hegemonial ambitions and obstruct Germany's 'natural' right to *Lebensraum* in the East. At the same time Hitler was also disappointed by the spinelessness of British appeasement policy between 1935 and 1938; their failure to act against Italy in East Africa, the non-intervention in the Rhineland and then in the Spanish Civil War, along with British support for the League of Nations all seemed to him to point to the flabby reflexes of a declining imperial power.[13] A powerful Britain had inspired his love and admiration. Its weakness aroused in him only contempt. Neither in its vacillating foreign policy nor in the hostility of the British press and public opinion to the antisemitic policies of the Third Reich, did England appear to be acting in what the Nazis regarded as its true national interests. The abdication of King Edward VIII, who was warmly regarded by the Nazi leaders as a key exponent of the pro-German orientation in Britain, confirmed Hitler in the belief that only a militant, aggressive stance could still bring about the desired Anglo-German alliance. From 1937 onwards, Hitler's foreign policy began to assume a more openly anti-British character. His fury at the 'unreasonableness' of British leaders in ignoring his advances was to be a major reason for his decision in 1939–40 to strike first against the West, after ensuring his rear through the Nazi–Soviet pact.

Hitler's love-hate relationship with the British was, however, not only a function of *Realpolitik* or of sentimental and ideological factors but also of his all-embracing antisemitism. Ever since the early 1920s the premise of an Anglo-German alliance had in his eyes been the victory of the 'Aryan' over the Jewish element in England. Both in *Mein Kampf* and in his *Secret Book* Hitler had raised what to him was the decisive question with regard to Britain's future: 'Will . . . the traditional forces of British statesmanship still be able to destroy the pernicious influence of the Jews, or not?'[14] As in Germany, Italy and France, Hitler imagined a bitter struggle for political control being waged between international Jewry and the *völkisch* circles within the nation. British hostility to Germany before and during the First World War had long been attributed by Hitler and the Nazi leaders to Jewish machinations. In *Mein Kampf* he had written: 'The annihilation of Germany was not an English interest, but primarily a Jewish one, just as today a destruction of Japan serves British State interests less than it does the widespread desires of the projected Jewish world empire. While England sweats to maintain her position in this world, the Jew organizes his attack for its conquest.'[15]

If England opposed Germany's *Ostpolitik* (which was directed primarily against Russia and France) then in Hitler's mind this could only be a manifestation of malevolence for its own sake, for such a programme did not clash with British commercial and maritime interests.[16] Hitler had already claimed in *Mein Kampf*: 'Jewish finance desires in opposition to the British State's welfare, not only the thorough economic dominance of Germany, but also its completed political enslavement.' British hostility must therefore be a sign that Jewish stock-exchange interests had gained the upper hand. If, on the other hand, England fulfilled Hitler's hopes by remaining aloof from Europe and granting Germany a free hand in the East, then this meant that the 'Aryan' nationalist element had assumed control. By 1937 Hitler was reluctantly becoming convinced that in this domestic struggle for influence, the 'non-Aryan' and anti-German interests were setting the tone. According to Nazi propaganda after September 1939, it was the Jews who were ultimately responsible for plunging Britain into a pointless war. Soon they would also be blamed for the British refusal to sue for peace on Hitler's terms.[17] Instead of linking the future of their Empire to a continental alliance with Germany and thereby stealing a march on their American competitors, the British had meekly allowed themselves to become agents of a diabolical Jewish world-conspiracy. English stubbornness in failing to see the 'inestimable advantages' which German hegemony in Europe would bring them could have no other explanation.

Hitler's wartime table talk was accordingly full of vehement and bitter outbursts against the folly of the English and the perfidy of the Jews, who step by step had allegedly seized control of the British press, manipulating public opinion and the decision-making elites. Britain was a warning example of Hitler's axiom that 'any and every nation which fails to exterminate the Jews in its midst will sooner or later finish by being itself devoured by them'.[18] What was happening in the Anglo-Saxon world during the Second World War reminded Hitler of the situation in Germany in 1918. The elites of Britain and America suffered from the typical bourgeois prejudice that 'no economic life is possible without the Jew – for, as they put it, without the Jew, money does not circulate'. In both countries the bourgeoisie and the clergy 'with the rope already round their necks, tremble at the idea of rebelling against him [i.e. the Jew] even timidly'.[19] The decadent ruling Anglo-Saxon elites, led by Churchill and Roosevelt, were blinded by 'Jewish' influence from grasping that the defeat of Nazi Germany could only mean Russian hegemony over Europe.[20] 'The policy represented by Churchill', Hitler insisted, 'is to nobody's interest, in short, but that of the Jews. But that people was chosen by Jehovah because of its stupidity. The last thing that their interest should have told the Jews to do was to enter into this war. All that they'll have gained by it is to be chased out of Europe, for the longer the war lasts, the more violently the peoples will react against them.'[21] In particular, Hitler hoped for an outburst of violent antisemitism in England. On 5 November 1941 he remarked: 'The English are engaged in the most idiotic war they could wage! If it turns out badly, antisemitism will break out amongst them – at present it's dormant. It'll break out with unimaginable violence.'[22]

Hitler's 'prophecy' in this respect was anchored in the expectations generated by the systematic Nazi effort to spread antisemitism to the Western world ever since 1937. The Nazi leadership was constantly looking for signs that this propaganda would take root and undermine opposition to its expansionist policy goals.[23] Goebbels noted, for example, in his diary entry of 13 May 1943: 'The Jewish question, in the Führer's opinion, will play a decisive role in England. . . .'[24] A month earlier he had recorded with satisfaction that 'antisemitism is growing rapidly even in the enemy States', especially Britain, and that it had been a shrewd propaganda move 'that we raised the Jewish problem again on the orders of the Führer'.[25] Goebbels was convinced that, deep down, the Anglo-Saxons were no less antisemitic than the Germans. With typical cynicism he had noted on 13 December 1942: 'I believe that both the English and Americans are happy that we are exterminating the Jewish riff-raff.'[26] On the other hand, when the British House of Commons rose in tribute to the massacred Jews of Europe on 17 December 1942 and Anthony Eden read out the first official Allied declaration condemning German mass murder, Goebbels dismissed him as 'thoroughly Jewish' in education and bearing. The House of Commons now reminded him of a stock exchange and the English were demoted to the status of 'the Jews among the Aryans'.[27]

Hitler, too, since July 1941 had ceased to regard the British as 'Aryan' kith and kin, related by a common blood and culture. Like Goebbels he became convinced that the Jews had acquired an extraordinary influence over public opinion and the ruling classes. His hopes for a new world order in which German continental hegemony would be supplemented by British naval power to ensure the dominion of the white race were fast receding. The 'Jew-infested' British, by making an alliance with Stalin, had 'forced' him into a two-front defensive war (Hitler in his misjudgement of England never asked why she should consolidate Nazi power for further use against herself) and were trying to sabotage his plans in Eastern Europe.[28] While the Germans were fighting for what he regarded as their legitimate right to living space, the decadent British elite under Churchill – a mere straw-man of the Jews – were objectively helping to bring about the victory of Bolshevism. In his wartime *Table Talk* Hitler never tired of lambasting what he called Churchill's 'suicidal' policy, which had in effect sacrificed the British Empire by its blind obstinacy. Instead of seeking to preserve the balance of power *vis-à-vis* the two emerging giants, Russia and the United States, by allowing the unification of Europe under German domination, Churchill had obstructed it.[29]

In Hitler's vision of the New Order, an alliance of 'the two Germanic Powers', Britain and Germany, could have kept both the Americans and the

Russo-Asiatic colossus from meddling in Europe. Even an aging enfeebled Britain, allied to a united Europe, could still have been an arbiter in world affairs, had it pursued a 'realistic' policy. The precondition would have been the eradication of the 'Jewish poison'; but the effete British elite ruled by Churchill ('this Jew-ridden, half-American drunkard') had rejected the honourable peace he offered them at the beginning of 1941.[30] Churchill was the punishment of Providence for Albion's past crimes and perfidy. For a long time he had been 'bound hand and foot to the Jewish chariot',[31] like his friend and ally, Roosevelt. The result would be the loss of the British Empire which might otherwise have been preserved by the forces of the German Reich once the 'Communist abscess' had been lanced. Three months before his own suicide, Hitler commented on what was for him one of the bitterest disappointments of his career: the failure of the British to ally with the Third Reich and their stubbornness in waging a war 'imposed on her by implacable allies', the Jews and Americans.[32] On 4 February 1945 he summed up his feelings: 'I had underestimated the power of Jewish domination over Churchill's England. They preferred indeed to perish by default, rather than to admit National Socialism to their midst. Under pressure, they might have tolerated a façade of anti-Semitism on our part. But our absolute determination to eradicate Jewish power root and branch throughout the world was too strong meat for their delicate stomachs to digest.'[33]

Hitler's view of the United States in some respects paralleled his attitude to Britain, though he had never seriously considered the Americans as potential allies or partners of the Third Reich. In *Mein Kampf*, the United States scarcely intruded as a political factor in Hitler's narrative, though in his *Secret Book*, written a few years later, he suddenly recognized the major international significance and dynamism of this 'new force which threatens to upset the existing balance of power among the nations'.[34] Thus in 1928 he favourably contrasted America as 'a young racially select people' to a Europe which had lost its best blood through war and emigration. North America had been invigorated and steeled by Nordic-German types who, unlike the white man in Central and Latin America, had 'mixed but little with the lower coloured peoples. . . .' This resistance to racial difilement which he had approvingly noted in passing in 1924–5, allied to the vast landmass and natural resources of the North American continent, convinced Hitler that the United States could one day become the most powerful nation in the world. Yet from the onset of the Depression years and in particular following the election of Franklin D. Roosevelt to the Presidency, Hitler dramatically reversed his earlier opinions. The American ethnic melting-pot and its vibrant democracy now became a symbol to the Nazis of the ruinous effects of race-mixing. America was not a real nation but the centre of a technological rootless 'civilization', of the Hollywood dream factory – a land of millionaires, gangsters, assassins, beauty queens, stupid records and bad taste;[35] its democratic political system was but a hollow façade for Mafia corruption and the rule of a Jew-ridden international plutocracy. This 'Judaized', negrified racial hodge-podge was now ridiculed by Hitler and the Nazis as a rubbish heap composed of the social débris of Europe washed up on its shores.[36] A country which 'had a concept of life inspired by the most vulgar commercialism' and no feeling for such sublime experiences of the human spirit as great music was no place for Hitler, as he confided to Mussolini during one of their wartime meetings.[37] A people which placed profit before blood consisted of the 'lowest kind of rabble'.[38]

The Nazis were undoubtedly influenced in their highly negative view of America by the conviction that 'Jewish' influence predominated in the politics, economy, media and cultural life of the United States. The hostility of American public opinion to the Third Reich and in particular to the persecution of Jews was already a major source of tension in 1933 when the threat of an anti-Nazi boycott made itself felt.[39] The 'Jewish question' continued to cloud German–American relations after 1933, leading to the recall of the US ambassador from Germany after the Crystal Night pogrom of November 1938. The Nazis naturally tried to argue that President Roosevelt did not represent the real feelings of the American people but only those of the 'Jewish' governing clique – as German Foreign Minister Ribbentrop informed the visiting South African Defence Minister, Oswald Pirow.[40] It eventually became standard Nazi propaganda to present President Roosevelt as a war-mongering psychopath, completely under the thumb of his Jewish advisers, who were determined to destroy the Reich. On 12 August 1941, before American entry into the conflict, Hitler told the Spanish ambassador: 'The chief blame for the war falls upon America, upon Roosevelt, surrounded by his Freemasons, his Jews and the whole of Jewish Bolshevism. . . .'[41] Two weeks later, speaking to Mussolini, 'the Führer gave a detailed analysis of the Jewish clique surrounding Roosevelt and exploiting the American people'.[42] Von Ribbentrop in diplomatic conversations was no less inclined to launch into diatribes against the Jews and plutocrats around Roosevelt, out to ruin the Third Reich. From a Nazi viewpoint, the entry of the United States into the war and the alliance between Roosevelt, Churchill and Stalin merely underlined what Hitler had proclaimed long before the event – the essential identity of interests between international 'plutocracy' and Bolshevism.

By 1939 Hitler had clearly abandoned his earlier hopes that the strength of the Germanic element in America might permit the successful transplantation of Nazism to the United States. Nazi doctrine had asserted that German-

Americans were part of a worldwide 100 million strong German *Volk*, whose first loyalty was to the Reich. The German-American Bund which was organized on this premise failed, however, to make a significant breakthrough into the mass of native-born or naturalized German-Americans.[43] Like the Nazi ideology itself, the German-American Bund was totally out of step with the multi-ethnic, pluralistic culture and national self-perception of most Americans. Hitler's failure to grasp this ethos was to lead him to a gross misreading of American political realities – one that was even more fateful for the success of his New Order than his illusions concerning Great Britain.

With the outbreak of war, Hitler systematically began to denounce Roosevelt as a tool of 'Jewish' influence, which, he observed, had steadily increased in America during the previous twenty-five years. Roosevelt, 'urged on by Jewry', had, in his view, long determined to go to war in order to annihilate National Socialism.[44] It was, moreover, 'Jewish'-interests which had pushed America into the war against Japan – a world power 'which had always sternly resisted contamination by the race of Jewry'.[45] Similarly, the same malevolent forces were responsible for the Anglo-Saxon war on his Germanic Reich, which had never threatened the great maritime empires and whose aspirations were directed exclusively to the East. The American war on Germany was therefore as devoid of a national foundation as that of the British. There would have been no conflict with the United States if it had not been for the fact 'that world Jewry has chosen just that country in which to set up its most powerful bastion. That, and that alone, has altered the relations between us and has poisoned everything.'[46]

On 24 February 1945, Hitler predicted that within a generation the American–Jewish symbiosis would rebound on both parties as it had in Germany. The Americans would realize what a handicap had been imposed on them 'by this parasitic Jewry, clamped fast to their flesh and nourishing itself on their life-blood'.[47] They would be dragged into adventures contrary to their national interest and 'within a quarter of a century the Americans will either have become anti-semitic or they will be devoured by Jewry'.[48] Hitler saw America as a young hybrid nation, lacking genuine homogeneity and national 'spirit', devoid of political sense and therefore easy prey for worldly-wise Jewish exploiters.[49] Hence, the cunning Roosevelt had been able to take advantage of their naive credulity and lead them into an unnecessary war. On the other hand, Hitler left open the possibility that the Americans would mature and eventually grasp the nature of the enemy within. Then they, rather than Europe, might take up his legacy of merciless struggle against the Jews.

If there was little place for America in Hitler's vision of a New Order, this was even more true of France, which had appeared to him in the wake of the Versailles Treaty as Germany's most dangerous enemy.[50] The goals of French policy were seen as rooted in a permanent and unchanging hostility to the idea of a German *Mitteleuropa*, the desire to Balkanize Germany itself and to re-establish French hegemony over the Continent. France was the traditional *Erbfeind* (hereditary enemy), determined to rob Germany of its vital strength and block its road to *Lebensraum*. It did not matter who ruled the country – Bourbons, Jacobins, Bonapartists, bourgeois democrats, clerical Republicans or red Bolsheviks – the objective was always to hold the Rhine frontier and guarantee it 'by means of a disintegrated and dismembered Germany'. Only through the 'obliteration of Germany' could a demographically declining and racially decadent France still maintain its world importance. To achieve their aims, the French had constructed a system of alliances in Central and Eastern Europe after the First World War intended to block and encircle Germany. But France was not just the most deadly adversary of the German people, it was also a peril to the 'existence of white humanity'. Its hybrid racial character, part Negro and part Jewish, testified to the degeneracy of *la grande nation*. 'This people, which is constantly becoming more negrofied, constitutes, by its tie with the aims of Jewish world domination, a grim danger for the existence of the European white race. For infection in the heart of Europe through negro blood on the Rhine corresponds equally to the sadistic perverse vengefulness of this chauvinistic hereditary enemy of our people, and to the ice-cold plan of the Jews thus to begin bastardizing the European continent at its core and, through infection by inferior humanity, to deprive the white race of the foundations for a sovereign existence.'[51]

Hitler saw, then, a clear connection between the 'negroification' (*Vernegerung*) of the French (especially their use of coloured troops in the post-war occupation of the Rhineland) and the sinister plans of Jewry to contaminate German-Aryan womanhood. Moreover, Jewish finance and French continental imperialism were symbiotically related – 'only in France is there today more than even an inner unanimity between the plans of the Jew-controlled stock exchange and the desires of a chauvinistically oriented national statecraft'.[52] Thus, according to *Mein Kampf*, in France, the struggle between 'Jewish' and 'Aryan' elements had already been resolved in favour of the former, whereas in Britain it was still undecided. Only in fascist Italy had national forces definitively overcome Jewish international interests – represented by freemasonry, Marxism and the liberal press. Hence it was no accident that Hitler looked to England and Italy as his natural partners against the ambitions of French hegemonism. Racial factors and *Realpolitik* merged in his early thinking on this issue. Italy was hampered by French economic and military power not only in Europe but in North Africa, which constituted its natural 'living space'. Its Mediterranean ambitions and hopes for a colonial empire clearly depended on a weakening of France. Hitler was therefore perfectly prepared, as he indicated in his *Secret Book* and in his subsequent policy, to abandon the Tyrolese Germans for the sake of an Italian alliance and Mussolini's support against France. Similarly he hoped to use British resentment of French hegemonistic aspirations in Europe and the legacy of traditional Anglo-French colonial rivalry for his own ends.

Hitler's attitude to the French underwent some modification following the Nazi rise to power and the need to consolidate his position at home. The dreams of a revanchist war and the crushing of France as a prelude to expanding eastwards at Russia's expense had to be shelved for a number of years. Hitler's 'peace' policy, which proclaimed reconciliation with France, was designed above all to prevent any armed intervention by his militarily more powerful neighbour before Germany had rearmed.[53] During the successive European crises between 1936 and 1939 as a result of which the Third Reich achieved a decisive military and political edge in Europe, Hitler still sought a *modus vivendi* with France in the hope that he would have a free hand for his projected war of conquest in the East. The Anglo-French insistence on honouring the guarantee to Poland inclined him, however, to return to his early conception of the 1920s – that France must first be destroyed as a major power before the Reich could achieve its broader aims. Nazi occupation policies in France after 1940 nonetheless suggested something of the continuing ambivalence and oscillations in Hitler's attitude to his western neighbour. The French were treated neither as 'Aryans' nor as subhumans; they were permitted a semi-autonomous regime in the South, though well before the Allied invasion of North Africa in November 1942 the economic *Gleichschaltung* of Vichy into the New Order had begun. Furthermore, in their Jewish as well as their general policy, the Nazis were considerably more ambivalent in France than in countries like Poland, which was in any case earmarked for obliteration as a nation. Whereas the Polish elites, Gentiles no less than Jews, were simply wiped out, the French elites were encouraged to adjust to German domination and some efforts were made not to ruffle their national pride and sensibilities.[54] The Vichy regime, rather than the Nazis themselves, initiated discriminatory legislation, and quotas of Jews for deportation and destruction were assigned to French policy officials. Whether this helped to slow down the implementation of the 'Final Solution' in France is problematic. But it is certainly arguable that the ambiguities of German racial policy toward the French had something to do with the dilatoriness of the Nazis in executing drastic measures against French Jews.[55]

Hitler never overcame his suspicions of France, though he sought to work with her during the war and to maintain the French colonial empire, even resisting Italian claims on Nice, Corsica and Tunis in 1940. By December 1942, however, he was telling the Italians that Germany had paid a high price for French 'collaboration'. France still remained a potential threat and its leaders, Hitler complained, sought only to gain time and obtain advantages for themselves at German expense.[56] They were *attentistes*, united only 'in the thought of freeing themselves from the Germans'.[57] In his *Table Talk*, Hitler expressed himself more sharply, remarking that France was endemically hostile – part of her blood 'will always be foreign to us'.[58] In his last utterances the suppressed bitterness against the French came pouring out as Hitler, facing utter defeat, returned to a reassessment of the basic racial-ideological premises that had originally guided his conception of a New Order. France 'was and is the mortal enemy of the German people', he declared on 2 April 1945. Though her former military might was now only a memory and she had declined to the level of a third-rate power, she remained a skilful blackmailer – a 'raddled old strumpet' with 'unlimited powers of corruption'.[59] Hitler concluded: 'Germany will always recruit her staunchest friends from among those people who are actively resistant to Jewish contagion. I am sure that the Japanese, the Chinese and the peoples of Islam will always be closer to us than, for example, France, in spite of the fact that we are related by blood. It is a tragedy that France has consistently degenerated in the course of centuries and that her upper classes have been perverted by the Jews. France is now condemned to the pursuit of a Jewish policy.'[60]

Hitler had returned once more to his hostile image of a completely 'Judaized' France, only this time from the perspective of radical disenchantment with European colonial policies. Now he cursed himself for listening to the old-school diplomats in the Wilhelmstrasse, who had failed to notice how France had changed since the nineteenth century into a nation of fossilized bourgeois, petty swindlers, profiteers and collaborators.[61] German policy should have helped the peoples subjected to the French colonial yoke in North Africa and the Middle East, instead of consolidating the crumbling overseas empire in Algeria, Morocco, Tunis and Syria.[62] Had the Germans 'emancipated the Moslem countries dominated by France', this would have had enormous repercussions in the Middle East which was still under Anglo-French domination. It would have led the Arabs to raise the standard of revolt against British rule, instead of allowing the British to pose as liberators in Lebanon, Syria, Cyrenaica and Tripolitania.[63] It was not only France but Italy which had made this policy impossible. The Italian alliance, Hitler now realized, had 'prevented us from pursuing a revolutionary policy in North

Africa'. Mussolini had never abandoned his design to inherit the territories of the French colonial empire in the Mediterranean and to make Italy the dominant power in the region. The Italian presence had paralysed Germany, creating 'a feeling of malaise among our Islamic friends, who inevitably saw in us accomplices, willing or unwilling, of their oppressors'.[64] Thus Hitler, a few weeks before his death, ruminating on these lost opportunities, convinced himself that because of his Latin partners he had missed the bus with Islam. Egyptians, Iraqis and other Arabs throughout the Middle East would have risen in revolt if only he had played 'our best card' against the British, instead of throwing his weight behind Italian and French imperial ambitions.

Though Hitler in February 1945 felt obliged to admit that his Italian ally, through its military failures, had been 'a source of embarrassment to us everywhere', he never fundamentally revised his admiration for Mussolini, even in the darkest moments of the war. There was no other living statesman to whom he felt a comparable sense of loyalty and whom he personally revered to the same extent. His 'deep friendship for this extraordinary man'[65] was not simply a product of the Rome–Berlin Axis, though it was during the Duce's visit to Berlin at the end of September 1937 that it found its most uninhibited public expression. The Führer acclaimed his visitor as one of those 'lonely men of the ages on whom history is not tested, but who themselves are the makers of history'.[66] He asserted that the Axis was solidly rooted not only in a community of views but in 'a community of action'. Fascist Italy 'through the creative activity of a man of constructive power has become a new Imperium', Hitler declared, just as National Socialist Germany had become 'once more a World Power'. The 115 million people bound together in these two empires 'form today the strongest guarantee for the preservation of a Europe which still possesses a perception of its cultural mission and is not willing through the action of destructive elements to fall into disintegration'.[67]

Hitler had in fact from the beginning of his political career regarded an Italian alliance as essential to Germany – in the first instance as a weapon against France and the hated Treaty of Versailles.[68] From 1920 onwards he had recognized that such an alliance ruled out any challenge to Italian control of the South Tyrol – a bitterly sore point with Pan-German nationalists and the *völkisch* Right as a whole.[69] His ideological sympathy with Mussolini's fascism further reinforced his determination to oppose the anti-Italian agitation in his own party. In *Mein Kampf* he denounced the fuss over the South Tyrol as a 'Jew-incited' bourgeois patriotic clamour designed to prevent a German–Italian understanding. In his *Secret Book* he went even further and claimed that the South Tyrol issue had been deliberately inflated by the Jews to discredit the fascist system which served the interests of the Italian nation rather than world Jewry.[70] Nothing must obstruct a *rapprochement* with the one truly national power in Europe, in which 'Jewish-Masonic' influence had ceased to be a factor. Mussolini's Italy was therefore a desirable ally to Hitler not only for reasons of power politics but also because fascism had dared to free itself 'from the Jewish-Masonic embrace and oppose a nationalistic resistance to this international world poisoning'. The Italian fascist assault 'against the three main weapons of the Jews is the best indication that the poison fangs of this supra-state power are being torn out, even though by indirect methods', Hitler wrote in *Mein Kampf*. 'The prohibition of Masonic secret societies, the persecution of the supra-national press, as well as the continuous demolition of international Marxism, and, conversely, the steady reinforcement of the Fascist state conception, will in the course of the years cause the Italian government to serve the interests of the Italian people more and more, without regard for the hissing of the Jewish world hydra.'[71]

Hitler's view on this issue was diametrically opposed to that of the leading Nazi Party ideologue and editor of the *Völkischer Beobachter*, Alfred Rosenberg, who was constantly attacking Mussolini's failure to deal with the 'Jewish question' and deploring the various manifestations of fascist 'philo-semitism'.[72] In his opinion, Mussolini had capitulated by the mid-1920s to the dictatorship of Jewish high finance.[73] Other leading Nazis from Julius Streicher to the 'socialist' Strasser brothers were no less convinced that the Italian fascist leader was a straw man in the hands of the Jews.[74] It took all of Hitler's authority to restrain the current of anti-Mussolinian and Italophobe feeling in the Nazi Party. Blinded by his own boyish admiration for the Italian dictator, Hitler seemed quite unaware of Mussolini's intellectual distaste for German racialism and *pangermanismo* which went back to his pre-1914 period as a revolutionary Italian socialist. The Duce was in fact never an antisemite in the German sense of the term, as Rosenberg and other Nazis had grasped more accurately than Hitler. As an Italian patriot and a rationalist intellectual, he resented the Nazi theory of a Nordic master-race as an insult to the Mediterranean peoples and especially to the dignity and intelligence of his own nation.[75]

Though Mussolini tolerated a few fanatic Jew-baiters like Preziosi and Farinacci in his own party he tended to dismiss Nazi racialism for what it was – pretentious, pseudo-scientific nonsense. However, until 1938 he skilfully managed both to avoid antagonizing Hitler on this issue and to maintain his reputation abroad as something of a 'philosemite'. The persecution of the Jews was in his eyes an embarrassing mark of German 'immaturity' but not sufficient reason to support an ideological crusade against a fraternal fascist dictator in Berlin. In moments of resentment against the Nazis, Mussolini could, however, express his repudiation of Hitler's antisemitism in un-equivocally angry terms. Thus he told Nahum Goldmann in a November 1934 interview (after the Nazi assassination of the Austrian Chancellor Dollfuss which had soured German–Italian relations) that the Jews were '*un peuple grand et eternel*': 'I know Herr Hitler', he informed Goldmann: 'He is an idiot, a' rascal, a fanatical rascal, an insufferable talker. It is a torture to listen to him. You are much stronger than Herr Hitler. When there is no trace left of Hitler, the Jews will still be a great people.'[76]

Mussolini, like Hitler, believed at this time in the reality of Jewish power, with the difference that he drew philosemitic conclusions from an antisemitic premise. World Jewry was in his eyes still a force that merited greater respect than the Third Reich. This situation began to change only in 1936 with Hitler's successful reoccupation of the Rhineland. Mussolini's own conquest of Ethiopia the previous year made him increasingly race-conscious and led to laws against miscegenation between Italians and natives. The co-operation between Italy and Germany during the Spanish Civil War drew Mussolini still closer to the Nazi orbit. The logic of this co-operation made it more difficult for Mussolini to contrast Italian fascism, as the product of a universalist Latin civilization and the humanist cultural traditions of the Italian people, with the 'savage barbarism' and 'unbridled militarism' of National Socialist Germany. While he still sought for a time to differentiate between the approaches of fascism and Nazism to the 'Jewish' question, by 1938 Mussolini had begun to align himself with Hitler's 'Aryan' myth. In part, this may have been connected with the drive of the regime to create a truly new *homo fascistus*, an Italian master-race in the totalitarian mould – efforts which intensified precisely around this period.[77] However, the Duce's sudden conversion to the 'Aryan-Nordic' racialism which he had always contemptuously dismissed in the past would appear to owe more to his decision to transform Italy into a full partner and ally of the Reich. Ideological *Gleichschaltung* on the Jewish problem was part of the self-imposed price that he was prepared to pay for the alliance. In this respect he preceded other allies of Nazi Germany like Rumania and Hungary with far more virulent antisemitic traditions, thereby sacrificing the Jews to the new alignment of forces in Europe. Discrimination against them was the pledge of his loyalty to the Axis. Thus the Italian Race Laws of July 1938 were unexpectedly to turn the German pattern of biological antisemitism into part of the official fascist creed.

Admittedly, for Mussolini this was little more than a tactical concession. He never shared Hitler's belief in 'superior' and 'inferior' races, his fanatical loathing for Jews, his obsession with blood purity or the eschatological struggle between the Aryan and Jewish people. Moreover, intermarriage between Jews and Gentiles had actually been encouraged in fascist Italy where official policy under his rule had favoured the integration rather than exclusion of Jews from Italian society. Mussolini was also well aware that among the established elites as well as the Italian masses there was little sympathy or support for his new Race Laws which were contrary to national traditions, to the Catholic universalism of Rome and popular sentiment. Given these factors it is not surprising that fascist policy *in practice* deviated sharply from the Nazi pattern. The numerous 'exemptions', the liberal Aryanization practices, and the readiness of the military authorities to protect persecuted Jews in the Italian-occupied territories of France, Yugoslavia and Greece during the Second World War, reflected the gulf between fascist and Nazi attitudes.

The German Nazis themselves became more and more infuriated by Italian half-measures in Jewish policy and the presence of 'Jew-tainted' Gentiles at various levels of the fascist party apparatus.[78] By the end of 1942 they became increasingly anxious that Jews were involved in acts of sabotage and espionage in Italy and the Italian-occupied territories. Goebbels noted in his diary on 13 December 1942: 'The Italians are extremely lax in the treatment of the Jews. They protect the Italian Jews both in Tunis and in occupied France and will not permit their being drafted for work or compelled to wear the Star of David. This shows once again that Fascism does not really dare to get down to fundamentals but is very superficial regarding problems of vital importance.[79] Von Ribbentrop on 25 February 1943 made an official complaint on this matter to Mussolini at the Führer's express wish. In a conversation with Goebbels on 23 June 1943, Hitler himself expressed his clear dissatisfaction with the fascist failure to deal with the Jewish question in a radical manner. According to the same source, following the overthrow of the fascist regime in Italy the Führer became profoundly disillusioned with the Duce. '. . . The Führer expected that the first thing the Duce would do would be to wreak full vengence on his betrayers. He gave no such indication, however, which showed his real limitations. He is not a revolutionary, like the Führer or Stalin. The Führer now realizes that Italy never was a Power, is no power today and will not be a Power in the future.'[80]

Hitler, however, attributed the failure of Italian fascism more to the lack of adequate material resources than to deficiencies of leadership or ideological weaknesses. For him Mussolini still remained the model of fascist demagogy, from whom he had first adopted the use of uniforms, coloured shirts and the arm-extended salute in the early 1920s. The paramilitary methods, the shock troops (Mussolini's *fascio di combattimento*), the *Führerprinzip*, the militarism, extreme nationalism and anti-Bolshevism were all innovations of the fascist movement adopted by the Nazis to their own needs. Mussolini was in these respects by far the most important political precursor of Hitler. The differences over the 'Jewish question' did nevertheless point to some fundamental ideological divergences between fascism and Nazism which had wider implications. Fascism was rooted, for example, in an idealist political philosophy, a cult of heroic vitalism and the desire to bring about a spiritual transformation of society within the framework of the nation-state. Nazism, on the other hand, was predicated on deterministic laws of Nature, belief in a Darwinian process of natural selection among individuals, groups and nations as well as a biologistic supranational concept of race. The fascist philosophy did not view politics or culture as having a racial basis determined by purity of the blood. 'Race' for Mussolini remained synonymous with nation and was perceived as a dynamic historical process rather than in the mythical static manner of Nazism.[81] There was nothing in Italian fascism to compare with Hitler's demonic juxtaposition of Aryan and Jew or his view that Slavs were a mass of helots born to be dominated by a master-race.[82]

Nonetheless both Nazism and fascism, though in different ways, dreamed of installing a New Order which would erase the 'shame of Versailles' or what the Italians regarded as the 'mutilated' victory in the First World War. Both built on the myth of the war experience, the trauma of defeat and the right of youthful, 'have-not' nations to assert themselves against an unjust imperialist partition of the globe. Both ideologies exalted youth, activism and movement as well as cultivating the nationalist mystique whose roots lay in nineteenth-century romanticism. Both thundered against the moribund bourgeois era while declaring a war to the death on Marxism. Both movements aimed to recreate powerful empires whose origins lay in the distant past – Hitler looking back to the myths of a Greater Germanic Reich and Mussolini to the example of ancient Rome. The myths of the past served, however, in both cases to disguise the break with respective national traditions of foreign policy and the conventions of power politics.[83]

This was particularly true in the case of Nazism, which, beyond its dream of an autarchic Germany aspiring to world dominion, ultimately intended the complete transformation of Europe on racial principles. These goals were in fact ideologically linked to the extent that Germany could only become impregnable, in Nazi terms, within a revolutionary new order based on biological principles. The process of cleansing had to begin from within by creating a healthy nation-state living off the yield of its own soil and territory. Nazism defined this notion of health in terms of racial cohesion (removing Jews as 'agents of decay') and the pitiless elimination of the physically weak, sick and mentally defective elements. The social order must overcome class divisions and acquire a crystalline hardness; Spartan values would have to be inculcated into youth; the weakened peasantry made secure in its own *Blut und Boden*, as the guarantor of the race. Finally, once the State had been re-armed and was led by an elite trained and bred to the ethos of unquestioning obedience, bravery and ruthlessness in battle, the German Reich would become the strongest ethnic community in the world.[84]

Space was, however, essential to the future of the Reich if it were to hold its own against the vast geographical expanses of Russia, America and the British Empire. Hitler regarded space not only as vital to the military and economic self-sufficiency of the Reich but as the *sine qua non* for the freedom and continued independent existence of the German people.[85] Like food and sex, it was an elementary necessity of life itself. Without territory for settlement, the nation could not be nourished nor could its frontiers be secured against surprise attack. Like war, this was a question of self-preservation, of being and non-being. Space would, moreover, have to be secured by war in order to correct the unfair distribution of the earth's riches and to adjust the size of its territory to Germany's population. In the Nazi conception, the plough would follow the sword. It was an iron law of existence that 'every being strives for expansion and every nation strives for world domination', Hitler told an audience of professors and students at Erlangen on 13 November 1930.[86] Nations would always have to wage eternal war for space, which by its very nature was limited and therefore a source of permanent conflict.

Indeed the basis of evolution and the meaning of history at its most elementary and fundamental level lay in the life-struggle of the nations for *Lebensraum* and the nourishing of their populations. Similarly the objective of politics was to safeguard the necessary living-space of each people, to provide it with the essential means for waging its struggle for life.[87] It was the task of the folkish state to educate its citizenry to heroic values that would enable them to emerge victorious in this merciless struggle. Democracy, pacifism and internationalism could only paralyse the natural strength of the instinct for self-preservation and were therefore wholly dysfunctional. What was decisive for the outcome in this battle for existence was less the strength of the army than the vigour of the leadership and the 'inner value' (*Volkswert*) of the people.[88] This in turn could only be secured by racial cleansing of the most radical kind.

Hitler's expansionist programme openly aimed at establishing in successive stages a Greater Germany, a New Order in Europe and World dominion; its goal of implementing the dawn of a great 'Aryan' civilization was clearly built on nineteenth-century social-Darwinian ideological premises. Though its basis was a wholly irrational belief-system, it was internally consistent to a surprising degree and remarkably constant in its methods, techniques and final aims. In the first stage, the Reich would expand to absorb racial Germans in the surrounding territories and restore its position as a major European power. In the next stage, Germany would have to pursue a determined policy of continental territorial acquisition to solve its overpopulation problem and acquire economic independence and a healthy social balance. This search for new soil and living space for its surplus population dictated a strategy of military conquest to the East at the expense of Russia. Having finally secured the food supply and *Lebensraum* of the German people, Hitler intended to develop its racial qualities in preparation for the aim of world conquest. Prussian traits of discipline and efficiency would be mobilized to check disunity and compensate for the historic lack of racial uniformity.[89] Germany would be reshaped in the image of a collective Nordic superman with emphasis on leadership, will-power, building of character and the military virtues alongside a policy of deliberate racial eugenics. The German folkish State as the vessel for breeding a new master-race would finally make the world safe for the flourishing of the creative Aryan genius. The Nazi Party as the implementor of this policy was to be the guardian of this millenial future – that of the thousand-year Reich. It would ensure the unity, cohesion and power of the purified race; the NSDAP was the delegate of the *Volk* and the Führer, whose historic task it was to prepare the Germans for their pivotal role in the coming struggle for global mastery.

Race was the alpha and omega of the New Order and the need for *Lebensraum* was decisively bound up with this premise. Germany could not become a world power without the wide-open spaces in the East. Similarly, the conquest of these territories and their settlement would foster the conditions for the creation of a pure race and a healthy *Volk*. The new spaces would be colonized by German peasants who would guarantee the Reich an independent food-supply and freedom from the constraints of foreign markets. The territories, but *not* their inhabitants, would be thoroughly Germanized. The lower, alien Slavic races (Russians, Poles, Czechs, etc.) would not be integrated but decimated and reduced to serfdom, to prevent the further hybridization of the German element. For the Jews there would be no place at all, for their very existence threatened Hitler's vision of a pre-ordained racial hierarchy, where the strong had the eternal right to subdue and enslave the weak. To allow them to live would be to sin against the laws of nature herself, to undermine the process of permanent selection by conflict, which Providence had willed; it would mean the abandonment of any attempt to purify the impure and achieve that physical perfection of race which was the highest mission on earth; it would mean final resignation in the face of the forces of decay and disintegration that had been operating throughout the history of civilization.

In Hitler's vision of the New Order it was the sacred mission of the Germans as a *Raumvolk* (people of space) to destroy the Jew, the people of time. The new *Herrenvolk* would have to conquer space in order to overcome time. Only a world where race was the final reality would also be one liberated from the tyranny of time. In the Nazi perception, the timeless, eternal Aryan race would then finally be recovered in its changeless purity.[90] The biological, genealogical past would subsume and conquer History in the permanent, indestructible framework of a Germanic *Grossraum*. Traditional hierarchies, structures and beliefs would be restored. The pagan gods of space would reassert their superiority over the obsolete Hebrew god of time. The true meaning of nature and history – the eternal struggle for food, territory and power – would find its consummation.

In his *Secret Book* Hitler had developed such ideas in a somewhat cruder, more materialistic form. His starting-point was the premise that 'the Jewish state was never spatially limited in itself; it was universally unlimited in respect to space, but it was restricted to the collectivity of a race. This is the reason why this people always form a State within other States.'[91] The unique position of the Jews as a people without a territory or specific national boundaries marked them off sharply from non-Jewish peoples. Whereas 'the foundation of the Aryan struggle for life is in the soil' and the conflict over *Lebensraum*, the Jewish people could not participate in this struggle, lacking as it did the productive forces for the construction of its own territorial state. Hence its fight for survival assumed unnatural forms; dependent on the work and creativity of other nations, it led a parasitical mode of existence. The 'ultimate goal' of its struggle for life was 'the enslavement of productively active people'. All nations were its enemy and the Jews therefore sought to systematically denationalize their host-peoples, lowering their racial level in order to facilitate the continuance of their parasitic exploitation. Egalitarianism, internationalism and pacifism were all stratagems in this war of survival of a Diasporic nation without a territorial base. In his *Secret Book* Hitler observed: 'In foreign policy he [the Jew] tried to bring nations into a state of unrest, to divert them from their true interests, and to plunge them into reciprocal wars and in this way to rise to mastery over them with the help of money and propaganda.'[92]

Jewish internationalism thereby obstructed the true purpose of nature – the racial war for *Lebensraum*. Hence, unless the Jews were first annihilated there could be no final struggle for living space: and without the conquest of new soil, the German people would inevitably be doomed to extinction. Thus the war for territorial expansion and the genocide of the Jews were from the outset organically related in Hitler's programme. The assault on Soviet Russia would be the climax of his mission, for at one blow he could solve the problem of German living space, destroy the greatest biological reservoir of Jewry and wipe out the citadel of Bolshevism. The strategy leading up to this climatic war would be dictated by the need to ally with nations like Britain, Italy or Japan, which in Hitler's eyes had retained sufficient racial value for expansion. The criteria for these alliances were not only dictated by the conventional conceptions of power politics but were to a remarkable degree determined by Hitler's racial doctrines. Hence, neither Nazi expansionism nor the resulting Holocaust can be properly understood simply in terms of the diplomatic relations of the period, military and geopolitical strategies, economic factors or Hitler's Machiavellian 'opportunism'. The key to resolving the apparent contradictions in Hitler's foreign and domestic policy and to comprehending his final goal of revolutionizing the global system lay in his perception of Jewry and its interaction with other actors on the international scene. The relentless drive towards the New Order in Europe, the system of alliances, the invasion of Russia and the 'Final Solution' were ultimately conditioned by Hitler's ideological obsessions.[93] Radical eschatological antisemitism and extreme Social Darwinism provided more than just a motor in Germany's bid for world power. They eventually became genocidal ends in themselves that devoured even the dream of global dominion.

# CHAPTER FOUR
# Nazis and Jews

In *Mein Kampf*, Hitler had defined the task of National Socialism as one of opening the eyes of the people to 'remind them again and again of the true enemy of our present-day world'.[1] He demanded that the fight against the Jew in Germany become 'a gleaming symbol of brighter days, to show other nations the way to the salvation of an embattled Aryan humanity'.[2] In countless speeches in the early 1920s he had made it clear that to save the nation 'the first thing to do is to rescue it from the Jew who is ruining our country. . . . We want to prevent our Germany from suffering, as Another did, the death upon the cross.'[3] From first to last, this was, as his biographer Alan Bullock put it, the most consistent theme of his career, 'the master idea which embraces the whole span of his thought'.[4] Nevertheless there was a difference between the rowdy antisemitism that went down well in the Munich beerhalls and at mass meetings and the tactical requirements of a party leader who was contending for national power. This was already apparent at the end of the 1920s when Hitler came to stress the theme of anti-Communism and play down his radical antisemitism, in order to win over the conservative elites, Reichswehr circles and the industrialists of the Rhineland. Significantly, in his January 1932 speech to the influential Industry Club in Düsseldorf, he avoided all talk of expropriating the big industrial concerns and did not even mention the Jews. The focus was on national renewal, on the authority principle, neutralizing the class-struggle and smashing Bolshevism.

Similarly in an interview with the *Times* correspondent in Berlin in October 1930 Hitler was careful to present National Socialism as a disciplined movement and even denied its violent antisemitism. 'He would have nothing to do with pogroms and that was the first word which had always gone forth from him in turbulent times. Their doctrine was 'Germany for the Germans' and their attitude towards Jews was governed by the attitude of Jews towards their doctrine. They had nothing against decent Jews, but if Jews associated themselves with Bolshevism, as many unfortunately did, they must be regarded as enemies. The Party was all against violence, but, if attacked, it was ready to defend itself.'[5] In the autumn of 1932, discussing the question of Nazi

69

propaganda in the United States, Hitler had suggested to Kurt Ludecke that 'the idea be disseminated that capitalism and Jewry need not look too fearfully toward a National Socialist regime'.[6] In an interview with Miss Ann O'Hare McCormick of the *New York Times* in July 1933 Hitler again made it clear that he did not regard it as expedient to be seen as an open antisemite in the Western democracies. He claimed that he would be 'only too glad if the nations which take such an enormous interest in Jews would open their gates to them'. It was true that there were 'discriminatory laws' in Germany, 'but they are directed not so much against the Jews as for the German people, to give economic opportunity to the majority'. Jews would have to share the privations of the whole nation. 'I cannot spare a Communist because he is a Jew', Hitler ingenuously declared.[7]

It was a theme to which Hitler would constantly return, especially for foreign consumption, in order to explain and gloss over his anti-Jewish policy. Thus a couple of months after the passing of the Nuremberg Laws in September 1935, in an interview with Mr Baillie of the United Press, Hitler stated: 'One of the principal reasons for the legislation in Germany is the necessity to combat Bolshevism. The legislation is not anti-Jewish, but pro-German. The rights of Germans are thereby to be protected against destructive Jewish influences. Nearly all Bolshevist agitators in Germany had been Jews: only a few miles separated Soviet Russia from Germany and continuous effective measures were needed to protect Germany from the intrigues of the agents of Bolshevism who were for the most part Jews.'[8] Hitler added that after 1918 the Jews had tried to monopolize the leadership of the people and had 'flooded the intellectual professions' such as law and medicine. 'The influence of this intellectual Jewish class in Germany had everywhere a disintegrating effect' which the Nuremberg Race Laws had been designed to halt. The objective was not antisemitic but to 'protect' the Jews by taking steps 'to establish a clear and clean separation between the two races'. Hitler claimed that since the passing of the restrictive measures 'anti-Jewish sentiment in the country had decreased. The Government was anxious to prevent self-help on the part of the people which might vent itself in dangerous explosions; its legislative measures were aimed at maintaining in Germany that calm and peace which had been enjoyed up to the present time.'[9]

Hitler's pose of 'moderation' on the Jewish question in the early years of the Nazi regime must be seen as a shrewd tactical move which was largely dictated by circumstances. But this compromise with reality did not mean that he had altered in the slightest his ideological commitment to expelling the Jews from Germany and then preparing for the final inevitable showdown with world Jewry. As he told Hermann Rauschning, in 1933 he had been 'compelled slightly to water down his attacks on the Jews';[10] for that very reason he was determined not to allow antisemitism to slacken, even as he and his leading party officials played down any official involvement in violent 'excesses' against Jews. The measures to expropriate German Jewry would be taken slowly but relentlessly. 'Everything we plan will be carried out, I shall not permit anyone to talk me out of it.' The Jews, he went on sarcastically, were 'Germany's best protection'. They were 'the pledge that guaranteed that foreign powers would allow Germany to go her way in peace'.[11] He informed Rauschning and company in 1934 that if the Western democracies did not withdraw their anti-Nazi boycott he would take from German Jews as much of their property as necessary to cover the damage caused by it. When there was nothing left to take, 'he would still hold their lives in the palm of his hand: their precious Jewish lives' – at which the company burst out laughing again. The Crystal Night pogrom, according to the same source, was no *ad hoc* response to the murder of von Rath in Paris but 'had been planned and considered long beforehand'.[12]

Hitler always distinguished sharply between the ultimate *goal* on which he was adamant and unmovable and the *means* by which it would be attained which were flexible and constantly open to adaptation and change. In a closed party forum he was more forthcoming in explaining this facet of his policy. Thus in April 1937 he told a meeting of party district leaders that the final aim of the regime's anti-Jewish policy was 'crystal clear to all of us. . . . You must understand that I always go as far as I dare and never further. It is vital to have a sixth sense which tells you broadly what you can and cannot do. Even in a struggle with an adversary it is not my way to issue a direct challenge to a trial of strength. I do not say: "Come and fight because I want a fight"; instead I shout at him, and I shout louder and louder! "I mean to destroy you." Then I use my intelligence to help me to manoeuvre him into a tight corner so that he cannot strike back, and then I deliver the fatal blow.'[13]

The purposiveness and devilish cunning of Hitler's approach to the 'Jewish question' have been consistently underestimated by most historians, who in this respect appear to have learned nothing from the past. Yet the truth was apparent from the beginning, after the first Nazi measures against 'non-Aryans' in the spring of 1933. Mussolini's ambassador in Berlin, Signor Vittorio Cerruti, had sought to intervene with Hitler on behalf of his master in Rome. In spite of all the genuine admiration he felt for his fascist mentor, Hitler angrily brushed aside the Italian protest, declaring that Mussolini knew nothing about racial problems. 'No one understands this problem better than I do, because I have made a thorough study of it and I know how dangerous the Jews in Germany are. . . . I refuse to alter a single point in my programme.'

To make sure his Italian friends would get the message, he shrieked that 'in five or six hundred years, the name of Hitler will be extolled throughout the world: the name of one who, once and for all, will have rid the world of the Jewish pest'.[14]

The fact that Hitler tolerated assorted 'solutions' to the Jewish problem between 1933 and 1939 should not blind one to the underlying consistency and determination of his resolve to destroy the Jews. Nor should Nazi policy in this regard be seen as a 'twisted road' of *ad hoc* improvisations without any common purpose or aim. On the contrary, ever since 1919 Hitler had regarded systematic anti-Jewish legislation as the model for his type of 'rational' antisemitism, which was no less cold-blooded and murderous for using the 'legal' framework of the State to accomplish its objectives. This early legislation designed to disenfranchise and isolate German Jewry within the Third Reich was, however, only a first step; one which neither Hitler nor the Nazi Party could ever have accepted as more than a partial and temporary 'solution', until conditions were ripe enough for implementing the more wide-ranging goals of National Socialism. Hitler's strategy in office was in fact no different from during the *Kampfzeit*: to advance step by step, always acting from a position of strength, ready to strike at the opportune moment. The grand design was in his head – the specific details of its implementation could be left to subordinates and were in any case dependent on domestic and foreign circumstances which could not be fully predicted in advance.[15]

In 1933 Hitler was obliged to partly disguise his true intentions, at least in public, because of the enormous economic difficulties and military weakness of the Reich. The massive unemployment, the shortage of foreign currency and imbalance of payments were the most pressing issues on which the Nazi regime might stand or fall. For this reason alone, as Hitler's extremely able Economics Minister Hjalmar Schacht pointed out, it was impossible to exclude the Jews from the German economy.[16] Thus, in the first four years of the regime, in spite of the pressure of radical party functionaries and the creeping persecution against local Jewish businesses (especially in the provinces), there was no systematic legislative effort to drive the Jews out of economic life.[17] Hitler recognized the force of Schacht's practical argument that unbridled, arbitrary actions against Jewry in this sphere might severely inhibit the rebuilding of the German economy – without which all his foreign policy goals would be unattainable. Moreover, he had to contend with considerable political constraints in these early years of the regime. They began with President Paul von Hindenburg's adamant opposition to the initial Nazi racial legislation at the end of March 1933 which dismissed Jewish judges, lawyers, teachers and civil servants from positions in government or the professions. What infuriated the ageing President in his letter to Hitler of 4 April 1933 was less the principle itself than the inclusion of former war veterans in such discriminatory legislation. 'For me personally, revering those who died in the war and grateful to those who survived and to the wounded who suffered,' wrote the former Field Marshal and Commander of the German Army in the First World War, 'this treatment of Jewish war veterans now in the civil service is intolerable.' He insisted that they must be allowed to continue in their professions, for 'if they were prepared to bleed and die for Germany, they deserve to be treated honourably by the Fatherland'.[18] Hitler replied the following day, reassuring von Hindenburg that any future solution would be carried out 'legally' and not in a capricious manner; the President's protest, motivated by 'noble motives', would be taken into consideration in framing new laws, especially with regard to war veterans. At the same time, Hitler respectfully pointed out that millions of brave, loyal National Socialists were being kept out of good jobs in the civil service by Jews.[19]

In these early months of the Nazi regime, Hitler had to manoeuvre carefully between the conservatives in his Cabinet, who, like von Hindenburg, disapproved of violent antisemitic measures, and the Nazi Party Radicals who demanded them. The first antisemitic legislation directed at Jewish professionals had been designed to satisfy and channel the Radical agitation – especially that of the SA rank-and-file who looked to benefit from the Nazi revolution at the expense of the Jews. Jewish doctors, lawyers, businessmen, civil servants, teachers and students had always been the special object of hatred for the *Mittelstand* and semi-proletarian element who to a large extent made up the Storm Troop battalions. Their call for action had somehow to be met and the pogrom mood controlled while acceding to the conservative demand for order and the image of respectability, so important to the creditworthiness of the regime and its international standing.

Addressing the Doctors' Union in April 1933, Hitler skilfully walked the tightrope between these different imperatives, whilst justifying the elimination of Jews from the German medical profession as a cleansing act of 'racial hygiene' and a firm foundation for future political development; it would create a new 'living space' and possibilities for young German doctors to exercise their profession in the midst of a great Depression. This was a 'natural' piece of affirmative action and an act of social justice, for Germany was entitled to an intellectual leadership inspired by the 'Aryan' or German spirit, which had been distorted in the past by an excessive number of Jewish professionals.[20] The United States, he emphasized, had no grounds to complain at such discrimination, since 'America's own immigration laws had excluded from admission those belonging to races of which America disapproved, while America was by no means prepared to open the gates to Jewish "fugitives" from Germany. As a matter of fact the Jews in Germany had not a hair of their heads rumpled.'[21]

In an interview in the same year published in the New York *Staatszeitung* Hitler returned to this theme, mocking the 'crocodile's tears' shed in the outside world over 'the richly merited fate of a small Jewish minority'. With pointed venom he asked Roosevelt and the American people: 'Are you prepared to receive in your midst these well-poisoners [*Brunnenvergifter*] of the German people and the universal spirit of Christianity? We would willingly give every one of them a free steamer-ticket and a thousand-mark note for travelling expenses, if we could get rid of them. Am I to allow thousands of pure-blooded Germans to perish so that all Jews may work, live and be merry in security while a nation of millions is a prey to starvation, despair, and Bolshevism?'[22] The challenge to Western (especially American) hypocrisy over immigration and their alleged indifference to German hunger and mass misery was one of Hitler's more cynically effective methods of combating foreign critics of his Jewish policy.

In 1933 Hitler and the Nazis had another special reason for singling out America as the object of their indignation, for it was from New York that the anti-Nazi boycott organized by American Jewry to help their beleaguered brethren took off. The giant anti-Nazi rally on 27 March 1933 in Madison Square Garden symbolized to the Nazis the beginning of the *bellum judaicum* designed by world Jewry to bring down the German economy and with it the Hitler regime. Goebbels expressed the fear of the German leadership in his diary: 'The horror propaganda abroad gives us much trouble. The many Jews who have left Germany have set all foreign countries against us. . . . We are defenselessly exposed to the attacks of our adversaries.'[23] A Jewish-led world-wide boycott of the regime was a weapon Hitler could not afford to ignore, given the economic crisis confronting his regime in the spring of 1933. Deprived of exports, Germany would also be denied foreign currency with which to purchase imported raw materials and be unable to borrow money abroad. Trapped in a cycle of depression without access to foreign markets, the Reich might be doomed to slow destruction. Hence the frantic agitation in the Nazi press against the 'atrocity' headlines (*Greuelpropaganda*) in the British and American media; the mobilization of German-Jewish leaders by Goering to be sent abroad to reassure world Jewry that there was no persecution; and the pre-emptive anti-Jewish boycott of 1 April 1933 in Germany, organized by the veteran antisemite, Julius Streicher.[24]

These 'defensive measures' of the Nazis were preceded by a rash of far from spontaneous acts of intimidation, violence, boycotting and expulsions. But

Hitler, in spite of the pressure of Goebbels and Goering, was forced to restrict the 1 April *aktion* to one day only, as a result of opposition from the non-Nazi majority in his cabinet led by Foreign Minister von Neurath who feared the economic consequences;[25] this opposition, reinforced by the Catholic Conservative von Papen and Schacht's expert financial advice, as well as the intervention of President von Hindenburg, gradually wore down Hitler's obstinacy. Though he refused to cancel the nation-wide anti-Jewish boycott, he did curtail its duration and scope, recognizing that in future he would have to proceed step by step, through the use of legal regulations, while at the same time ensuring German economic viability. The foreign anti-Nazi boycott would eventually be broken by other means, not least by the transfer agreement negotiated with the Zionist movement and by the unwillingness of the Western democracies to stop trading with the Third Reich.[26]

Hitler's caution was reflected in the terminology of the initial racial legislation, which still used the clumsy term 'non-Aryan' rather than Jew and restricted its attack to removing Jews from the free professions and cultural life. The brunt of Nazi terror at this stage of consolidation was in any case directed at finally smashing the Communists, Social Democrats, trade unions and liberal Republicans – an issue on which there was a greater consensus between Nazis and conservatives, than over the Jews. Hugenberg's right-wing national party (DNVP) had always stressed the Marxist rather than the 'Jewish' danger, regarding the latter almost as a distraction from dealing with the real enemy on the Left.[27] The conservative nationalists were ready to support a 'respectable' antisemitism which restricted the freedom of Jews to engage in cultural and political activity. They even agreed with the Nazis that Jews had been largely responsible for the twin evils of finance capitalism and socialism – this was, after all, part of the heritage of late nineteenth-century Prusso-German conservatism.[28] At the same time, they feared the *Radauanti-semitismus* of Nazi extremists and the social radicalism of the SA which threatened the entire middle-class, capitalist structure of Germany.

They looked to Hitler to tame this Nazi violence and disorder, to keep National Socialism within the bounds of bourgeois morality, law and order and an authoritarian state efficiently run on Prussian lines. Within the limits of this conservative world-view, non-Nazi members of the government like Hugenberg, von Papen, von Neurath and Schacht tried to restrain Hitler's antisemitism, to differentiate between useful and harmful Jews, to emphasize the importance of world opinion and the priorities of national economic recovery. Their attachment to a free market economy succeeded in preventing the institutionalization of apartheid in this sphere until 1937–8; their influence further helped to hold at bay the incessant pressures of the 'little' Nazis, the

*Mittelstand* rank and file and radical elements who had been disappointed by the promises of an anti-capitalist revolution which had simply not materialized.[29]

Many of the Nazi rank-and-file in the mid-1930s simply could not understand why any Jewish banks, department stores, export houses and industrial enterprises should continue to flourish in a National Socialist state reputedly at war with world Jewry.[30] Since 1933 they had in any case engaged in continual harassment and unofficial boycotts of local Jewish businesses whose liquidation or 'Aryanization' they greedily anticipated. Sometimes they had taken the law into their own hands and made unsanctioned assaults on Jews and Jewish property. These *Einzelaktionen* were periodically condemned by leading party officials in the first two years of Nazi rule, when the emphasis was on consolidation of power and the breaking of revolutionary enthusiasm. The tone had already been set from the top in a ministerial discussion of 25 April 1933 when Goering quoted Hitler to the effect that 'we must hit the Jews hard' but not allow them to malign Germany 'in places where it could be interpreted in the wrong way'.[31] The need to take world opinion into account, deference to President Hindenburg and conservative views in the Cabinet, fear of economic reprisals abroad and the desire to keep the SA under control ultimately determined the official policy during this phase. Jewish doctors could be prohibited from working in hospitals, the *numerus clausus* was instituted in schools, colleges and universities, but as Minister of the Interior Wilhelm Frick put it in January 1934, the letter of the law had to be respected.[32] In April 1935, Deputy Leader Rudolf Hess, citing Hitler's need to refute 'allegations of atrocities and boycotts made by Jews abroad', gave a confidential order to party militants not to engage in acts of terror against individual Jews:[33] 'The political police can in such cases only follow the strict instructions of the Führer in carrying out all measures for maintaining peace and order. . . .'

These warnings, which had Hitler's explicit authority behind them, revealed just how determined the Nazi leadership was to protect the economy from disruptive measures. The shotgun approach of the SA, eager for blood and spoil, was to be carefully controlled so as to preserve the legitimacy of the regime and its projected image of discipline and order; the massacre of the SA leadership in June 1934 had already shown that in this respect Hitler meant business. In Jewish policy, too, the party radicals who disdained the slower methods of the German bureaucracy would have to learn the facts of life and subordinate their activism to the requirements of *raison d'état*. The failure of the 1 April boycott had taught Hitler an important lesson regarding the inadvisability of a frontal assault on Jewry which he would not quickly forget.

In the phase of economic and military consolidation, radical antisemitism would have to be toned down.

Hitler's tactical retreat on the Jewish question in the early years of Nazi rule was only one of a number of concessions which he had to make to the realities of power. The fear of adverse international repercussions and internal economic collapse was the most obvious restraining factor. But he could also not afford to dispense with the co-operation of such established institutional structures as the bureaucracy, the army, the churches and big business and it would take a number of years before these were sufficiently 'Nazified'. Furthermore, he had still to take some account of German public opinion, which was by no means universally enthused by official antisemitic propaganda.[34] Even in the Nazi Party there were different shades of opinion on this issue.[35] Finally there was the practical problem of what to do with German Jewry – a question which had never been clearly thought out in the years before 1933 and which became inceasingly urgent in the wake of Nazi persecution.[36] These unforeseen complexities inevitably led to a certain confusion in policy. This tendency was accentuated by the somewhat anarchic power-structure in Nazi Germany with its myriad organizations and 'contra-dictory mosaic of antagonistic interests and directions'.[37] Though Hitler was himself temperamentally allergic to formal bureaucracy and the restraints of the legal framework, he could not yet break free from its straitjacket. The resistance of the moderate nationalists, the old-school civil servants and influential commercial circles was still too powerful. Moreover, the Foreign Office and the Ministries of Economics, Finance and Defence were to remain in non-Nazi hands until 1938. Only then, with the dismissal of 'moderates' like Schacht, von Neurath, von Blomberg and von Fritsch, the upturn in the economy, the rise of the SS and the radical change in the international situation of the Third Reich, was the road clear for Hitler. He could now afford to tighten the administrative and legal noose around German Jewry, finally drive them out of the economy, permit state expropriation in the form of 'Aryanization' and let loose the party radicals in the Crystal Night pogrom.

Hitler's caution in the years between 1933 and 1938 did not mean, however, that he had no specific design in his Jewish policy or that he had abandoned antisemitism once he stepped inside the portals of the Chancellery.[38] Unlike his first political mentor, Karl Lueger, or his fascist model, Benito Mussolini, Hitler *was* deadly serious when it came to the Jews. It was for this reason that he had brought about the Nazi revolution in the first place and it was also to be a major driving force behind his preparations for war. His emotional sympathies even in the early years of Nazi rule had been with his old comrade, the rabidly antisemitic editor of *Der Stürmer*, Julius Streicher, whose semi-pornographic publication was among Hitler's favourite reading matter.[39] Even as he temporarily bowed to the constraints of economic necessity, the Führer gave Streicher a free hand to nourish and develop the most lurid themes of traditional anti-Jewish propaganda, from ritual murder to racial defilement and white slavery. During the 1930s *Der Stürmer* achieved a circulation of almost half a million readers. Its display cases replete with slogans like 'Jewry is Criminality', 'German Women and Girls: The Jews are your Destruction' or 'He who Buys from Jews is a Traitor to the Third Reich' became part of the urban landscape in Nazi Germany.[40] Streicher's indoctrination campaigns and especially his 'Pillory' columns with their popular appeal to sadistic instincts did a great deal to spread antisemitism among Germans and establish a general atmosphere of intimidation. Invariably his calls for a total social and economic boycott of Jews, for banning them from public baths or places of entertainment and his endless warnings against racial defilement (*Rassenschande*) left their mark on the German public and acted as a form of pressure to escalate legal measures against German Jewry. Not surprisingly, Hitler regarded Streicher as 'irreplaceable' and did not share the resentment of many party comrades or the more 'respectable' sectors of public opinion at the Franconian Gauleiter's vulgar perversions. If anything, he found the *Stürmer* too mild. 'Streicher is reproached for his *Stürmer*', Hitler observed during the war. 'The truth is the opposite of what people say: he *idealised* the Jew. The Jew is baser, fiercer, more diabolical than Streicher depicted him.'[41]

If Hitler's heart was with the more fanatical antisemites like Streicher, Goebbels and Ley, his head still told him that the time was not yet ripe for the total implementation of his plan for a *judenrein* Germany. The Nuremberg Race Laws of September 1935, for which Streicher had insistently agitated, were Hitler's interim compromise between the countervailing pressures confronting him and his will to execute, at least in part, the principles of his racial ideology. The declared object of the laws he announced on 15 September 1935 to the Nuremberg Party Congress was to find a 'solution' by *legal* means to an essential problem.[42] By disenfranchising those German subjects (i.e. Jews) who were not of German 'blood' and forbidding marriage and extra-marital sexual intercourse between Germans and Jews, Hitler was fulfilling the NSDAP programme of 1920 in an 'important point': namely that only *Volksgenossen* (racial comrades) could be 'citizens of our State' and that no Jew could be regarded as a *Volksgenosse*. He was, moreover, anchoring the dogma of the 'purity of German blood' in official legislation. Henceforth, according to the basic Reich Citizenship Law, a *Reichsbürger* (citizen of the Reich) would have to be of 'German or cognate blood' while Jews were treated as subject to the equivalent of an Aliens Law. In addition they could not employ 'Aryan' domestic maidservants under the age of forty-five (another pointer to Nazi sexual phobias) or fly the German national colours (*Flaggengesetz*). The Jews were thus placed outside German society as a whole. Their position as a pariah group was formally institutionalized, though the complex question of *Mischlinge* (the 'mixed' offspring of Germans and Jews) was not yet resolved.[43] On the other hand, a legal basis had seemingly been laid for the continued existence of a Jewish community in Germany, one which was reduced to separate, second-class status but not yet deprived of its means of livelihood. Jewish existence was severely circumscribed but there was still the hope that wildcat boycott action might come to an end and propaganda assaults be curbed.

German Jewry had been given the misleading impression that in spite or perhaps because of the biological separation of the races, they might yet find a small niche within the Third Reich. In part these expectations were aroused by passages in Hitler's Reichstag speech which condemned arbitrary acts of violence (*Einzelaktionen*) and which affirmed: 'The German government is guided by the thought that it might still be possible to find a separate, secular solution [*eine einmalige sakuläre Lösung*] for building a basis upon which the German nation can adopt a better attitude towards the Jews' (*ein erträgliches Verhältnis zum jüdischen Volk*).[44] Hitler ominously warned, however, that in the case of a repeated breakdown in workable arrangements with the Jews, it might be necessary to pass a law 'handing the problem over to the National Socialist Party for final solution' (*zur endgültigen Lösung*).[45]

It was, however, less the intentional ambiguity in Hitler's remarks or their implicit threat that the legal phase might soon come to an end, which attracted the attention of German Jews, than the hope for a stabilization of their status. In this vain belief they were encouraged by a number of reassuring remarks made at the time by top Nazi officials. Thus, writing in the organ of German jurists, Interior Minister Wilhelm Frick declared in December 1935: 'The Citizenship Law and the law for the Protection of the Race and the regulations concerning their implementation are not intended to harm the members of the Jewish race on the grounds of racial origin. The Jews will not be deprived of the possibility of living in Germany.'[46] Hans Frank, speaking before the Academy of German Law, stated that 'the publication of the Nuremberg Laws brings to an end, for the moment, the process of revolutionary development in Germany'.[47] German Jews could remain and function as a Jewish body without harassment in the Reich on the basis of separate racial development. The Director of the German Press Agency, Brandt, put an even brighter face on this policy of apartheid. As a result of the new laws, the Jewish 'national' minority would gain an independent cultural and national existence which would be beneficial and regenerative for Judaism. 'Germany is helping Judaism to strengthen its national character and is making a contribution towards improved relations between the two peoples.'[48] Jewry would now enjoy a degree of cultural autonomy under the auspices of the Nazi state, and as a result of the Nuremberg Laws they could even fly their own national flag (the Star of David) without hindrance.

Many German Jews were indeed reassured by these deceptive promises of a tranquil co-existence between Germans and Jews within a 'legally protected' framework. Though the Nuremberg Laws had given official sanction to stripping German Jewry of equal civil rights and had confirmed their isolation from the rest of the population, they did not appear to deny Jews the right to reside in Germany. The main thing in the eyes of German Jewry was that their position had been clarified and the uncertainty surrounding their legal status dissipated to some degree. Thus when the head of the organization of 'State Zionists', Georg Kareski, was interviewed in Goebbels' newspaper *Der Angriff* in December 1935 he stressed the positive theme of a possible *modus vivendi* between Germans and Jews and the opportunities for increased cultural activities rather than the restrictions on civil rights. From a Zionist standpoint the Nuremberg Laws had the advantage of having destroyed the illusion of assimilation which Jewish nationalists had always rejected on principle. A German Zionist might even (as Kareski did in a rather degrading way) theoretically approve of the separation of the two races as long as this was done on the basis of 'mutual respect'.[49]

For the majority of non-Zionist German Jews such an attempted ideological *Gleichschaltung* was not so easily accomplished, though some German nationalist Jewish veterans' organizations had vainly attempted this since the 1920s.[50] Max Naumann, founder of the numerically insignificant but militant *Verband nationaldeutscher Juden*, the only Jewish group to support a Nazi-led national revolution, found, much to his chagrin, that even extreme assimilationism of a fascist character was unwelcome. The Nazis were totally unimpressed by his denunciations of Zionists and *Ostjuden* as alien enemies of the German *Volk*. The last thing Hitler and the Nazis desired was to assimilate German nationalists of Jewish origin.[51] This would in their terminology have been equivalent to exposing themselves to 'racial poison' within their own ranks. Significantly, in 1935 the Nazis dissolved Naumann's organization for attitudes 'hostile to the State', some time before they began their all-out assault on German Jewry.

The Nuremberg Laws did at least outwardly appear to confirm German Jewry's expectations, by bringing to a halt a wave of antisemitic terror by SA and SS units in the summer of 1935. The radical elements in the NSDAP, however, were far from dissatisfied. They had the opportunity of seeing their racial antisemitism anchored for the first time in the socio-political reality of the Third Reich; their earlier disappointment with the regime's apparent lack of a clear policy line abated. In conservative circles, on the other hand, the concern with economic reprisals provoked a much more muted response to the new legislation. Religious opinion, especially in the Catholic sector, generally disapproved, as did the remnants of the liberal bourgeois and left-wing intelligentsia. 'Public opinion' in general was more neutral, though there appears to have been a widespread feeling, according to secret SD reports, that the legislation might provide some stability and perhaps even a permanent solution to the Jewish problem.[52]

The fraudulent façade of a law-abiding, peaceful State was particularly important for Hitler and the Nazi leadership to preserve at this time in view of the forthcoming Olympic Games in Berlin. With the Winter Olympics due to begin in February 1936 it was essential to maintain the best possible image of the Reich abroad. Even the Nuremberg Race Laws were soft-pedalled for the occasion to convince the International Olympic Committee that in the field of sport, at least, Nazi Germany did not differentiate between 'Aryans' and 'non-Aryans'. In fact such transparently cosmetic operations only deceived those who did not wish to see that Nazi 'moderation' was but a lull before the storm. The Berlin correspondent of *The Times* had already noted shortly after the Nuremberg Laws that 'like so many Nazi catchwords, "*Juda Verrecke*" – "May Jewry Perish" – was meant literally and will be literally brought to pass if the fanatics have their way'.[53] Hitler himself had unveiled his true intentions towards the Jews before a small circle of intimates at about this time: 'Out with them from all professions and into the ghetto with them; fence them in somewhere where they can perish as they deserve while the German people look on, the way people stare at wild animals.'[54] In February 1936, after the assassination of Wilhelm Gustloff, head of the Nazi Party in Switzerland, by a young Jew, David Frankfurter, Hitler had considered a collective punishment and fine for German Jewry, but postponed the plan. Germany remained relatively quiet but Hitler encouraged the uninterrupted flow of amendments to the Nuremberg Laws which continued into 1938. Within two years, Jews were no longer to be admitted to public offices, hospitals, pharmacies, restaurants, schools and universities. They were ineligible for government or tax aid. By the end of 1938, they would be banned from theatres, concerts, museums, athletic fields and public baths. They would be barred from ownership of gold, silver or jewels and the possession of radios and telephones by Jews would be made illegal. All these discriminatory measures were carried

As Hitler told an assembly of regional Nazi leaders (*Kreisleiters*) on 29 April 1937, he did not need any pressure in pursuing his Jewish policy. Referring to an article in a provincial newspaper in which the editor had called on the party to establish some means of distinguishing Jewish from German firms, Hitler retorted: 'From whom is he demanding this? Who can give the necessary orders? Only I can give them. The editor, in the name of his readers, is asking me to act. First, I should tell you that long before this editor had any inkling about the Jewish problem, I made myself an expert on the subject. Secondly, this problem has been under consideration for two or three years, and will, of course, be settled one way or the other in due course.'[55] By the end of 1937 the first outlines of this 'settlement' were becoming clearer as the mechanisms for expropriating German Jewry were set in motion. Hitler had already envisaged in his secret 1936 memorandum on the Four Year Plan that in the event of Germany going to war, the Reichstag would pass an expropriation law. The whole of German Jewry would be made responsible 'for all damage inflicted by individual specimens of this criminal community upon the German economy. . . .'[56] As Hitler stepped up his preparations for war, so too he intensified his propaganda against the world citadel of 'Jewish Bolshevism' in Moscow and tightened the noose around German Jewry.

The resignation of Schacht from the Economics Ministry late in 1937 and the removal of von Blomberg, von Fritsch and von Neurath from the Army and Foreign Ministry in February 1938 had cleared the road for a more activist foreign policy. At the same time it made the implementation of an aggressive policy of expropriating German Jewry easy to accomplish. By the end of 1937 many Jewish workers and employees, professionals, civil servants and artists had already lost their means of income. Early in 1938 a systematic plan for the 'Aryanization' of larger Jewish firms was initiated by Hermann Goering, as the overseer of the Four Year Plan. A decree of 26 April 1938 obliged all Jews to report their total assets; further decrees defined the character of a Jewish enterprise, and in mid-June 1938 drafts for the obligatory 'Aryanization' of Jewish businesses were already circulating in the Interior Ministry. The connection between accelerated rearmament and the complete removal of Jews from the economy – including previously exempt import-export businesses, big banks and Jewish firms involved in rearmament – was made clear by Goering at a meeting of senior civil servants in October 1938.

The flood of anti-Jewish legislation beginning in February 1938 and intensifying throughout the year was a sign of the increasing radicalization of the regime both at home and abroad. Only this time the Nazi state was determined to centralize all measures concerning the 'Jewish question' so that

82

the depleted Treasury rather than local *Gauleiters* and the party rank-and-file would profit.[57] 'Aryanization' was intended to serve war preparations, not to enrich ordinary party members, though big business interests greedily joined hands with the Nazi state in exploiting opportunities to indulge in thievery on a grand scale.[58] Goering, who now supervised the legislative measures for driving the Jew from the economy and bringing about a *judenrein* Germany, was determined to keep the 'Jewish question' out of radical Nazi hands. Like Himmler and Heydrich, who respectively controlled the German police and security services (SD), he opposed uncontrolled violence and preferred to tighten the net around German Jewry by administrative measures. In July 1938 all Jews were required to apply for identification cards; in August it was announced that, as from 1 January 1939, all Jewish males were to take the name of Israel, and all Jewesses that of Sarah. On 5 October a law announcing the designation of Jews as such on their passports was issued; as the net was squeezed, international tensions were also growing. Hitler's plan for the dismembering of Czechoslovakia was only temporarily diverted by Chamberlain's appeasement policy at the Munich Conference of 29 September. Then, on 7 November 1938, the shooting of secretary von Rath in the German Embassy in Paris by a young Polish Jew, Hershl Grynszpan, gave the regime a perfect pretext to trigger off the Crystal Night pogrom two days later. The burning of Jewish synagogues and institutions all over Germany, the destruction of over 7,000 businesses, the murder of almost 100 Jews and the incarceration of about 30,000 Jewish males in concentration camps was the direct result.

To a large extent the pogrom had been incited and master-minded by Propaganda Minister Goebbels, though he could scarcely have acted in opposition to Hitler's wishes. The Führer had no objections as long as the pogrom could be given the appearance of being a 'spontaneous' expression of popular wrath against the Jews, of which there had indeed been some evidence in previous months. There were definite advantages to the regime in allowing the SA and more radical party members one last fling.[59] Hitler knew well enough that for five years he had done little to satisfy the pent-up energies and economic aspirations of his lower middle-class followers. He had carefully avoided a frontal assault on the Jews and opted for a more shadowy role behind the scenes.[60] Even with regard to the events of the *Kristallnacht* he still preserved an attitude of aloof detachment, officially neither approving nor disapproving as German Jewish institutions were ignited by the party mobs. Goebbels' initiative, designed in part to recapture the limelight for himself and to establish his own *locus standi* in Jewish policy, had, however, the advantage of allowing Hitler to accelerate still further the pace of expropriation.

Though Goering, Himmler and Heydrich were momentarily infuriated at the disorderly looting and the impudence of Goebbels in intruding on their fiefdom, they soon turned the situation to account. On 12 November 1938 a meeting at Goering's offices in the Reich Air Ministry was held to complete the process of eliminating the Jews from the economy and to co-ordinate the confiscation of all remaining Jewish factories and businesses. A decree was issued to exclude Jews from the retail trade, crafts, and sales agencies (*Bestellkontoren*), from offering business services of any kind, from managing firms or from membership of a co-operative (*Genossenschaft*). At the same time a fine of one billion marks was levied on German Jewry for its 'hostile attitude' to the German *Reich* and its people. Not only were the German Jews to be paid no compensation for the massive damage they had sustained as a community, they were to be collectively penalized in the harshest possible way. Goering could rest here on the Führer's authority, for he had opened the meeting by announcing that he had orders that 'the Jewish question be now, once and for all, co-ordinated and solved one way or the other'.[61]

The various suggestions raised by Goebbels, Goering and Heydrich at the meeting, from expelling Jewish children still in German schools to banning them from all public places and imposing curfew restrictions, would soon be implemented with the Führer's approval. Heydrich's suggestion that the SS methods of forced emigration used so successfully by Eichmann's office in Vienna after the *Anschluss* should be applied to German Jewry was a further pointer to the new radicalization of Nazi policy. Goering's closing threat, with its unmistakable echoing of Hitlerian rhetoric, reflected the accelerated drive to a radical solution. 'If, in the near future, the German Reich should come into conflict with foreign powers, it goes without saying that we in Germany should first of all let it come to a showdown with the Jews'.[62] Goering added that 'the Führer shall now make an attempt with those foreign powers which have brought the Jewish Question up . . . [a reference to Polish and French interest in the Madagascar project]. . . . He has explained it all to me on 9 November. There is no other way. He'll tell the other countries "what are you talking about the Jew for? – Take him." Another proposal may be made. The Jews, gotten rid of, may buy territory for their "co-religionists" in North America, Canada, or elsewhere.'[63]

The increasing militancy of the National Socialist leadership as it prepared for war found an even more ominous echo in the SS journal, *Das Schwarze Korps*, which 'prophesied' on 24 November 1938 that Germans were no longer prepared to tolerate hundreds of thousands of 'criminals' in their country. In what sounded like a trial-balloon for the 'Final Solution', the SS organ added: 'We would be faced with the hard necessity of exterminating the Jewish underworld in the same way as, under our government of Law and Order, we are wont to exterminate any other criminals, viz. by fire and sword. The result would be the factual and final end of Jewry in Germany, its absolute annihilation.'[64]

Hitler himself still relied for the moment on more veiled language in his public appearances. In his closing speech to the Nuremberg Party Congress (12 September 1938) he had claimed that National Socialism fought 'the Jewish element in Germany so fanatically, and has pressed and still presses so urgently for its removal . . .' because it wished 'to establish a real community of the people'.[65] The unconditional authority of the leadership was the product of a united body in which 'the most capable sons of the people', regardless of their origin or social position, could reach the highest positions. There was no conflict between rulers and ruled in the Third Reich because the peasant and worker knew that his leaders 'are his own flesh and blood'. Thus, according to Hitler, 'the strongest evidence for the truly Socialist character of the National Socialist Movement is its struggle against an alien leadership which has not sprung from its own people'.[66] The myth of the *Volksgemeinschaft* had long been a powerful weapon in Hitler's world-view, which in the early 1920s had already sought to synthesize nationalism, socialism and antisemitism in an unholy trinity. Since coming to power in 1933 he had often struck a pseudo-egalitarian pose in justifying his anti-Jewish policies, which were presented as an exercise in encouraging social mobility for deserving *Volksgenossen* (racial comrades).

Nevertheless, until the summer of 1938 when the material incentives increased, there is little firm evidence that a majority of Germans were enthusiastic supporters of the regime's rabid antisemitism. Indifference and dislike of Jews were widespread enough, but the masses by and large lacked interest in ideological and political issues.[67] Commercial relationships between Jewry and non-Jews had continued to flourish in the first few years of the Third Reich, highlighting the gap between Nazi propaganda and the populace at large. This lack of 'racial' consciousness manifested by Germans shopping in Jewish stores or trading with Jews was constantly denounced by party officials. In spite of massive indoctrination, they still had difficulty in persuading ordinary Germans of 'the need for active discrimination and persecution of the Jews'.[68] Even during the November 1938 pogrom, 'the general public failed to take any leading part at all', as one historian has noted.[69] On the contrary, the wanton destruction of property during the *Kristallnacht* provoked widespread criticism and disapproval. Mostly this was directed to the pragmatic issue of the damage caused to the economy rather than sensitivity to the treatment of the Jews as such, though in 'opposition' circles – whether left-wing, liberal, conservative or religious – there was a greater awareness of the moral dimension.[70] Though it was never in itself the cause of internal revolt against the Nazi regime, persecution of the Jews (especially after November 1938) could become an additional rallying-point for the clandestine opposition.

This fact may also have had some bearing on the radicalization of Nazi policy apparent since the end of 1937, given Hitler's conviction that the Jews were 'a ferment of decomposition' both at home and abroad. The first sign of internal opposition was liable to be interpreted by Hitler, the top Nazi leadership and the security services as a product of 'Jewish' intrigues – whether local or foreign. Thus any dissatisfaction in working-class circles or among the conservatives, any rumblings in the Army or the churches, would automatically be seen in terms of a potential 'Jewish' threat to overthrow the regime. The coincidence between Hitler's more aggressive foreign policy and the drastic legislation against Jews in 1938 has therefore been related by some recent commentators to a feeling of crisis and stagnation felt by the regime and its need to break out of this impasse by taking radical measures.[71] But the new élan of German anti-Jewish policy from the end of 1937 onwards seems to me much more a result of the restoration of Nazi self-confidence and their power-lust than of a sense of internal weakness felt by the regime. Many of the tactical restraints which had operated in the past could now be dispensed with, as Germany rearmed and attained full employment while successfully asserting herself against her neighbours and the Western democracies. Germany was by 1938 economically and militarily stronger than at any time since 1918. The limitations on its freedom of action were fading fast.

The *Anschluss* with Austria in March 1938 was, in my view, the crucial turning-point, for in addition to its 'strategic' significance it realized Hitler's oldest dream – the establishment of *Grossdeutschland* and the reunion of his former homeland with the Reich. Austria was rapidly turned into an SS Gestapo laboratory for carrying out new and more ruthless 'solutions' of the Jewish question, by quick-fire 'Aryanization' measures and forced emigration. It was no accident that Adolf Eichmann learned the tricks of his trade in Vienna during 1938, experience that proved invaluable in carrying out the 'Final Solution' from the Reich Security Main Headquarters in Berlin three years later. The *Anschluss* had, however, added another 200,000 Jews to the Reich, which virtually equalled the number who had emigrated from Nazi Germany in the previous five years. Thus the Nazis had made no progress as far as the immediate objective was concerned – ridding the Reich of its Jews. The vicious circle of territorial expansion and with it a growing Jewish population had begun – one that increasingly neutralized the value of an emigration policy based on gradual pressure as a 'solution' to the Jewish question. The alternative solution of physical destruction, which Hitler had always harboured as his deepest urge and motivation, therefore began to appear, by force of circumstances, more feasible. By the end of 1938 the Jews of Germany and Austria had already been uprooted from all fields of activity and reduced to the status of outlaws in the Reich. They were no longer necessary to the economy and with that their only *raison d'être* in Nazi eyes had already disappeared. Moreover, their last possible protectors among the Old Guard in the Army, Economics Ministry and Foreign Office had been dismissed. The regime had militarily consolidated and was now about to dismantle Czechoslovakia as its next move on the European chessboard.

The reaction of the Western democracies against his discriminatory measures was already a matter of growing indifference to Hitler.[72] During the visit of the South African Defence Minister Oswald Pirow to Berlin on 24 November 1938, Hitler had rejected his guest's proposals to mediate between Germany and Neville Chamberlain over the 'Jewish question'. The British were full of humanitarian intentions, the Führer pointed out, but they did nothing to solve the problem. Hitler categorically rejected Pirow's suggestion that the Jews be removed to the former German colony of Tanganyika for resettlement. The German people would never hand over to their bitterest enemies any area in which German blood has been spilt. Moreover, the Jews would never work as settlers in East Africa anyway. 'The last thing that world Judaism wants', he told his (pro-German and antisemitic) guest, 'is to see the Jews disappear from Europe. On the contrary it looks on the Jews in Europe as the advance troops for the bolshevization of the world.'[73] In response to Pirow's plea that he offer a workable solution in the interests of an understanding with Britain's Prime Minister Chamberlain, Hitler referred heatedly to the Jewish 'invasion' from the East and the scale of their assets in Germany. 'But the problem would soon be solved', he insisted. 'On this point his mind was irrevocably made up. . . . One day the Jews would disappear from Europe' (*die Juden würden . . . aus Europa verschwinden*).[74]

The interview with Pirow was a sign that Hitler felt he could now state his long-held convictions more openly and without reservations, even to foreign visitors. He had already achieved the necessary freedom of manoeuvre in foreign policy to cast off most of the diplomatic double-talk of the past five years. Admittedly, his former Economics Minister Schacht would still be sent on one last trip to England to see if he could reach an agreement with the American negotiator, Rublee, over ransoming German Jewry.[75] Hitler had voiced no objection to a plan which envisaged world Jewry raising a loan to free his Jewish hostages detained in Germany, in return for helping German exports. Why should the Nazis not be rewarded economically for their policy of expropriating and ultimately expelling the Jews? But Hitler's cunning if twisted mind had long since grasped that the countries of potential immigration, beginning with the wide expanses of the British Empire and the United States, were most unlikely to accept additional Jewish refugees. This hard fact was almost certain to kill the Schacht plan, which had envisaged the emigration over five years of two-thirds of German Jewry. When Schacht was relieved of his post as President of the Reichsbank on 20 February 1939 the last slim hope of a negotiated transfer to save the by now impoverished community of German Jewry had faded. Even if the Western democracies had been more forthcoming, it is doubtful whether Hitler at this stage would have allowed economic considerations to prevail over his ideological and political imperatives. While Jews could still be used as counters in the great-power bargaining between Nazi Germany and the West, their fate was basically sealed from the moment that Hitler's preparations for war were ripe.

The connection was made crystal-clear in the Führer's Reichstag speech of 30 January 1939, delivered eight months before the German invasion of Poland. In this 'prophecy' the imminence of the world war and the Holocaust were linked in the most ominous manner. 'One thing I should like to say on this day which may be memorable for others as well as for us Germans: in the course of my life I have very often been a prophet, and have usually been ridiculed for it. During the time of my struggle for power it was in the first instance the Jewish race which received my prophecies with laughter when I said that I would one day take over the leadership of the State, and with it that of the whole nation, and that I would then among many other things settle the Jewish problem. Their laughter was uproarious, but I think that for some time now they have been laughing on the other side of their face. Today I will once more be a prophet: If the international Jewish financiers in and outside Europe should succeed in plunging the nations once more into a world war, then the result will not be the bolshevization of the earth, and thus the victory of Jewry, but the annihilation of the Jewish race in Europe!'[76] Decoded back into normal speech, Hitler was informing his audience and the rest of the world: 'I am preparing to unleash a second world war and to murder European Jewry.'

## CHAPTER FIVE
# Antisemitism as a Global Weapon

At the annual general meeting of the Nazi Party in September 1928 Hitler told his assembled audience, to enthusiastic applause, that antisemitism was growing as an idea. 'What was hardly there ten years ago is there today: the Jewish question has been brought to the people's notice, it will not disappear any more and we shall make sure that it becomes an international world question; we shall not let it rest until the question has been solved. We think we shall live to see that day.'[1] Hitler had always seen the 'Jewish question' in global terms as involving a direct confrontation with the liberal democracies and Moscow's drive to 'Bolshevize the earth', not just as a narrow national issue involving the Jews of Germany,[2] for behind the foreign and internal enemies of a new National Socialist order stood the invisible forces of world Jewry, which would never give up their bastion in Germany without a fight. Antisemitism by definition would therefore have to develop an international power-base such as the Jews had secured for themselves in Soviet Russia. If it were successfully to resist the forces of disintegration sapping the marrow of 'Aryan' existence and to halt the decline of the West, National Socialist Germany would ultimately have to conquer the world.

The despotic imperialism of the Nazis was in many respects conceived as a mirror-image of the 'Jewish-Bolshevik' International. More specifically, it borrowed from the methods, techniques and terminology of the *Protocols of the Elders of Zion* – the turn of the century Tsarist secret-police forgery which claimed to disclose the international Jewish conspiracy for world-domination. In Germany the *Protocols* had made an enormous impact precisely in the years between 1919 and 1923 when Hitler embarked on his career as a political agitator.[3] He was familiar not only with their contents but also with the numerous commentaries by Alfred Rosenberg on the subject and with the American millionaire Henry Ford's *The International Jew*, which had a great influence in Germany. Hitler, who kept a photograph of Ford by his desk in those early years, looked in 1923 to his American idol as 'the leader of the growing fascist movement in America' – hopes which were soon to be disappointed.[4] But the reading of the *Protocols* had a more lasting impact. In

*Mein Kampf* Hitler had written that they disclosed the fundamental lie on which the existence of the Jewish people was based. If 'Jewish' liberal newspapers like the *Frankfurter Zeitung* proclaimed the *Protocols* to be a forgery that was the surest proof of their veracity. 'What many Jews do perhaps unconsciously is here consciously exposed. But that is what matters. It is a matter of indifference which Jewish brain produced these revelations.' What was important was the fact that 'the historical development of the last hundred years' confirmed their truth. The *Protocols* had uncovered 'the nature and activity of the Jewish people', they had exposed the forces of darkness in their inner logic and final aims.[5] In his conversations with Hermann Rauschning at the time of the Great Depression, Hitler returned to the theme. 'I have read the *Protocols of the Elders of Zion* – it simply appalled me. The stealthiness of the enemy, and his ubiquity! I saw at once that we must copy it – in our own way of course. . . . It is in truth the critical battle for the fate of the world.'[6] Hitler once again made it clear that it was 'the intrinsic truth' of the *Protocols* and not their authenticity which made them so persuasive. In other words, it was the myth not the reality which counted.

For Hitler, not only Soviet Communism but also the world capitalist system was a devilishly ingenious invention of the Jews to destabilize the Gentile world, in preparation for the future seizure of power foretold by the *Protocols*. 'The economic system of our day is the creation of the Jews. It is under their exclusive control. It is their super-state, planted by them above all the states of the world in all their glory. But now we have challenged them with the system of permanent revolution. . . .'[7] As this passage reveals, Hitler, depending on his audience, could simultaneously sound like a pseudo-Bolshevik revolutionary and a rabid right-wing reactionary, an 'Aryan' internationalist and a narrow *völkisch* nationalist. What gave unity to these seemingly incompatible postures was the Nazi belief in the world-Jewish conspiracy, a myth which permitted the resolution of all contradictions. Both capitalism and Communism no less than Christianity or liberalism were merely different historical masks for the occult power that sought to bastardize and denationalize the Gentiles. The resultant racial mishmash, the impure breeds of subhumanity whose leader was the 'eternal Jew', could only be thrown back by a concerted *international* policy. The Nazis would therefore copy their world-enemy by organizing the struggle against 'the international Jewish financiers' on a supra-national basis. The *Protocols* would serve as the primer for their own politics of conspiracy and subversion, of intrigue and mass destruction in the ruthless struggle for world-domination.[8]

The international dimension of Nazi antisemitism was to take on a sharper and more concrete dimension after the seizure of power in 1933. The war on the Jews was now escalated in practical terms from a predominantly domestic issue to a central problem of German foreign policy. In terms of Hitler's political logic, the 'Jewish question' could on no account be separated from the network of international relations in which the Third Reich was enmeshed. Friends and enemies, potential allies and rivals, were henceforth judged in terms that had previously been remote from the mainstream of German and European foreign policy. Whether foreign leaders were considered to be agents, collaborators or clients of the international Jewish conspiracy had now become a material factor in the foreign policy calculations of a leading European state. Not only was the outside world subdivided into countries which were to a greater or lesser degree subject to 'Jewish' influence, but German diplomatic initiatives frequently depended on the same criteria.[9] Indeed, Hitler's foreign policy after 1933 cannot be properly understood without regard to his determination to build a countervailing power to that of world Jewry. The creation of such a *Gegenmacht* was not only a question of building up a powerful military machine capable of conquering Europe. It involved using subversive techniques to destabilize the world-enemy and weaken him from within – the 'Jewish' methods that Hitler had learnt from the *Protocols* and from his Bolshevik adversaries.

In this political warfare antisemitism played a decisive role. Not only within Germany had it proved itself an indispensable weapon against internal enemies such as the organized Left, the liberals and the Catholic centre: in foreign policy, too, Hitler perceived the spread of antisemitism as the key to his strategy of undermining opponents, spreading German influence and acquiring a power-base abroad. In the long-term confrontation with the occult forces controlled by world Jewry, the internationalization of the 'Jewish question' as a life and death issue for the nations of the world was essential. Nazi antisemitism ultimately aimed at creating a broad-based *universal* front against Jewry and its 'stooges'. Once this was accomplished the 'Jewish peril' could be neutralized and finally liquidated by military means. Thus German power politics and the universalization of antisemitism were two sides of the same coin, essential parts of one and the same strategy of domination.

It was no accident that both components in Hitler's grand strategy began to emerge into the foreground between 1936 and 1938. Nazi Germany had by then already re-established itself as a major force in European diplomacy. A string of domestic and foreign policy successes beginning with the re-occupation of the Rhineland had dramatically strengthened Hitler's own position as a statesman of world stature. The situation now seemed ripe for taking on the hidden world-enemy and for raising the stakes as well as escalating tensions in the international sphere. A significant increase of antisemitism abroad was a *sine qua non* for the success of this policy and the achievement of greater understanding for National Socialist Germany and its policies. In his closing speech to the 1937 Nuremberg Party Congress, Hitler had already hinted at the broad outlines of his strategy. Denouncing 'Jewish Bolshevism' in Moscow as the fountainhead and source of all unrest and revolt around the globe, he presented Communism as *a world-question* because the Jews were using it as their base of operations for expansion. Behind the Communist International, the Social Democratic parties and Popular Fronts in the West, there was one common denominator – the 'Jewish racial community'. The Jews represented the advance-guard of the world-revolution not only in Moscow but in the midst of the bourgeois democracies. Their ultimate aim, as in Soviet Russia, was to proceed 'to a bloody annihilation of the former intellectual upper class' in order to pave the way for Jewish-Bolshevik dictatorship of the masses.[10] In Germany, Hungary and more recently in Spain they had temporarily succeeded. But the rise of National Socialism and its victory in 1933 had frustrated their efforts to exploit democracy in Germany, where 'the Marxist parties of the proletariat' had been their battering-ram.[11]

Since 1936 Hitler had been able to use the Spanish Civil War as a convenient symbol for intensifying this stock propaganda assault on Moscow and 'Jewish Bolshevism'. Just as he had saved Germany from Bolshevist chaos and as Mussolini before him had crushed the Reds in Italy, so now the Francoist forces in Spain were heroically combating the efforts of the 'Jewish international' to destroy European civilization.[12] The solidarity of the fascist dictators in the face of the common enemy was an important achievement in Hitler's eyes, for it represented a closing of ranks against the forces of decomposition and racial decay. The linking of the war in Spain with the machinations of 'Jewish Bolshevik' plotters in Moscow had been elaborated on in a similarly apocalyptic vein by Goebbels at the Nuremberg Party Congress in September 1936. 'It is a matter for all statesmen of all nations who must deal with this question unless they want to accept the responsibility for plunging Europe by their own fault into the deepest crisis and destruction. Yes, the problem of Bolshevism is the problem of Europe's very survival. Here is the parting of the ways, here one must take sides for or against . . . Jewry knows the significance of the hour. In a last convulsion it seeks to mobilize all forces against Germany. It has established itself comfortably and, as it thought safely in Russia. . . . The *arriviste* Jews who now have the chance to enlarge their once petty swindles to grandiose dimensions on the backs of a people of one hundred and sixty millions are the most bloodthirsty tyrants; they have no ideals but merely make the nations suffer, a true scourge of God.'[13]

The Nazi leadership repeatedly announced that its intervention in Spain was preventing the emergence of a second 'Jewish-Bolshevik' base in Europe. This conviction found a certain echo in fascist Italy, where Mussolini's troops were becoming bogged down on Franco's side in the Spanish Civil War and the Duce discovered a convenient scapegoat in world Jewry.[14] Indeed, all over Europe fascists and right-wing conservatives from the mid-1930s began to imitate Nazi antisemitism in their own way, encouraging Hitler in his long-held belief that singling out Jews for attack could only favour German policy objectives. For example, in the Danubian basin, especially in Rumania, Hungary and the Slovak regions, radical antisemitism was making steady headway along with a pro-German political orientation. In December 1937 Rumania already had a government with an antisemitic programme; in Hungary during the following year the first anti-Jewish legislation was passed. The creation of the satellite Slovak state in 1939 led to racial laws on the German pattern.[15] As in Poland, there was a long tradition of indigenous antisemitism in each of these East European states, as well as a clear trend to authoritarian dictatorship between the wars. Nationalism in countries like Rumania, for example, was virtually synonymous with antisemitism. The Nazi slogans equating Jewry with Communism, capitalism and plutocracy fell here on fertile soil.[16] In Hungary, too, there was considerable admiration for the social achievements of the Nazi regime as well as sympathy for the German policy of despoiling the Jews.[17] But with or without German support, Nazi-type movements were sprouting and flourishing all over Eastern Europe throughout the 1930s. In the matter of antisemitism, Hungarians, Poles, Rumanians and Slovaks believed that they needed no lessons from the Nazis.[18] On the other hand, before 1939 none of the governments had yet adopted such drastic measures as were employed in the Reich; it was at least partly under German pressure that they began during the war to escalate their anti-Jewish policies in a racist direction.

Though their virulent nationalism did lead Central and East European fascist movements like the Rumanian Iron Guard and the Hungarian Arrow Cross to carry out horrifying massacres of Jews, the cold-blooded bureaucratic efficiency and totality of the 'Final Solution' was nonetheless a German, not an East European, phenomenon. Authoritarian conservative rulers like Admiral Horthy in Hungary and Marshal Antonescu in Rumania were, in spite of their harsh antisemitic measures, frankly reluctant to co-operate with the Nazis in implementing mass murders, especially as the tide of war turned against Germany.

In the case of Hungary, political opportunism was clearly a decisive factor. The hopes of overthrowing the Versailles peace settlement and recovering lost provinces had been a primary factor in co-operating with Hitler. In addition, Germany was an economically indispensable partner and the chief supplier of arms to the Hungarians. Nevertheless Hungarian opinion was not unanimous about the advisability of linking its fate to Nazi Germany. The Hungarian fascists and antisemites who sought an open alliance with the Reich wanted to please Hitler, above all by internal measures against the Jews; but those who opposed this course feared Hungary's reduction to satellite status and her being compromised in the eyes of the West.[19] In practice, however, all Hungarian governments, whatever their inclinations, had to pay for German economic, political and military assistance in the currency of anti-Jewish legislation. Moreover, they faced constant internal pressure from the violently antisemitic fascist parties whose slogans and ideologies, while rooted in the Hungarian counter-revolution of 1919, borrowed freely from both Hitler and Mussolini.

By the beginning of 1939 the Nazi-type Arrow Cross movement had a quarter of a million members and had gained 25 per cent of all votes in the first elections by secret ballot in Hungary.[20] However, their influence was partly neutralized by the more 'moderate' antisemitic measures of the government, and the local Nazis were not put in power until the last months of the German occupation. Indeed, until the Nazi invasion of Hungary in March 1944, the Jews were paradoxically less molested there than almost anywhere else in Axis-controlled Europe. This was a constant sore point with Hitler who, according to Horthy, as late as 18 March 1944 had bitterly complained that 'Hungary did nothing in the matter of the Jewish problem, and was not prepared to settle accounts with the large number of Jews in Hungary'.[21]

The case of Rumania, along with Tsarist Russia one of the two most antisemitic countries in Europe before 1914, is no less paradoxical. Unlike Hungary, it had emerged as an enlarged state after the collapse of Austria-Hungary, with nearly a third of its population belonging to ethnic or religious minorities. A long-standing nationalistic and economic antisemitism was exacerbated by the post-war national minority tensions and the identification of Jews with Communism, following the revolutions in neighbouring Russia and Hungary between 1917 and 1919. Though the Iron Guard fascist movement did not initially have many ideological or financial contacts with Rome or Berlin, the Spanish Civil War inspired it with the belief that it was engaged in a mortal combat with the forces of 'Judeo-Communism'.[22] After the *Anschluss* and especially after the Munich agreements in September 1938, the Guard began to enjoy open German support. Its credo, which included fanatical antisemitism, destruction of the Bolsheviks and ruthless elimination of all opponents, was drawing closer to the Nazi model. But the Guard's ally,

Marshal Antonescu, who established his power at the end of 1940 with German support, did not in fact adopt the racist antisemitism of the Guardists. His war on the Soviet Union as Hitler's ally was not so much a crusade against the 'Jewish-Bolshevik' conspiracy as an attempt to liberate lost Rumanian territories. Though Hitler, a great admirer of the Rumanian dictator, could remark to Goebbels in August 1941 that 'a man like Antonescu proceeds in these matters [i.e. anti-Jewish legislation] in a far more radical fashion than we have done up to the present', he was in fact mistaken.[23] Rumanian Jews were persecuted and during the liberation of Bessarabia and Transnistria even massacred as accomplices of Communism, but they still fared better than Jews in most countries of Nazi-occupied Europe. Antonescu successfully resisted subsequent Nazi pressures to exterminate Rumanian Jewry, not only for reasons of political opportunism but also because it did not fit his conception of solving the 'Jewish question'.[24] Significantly, too, Antonescu supported projects of Jewish emigration to Palestine and other places in 1942, in order to prevent the Nazi 'Final Solution'.[25] Rumania became one of the few outlets for such emigration during the war. Though this policy was doubtless inspired by the popular pre-war antisemitic slogan 'Yids to Palestine', its results were incomparably better than the alternative of deporting Jews to Auschwitz. As a result, nearly half of Rumania's 850,000 Jews survived the Holocaust and many of them found their way to Israel.

Like the pre-war Rumanian government, Poland had made it clear enough in official proclamations during the 1930s that it wished to get rid of as many of its Jews as possible. It was no accident, for example, that the Polish authorities were enthusiastic advocates of such fantastic solutions to their Jewish problem as the Madagascar plan or, more feasibly, a Jewish state in Palestine. The Polish incentive for supporting massive emigration was only too evident. No other country in Europe had a Jewish minority comparable to the three million Jews who constituted 10 per cent of the inter-war population of Poland – one third of whom belonged in any case to national minorities. Moreover, after 1930 Poland came under the control of increasingly authoritarian regimes who in conditions of economic crisis were more than willing to look for scapegoats. The rise of Hitler gave a great impetus to the growth of fascist antisemitic trends in Poland, which further intensified after Marshal Pilsudski's death in 1935. For example, the ONR-Falanga movement, extremely nationalistic, Catholic and antisemitic as well as being hostile to the minorities in general, openly looked to fascist and even Nazi models, though its impact was mainly restricted to the universities and high schools. German–Polish antagonisms made it difficult, however, for such groups to develop direct links with the Nazis, and the 'collaboration' even of the most extreme Polish fascists with the

German occupiers after the invasion of September 1939 was never a real option.[26]

But if the vehement anti-German nationalism of the Polish Right and the racialist attitudes of the Nazis towards the Poles as a whole excluded practical co-operation, there were remarkable parallels in their respective attitudes to the 'Jewish question'. Since the turn of the century the Polish National Democratic Party (Endecja) had placed antisemitism at the centre of its nationalist world-view. After the proclamation of Polish independence in 1918, the influence and political muscle of the Endecja steadily grew and forced even the comparatively enlightened Marshal Pilsudski to accommodate some of its demands by restricting Jewish rights. Polish Jews gradually found themselves excluded from certain occupations, objects of perpetual harassment, boycotts and pogroms. The *numerus clausus* in the universities blocked access for Jews to many careers. By the late 1930s openly fascist terror and physical assaults on Jewish students were commonplace at institutions of higher learning. Professional associations of physicians, architects and engineers barred Jews on the basis of 'Aryan' paragraphs formulated on the German Nazi pattern.[27] Increasingly, Polish antisemitism appeared indistinguishable from the practices of the Third Reich, at least until the Crystal Night pogrom. Like the National Socialists, the Endecja openly aimed at ensuring the racial purity of the Polish state by driving the Jews out of economic life and forcing them to emigrate *en masse*. Like the Nazis, they had a pathological fear of Jewish economic and cultural influence which could only be contained by a radical policy of racial separation or expulsion. Moreover, unlike their German counterparts before 1938, the Endeks had actually taken part in the bloody pogroms which had swept Poland between 1918 and 1920, and then again during the mid-1930s.

Furthermore, the Polish government itself in the late 1930s embarked on policies which were scarcely different from those of the Endecja or the German Nazis, even as it hypocritically condemned such methods as being contrary to Polish Catholic traditions. The policy followed by the ruling party, the Camp of National Unity (OZN), as set out in its 'Thesis on the Jewish Question' in 1937, makes this plain enough: 'The Communist party of Jewry is the open enemy of our Nation and State: the conservative portion is, through its cultural and ethical differences, a heavy burden upon our national and state life. It is a foreign body, dispersed in our organism so that it produces a pathological deformation. In this state of affairs, it is impossible to find a way out other than the removal of this alien body, harmful through both its numbers and its uniqueness.'[28] Significantly, apart from the Polish Socialist Party (PPS) all Polish political parties as well as the Catholic Church similarly regarded Jews as a harmful, alien group whose influence had to be eradicated from commerce, industry, the professions and cultural life. These depressing realities and the massive *de facto* discrimination in employment were ultimately more significant than the fact that the Polish parliament had not formally enacted anti-Jewish laws similar to those in the Third Reich, Horthy's Hungary, Rumania or Vichy France.[29] Hence, it was probably no accident that the Nazis chose Poland rather than any other country as the site for their death camps, knowing only too well how to exploit the indigenous antisemitic traditions of the area.

Some observers, including one of the leaders of the Jewish underground in occupied Poland, Mordekhai Tennenbaum, even believed that without the active and passive aid of Poles, 'the Germans would never have dared to do what they did'. It was the Poles 'who called out "Yid" at every Jew who escaped from the train transporting him to his death, it was they who caught the unfortunate wretches, who rejoiced at every Jewish misfortune – they were vile and contemptible.'[30] Indeed, it was not uncommon for Poles under the occupation to express the view that Hitler, whatever his crimes against Poland, had at least 'liberated' the country from the Jews. Though there were also examples of warm-hearted sympathy for persecuted Jews, of idealists who risked their lives to save Jews from destruction, the German invasion in the long run undoubtedly exacerbated the virulence of Polish antisemitism.[31] The younger generation of the Endecja openly approved of Hitler's programme for eliminating Poland's Jews. The ONR regarded hiding Jews as an anti-national act detrimental to Polish interests.[32]

The middle-class population as a whole, according to Emmanuel Ringelblum's eyewitness account, 'rejoices at the Nazi solution to the Jewish problem in Poland. Thanks to Hitler, the Polish middle class, in debt to Jewish bankers, tradesmen etc., immediately got rid of its unwanted creditors. Thanks to the mass slaughter of the Jews, the programme of *numerus nullus* in industry, handicrafts, trade and economic life in general has been carried out to the full. Thanks to the liquidation of the Jews, the Christian "men of straw" [*Strohmänner*] suddenly became the owners of numerous industrial and commercial enterprises, and partners freed themselves of their Jewish co-partners. Thanks to the liquidation of Polish Jews, Aryan depositaries became the owners of belongings and goods left with them by the Jews. Thanks to all this, tens and hundreds of thousands of Aryans were able to obtain objects of everyday use dirt cheap: clothing, machines, tools, etc. Thanks to all this, the Polish middle class was able to obtain market stalls without a struggle and take over petty trading after the Jews were gone. Thanks to Treblinka, Jewish fortunes worth millions, which had been amassed over the centuries, passed into Aryan hands.'[33]

The material aspects of the situation in Poland were a microcosm of the greedy despoliation and robbery which motivated much of the antisemitism throughout Nazi-occupied Europe. Yet it is doubtful if anywhere, except perhaps for the Baltic States and the Soviet Ukraine, the mass murder of the Jewish population was seen to the same degree as a gain for the local population.[34] The Polish Socialists, the one group who had consistently opposed pre-war antisemitism in their country, understood perfectly that the local population was being corrupted by the 'Aryanization' process (the clearing-out of Jews) and that local resistance to the invaders was thereby substantially weakened. Antisemitism was the wedge successfully driven by Hitler's system between Poles and Jews. The Polish nationalists fell only too eagerly into the trap, readily combining their traditional hatred of Germans with enthusiasm for Hitler's ghettoization policy and then his liquidation of Jews. As *Barykada Wolnosci* (a PPS organ) noted on 15 February 1942: 'According to the notions of a Polish nationalist, Hitler is a two-faced deity; when he shows his anti-Polish visage the nationalist shakes his fist at him, but when he revolves to show his anti-Jewish countenance he bows down and worships him.'[35] Such common attitudes played into the hands of the German conquerors as they had in other occupied European states, including Austria, Czechoslovakia and France. Ringelblum summed up Hitler's war strategy *vis-à-vis* Poland in words that perhaps explain why that country had been selected as the first victim of his genocidal war. 'He therefore made the greatest efforts to conquer it from within before conquering it by military means. These efforts, supported by local elements to a large extent, bore fruit during the war. Fragmented socially, torn by nationalist hatred, demoralized by the campaign against ritual slaughter, the programme for market stalls, boycotts and similar antisemitic farces, Poland was easy prey for Hitler. In 1939 the downfall of Poland was brought about not only by an external enemy force but also by an inner enemy that had shattered the unity of the State, its defence system and inner cohesion. This enemy was Polish Fascism allied to antisemitism.'[36]

Hitler understood only too well the destabilizing global effects of his racist antisemitic ideology, especially in neighbouring Central and Eastern European countries like Poland and Czechoslovakia. He had always seen it as a force capable of harnessing widely different circles to the chariot of German policy. The spectre of International Jewry and the 'Jewish Bolshevik' bogey were guaranteed to attain a broad public resonance throughout the Continent, but nowhere more so than in Eastern Europe.[37] Hence in their foreign propaganda and in diplomatic negotiations with Polish, Czech, Slovak, Hungarian, Rumanian and in 1939 perhaps even with Russian statesmen, the

Nazis constantly stressed the centrality of the 'Jewish question' and the need to uproot the Jews from Europe once and for all. At the same time Hitler could use the antisemitism of his ideological allies on the Right – the local fascist movements in Eastern Europe – as a weapon not only against the Western democracies and Bolshevik Russia but also against insufficiently pro-German regimes in the neighbouring countries. Still more ominously, the rampant antisemitism of the East European states could only reinforce Hitler's conviction that there would be no significant obstacles to the German implementation of a 'Final Solution' in the eastern territories.

In a Foreign Office circular reviewing 'The Jewish Question as a Factor in Foreign Policy in 1938', which was addressed to all German Diplomatic Missions and Consulates abroad, the satisfaction of the Nazis at the rapid spread of antisemitism throughout Europe and more remote parts of the globe was made evident. 'In North America, South America, France, Holland, Scandinavia and Greece – wherever the Jewish migratory current flows – a marked growth of antisemitism is already noticeable. It must be a task of German foreign policy to encourage this antisemitic wave. This will be accomplished less by German propaganda abroad than by the propaganda the Jews are forced to spread in their own defense.' The circular then proceeded to give various examples, including the press and official reports in North America, stressing that the audience of the antisemitic Catholic 'radio priest' Father Coughlin had jumped to over 20 million.[38] It cited the growing reaction against Jewish immigration in France, Holland and even Norway, where the German Legation reported that the local press had finally 'become aware of what it means when the children of Israel suddenly invade a country like locusts'.[39] The examples could have been multiplied many times over, and for the German Foreign Office they confirmed that other countries were now beginning to understand what the 'Jewish threat signifies for their own existence'.[40]

The Foreign Office circular pointed out that 'it is probably no coincidence that 1938, the year of destiny, has not only brought the realization of the concept of a Greater Germany, but at the same time has also brought the Jewish question closer to solution. For the Jewish policy was both cause and consequence of the events of 1938'.[41] The precondition for consolidating the Greater German Reich 'against the will of the whole world' had been the curing of the body politic from paralysing and corrupting Jewish influences – a threat more dangerous 'than the opposition of our former World War enemies'.[42] The Jews had, in fact, so the circular argued, 'underestimated the consistency and strength of the National Socialist idea'. It was no coincidence, therefore, that the Versailles system which was intended 'to keep Germany down' had collapsed in 1938 at the same time as 'the dominant Jewish positions in Vienna and Prague'. World Jewry, along with its American allies, naturally regarded the Munich agreements as signifying 'the collapse of the democratic front in Europe' and therefore as its own defeat. Parliamentary democracy had always 'helped the Jew to obtain wealth and political power at the expense of the host peoples'. But the year 1938 had brought about the crumbling of this Jewish-democratic system and 'probably for the first time in modern history Jewry now has to retreat from a secured position'.[43] The Foreign Office memorandum further noted that in 1938 anti-Jewish *legislation* was everywhere on the rise among Germany's neighbours. 'Italy took her place at Germany's side in the struggle against Jewry. In Bucharest Professor Goga, an expert on the Jewish question, took over the government with a programme directed against Jewry – without, however, being able to prevail against the overwhelming international pressure from Paris and London. In Hungary and Poland the Jews were subject to special laws. Now the German political success at Munich, like an earthquake with its distant tremors, is beginning everywhere, even in remote countries, to shatter the position which the Jews have consolidated for centuries.'[44] The Foreign Office observed that as a result of German foreign policy, 'the Jewish question will expand into a problem of international politics when great masses of Jews from Germany, Poland, Hungary and Rumania are put on the move by the growing pressure of their host peoples'.[45]

The self-proclaimed goal of German foreign policy was now 'the emigration of all Jews living on German territory' and through this means, the export of antisemitism so that all peoples would come to recognize 'the danger which the Jews represent for the racial preservation of the nations'. Schumburg's Foreign Office memorandum set out the cold-blooded calculation behind Nazi emigration policy: 'The poorer the immigrant Jew and thus the greater the burden he is to his country of immigration, the more strongly will the host country react and the more desirable will be the effect in the interest of German propaganda.' Moreover, in contrast to those who still advocated a Jewish state in Palestine as a solution to the 'Jewish question', the Foreign Office now formally stated that Nazi Germany 'has a major interest in seeing that the Jews continue to be dispersed'.[46] The dispersal and influx of destitute Jews, stripped of their property and assets, could only arouse the resistance of the native population in lands of emigration across the globe and thereby provide the best justification for Germany's Jewish policy. Indeed, the more anti-semitic the Gentile world became as a whole, the greater the understanding there would be for National Socialist Germany and its foreign policies. Ominously, however, as the circular pointed out, emigration and the export of

Judeophobic sentiments were not considered the last stage. 'The Jewish question will not be settled for Germany, either, when the last Jew had left German soil.' The Schumburg circular did not specify what might constitute a final settlement, merely hinting vaguely at 'an international solution of the Jewish question in the future'.

The Nazi leaders when they spoke of such 'solutions' did not of course mean that they were interested in co-operatiiong with international organizations like the League of Nations' High Commission for Refugees. Nor did they respond to the various protests lodged by other governments against the expulsion of Jews from Germany and the aggravation of the refugee problem at a time when migration restrictions were reaching their peak.[47] The Great Depression had already encouraged restrictionism in admission policies even in traditional lands of immigration like the United States, Canada, Latin America, Australia and New Zealand. Nor did Alien laws, economic nationalism and fear of exacerbating antisemitic reactions facilitate the absorption of Jews in the liberal democracies of Northern and Western Europe. The Nazis, however, were not overly worried by the practical difficulties that their own brutal policies might be causing. On the contrary, the more chaos they could sow in the outside world by expelling impoverished Jews the better for German interests; the restrictive backlash of the Western democracies – the failure of the Evian Conference and the British White Paper on Palestine – merely gave them further arguments with which to justify their cruelty and to expose the 'hypocrisy' of their critics.

Hitler's notorious Reichstag speech of 30 January 1939, which *inter alia* mocked the democracies for refusing to accept German Jewish refugees, 'with every imaginable excuse', was a case in point. It was a 'shameful spectacle', Hitler declared, 'to see how the whole democratic world is oozing sympathy for the poor tormented Jewish people, but remains hard-hearted and obdurate when it comes to helping them – which is surely, in view of its attitude, an obvious duty'.[48] The arguments put forward by the democracies 'as an excuse for not helping them actually speak for us Germans', he added. According to the Führer, the democratic empires had only a handful of inhabitants per square metre, while far more densely populated Germany, which had 135 inhabitants to the square metre, was expected to have room for Jews. In fact, the Reich was not acting in an inhumane manner but 'merely paying this people for what it deserves' – revenging itself on the Jews for having robbed, corrupted and paralysed the Germans after the First World War. It could not tolerate the presence of a foreign people 'which was capable of snatching for itself all the leading positions in the land' and within German culture – which were now once again open to the sons of peasants, workers and intellectuals.

Moreover, it was 'Jewish' warmongers and agitators who had for decades continuously stirred up hatred for Germany, which had desired nothing but peace with Britain, the United States and France. The rest of the world might cry crocodile tears and denounce 'this barbaric expulsion from Germany of such an irreplaceable and culturally eminently valuable element'. Yet, with heavy irony, Hitler remarked that they did not welcome 'these precious apostles of culture', though they had not a single reason (according to their own declarations) for refusing to receive 'this most valuable race in their own countries'.[49] The world had 'sufficient space for settlements' to accommodate Jews ready for productive work. But Hitler warned that 'the Jewish race will have to adapt itself to sound constructive activity as other nations do, or sooner or later it will succumb to a crisis of an inconceivable magnitude.[50]

Hitler's Reichstag speech contained a sarcastic juxtaposition of the Western refusal to liberalize immigration policies with a grim prophecy of the imminent 'annihilation of the Jewish race in Europe' in the event of war. It suggests that emigration and extermination were really parts of one and the same continuum in his mind by the end of the 1930s. 'Emigration' was, indeed, essentially a prelude to physical destruction. They were not alternative solutions but different stages within a single solution. For years the goal of *Vernichtung* (destruction) of the Jews had been present in Nazi propaganda and had represented its *ultima ratio*. But until the end of 1938 it had been 'subdued by the *reality* principle of economics and politics'.[51] Now, as Hitler explained it to an enthusiastic Reichstag audience on 30 January 1939, the time of reckoning had come. 'National Socialist Germany and Fascist Italy have institutions which enable them when necessary to enlighten the world about the nature of a question of which many nations are instinctively conscious but which they have not yet clearly thought out. At the moment the Jews in certain countries may be fomenting hatred under the protection of the Press, the films, wireless propaganda, the theatre, literature etc., all of which they control. If this nation should once more succeed in inciting the millions which compose the nations into a conflict which is utterly senseless, then there will be revealed the effectiveness of an enlightenment which has completely routed the Jews in Germany in the space of a few years. The nations are no longer willing to die on the battlefield so that this unstable international race may profiteer from a war or satisfy its Old Testament vengeance. The Jewish watchword, "Workers of the world unite", will be conquered by a higher realization, namely, "Workers of all classes and of all nations, recognize your common enemy".'[52]

As Hitler's own preparations for further military expansion ripened, his trusted propaganda line that the Jews always tried 'to bring nations into a state of unrest', and 'to plunge them into reciprocal wars' was intensified.[53] So, too, was the claim that 'the Jewish question was today no longer a German problem' – it had become 'a world problem' as Hitler bombastically announced in a Munich speech to the *Alte Kämpfer* on 24 February 1939.[54] If European harmony was ever to be achieved, the Gentile nations would have to unite and solve the 'Jewish question'. In Wilhelmshaven on 1 April 1939, Hitler became even more explicit. 'Only when this Jewish bacillus infecting the life of people has been removed can one hope to establish a co-operation among the nations which shall be built on a lasting understanding.'[55] Two months earlier, Alfred Rosenberg in an address to foreign diplomats had stated that 'the solution of this question is a necessity for all nations'.[56] The multiplication of such declarations in the months immediately preceding the outbreak of the Second World War simply underlined the indissoluble nexus that now existed for the Nazi leadership between their global political objectives and the elimination of European Jewry. What had previously been an abstract final goal was coming closer to concrete realization as an operational plan.

The Nazis were, of course, well aware that since 1933 their emigration policy had been complicated by the fact that large numbers of Jews in Poland, Hungary and Rumania as well as Germany, Austria and Czechoslovakia were intent on getting out and that their governments were giving them every encouragement.[57] This growing pressure from Eastern Europe clashed with Germany's own interest in an accelerated emigration, especially as the doors of most Western countries remained firmly closed. Even Palestine after the mid-1930s was increasingly subject to restrictions as a result of British submission to Arab pressures, and no longer appeared to offer a rapid solution to the Nazi aim of a *judenrein* Germany. In Palestine, moreover, Polish Jews were competing with their German brethren for the limited quota of immigration certificates. As a result, the Nazis began in 1939 to contemplate the option of some remote and isolated territory where the Jews might be confined. On 5 January 1939, Hitler mentioned to Colonel Beck, the Polish Foreign Minister, the possibility of an African territory for German and Polish Jews.[58] Rosenberg on 7 Februrary 1939 had evoked the idea of a reserve in which the Jews of Europe might be concentrated, in a speech before the foreign press in Berlin. 'What territories', he rhetorically asked, 'are the democracies willing to provide for the purpose of settling some fifteen million Jews?' The Jewish multi-millionaires would have to provide the means and the colony should be 'placed under administrators trained in police work'. 'There is no question', Rosenberg added, 'of establishing a Jewish State, but only of a Jewish reserve.'[59] It was not all that clear *where* this penal colony under police supervision would be – though both Madagascar and British Guiana had been evoked over the past year in diplomatic encounters with foreign officials.

It was, however, increasingly obvious to Hitler that the German policy of trying to expel unwanted Jews across the border into neighbouring European states, which had begun in October 1938, offered no solution. The Czech Foreigh Minister, Chvalkovsky, had told him at a reception on 21 January 1939 that he was 'wondering where and across what frontiers he was to send the Jews. He could not dump them on the German territories, nor on the Polish or Hungarian frontier . . . they had been driven back by the military. . . .'[60] The British, who had promised to let some of these Czech Jews emigrate to Australia and New Zealand, had done nothing to remove them. Hitler's reply 'pointed to the possibility that interested states might take some spot in the world, put the Jews there, and then say to the Anglo-Saxon states oozing with humanity: "Here they are: either they starve to death or you put your many speeches into practice".'[61] But what concerned Hitler over and above a further opportunity to condemn Anglo-American two-facedness was to use the 'Jewish question' as a means of pressuring Czechoslovakia and moving it into the National Socialist rather than the Western democratic camp. He warned Chvalkovsky that 'the Jews in Czechoslovakia were still poisoning the nation' and that it was impossible to give a German guarantee for the frontiers of a state which did not eliminate the Jews. According to the French ambassador in Prague, who spoke with Chvalkovsky after his return from Berlin, both Hitler and von Ribbentrop had told the Czech Foreign Minister: 'Our kindness was nothing but weakness, and we regret it. This vermin must be destroyed. The Jews are our sworn enemies, and at the end of this year there will not be a Jew left in Germany. Neither the French, nor the Americans, nor the English are responsible for the difficulties in our relations with Paris, London, or Washington. Those responsible are the Jews. We will give similar advice to Rumania, Hungary, etc. . . .'[62] According to Chvalkovsky's account, Hitler and his Foreign Minister had added that Germany would seek 'to form a bloc of anti-Semitic States, as she would not be able to treat as friends the States in which the Jews, either through their economic activity or through their high positions, could exercise any kind of influence'.[63]

There is no doubt that from the end of 1938 Hitler and other German policy-makers had indeed come to see the 'Jewish question' as an area of possible entente with East European states and as a major instrument of foreign policy in general. Hitler had already told Oswald Pirow on 24 November 1938 that antisemitism was the one idea which the National Socialists exported.[64] On the level of propaganda, Hitler clearly believed in its efficacy. Moreover, as he told the Hungarian Foreign Minister, Count Csaky, on 16 January 1939, the 'Jewish question' was not just an affair that concerned

Germany. The Third Reich would readily help every nation which committed itself to the struggle against Jewry. But these ideological convictions, however sincerely held, did not necessarily translate into political action or diplomatic alliances with East European states. With regard to Poland and Czecho-slovakia, they were primarily intended to sap internal resistance to German designs. In the case of Nazi policy towards the Czech state, antisemitism, like the manipulation of national self-determination for the Sudeten Germans, was clearly a useful weapon to remove the last bastion of democracy in Central Europe and tie it more closely to the Third Reich. Even with future allies like Hungary and Rumania, the interests of Nazi Germany did not necessarily converge when it came to Jewish emigration. The more the Germans stirred up antisemitism, the more these countries were encouraged to expel their Jews, which in turn increased pressure on potential lands of emigration and made it difficult to accomplish the Nazi objective of a Germany that was *judenrein.*[65] In that sense the German policy of exporting antisemitism had actually become self-defeating. Furthermore, what could an 'international' solution mean as long as the west was unwilling to accept masses of destitute Jews and no territory was available which could absorb them? One must remember that Nazi policy since 1937 had ruled out a Jewish state in Palestine – which would have been acceptable to the Poles, Rumanians and Hungarians – as contrary to German interests. Even had this not been the case, both the British mandatory authorities and the Palestinian Arabs would have resolutely resisted any radical Zionist solution to the European Jewish problem.

Thus, on the eve of the Second World War, Hitler's policy appeared to have led to an impasse. Antisemitism, it is true, had proved its efficacy as a catalytic agent in German strategy at home and abroad. An international refugee problem had indeed been created and the Western democracies had been proved incapable of dealing with it. Furthermore, those foreign governments in Europe which were becoming increasingly anti-Jewish tended to drift into the German orbit of influence. A further plus was that the Reich had outwardly never appeared to be as self-confident and secure as it did in 1939, though beneath the surface the domestic situation was far less stable. The intensification of Hitler's antisemitic policy at home, moreover, had driven German Jews to the edge of ruin. Excluded from the German economy, deprived of civil rights, reduced to the status of social pariahs, they scarcely posed any threat to the 'purity' and cohesion of the Reich. Their fate now lay in the hands of the German police and security services. Yet Hitler and the Nazi leadership remained manifestly dissatisfied, in spite of the flood of anti-Jewish legislation which had engulfed Germany (and then Austria) since their rise to power. The hoped-for mass exodus of German Jewry had not yet taken place, in spite of Nazi persecution and harassment. The *Anschluss* and then the occupation of Bohemia and Moravia had simply increased the number of Jews under German control. The conquest of Poland in the autumn of 1939 by the Wehrmacht would magnify this problem to an unprecedented degree, adding a further 3.2 million East European Jews to the Reich. Further military victories and the extension of German *Lebensraum* could only aggravate the self-created dilemma, as more and more Jews would find themselves under the Nazi boot. Where, then, was the solution to this vicious circle?

The first answer proposed was the evacuation *en masse* of European Jews to the East African tropical island of Madagascar where they would be cut off from all contact with the rest of the world. Following the defeat of France in June 1940, Franz Rademacher, an official responsible for Jewish Affairs at the Foreign Office, drew up the Madagascar Plan in the framework of an anticipated peace treaty with France.[66] The project envisaged the mass deportation of 4 million Jews from Europe and their resettlement on the French island, which it was anticipated would be transferred to Germany as a mandate. The funds would naturally be provided by the despoiled Jews. They would nominally enjoy self-government 'in the fields of culture, economics, administration, and justice' but would be 'placed under the administration of a German policy governor, who will be under the control of the *Reichsführer SS*'. The deported Jews who lived there would not enjoy German citizenship or that of any other European country. They would be citizens of the Madagascar mandate. 'This arrangement will prevent the possible establishment of a Vatican State of their own in Palestine by the Jews, thus preventing them from using for their own purposes the symbolic value which Jerusalem has for the Christian and Mohammedan portions of the world.' More ominously, Rademacher added, 'the Jews will remain in German hands as a pledge for the future good conduct of the members of their race in America'.[67] The Rademacher plan had the approval of Foreign Minister von Ribbentrop and Reinhard Heydrich, head of the security services; it appears to have enjoyed serious consideration among the SS bureaucrats during the summer and autumn of 1940.[68] There is also some evidence that Hitler took it into account at this time.[69] On 18 June 1940 he told Mussolini in Munich that, in the context of a new African colonial order, a Jewish 'state' might be set up in Madagascar. But the idea of a Jewish reservation in Madagascar under SS rule, while its insular, remote character would have provided the secrecy necessary for eventually implementing a 'Final Solution', was obviously impractical as long as Great Britain controlled the sea-lanes and had not abandoned the struggle against Nazi Germany. The plan only made sense, after all, in the context of a German colonial Reich in Africa, established *in co-operation* with England after a peace treaty. By the winter of 1940, with this hope disappointed and as the Führer began drawing up his instructions for the invasion of Soviet Russia, thoughts of a 'final solution' in the eastern territories had already taken precedence over SS and Foreign Office fantasies of quarantining European Jewry in an African reservation.[70] On 10 February 1942, the Foreign Office Departments finally received a new ruling from Rademacher which officially confirmed what had in fact long since been Hitler's conclusion. 'The war with the Soviet Union has in the meantime created the possibility of disposing of other territories for the Final Solution. In consequence, the Führer has decided the Jews should be evacuated not to Madagascar, but to the East. Madagascar need no longer therefore be considered in connection with the Final Solution.'[71]

# CHAPTER SIX

# Hitler and the 'Final Solution'

Since the early 1920s, Hitler had always envisaged a war in the East against the Soviet Union as indispensable to his long-term objectives of establishing living space for a Greater German Empire; such a project involved decimating the Slavic masses, destroying Bolshevism and wiping out its biological roots in East European Jewry. Yet on 23 August 1939 Nazi Foreign Minister von Ribbentrop signed a pact with Stalin in Moscow which outwardly appeared to contradict one of the cardinal pillars of Nazi doctrine. Five days later at a meeting with top party officials Hitler tried to alleviate the consternation by presenting the alliance as a 'pact with Satan so as to drive out the devil'.[1] It was clear to him that the imminent invasion of Poland demanded the securing of Germany's eastern flank, given the possibility of an Anglo-French intervention in the west. If the partition of Poland and the drawing up of spheres of influence in the Baltic States (Lithuania was assigned to Germany, the rest to Russia) was undoubtedly the immediate goal, the partnership between Hitler and Stalin nonetheless had some potentially far-reaching implications. For a pact with the citadel of world-Bolshevism could mean both that Hitler was ready to abandon his racial principles and that he no longer regarded the Jews as being in control of the Soviet Union.

Over the years there had in fact been occasional indications that Hitler doubted the 'Jewishness' of the Soviet regime, especially after the defeat of Trotsky and the Left opposition in 1927. In his *Secret Book*, written in the following year, he had predicted that Pan-Slav anarchism might eventually sweep away the Jewish ruling elite in Moscow.[2] In 1931 in his conversations with the conservative newspaper editor, Richard Breiting, Hitler had suggested not only that Stalin might have already broken Jewish domination in Russia but that 'at bottom the Jews are averse to Communism for racial and financial reasons'.[3] Several years earlier, the young Goebbels, then on the left wing of the NSDAP, had argued, in similar vein, that it was 'improbable that the capitalist Jew is identical with the Bolshevist Jew'.[4] Goebbels argued that the Soviet system was essentially national rather than based on Marxist internationalism and that Russian Pan-Slavism was the driving force of

Bolshevism. Hitler, who was generally closer to Alfred Rosenberg's dogma of 'Soviet Judea' than to Goebbels' earlier scepticism on this key issue, nonetheless kept something of an open mind. In conversations with Hermann Rauschning, shortly after taking power, he suggested that it was not Germany that would turn Bolshevist 'but Bolshevism that will become a sort of National Socialism' – one of his more prophetic utterances.[5] There was 'more that binds us to Bolshevism than separates us from it', Hitler remarked, pointing bizarrely to the genuine revolutionary feeling alive everywhere in Russia 'except where there are Jewish Marxists'.[6] Former Communists, he added, made better National Socialists than petit-bourgeois Social Democrats and trade-union bosses. By the end of 1933, having broken the German Communists, it would appear that Hitler no longer feared Marxism. Furthermore, he saw no reason why he should not make a pact with Russia if it would improve his international position. Such an alliance would perhaps be unavoidable – in any case he would keep it up his sleeve as a trump card.

On the other hand, Hitler also understood that a Nazi–Soviet pact (perhaps the 'decisive gamble of my life') could not last if Germany wished to become a great world-conquering power.[7] 'Only *one* can rule', he told Rauschning. 'If *we* want to rule we must conquer Russia.' This would be the decisive battle that cannot be escaped, for Russia was not only 'Bolshevik' but 'also the greatest continental empire in the world, enormously powerful and capable of drawing the whole of Europe into its embrace'.[8] The danger to Germany in even a temporary alliance with this giant partner was that it would be absorbed and lose its national identity. Germany's rise to becoming a world-power would be impossible as long as it lay under the shadow of the Eastern Slav Empire. The task of National Socialism, once German aims in the West had been achieved, would be 'to shatter for all time the menacing hordes of the Pan-Slav Empire'.[9] There was an eternal abyss which no mutual political interests could bridge between 'German race ideals' and 'Pan-Slav mass ideals'; the fight for victory of Germanic racial consciousness meant the right to dominate the Slavic masses in the East 'eternally fated to serve and obey' – a natural right that could only be achieved by conquering the great continental spaces of Russia.

After his accession to power Hitler had nevertheless maintained existing economic and political ties with Moscow – even receiving Stalin's Jewish ambassador Lev Khinchuk in Berlin on 28 April 1933.[10] Though he continued to utilize the slogan of 'Jewish Bolshevism' in the mid-1930s as one of his most effective foreign policy devices, it is possible that this was in part a cloak for his imperialistic *Drang nach Osten*. On the other hand, Hitler gradually came to believe that Stalin was an antisemite rather than a lackey of the Jews and furthermore a potential short-term ally of the Third Reich in its fight to overthow the Versailles settlement. The intense propaganda crusade after 1935 against 'Jewish Bolshevism' looks in this respect to have been a clever deception. Intended to create a united front at home and to neutralize Western opposition to German rearmament, it peaked just at the moment when most of the 'Jewish' Old Bolsheviks were being liquidated in 1937. Hitler undoubtedly regarded the purges as a positive sign of Stalin's antisemitism, though the eclipse of Jews in high party or Soviet government positions might – so he feared – always be reversible. The dismissal by Stalin of Maxim Litvinov as Soviet Foreign Minister on 3 May 1939 was, however, for Hitler a decisive indicator that Jewish influence in the USSR was really declining.[11] The last ideological obstacle to a temporary accommodation with Stalin appeared to have vanished. To satisfy the apprehensions of his Italian ally, Hitler explained to Count Ciano that Russia had given up her world-revolutionary goals, so that previous objections to co-operation with Moscow were invalid.

Mussolini was far from happy with this unexpected somersault, reproaching Hitler on 3 January 1940 with betraying the principles of National Socialism to tactical exigencies and abandoning 'the anti-Semitic and anti-Bolshevist banner which you have been flying for twenty years'.[12] Hitler's task, the Italian dictator suggested, was 'to defend Europe from Asia' and to demolish Bolshevism. 'The solution of your *Lebensraum* problem is in Russia and nowhere else.'[13] Mussolini even presumed to criticize Nazi treatment of the 'Aryan' Poles; they deserved better than to be put on the same level as Polish Jews who had been unceremoniously shunted into the Lublin reservation. On 8 March 1940, Hitler, irritated by this Italian lecture in ideological purism to the antisemitic Reich, replied that there had been an *epochal change* in Russia;[14] following Litvinov's replacement by Molotov, conditions for a reasonable relationship now existed. National Socialism had in the past been a mortal enemy of Communism because of its 'Jewish-international leadership with its avowed goal of destroying the non-Jewish nations'.[15] But Stalin was a Russian nationalist who had modified Bolshevik principles and rid the Soviet system of its 'Jewish' character. If Bolshevism developed 'into a Russian national State ideology and economy', Hitler told Mussolini, 'it constitutes a reality which we have neither interest nor reason to combat'.[16] On the contrary, Stalinist Russia could assist the Third Reich in the struggle 'against the blockade of the world by the plutocratic democracies'. Furthermore, Russian raw materials complemented German industrial production and both nations had a long tradition of peace and friendship. Hitler concluded this remarkable turnabout by observing that the aim of the 'plutocratic clique of war criminals' in England and France was 'the annihilation of the totalitarian people's state, and thus of Germany'.

A conversation in Rome two days later between Mussolini and Reich Foreign Minister von Ribbentrop amplified Hitler's remarks.[17] Von Ribbentrop lashed out against the 'Jewish plutocratic clique whose influence, through Morgan and Rockefeller, reached all the way to Roosevelt'; the American plutocrats, along with their British and French counterparts, were filled with boundless hatred for National Socialism. On the other hand, during his two visits to Moscow the Reich Foreign Minister had felt it was 'just like talking with old party comrades'.[18] Russia had renounced the idea of world-revolution. The Comintern now confined itself to mere propaganda and information work and was gradually 'becoming a normal nation-state'. 'There were no more Jews in the central agencies, and even Kaganovich, who had always been said to be of Jewish blood . . . looked more like a Georgian. After Litvinov's departure all Jews had left the key positions.'[19] Stalin had utilized the traditional methods of the Russian Tsars to give the Empire a centralized organization. The Politburo now consisted of hundred per cent Muscovites, mostly uninterested in foreign countries and with 'the tendency to isolate their country from the rest of the world'. The new men, like Molotov and Beria, 'would have nothing to do with Paris, London or Washington'. They were Russian isolationists rather than Pan-Slav nationalists, with certain 'revisionist' (in the territorial sense) aspirations.[20] These new men were no threat to Nazi Germany or to Italian fascism. They did not intend to meddle in German internal affairs or to interfere actively in the international field. Above all, they were interested in the trade agreement with Germany. By signing the pact, Germany therefore had nothing to fear and she had been able to release a sizeable number of divisions for use against the West.

Von Ribbentrop's enthusiasm for the Russian 'comrades' appears to have overcome Mussolini's doubts, for the Duce concluded that the Führer was indeed correct and that the end of the Communist *world* movement was at hand.[21] In their meeting of 18 March 1940 at the Brenner Pass, Hitler again stressed to Mussolini that Russia was moving away from Jewish international Bolshevism and towards Slav Muscovite nationalism.[22] She was undergoing a great transformation under Stalin, who was an out-and-out autocrat, a Russian Tsar. 'The Jews, too, were being increasingly forced out of key positions in the Russian administration.'[23] They had played a certain part in the occupied Polish territories 'but had then all been deported to Siberia' (the source for this strange claim is unclear). Hitler nonetheless admitted that only 'bitter necessity' had made him join forces with Russia. It was British policy which, by setting limits on German *Lebensraum* eastwards and on her colonial aspirations, had forced his hand. He had only wanted peace whereas Britain and France sought the 'annihilation of Germany'.[24] In these circumstances,

Russia provided the 'only protection for the rear'. Indirectly, Hitler also answered Mussolini's concern for the ill-treatment of Poles by fabricating a story about their 'atrocities' and the 'torment of the German minority' in Poland. Furthermore, Hitler gave the deliberately misleading impression of territorial satiety by claiming that he 'would need forty to fifty years to develop the territories which now belonged to him again'.

Hitler had initially decided on the pact with the Soviets in order to avoid the spectre of a two-front war and to secure the conquest of Poland. Addressing his generals on 22 August 1939, he had counted Stalin along with Mussolini and himself as one of the three great statesmen in the world, adding that 'Stalin and I are the only ones who can visualise the future'.[25] Therefore, Hitler explained, he had undertaken to redistribute the world with Stalin's assistance. Poland would be depopulated and settled with Germans. The fate of Russia would eventually be the same, though the USSR might not be ripe for destruction until after Stalin's death. This prognosis reveals not only his own treacherous intentions but also Hitler's high appreciation of Stalin, which runs right through his wartime table talk. Stalin is depicted there as the new Genghis Khan (a compliment in Hitler's book), 'half beast, half giant', who towered above Churchill and Roosevelt. His industrial planning, his political genius and transformation of Russia into a military power, his ruthlessness toward his own people and his antisemitism aroused the Führer's unstinting admiration. On 20 January 1941 in the presence of the German and Italian foreign ministers as well as leading Axis generals, Hitler declared that 'as long as Stalin lives, there is probably no danger; he is intelligent and careful. But should he cease to be there, the Jews, who at present only occupy second and third-rank positions, might move up again into the first rank. It therefore behoves us to be careful.'[26] The greatest potential danger to the Axis was therefore not America but 'the gigantic block of Russia' which would have to be watched constantly. She had completely absorbed the Baltic States and one-sidedly interpreted the treaty with regard to Lithuania; moreover the vital Rumanian oilfields were dangerously exposed to her air force. As he had monitored these Russian moves and the threats from Moscow against Bessarabia and Finland, Hitler felt more and more that they demonstrated a clear Russian resolve to expand into Europe rather than eastwards into Asia.[27] Bolshevism appeared to be a cover for continuing the traditional aims of Tsarist Pan-Slav imperialism which would inevitably clash with the Third Reich's own sphere of influence in the Baltic, the Balkans and Eastern Europe.

Looking back in February 1945 on the interlude of the Nazi–Soviet pact, Hitler asserted that after the Russian behaviour in the Baltic States and Bessarabia in the summer of 1940 he already had 'no illusions regarding their intentions'. Molotov's visit to Berlin in November 1940 had confirmed Hitler in his belief that war with Russia was inevitable. Throughout the winter and into the spring of 1941, he recalled, 'I was haunted by the obsession that the Russians might take the offensive'.[28] In this context, he commented shortly afterwards that for a whole year he had still hoped that an entente could be established between Stalinist Russia and the Third Reich, in the spirit of 'implacable realism on both sides'. This entailed defining zones of influence precisely, co-operating on economic matters and at the same time keeping one's finger on the trigger. 'I imagined that after fifteen years of power Stalin, the realist, would rid himself of the nebulous Marxist ideology and that he was preserving it merely as a poison reserved exclusively for external use. The brutal manner in which he decapitated the Jewish intelligentsia who had rendered him such signal service in the destruction of Tsarist Russia encouraged one in that belief. I presumed that he did not wish to give these same Jewish intellectuals the chance of bringing about the downfall of the totalitarian empire which he had built – that Stalinist empire which, in all its essentials, is only the spiritual successor to the empire of Peter the Great.'[29]

The astonishing implication in these words is that it was Stalin's *anti-Jewish* policy which had ultimately determined the feasibility of the Russo–German pact. Soviet territorial expansionism in 1940 had, on the other hand, finally indicated to Hitler that neither 'Jewish-Bolshevik' objectives of world revolution nor traditional Pan-Slavic imperialism had truly been abandoned by Stalin. Furthermore, in practical terms the price of the agreement with Russia was very substantial, as Mussolini had already pointed out to Hitler in 1940. Latvia, Lithuania and Estonia, along with half of Poland, had been handed over to the USSR which had strengthened its position in Eastern Europe even more than the Germans. On the other hand, Hitler had secured important raw materials from Russia, weakened Britain and France and left himself the chance to concentrate all his forces against the West. The success of the German armies in the West was indeed in his eyes the precondition for any future confrontation with Russia; and as early as July 1940, following the defeat of France, Hitler had thought of striking eastwards at once and shattering the Russian state 'to its roots with one blow'.[30] The first directives for the invasion plan (Operation Barbarossa) were already prepared in the autumn of 1940 and presented for Hitler's approval in December. The decision to attack the Soviet Union was therefore by no means impulsive but represented a result of careful calculation in which ideological, military, political and economic factors were all involved. Molotov's visit to Berlin on 12 November 1940, which raised the question of Soviet territorial ambitions in the Balkans, the Black Sea and Finland, accentuated all of Hitler's brooding suspicions about his ally.[31] The Soviet demands indicated that his hopes of diverting Russia away from Europe to areas such as the Persian Gulf and the Indian Ocean (where she could inherit the position of the British Empire) had failed; given his own treacherous intentions *vis-à-vis* Russia, Hitler could all the more easily convince himself that the new Soviet demands meant that Stalin was preparing to attack Germany.[32]

On 18 December 1940 Hitler signed Directive No. 21 for Operation Barbarossa, which stated that 'the German Armed Forces must be prepared to crush Soviet Russia in a quick campaign even before the end of the war against England'. Though the order to advance would still be delayed for slightly over six months, Hitler was by the end of 1940 mentally attuned to consummating his imperial dream of a European New Order.[33] Convinced, as he told Jodl, that Russia would in any case collapse within two or three months ('We have only to kick in the door and the whole rotten structure will come crashing down'), Hitler could now safely return to the basic principles of his creed. Significantly, in his last big speech of the winter, delivered in the Berlin Sportpalast, after denouncing the British for seeking 'to exterminate the German nation' Hitler concluded with a 'prophecy': 'I am convinced that 1941 will be the crucial year of a great New Order in Europe. The world shall open for everyone. Privileges for individuals, the tyranny of certain nations and their financial rulers shall fall. And, last of all, this year will help to provide the foundations of a real understanding among peoples, and with it the certainty of conciliation among nations. When the other world has been delivered from the Jews, Judaism will have ceased to play a part in Europe. . . . Those nations who are still opposed to us will some day recognize the greater enemy within. Then they will join us in a combined front, a front against international Jewish exploitation and racial degeneration.'[34]

As the prospect of a gigantic world-struggle with the USSR approached, Hitler began increasingly to return to the themes of *Mein Kampf* and his early years as an antisemitic agitator in Munich. The rhetoric of racial eschatology which was to characterize the 'Final Solution' more and more entered into the language of top-secret military briefings and directives. At a conference early in March 1941 where Hitler justified the coming invasion of the USSR as a preventive action against Russian imperialist designs in the Balkans and the Baltic region, he stressed that it would not be conducted in a chivalrous manner. 'This struggle is one of ideologies and racial differences and will have to be conducted with unprecedented, merciless and unrelenting harshness. All officers will have to rid themselves of obsolete ideologies. . . . The [Russian] commissars are the bearers of an ideology directly opposed to National Socialism. Therefore the commissars will be liquidated.'[35] On 13 March 1941 a special directive issued by Field Marshal Keitel provided that 'in the area of army operations the Reichsführer-SS will be entrusted, on behalf of the Führer, with special tasks for the preparation of the political administration – tasks entailed by the final struggle that will have to be carried out between two opposing political systems. Within the framework of these tasks, the Reichsführer-SS will act independently and on his own responsibility.'[36] In other words, Himmler and the SS were to be given a free hand in stamping out all Jews and Bolsheviks in the eastern territories. On 30 March 1941 Hitler informed his generals and top commanders that war with the Soviet Union was inevitable. It would be a 'struggle between two opposing world outlooks' (*Kampf zweier Weltanschauungen gegeneinander*) in which there was no room for 'soldierly comradeship'. This would be 'a war of destruction' (*Vernichtungskampf*) conducted 'against the poison of decomposition'. The struggle against Russia meant the liquidation of the Bolshevik Commissars and the Communist intelligentsia.[37] It would be totally different from the war in the West.

The same brutal tone appeared in the *Kommissarbefehl* of 6 June 1941 which revealed how far the Wehrmacht had already become indoctrinated by National Socialist ideology. The troops were told that 'consideration and respect for international law' with regard to political commissars of all kinds was wrong. These 'originators of barbaric Asiatic methods of warfare' (*barbarisch asiatischer Kampfmethoden*) were a danger for German security and 'for the rapid pacification of conquered territory'. Hence they would not be treated as prisoners of war but 'executed forthwith'. (*Sofort mit der Waffe zu erledigen*).[38] Further guidelines for the troops in Russia, drawn up before the invasion, followed the same pattern, calling for ruthless elimination of Bolshevik agitators, guerrillas, saboteurs and Jews.

The 'Final Solution' was indissolubly linked in Hitler's mind with this coming war for *Lebensraum* in the East. The invasion of Poland and then the crushing of France had been conceived as a necessary launching-pad for carrying out this ultimate reckoning, following the refusal of the British to co-operate with his plans for German hegemony in Europe. In the meantime, during the period before June 1941, various partial solutions for dealing with the 3.3 million Jews of Poland as well as those of Western Europe had to be improvised. Already in October 1939 the head of the SS, Heinrich Himmler, had been appointed Reich Commissioner for the strengthening of Germandom and began to carry out racial policies in Poland designed to expel Jews and Poles from areas to be annexed to the Reich. These areas were to be settled exclusively by racially pure Germans from the *Altreich* and *Volksdeutsche* from the Baltic lands and outlying parts of Poland. Meanwhile the Generalgouvernement under its civilian Governor-General Hans Frank was assigned as a vast dumping ground mainly for Jews from Germany, Austria and the annexed territories, who were to be concentrated in a few large towns and segregated as far as possible from their non-Jewish neighbours. Responsibility for this task was assigned to Reinhard Heydrich and his mobile paramilitary police force, the *Einsatzgruppen*.[39] Already during the Polish campaign they had carried out wholesale murders of Poles and Jews, which led to friction with some shocked Army commanders. In 1939–40 close to 10,000 Polish intellectuals, members of the nobility and clergy, were killed by the *Einsatzgruppen* as part of a deliberate policy of breaking Polish national resistance. With regard to Jews, Heydrich's special directive of 21 September 1939, which was circulated among the higher military administration in Poland, already provided a first step towards the 'Final Solution' of the Jewish problem in the occupied territories.[40] Two years before the death camps began to function in Poland, it was emphasized by Heydrich that all Polish Jews must be concentrated in as few urban areas as possible, at rail junctions or locations along railway lines 'to facilitate subsequent measures'. Jewish Councils (*Judenräte*) were to be set up, headed by an 'Eldest', who were fully responsible for the transportation or reception of Jews who were to be moved, for providing food supplies and for housing. The Jews would be concentrated in ghettos as a preparation for the 'final aim' which, as Heydrich indicated, was 'to be kept strictly secret' and would require a longer period of time to implement. Heydrich did not yet reveal the nature of the *Endziel* and it is just possible that this was still conceived in the context of a 'Jewish reservation' in the Lublin district.[41] But by March 1940 the Lublin project had been abandoned as impractical. The alternative 'solution' of a reservation in Madagascar was not seriously considered by Hitler *after* the summer of 1940. Meanwhile the Jews of Poland were being systematically isolated in ghettos, including that of Lodz, and then in the autumn of 1940 the Warsaw ghetto was established, in which about 500,000 Jews were eventually concentrated. Here they suffered from acute overcrowding, chronic shortage of food and sanitation, outbreaks of typhus and other infectious diseases. Many died in these appalling conditions or in the labour camps to which they were transported. Nevertheless, in 1939–40, systematic mass murder was not yet official German policy. If Poland, in Lucy Dawidowicz's words, was the 'testing laboratory not only for the execution of the Final Solution, but for all of Hitler's racial and imperial ambitions', Russia would become the arena for the final struggle, 'the prelude to the millennium'.[42]

On 31 July 1941, almost six weeks after the invasion of Russia and the murderous assaults of the mobile killing units had begun, Goering, as

Plenipotentiary of the Four-Year Plan, referring back to his earlier commission of 1939, instructed Heydrich to 'carry out all preparations with regard to the organisation, the material side and financial viewpoints for a total solution [*Gesamtlösung*] of the Jewish question in those territories of Europe which are under German influence'.[43] In the same document, Heydrich was further requested to submit a draft 'showing the administrative, material and financial measures already taken for the execution of the intended final solution [*Endlösung*] of the Jewish question'.[44] Goering's letter to Heydrich was almost certainly the response to a secret order from Hitler to prepare an extermination plan.[45] The commission to draw up a 'total solution' for the Jewish question in all areas under German control (or influence) amounted to nothing less than planning the physical destruction of European Jewry, though the modalities for implementation were still not in place. This is confirmed, among other evidence, by the testimony of SS personnel like Rudolf Höss, the Commandant of Auschwitz, and Adolf Eichmann himself, both of whom first heard of the Führer-Order for the 'Final Solution' between the summer and autumn of 1941.[46] Höss's autobiography recounts that Himmler personally told him of the *Führerbefehl* to liquidate all European Jews in the summer of 1941 and that he was then visited by Eichmann with whom he discussed the inadequacy of shooting and gas-vans as extermination methods.[47]

Eichmann, for his part, maintained that he was informed by Heydrich late in the summer of the same year and then sent on a mission to Odilo Globocznik, the SS Commander in Lublin, to witness the killing methods being carried out in the East.[48] In his interrogation by Captain Avner Less of the Israeli police in 1960, Eichmann affirmed that two or maybe three months after the invasion of the USSR (i.e. in August/September 1941) Heydrich had told him point-blank: 'The Führer has ordered physical extermination.'[49] Questioned further, Eichmann agreed that Heydrich must have received instructions from his immediate superior, the Reichsführer-SS, and 'Himmler must have had express orders from Hitler. If he hadn't had orders from Hitler, he'd have been out on his ear before he knew what hit him.'[50] Eichmann agreed that he had never seen a *written* order from Hitler or Himmler concerning the physical extermination of European Jewry. This did not in the least surprise him. From his knowledge of Himmler and the SS a written order on such a subject would have been *out of the question*. 'Herr Hauptmann, I can't imagine Himmler putting that in writing', he told his Israeli interrogator. 'To me that is inconceivable.'[51]

The balance of avilable evidence indicates that by October or November 1941 at the latest, Hitler had approved the outline of the extermination plan which he had requested through Goering in July.[52] The essential pre-conditions – i.e. special reception camps in the East for deported Jews and plans for gassing facilities – were being intensively discussed in the autumn of 1941 in the SS, the Foregin Office, the Führer's Chancellery and the Ministry for the Eastern occupied territories.[53] It was already evident that the *Einsatzgruppen* massacres of Russian Jews which had been going on since the beginning of the German invasion in June 1941 could provide no solution to the European Jewish question *as a whole*.

On the other hand, they did offer a quick answer to the immediate problem of dealing with the millions of Soviet Jews who had come under German rule as the Wehrmacht struck deep into Russia. On 12 September 1941 Field Marshal Keitel reminded German troops in the occupied eastern territories that 'the struggle against Bolshevism demands ruthless and energetic measures, above all against the Jews, the main carriers of Bolshevism'.[54] The Commander-in-Chief of the Sixth Army, Walter von Reichenau, told his men on 10 October 1941 that they 'must have full understanding for the necessity of a severe but just atonement on Jewish sub-humanity' (*Sühne am jüdischen Untermenschentum*).[55] The German soldier in the East was not 'merely a fighter according to the rules of the art of war, but also the bearer of an inexorable national idea [*einer unerbittlichen völkischen Idee*] and the avenger of all bestialities inflicted upon the German people and its racial kin'.[56] The aim of the entire campaign 'against the Jewish-Bolshevist system', according to von Reichenau's directive (which Hitler found 'excellent'), was the 'complete crushing of its means of power and the extermination of Asiatic influence in the European region'.[57] Even one of the most brilliant German commanders in the Second World War, Field Marshal Erich von Manstein, passed on to his soldiers a directive identical to that of von Reichanau on 20 November 1941, adding that: 'The Jews are the mediators between the enemy in our rear and the still fighting remnants of the Red Army and the Red leaders. . . .'[58] Hitler himself had indicated on the evening of 25 October 1941 that the massacres in the East had his full approval. Recalling his Reichstag prophecy that 'the Jew would disappear from Europe', he told Himmler and Heydrich: 'It's not a bad idea, by the way, that public rumour attributes to us a plan to exterminate the Jews. Terror is a salutary thing.'

By November 1942 over a million Russian Jews had been murdered by the *Einsatzgruppen* and their support groups.[59] There is no doubt that this bloodbath corresponded exactly with Hitler's intentions. In a public speech on 8 November 1942 he had declared: 'People always laughed at my prophecies. . . . Among those who laughed then are innumerable persons who no longer laugh today, and those who are still laughing will probably soon stop.' Hitler's prophecies invariably referred to the murder of Jews. Sixteen months earlier, at a planning conference on 16 July 1941 dealing with future occupation policy, he had openly advocated shooting 'anyone who so much as looks like giving trouble' as part of general pacification methods in the conquered Russian territories. The partisan warfare of the Soviets was 'not without its advantages as far as we are concerned', he commented, 'since it gives us a chance to wipe out anyone who gets in our way'.[60] Under the cover of protective security measures, a pitiless genocidal operation ordered by Hitler was to take place in the coming months with the complicity of the top Army command.[61] The destruction of Bolshevism was, after all, a common goal shared by the conservative Army leaders with the Nazi Party; they were now also ready to pay the price of involvement in extermination policies against Jews and Slavs to preserve their position in the New Order, just as they were willing to cold-bloodedly allow the death of 3.5 million Soviet prisoners-of-war in German captivity.[62]

The 'Final Solution', which emanated at source from Hitler and whose execution was passed down through Himmler and Heydrich to top police and SS bureaucrats at Reich Security Headquarters like Heinrich Müller, Ernst Kaltenbrunner and Adolf Eichmann, was to depend on innumerable complicities of this kind. Without the active co-operation with the SS of the Army, the Foreign Office, the bureaucracy, big industry and party officials at every level and the lack of resistance by the German people as a whole, it could never have been implemented.[63] The process of mass murder needed literally thousands of participants who were not directly involved in killing anyone, yet made it possible by never deviating from their daily routines or regular tasks. They included diplomats, lawyers, physicians, accountants, engineers, bankers, clerks and the hundreds of railway workers and officials without whom the trains to Auschwitz from all over Europe would never have run on time.[64] Even a single transport of German Jews involved the co-operation of not only the local police but of many municipal authorities. Officials from the Finance, Labour and Housing offices had to collect appropriate documents from the deportees while local railway authorities provided an assembly and loading area. As Raul Hilberg has pointed out: 'The machinery of destruction, then, was structurally no different from organized German society as a whole; the difference was only one of function. The machinery of destruction *was* the organized community in one of its special roles.[65] The Nazi Holocaust cannot therefore be explained by Hitler's personality and politics or by ideological factors alone. It could not have happened except in a highly organized, bureaucratized industrial society which had reached a certain level of technological achievement.[66] In particular, the methodical, bureaucratic approach which characterized the German solution to the 'Jewish question', with its deliberate fragmenting of responsibilities and routinizing of operations, gave to the Holocaust its extraordinary quality of depersonalized violence. This administrative-bureaucratic approach was not superseded by the SS ascendancy and control of Jewish policy after 1939.[67] On the contrary, Himmler's SS and police had always favoured a comprehensive and 'rational' handling of the 'Jewish question'. The senior SS and police leaders were sometimes fanatics but more often tended to be younger well-educated middle-class professionals, who were also party members.[68] They performed their job of 'extermination' as much out of careerist reasons, the habit of obeying orders or the fear of being different, as from ideological conviction.

But recognizing these structural realities should not lead one to forget that the depersonalized behaviour of Nazi bureaucrats and of the SS was itself the product of a long process of ideological indoctrination. The willingness of Germans to participate in the mass murder of Jews had been conditioned by a totalitarian propaganda apparatus which for years had portrayed the Jews as vermin to be mercilessly eradicated. Hitler had a decisive hand in this ideological conditioning-process without necessarily initiating every single step along the road to destruction.[69] His charismatic authority gave a normative character even to utterances of a predominantly visionary or utopian character that might otherwise have remained without practical consequences.[70] Moreover, during the years between 1933 and 1939 when he had allowed subordinates greater scope in defining Jewish policy, he had always been the ultimate source of authority.[71] This was, in my view, even more the case after 1939 when Hitler had at his disposal a perfected instrument in the SS bureaucracy which, through its security services, police formations and concentration camp system, was ideally suited to carrying out deportations and mass murder in conditions of wartime. Heinrich Himmler and his deputy Heydrich were designated to operate this killing machine and could be relied upon to carry out their dirty job obediently without written orders. Neither of them would have dreamed of initiating the 'Final Solution' on his own.

Himmler was, however, given the widest authority, already before the invasion of Russia, to implement his 'security functions' in the eastern occupied territories. It was in his name that Gestapo chief Heinrich Muller issued the fateful circular of 23 October 1941 banning 'all further Jewish emigration, with immediate effect'.[72] It was Himmler who had informed the *Gauleiter* of the Wartheland, Arthur Greiser, on 18 September 1941 that it was 'the Führer's wish that the Altreich and the Protectorates should be cleared of Jews from west to east. I am therefore doing all I can to see that the deportation of the Jews out of the Altreich and the Protectorates into the territories assimilated into the Reich during the past two years is completed during this year as a first stage, preparatory to their being sent further east early in the new year.'[73] It was Himmler who had overall responsibility for the mass deportation, the destruction of the ghettos, the building of death camps in Poland and the machinery of extermination. In all these tasks he was the faithful executor of the Führer's will, as he admitted on several occasions. Thus in a letter to *SS-Gruppenführer* Gottlob Berger on 28 July 1942 warning against dogmatic definitions of the term 'Jew' which would unnecessarily tie their hands, Himmler added: 'The occupied territories will be cleared of Jews. The Führer has charged me with carrying out this very difficult task. No one can relieve me of this responsibility. I cannot allow myself the luxury of discussing it.'[74]

The instructions for mass murder which Himmler, too, had to translate into formal though unwritten orders relied on the force of law which *Führerbefehle* enjoyed in the Third Reich. Thus Himmler and Heydrich would if necessary assure commanders and SS personnel that the mass executions of Jews were the 'wish of the Führer' (*des Führers Wunsch*) – a semantic formula which, as Gerald Fleming has shown, acquired a life of its own during the Holocaust.[75] Hitler, as an international statesman, could simply not afford to saddle himself publicly with the actual killing, though, to quote Heydrich's words to Admiral Canaris, the shootings in Russia were 'due exclusively to the personal orders of the Führer Adolf Hitler'.[76] Though he had openly proclaimed throughout his career that the Jews must be exterminated, the horrible reality of its implementation was something that Hitler preferred to be carried out secretly outside Germany and with a minimum of discussion. The Jews of Europe were to be 'evacuated', 'transported to the East' or 'resettled' – some of the various code-words devised by Himmler and Heydrich to disguise the terrible truth. The Führer would never issue a direct formal order for their death, but it was ultimately his implacable will that drove the machinery of destruction.[77]

Where Himmler and other subordinates might have been tempted to crack under a burden of such monstrous weight, Hitler was always there to force the pace. For the Führer it was seen as his most sacred mission in a World War where the best blood of the white races was being shed. Unless Nazi Germany was victorious, Hitler believed, the destructive forces of Jewry would finally gain the upper hand. According to Himmler's account of a conversation with Hitler, as retold to an SS *Sturmbannführer* who had visited Auschwitz in the spring of 1943, the 'Final Solution' was therefore undertaken to protect future generations. Hitler had decided 'after long reflection to eradicate once and for all the biological strength of Jewry [*die biologischen Schwerpunkte des Judentums ein für allemal auszutilgen*], so that even if the Aryan peoples emerge weakened from this struggle, at least we shall put an end to those forces'.[78] This was certainly consistent with other statements relating to the 'Final Solution' made by Hitler during the war, whether in public speeches, to visiting allies or in his table talk. Though the language is sometimes abstract or metaphorical and Hitler never enters into specific details about the mass slaughter taking place, his will to exterminate the 'Jewish plague' is always apparent. Thus on 21 July 1941, speaking to the Croatian Foreign Minister, General Slavko Kvaternik, he described the Jews as 'the scourge of humanity'. This was shortly after the mass shootings of Jews by the *Einsatzgruppen* had begun. Hitler told his Croatian ally: 'If the Jews were given their way, as they are in the Soviet paradise, they would carry out the maddest plans. That is how Russia has become a plague centre [*Pestherd*] for humanity. If only one country for whatever reasons tolerates a Jewish family in it, that family will become the germ centre [*der Bazillenherd*] for fresh sedition. If there were no longer any Jews in Europe, the unity of the countries of Europe would no longer be disturbed.'[79]

On 23 January 1942 Hitler returned to this theme in his table talk. 'One must act radically. When one pulls out a tooth, one does it with a single tug, and the pain quickly goes away. The Jew must clear out of Europe. Otherwise no understanding will be possible between Europeans. It's the Jew who prevents everything. When I think about it, I realize that I'm extraordinarily humane. . . . I restrict myself to telling them to go away. If they break their pipes on the journey I can't do anything about it. But if they refuse to go voluntarily, I see no other solution but extermination.'[80] Hitler went on to compare the Jews to the Russian prisoners-of-war who were dying in large numbers in German camps.[81] 'It's not my fault', he pathetically insisted. 'I didn't want this war or the P.O.W. camps. Why did the Jews provoke this war?'[82] Four days later Hitler amplified what was by now becoming an obsessive theme even by his monomaniac standards. 'The Jews must pack up, disappear from Europe. Let them go to Russia. Where the Jews are concerned, I'm devoid of all sense of pity. They'll always be the ferment that moves peoples one against the other. They sow discord everywhere, as much between individuals as between peoples. They'll also have to clear out of Switzerland and Sweden. It's where they're to be found in small numbers that they're most dangerous. Put 5,000 Jews in Sweden – soon they'll be holding all the posts there. . . . It's entirely natural that we should concern ourselves with the question on the European level. It's clearly not enough to expel them from Germany. We cannot allow them to retain bases of withdrawal at our doors. We want to be out of danger of all kinds of infiltration.'[83]

On 30 January 1942 in a speech delivered at the Berlin *Sportpalast*, Hitler was even more explicit, declaring that 'the result of this war will be the complete annihilation of the Jews. Now for the first time they will not bleed other people to death; rather . . . [the old] law – eye for eye etc. will be applied . . . and the hour will come when the most evil world-enemy of all times, or at least of the last thousand years, will have played his part to the end.'[84] In the same speech Hitler was, not for the first or last time, reiterating the 'prophecy' he had made on 30 January 1939. Significantly, he confused the date of his earlier prophecy with his Reichstag speech of 1 September 1939 – thereby inadvertently revealing the connection in his mind between the launching of the *Blitzkrieg* on Poland, the Second World War and the 'Final Solution' of the Jewish question. This confusion of dates which Hitler repeated each time he recalled his annihilation threat of January 1939 was too consistent to be accidental. Moreover, in each case the promise of destruction was couched in terms of the same antithetical pairing; *either* the Aryan peoples would be wiped out *or*, as in the 30 January 1942 formulation, '*Jewry vanishes from Europe*'. The novelty in the January 1942 *Sportpalast* speech lay only in the usage of the biblical saying, 'an eye for an eye, a tooth for a tooth', probably inserted for greater emphasis. Interestingly enough, according to secret SD reports, the German public appeared to be aware of the drastic implications of this speech; it was widely interpreted to mean 'that the Führer's battle against the Jews would be followed through to the bitter end with merciless consistence and that very soon *the last Jew would be driven* off European soil'.[85] As an Israeli researcher who uncovered this SD report has pointed out, the mass deportations of Jews from Germany had been going on for some three months before the speech. Though they aroused little response from the German public, the connection with Hitler's threats was too obvious to be missed.

Hitler's speech was made, significantly enough, only ten days after the notorious Wannsee Conference which extended the 'Final Solution' to *all* of European Jewry. The conference had been organized by Reinhard Heydrich in order to co-ordinate with the various Reich ministries and service chiefs a pan-European plan.[86] It had been intended to meet on 8 December 1941, but the conference was postponed until 20 January 1942. There were five representatives of the SS and police present (including Heinrich Müller and Adolf Eichmann) and nine civilians representing among others the Ministry of the Interior, the Ministry of Justice, the Reich Chancellery, the Ministry of the Eastern Territories, the office of the Four-Year Plan and the Foreign Ministry.[87] The support of the Foreign Office was especially important in view of the intention to exterminate the Jews not only in areas directly controlled by the Reich but throughout the *whole* sphere of German influence.

Heydrich referred back to the commission he had received from Goering on 31 July 1941 to prepare a 'final solution to the European Jewish question' (*Endlösung der europaischen Judenfrage*); he mentioned the ban which Himmler had meanwhile placed on emigration as a result of 'the possibilities offered by the eastern territories' and explained: 'In place of emigration, a further possible solution has now begun in the shape of the evacuation of the Jews to the east, in accordance with the prior approval of the Führer' (*nach entsprechender vorheriger Genehmigung durch den Führer*).[88] Heydrich emphasized that the deportations to the East were a temporary expedient on the road to 'the coming final solution of the Jewish question' (*die kommende Endlösung der Judenfrage*).[89]

According to the overblown estimates of the Central Security Department of the Reich (RSHA), the 'final solution' would involve about 11 million Jews in Europe (England, Ireland and Turkey were significantly included). Heydrich then detailed the 'special administrative and executive measures' which would apply to the conscription of Jews for labour (*Arbeitseinsatz*) in the eastern territories. 'Large labour gangs of those capable of work will be formed with the sexes separated, which will be brought to those areas for road building in which task a large part of them will undoubtedly fall out through natural elimination [*durch natürliche Verminderung ausfallen wird*]. Those that remain alive – since they are unquestionably those with the strongest resistance – must be treated accordingly. If they should be allowed to go free, these people, representing a natural selection of the fittest, would form the germ-cell [*Keimzelle*] of a new Jewish development (History teaches that).'[90] In spite of Heydrich's veiled language, it was clear to all concerned that most of the deported Jews would be 'unfit for work' and therefore disposed of immediately. Those with 'the greatest powers of resistance' would also eventually be killed, or in the Nazi euphemism receive 'special treatment' (*Sonderbehandlung*). The Wannsee Conference did not resolve all problems (the question of 'half breeds and mixed marriages', for example, was exhaustively discussed without any final conclusion being reached), but it did set out in circumlocutionary bureaucratic language one of the central objectives of Hitler's New Order – namely, the systematic murder of the Jewish people.

With regard to the Führer's wishes, it had been intended to give priority to deportations of Jews from Reich territory and the Protectorate. In the meantime pressure had been building up in the Generalgouvernement where Hans Frank had been lobbying for the elimination or disappearance of the Polish Jews. A few weeks before the Wannsee Conference, to which he was to send a representative, the Governor General had given expression to his impatience: 'We must destroy the Jews wherever we meet them and whenever opportunity offers so that we can maintain the whole structure of the Reich here. . . . The Jews batten on to us to an exceptionally damaging extent. At a rough estimate we have in the Generalgouvernement about 2.5 million people with Jewish connexions, and on top of that – and this is the point – we now have 3.5 million Jews. We can't shoot these 3.5 million Jews, and we can't poison them, but we can take steps which, one way or the other, will lead to extermination, in conjunction with the large-scale measures under discussion in the Reich.'[91] Frank was well aware of the measures planned at the coming Wannsee Conference. He was hopeful that they would lead to a large-scale Jewish 'migration' (i.e. extermination) so that the Generalgouvernement would at least be 'as free of Jews as the Reich itself'.

Already in October 1941 plans for construction of gassing apparatus had been discussed between Eichmann, Alfred Wetzel, the Jewish expert of the *Ostministerium*, and the supervisor of the euthanasia programme in the Führer's Chancellery, Viktor Brack.[92] It had been agreed that 'there is no reason why those Jews who are not fit for work should not be removed by the Brack method [i.e. gassing]. . . . The workworthy on the other hand will be transported to the East for labour.'[93] Riga and Minsk were mentioned as destinations for deported Jews from the Altreich who would be turned over to the *Einsatzgruppen* commanders, already supervising the murder of Communists and Jews. Heydrich, at a conference in Prague on 10 October 1941, had also confirmed that it was 'the Führer's wish' that the German Jews be deported to Lodz, Riga and Minsk by the end of the year, if possible.[94] Hitler had resolved in September 1941 that the whole of the Old Reich and Protectorate be made *judenfrei*, even before the *Endlösung* for all of Europe could be implemented.[95] The deportation programme was clearly a sentence of death. The Germans had no intention of feeding a mass influx of deported Jews incapable of hard labour, who would be sent eastwards. The only real question was *where* and *how* the deported Jews would be killed and which categories might be temporarily exempted. Between November 1941 and March 1942 major death camps on Polish soil – Chelmno, Belzec and Auschwitz – were constructed, and the first gassings in these camps probably began in January 1942.[96] In Chelmno (Kulmhof), where euthanasia personnel had been reassigned by Viktor Brack of the Führer's Chancellery, gassing by exhaust gas began a month earlier.[97] Belzec, the first extermination camp to be equipped with permanent gas chambers, was established in mid-March 1942.[98] It was to be followed by the construction of similar facilities in Sobibor (May 1942), Treblinka (July 1942), and Majdanek (autumn 1942). None of these concrete steps could have been taken without the prior authorization by Hitler of an extermination plan, before the end of 1941.

The 'Final Solution' was henceforth to have priority over all pragmatic considerations that might have slowed down its implementation. Already on 18 December 1941, in reply to an inquiry from Heinrich Lohse, Reich Commissioner for Ostland, as to whether 'all Jews, regardless of age and sex, or their usefulness to the economy' were to be liquidated, the Ministry for the Eastern Territories had replied in the affirmative. There were to be no exemptions even for skilled workers in the Wehrmacht's ordnance factories. 'The rules relating to the problem require that the demands of the economy be ignored.'[99] The 'Final Solution' had in principle to be carried out in a 'radical' uncompromising manner and with all possible speed, even if it conflicted with Germany's war needs. This conviction that speed was essential came from the very top and was passed on by Himmler to Odilo Globocnik, the Austrian-born Lublin *SS und Polizeiführer* in charge of the murder campaign in Poland. By early 1942 'resettlement' (the euphemism for extermination) was in full swing. Goebbels noted in his diary on 27 March 1942: 'Starting with Lublin, the deportation of the Jews from the Government General to the east has been set in train. It is a pretty barbarous business – one would not wish to go into details – and there are not many Jews left. I should think that one could reckon that about 60 per cent of them have been liquidated and about 40 per cent taken for forced labour. The former *Gauleiter* of Vienna [Globocnik], who is in charge of the operation, is carrying it out with a good deal of circumspection, and his methods do not seem to be attracting much publicity. . . . One simply cannot be sentimental about these things. . . . The Führer is the moving spirit of this radical solution both in word and deed. . . .'[100]

Goebbels' diaries confirm what is known from other sources concerning Hitler's decisive role in the conception and acceleration of the 'Final Solution'. On 14 February 1942 he recorded, after a meeting with Hitler, that world Jewry would suffer a great disaster. 'The Führer once more expressed his determination to clean up the Jews in Europe pitilessly. There must be no squeamish sentimentalism about it. The Jews have deserved the catastrophe that has now overtaken them. Their destruction will go hand in hand with the destruction of our enemies. We must hasten the process with cold ruthlessness. We shall thereby render an inestimable service to a humanity tormented for thousands of years by the Jews. This uncompromising antisemitism must prevail among our own people despite all objections. The Führer expressed this idea vigorously and repeated it afterwards to a group of officers who can put that in their pipes and smoke it.'[101] Hitler's radical extremism was very much to Goebbels' own taste. On 6 March 1942 the Propaganda Minister wrote that the Jews were busy stirring up trouble again in Russia; his solution was simple – 'the greater the number of Jews liquidated, the more consolidated will be the situation in Europe after this war'.[102] Two weeks later, following another discussion with Hitler when the 'Jewish question' was touched on towards the end, Goebbels observed with obvious satisfaction: 'Here the Führer is as uncompromising as ever. The Jew must be got out of Europe, if necessary by applying the most brutal methods.'[103] One week later, Goebbels acknowledged, as we have seen, that the 'evacuation' meant in fact the mass murder of the Jews. 'The prophecy which the Führer made about them for having brought on a new world war is beginning to come true in a most horrible manner.'[104] No other government, according to Goebbels (mimicking Hitler), would have had the strength for such a *global* solution. 'Here, too, the Führer is the undismayed champion of a radical solution necessitated by conditions and therefore inexorable. Fortunately, a whole series of possibilities presents itself for us in wartime that would be denied us in peacetime. We shall have to profit by this.'[105]

Through 1943 Goebbels continued to record some of Hitler's rantings on the 'Jewish question' while the gassings in the Polish death camps continued at full pace. On 24 February 1943 Hitler had confidently announced: 'This struggle will not end with the annihilation of Aryan mankind, but with the extermination of the Jewish people in Europe.' Goebbels was fond of observing that the Führer's prophecies were coming true. At the time of the Warsaw ghetto uprising, he cryptically noted: 'The Fuehrer would like to talk to me before I go on leave, especially to discuss the next measures in the Jewish question of which he has great expectations.'[106] Other entries recorded Goebbels' immense personal delight at making Berlin *judenfrei* ('one of the greatest political achievements of my career') and his hopes – shared by Hitler – that antisemitism would take root in England and America. On 8 May 1943 Goebbels recorded that Hitler attached a great deal of importance to the antisemitic movement in England, even though it was not yet a political factor.[107] The Führer had argued, moreover, that 'the antisemitism which formerly animated the Party and was advocated by it must again become the focal point of our spiritual struggle'.[108] Two days later, after noting that 70–80 per cent of his own ministry's propaganda broadcasts were devoted to the 'Jewish question', Goebbels added: 'The Fuehrer attaches great importance to a powerful anti-Semitic propaganda. He, too, regards success as depending upon constant repetition. He is immensely pleased with our sharpening up the anti-Semitic propaganda in the press and radio.'[109]

The picture of Hitler that emerges from the Goebbels' diaries in the crucial years between 1942 and 1944, when the 'Final Solution' entered into full swing, does not support the view that the Führer was only marginally involved in its implementation. Nor does it give any credence to the idea that the

'Jewish question' had ceased to be a central driving force in his world-view.
Both Hitler and Goebbels were united in the conviction that to eradicate the
Jewish peril there was 'no other recourse left for modern nations except to
exterminate the Jew. . . .'[110] Furthermore, Hitler remained convinced that
'the nations that have been the first to see through the Jew and have been the
first to fight him are going to take his place in the domination of the world'.[111]

Not all his military allies, however, were persuaded by Hitler's insistence
on the necessity for the most stringent measures against the Jews, i.e.
deportation to the death camps. The seventy-five-year-old ruler of Hungary,
Admiral Horthy, for example, appears to have been unimpressed during a
meeting with Hitler at Klessheim Castle on 17 April 1943. Indeed, Goebbels,
for one, complained bitterly of the slack attitudes of the Hungarian state
('permeated with Jews') and the humanitarian arguments of Horthy (whose
family was 'stark jüdisch verfilzt', according to the Propaganda Minister).[112]
Goebbels observed somewhat pathetically that 'the Fuehrer made every effort
to win Horthy over to his standpoint but succeeded only partially'.[113] The
extant record of Hitler's remarks shows that he had referred to the situation in
Poland (which had been 'cleared up thoroughly') in such a way that his
knowledge of what was actually happening there can scarcely be doubted. 'If
the Jews there [i.e. in Poland] did not want to work, they were shot. If they
could not work, they had to succumb. They had to be treated like tuberculosis
bacilli with which a healthy body may become infected. This was not cruel, if
one remembered that even innocent creatures of nature such as hares and
deer, have to be killed so that no harm is caused by them. Why should the
beasts who wanted to bring us Bolshevism be spared more? Nations which did
not rid themselves of Jews perished.'[114] Von Ribbentrop was even more
blunt, telling Horthy during the same encounter that 'the Jews must either be
exterminated or taken to concentration camps'.[115] The Nazi leaders clearly
saw in Horthy's refusal to co-operate adequately on the 'Jewish question' a
sign of Hungarian unreliability and the regime's secret desire to make peace
with the Western Alliance. Horthy, for his part, had argued that because of the
large number of Jews in Hungary, the problem could not be solved by
'deportations'. He told Hitler that 'he had done everything that could be done
against the Jews, but one couldn't murder them or let them die, after all'.[116]

The intensity of Hitler's personal involvement in the 'Final Solution' was
shown by his refusal to accept Horthy's stubbornness. In the summer of 1944,
after German troops had occupied Hungary, he insisted that there should be
no prevarication in measures to deport Hungarian Jews to Auschwitz. On 16
July 1944 von Ribbentrop conveyed to the Reich Plenipotentiary in Hungary
that 'the Führer expects that henceforth the measures against the Jews of

Budapest will be carried out by the Hungarian government without any further delay. . . .'[117] Similar pressures, exerted with more tact but with less success, were directed against Marshal Antonescu of Rumania, whom Hitler also came to suspect, with some reason, of no longer believing in an Axis victory.[118] Both Horthy and Antonescu, like Marshal Pétain, General Franco or President Salazar, were not revolutionaries or even genuine fascist rulers. They rejected the radical extremism behind Nazi racism and still thought in terms of traditional, inherited hierarchies.[119] Distrustful of mass movements and the dynamic nihilism that impelled Nazi activism, they sought to preserve the status quo by relying on the army, the church and the traditional ruling classes. None of these reactionary right-wing dictators regarded the eradication of Jewry as a vital goal, in spite of the powerful antisemitic traditions in East European countries like Rumania and Hungary and to a lesser extent in France. They were prepared to sacrifice foreign Jews without compunction (as did the Vichy regime in France) but protected their own native Jews from Hitler's clutches out of the same conservative nationalist reflex which guided the rest of their policies.

In contrast to the views of all other fascist, semi-fascist and conservative rulers in occupied Europe, Hitler's antisemitism stood out in its ideological inflexibility and systematization as well as the ruthlessness of its implementation. Far more obsessively than his antisemitic predecessors in Germany and elsewhere in Europe, Hitler insisted on identifying the Jews with microbial infection, and his struggle against them resembled a frenetic ritual of purification. The Jews were 'propagators of infections', germs of a deadly plague which decomposed the body of the people unless it was eradicated in time. At a dinner on the evening of 22 February 1942, Hitler announced with truly grotesque pomposity: 'The discovery of the Jewish virus is one of the greatest revolutions the world has seen. The struggle in which we are now engaged is similar to the one waged by Pasteur and Koch in the last century. How many diseases must owe their origins to the Jewish virus! Only when we have eliminated the Jews will we regain our health.'[120] The biological metaphor was one much favoured by Hitler, Himmler, Goebbels, Streicher and other Nazi leaders. By perpetually comparing the Jews to a bacillus, a plague, a world pest or a fatal infectious disease, they had already created an alibi for genocide long before the event itself. In his first political statement of 1919 Hitler had already described the Jewish people as a 'racial tuberculosis of the peoples' (*Rassentuberkulose der Völker*). During the war years Hitler returned to the theme as millions of Jews were destroyed on his orders like vermin, with the help of the pesticide Cyklon B. For Hitler and Himmler, the Jews were simultaneously mythical supermen endowed with demonic powers and a kind of deadly bacteria or parasite belonging to the lowest level of the organic world.[121] Whether in the guise of devils or bacillae, they were thrust outside the human realm altogether into a special category of their own. They belonged neither to humanity nor even to nature. The drastic 'security measures' taken against them therefore necessitated total segregation, purification and finally liquidation – terms properly applicable to an extremely harmful and dangerous alien species.

Heinrich Himmler, the meticulously efficient *Reichsführer-SS* who organized the Holocaust, saw his monumental task in precisely these clinical terms. Like Hitler a fanatical disciple of race theory, though more deeply imbued with the cult of Nordic mysticism, he brought to his genocidal mission the talents of an extremely able administrator and politician. The destruction of the Jews was for Himmler the indispensable prerequisite for implementing his romantic dream of a race of blue-eyed blond heroes, incarnated by the SS elite which he commanded.[122] In addition to wiping out Jews, the systematic decimation of Poles and Russians also became an integral part of the great experiment in genetic engineering which Himmler was assigned to organize in the eastern territories.[123] To these genocidal aims the *Reichsführer-SS* brought a strange kind of apocalyptic 'idealism' which typified the SS. Mass murder was rationalized as a form of martyrdom and harshness towards oneself. To rule, to oppress and murder masses of people in a sacred mission, became the necessary crucible for creating a new ruling aristocracy, embodied in the ideal type of the 'SS Mann'.[124] In this context, whatever his private feelings, Himmler saw the 'Final Solution' as a great historical achievement of the SS.[125] On 6 October 1943 in Posen he told over a hundred assembled SS and police officials: 'I also want to talk to you quite frankly on a grave matter. Among ourselves it should be mentioned quite frankly and yet we will never speak of it publicly. . . . I mean the evacuation of the Jews, the extermination [*Ausrottung*] of the Jewish race. It is one of the things it is easy to talk about. 'The Jewish race is being exterminated', says one party member, it is quite clear, it is in our programme – elimination of the Jews; and we are doing it, exterminating them. And then they come, eighty million worthy Germans, and each one has his decent Jews. Of course, the others are vermin, but this one is an 'A1' Jew [*ein prima Jude*]. Not one of those who talk this way has witnessed it, not one of them has been through it. Most of you must know what it means when a hundred corpses are lying side by side or five hundred or a thousand. To have stuck it out and at the same time – apart from exceptions caused by human weakness – to have remained decent men [*anständig geblieben zu sein*], that is what has made us hard. This is a page of glory in our history, which has never been written and never is to be written.'[126] Himmler further explained to the distinguished gathering that the extermination was a necessary preventive measure, 'for we know how difficult we should have made it for ourselves if, with the bombing raids, the burdens and deprivations of war, we still had the Jews today in every town as secret saboteurs, agitators and trouble-makers. We would now probably have reached the 1916–17 stage when the Jews were still part of the body of the German nation.'[127] Himmler even presented the murderous actions of the SS as the fulfilment of a *duty* to the German people ('We had the moral right to destroy this people which wanted to destroy us') and as an act of moral idealism, since there had been no personal enrichment involved.[128] Above all, the 'Final Solution' was a *hygienic* measure (*'eine Reinlichkeitsangelegenheit'*).[129] 'We have exterminated a bacterium because we do not want in the end to be infected by the bacterium and die of it. I will not see so much as a small area of sepsis appear here or gain a hold. Wherever it may form, we will cauterize it.'[130]

Himmler's insistence on 'total purification' of the territories that had to be Germanized in the future was expressed in several documents relating to the 'Final Solution'. For example, on 19 July 1942 he had written from Lublin to SS police leader Friedrich Krueger that 'the resettlement of the whole Jewish population of the General Government is to be completed by 31 December 1942'. The accelerated measures were essential 'if the ethnical division of races and peoples contemplated in the new order in Europe is to be accomplished, and the safety and racial purity of the Reich and its satellites assured. Any relaxation of this ruling would constitute a threat to law and order in the territories under German sovereignty, would provide a rallying point for the forces of resistance, and would serve as a centre of contagion, both morally and physically.'[131] Himmler's concern for Jewish 'contagion' extended even to women and children. On 6 October 1943 in Posen he told the Reich and *Gauleiters*: 'I have decided that this too requires a clear answer. I did not consider that I should be justified in getting rid of the men – in having them put to death, in other words – only to allow their children to grow up to avenge themselves on our sons and grandsons. We have to make up our minds, hard though it may be, that this race must be wiped off the face of the earth.'[132] Himmler's determination to carry through his task was undoubtedly based on strongly-held ideological convictions. But without the constant prodding from Hitler there is little doubt that the 'Final Solution' would never have been conceived or implemented. Himmler's hand-written record of his discussions with Hitler at Obersalzburg on 19 June 1943 provides further confirmation of what is also evident from other sources. 'The Führer talked to me about the Jewish problem', Himmler noted, 'and said that the deportation of the Jews must go on regardless of any unrest it might cause during the next three or four months, and that it must be carried out in an all-embracing way' (radikal durchzuführen).[133] Himmler did finally crack and in November 1944, on his own initiative, ordered a halt to the gassing of Jews in the hope that he could secretly come to terms with the West.[134] It was an enraged Hitler who intervened and called on Kaltenbrunner (head of the RSHA) and Müller to carry the 'Final Solution' through to the bitter end.

In Hitler's mind the desperate military situation was evidently subordinate to the absolute priority he now attached to the implementation of his racial policy. Whereas before 1939 the anti-Jewish measures of the Third Reich had been weighed and sometimes modified in terms of their practical conse-quences, all inhibitions and restraints were thrown to the winds after the summer of 1941. Following the attempt on his life on 20 July 1944, Hitler's attitude to the 'Jewish question' reached new peaks of irrationality. He ordered all officers with two Jewish grandparents, or whose wives came into that category, to be instantly dismissed from the Wehrmacht.[135] Naturally, no officers of Jewish ancestry had been involved in the July plot. But by now Hitler regarded anyone of partly Jewish blood or with a remote non-Aryan ancestor as suspect.[136] The expulsions were carried out, moreover, at a time when the authorities were desperately scraping together the last reserves fit for military service. This measure was followed by a new racial purge of the civil service. On Hitler's orders, Martin Bormann, 'Secretary to the Führer', informed the Reich Chancellery at the beginning of November 1944 that it was necessary 'to remove from leading offices in the Reich all men whose origin is such as to give rise to doubts about their National Socialist bearing and ideological firmness. . . .'[137] Hitler was henceforth determined at whatever cost to root out the persons of mixed descent (Mischlinge) and those married to Jewish partners, whose fate had not been definitively resolved by earlier Nazi legislation. The goal was to eradicate all 'half-Jews' and persons in mixed marriages from the civil service on the grounds that they constituted a mortal threat to National Socialist ideology. A minority of Mischlinge, who would be allowed to remain in the Reich, would have to agree to compulsory sterilization, according to an earlier recommendation of the Nazi Party Bureau. This had originally been made in March 1942 and was now reactivated by Hitler's witch-hunt.[138]

The biologistic insanity which marked off Nazism from previous varieties of antisemitism and also from all contemporary forms of fascism had always been at the core of Hitler's programme.[139] It was a modern racial form of Manicheism which lifted the age-old disease of Judenhass to a new extreme and turned it into a cosmic principle. For Hitler and all the leading Nazis, the Jew was no longer a human being at all but a purely mythical figure – 'a grimacing, leering devil invested with infernal powers, the incarnation of evil'[140] – against whom they projected all their phobias, their hatreds, anxieties and desires. But none of the other Nazi leaders ever showed the same unwavering sense of purpose or terrifying resolve displayed by Hitler in turning antisemitic myth into literal reality. As his British biographer, Alan Bullock, pointed out: 'He meant to carry out the extermination of the Jewish race in Europe, using the word 'extermination' not in a metaphysical but in a precise and literal sense as the deliberate policy of the German state. . . .'[141] *Judah Verrecke* ('Perish Judah!'), the Nazi slogan of the 1920s, had been meant quite literally. In that sense, the physical destruction of European Jewry between 1941 and 1945 was only the last stage of a process which was almost certainly built into Nazi ideology and Hitler's politics from the beginning. It was the world war which after 1941 fully activated this genocidal dynamic in National Socialism – a war which was limitless in its aims, at least in the East, and involved the uprooting and decimation of whole populations, beginning with the Jews but also including Slavs, gypsies and other 'lesser breeds'. The Holocaust was not, however, a 'war crime' nor was it merely a product of *ad hoc* improvisations in the chaotic conditions of wartime. The promise of 30 January 1939, that in the event of war the Jews would be exterminated, was in fact a *self-fulfilling prophecy*. Hitler did not kill the Jews because a world war he had never intended accidentally broke out; on the contrary, he *had* to wage that war to forge the *Lebensraum* on which he believed Germany's future depended and in order to destroy European Jewry, whose demise always had been the supreme aim of his existence.

Hitler did not repudiate the Holocaust; indeed he gloried in it, ostentatiously repeating his 'prophecies' with an astounding, monotonous insistence during the war years. There was no need for him to enter into the gory operational details – that could be left to trusted subordinates like Himmler and Heydrich. What was important to Hitler was to ensure his own legend as a major historical figure with a sense of Faustian destiny. In his own eyes the killing of the European Jews was the achievement which entitled him to this special position. It was not only the consummation of his fundamental beliefs and convictions and the fulfilment of National Socialist ideology; the Holocaust was at the same time the logical culmination of Hitler's messianic self-conception. Moreover, the very finality of the 'Final Solution' gave it a kind of irresistible appeal to the perverted religiosity that animated Hitler's politics. No one has expressed this aspect of Nazism better than Lucy Dawidowicz: ' "Final" reverbates with apocalyptic promise, bespeaking the Last Judgement, the End of Days, the last destruction before salvation, Armageddon. "The Final Solution of the Jewish Question" in the National

Socialist conception was not just another anti-semitic undertaking, but a metahistorical program devised with an eschatological perspective. It was part of a salvational ideology that envisaged the attainment of Heaven by bringing Hell on earth.'[142]

In the last weeks of his life, Hitler dwelt obsessively on the services he had rendered to humanity by exterminating the 'Jewish pest'. Thus on 13 February 1945 he emphasized: 'National Socialism has tackled the Jewish problem by action and not by words. It has risen in opposition to the Jewish determination to dominate the world; it has attacked them everywhere and in every sphere of activity; it has flung them out of the positions they have usurped; it has pursued them in every direction, determined to purge the German world of the Jewish poison. For us, this has been an essential process of disinfection, which we have prosecuted to its ultimate limit and without which we should ourselves have been asphyxiated and destroyed.'[143] The Jews had organized a life-and-death struggle against Germany, recognizing the danger that National Socialism represented to them on a global scale. Hitler had 'at least compelled them to discard their masks'. This was in itself an achievement, for, according to the Führer, he had 'opened the eyes of the whole world to the Jewish peril. . . .' Hitler's conscience was clean: 'I have always been absolutely fair in my dealings with the Jews. On the eve of the war, I gave them one final warning. I told them that, if they precipitated another war, they would not be spared and that I would exterminate the vermin throughout Europe, and this time once and for all. To this warning they retorted with a declaration of war and affirmed that wherever in the world there was a Jew, there, too, was an implacable enemy of National Socialist Germany. Well, we have lanced the Jewish abscess; and the world of the future will be eternally grateful to us.'[144]

Hitler's political testament, dictated on the morning of 29 April 1945 as the Reich Chancellery was being bombarded by Soviet artillery fire, summed up what had always been the central existential question of his career. In this document for posterity he defended his work and career, prepared his alibi before the court of history, and blamed the outbreak of the Second World War on 'International Jewry'. He had never wished that 'after the first fatal world war' a second war should break out against England or America.[145] 'Centuries will pass away, but out of the ruins of our towns and monuments the hatred against those finally responsible whom we have to thank for everything, International Jewry and its helpers, will grow.'[146] His peace offers had been rejected mainly because of Jewish propaganda and its influence on English politics. The culprit therefore had to pay the price. 'I have also made it quite plain that, if the nations of Europe are again to be regarded as mere shares to be bought and sold by these international conspirators in money and finance, then that race, Jewry, which is the real criminal of this murderous struggle will be saddled with the responsibility.'[147]

The gassing of the Jews as Hitler now presented it in his last Testament, in typically paranoid and circumlocutory language, was rationalized as his revenge for the Allied bombing of Germany. 'I further left no one in doubt that this time not only would millions of children of Europe's Aryan people die of hunger, not only would millions of grown men suffer death, and not only hundreds of thousands of women and children be burnt and bombed to death in the towns, without the real criminal having to atone for this guilt, even if by more humane means.'[148] Translated back from totalitarian into normal language, this meant that gassing in the death camps was Hitler's 'humanit- arian' response to the Anglo-American bombing raids and Soviet counter- offensives organized by the Jews! In the second part of his Testament, after expelling Goering and Himmler from the party for 'secret negotiations with the enemy', Hitler closed with the sentence that literally contained his last words to posterity. 'Above all I charge the leaders of the nation and those under them to scrupulous observance of the laws of race and to merciless opposition to the universal poisoner of all peoples, International Jewry.'[149] There could scarcely be a more succinct epitaph for the murderous design to which he had so fanatically adhered since his entry into politics in 1919.

# CHAPTER SEVEN

# The Nemesis of Christianity

Hitler's Holocaust has been described by a distinguished Christian theologian as a '*caesura* in Western civilization', a credibility crisis in Christianity.[1] From a Christian viewpoint 'it stands as a sign of the final blasphemy of the baptized Gentiles, an open revolt against the God of Abraham, Isaac and Jacob. . . .'[2] From this perspective Nazism represented the culmination of the 'spiritual treason of Christendom'. In Franklin H. Littell's words, 'it exposed the thinness of the veneer that covered with a sham Christianity the actual devotion of the European tribes to other gods'.[3] Alongside this neo-pagan eruption, it was above all the deicide myth, the claims that the Church as the 'New Israel' had superseded the Jewish people (who therefore had no more *raison d'être*) and the 2,000-year-old history of *Judenhass* within Christendom, which prepared the ground for the modern secular antisemitism that found its ultimate expression in the Nazi atrocities. Without this background of centuries of Christian history, six million Jews would not have perished. Though Hitler and his movement expressed a world-view that was ultimately anti-Christian, their antisemitism was, to quote Emil Fackenheim, 'the nemesis of a bimillenial disease within Christianity *itself*, transmuted when Nazism turned against the Christian substance'.[4] As Fackenheim has pointed out, this metamorphosis was already latent in the diatribes of such anti-Jewish 'saints' as Chrysostom, Augustine and Luther.

The Nazi murder camps were 'the apocalyptic nemesis of an anti-Jewishness that has persisted, at times dormantly, at times violently, among Christian saints through the centuries'.[5] At the same time there can be little doubt that, had Hitler's war been successful, a 'final solution' would also have been sought for the Christian churches.[6]

The Janus-face of Nazism *vis-à-vis* the Christian faith is perhaps best epitomized by two remarks of Hitler himself: the first, in *Mein Kampf*, explicitly appropriated the Christian anti-Jewish tradition for his own ends – 'in defending myself against the Jews I am acting for the Lord' (*vollziehe ich das Werk des Herrn*).[7] Seventeen years later, shortly after the gassings of Jews had begun, he expressed in Himmler's presence his fundamentally anti-Christian outlook. 'The sensational event of the ancient world was the mobilization of the underworld against the established order. This enterprise of Christianity had nothing more to do with religion than Marxist socialism has to do with the solution of the social problem. The notions represented by Jewish Christianity were strictly unthinkable to Roman brains. . . . The Jew who fraudulently introduced Christianity into the ancient world – in order to ruin it – reopened the same breach in modern times, this time taking as his pretext the social question. It's the same sleight-of-hand as before. Just as Saul has changed into St. Paul, Mordechai became Karl Marx.'[8]

Whereas the early Hitler appears to have consciously built on traditional Christian anti-Judaism, his rambling wartime monologues suggest that hatred of Christianity and Judaism had become inextricably connected in his later years. In this respect Hitler's relationship to Christianity reflected the two antithetical yet related currents of Christian anti-Judaism and anti-Christian racialism which had co-existed in the German-speaking world since the end of the nineteenth century.[9] Both currents played their part in inspiring the new *ersatz* religion of National Socialism in which the Führer's position as the 'eschatological saviour' as well as political leader of Germany was so central.[10] As redeemer of the new Reich, Hitler combined in classic Wagnerian fashion the roles of Christ and Siegfried. Allusions to the New Testament could mix (however grotesquely) with Aryan myths and a Darwinian view of Nature. Being himself rather sceptical about some of the romantic neo-pagan cults which flourished in Germany both before and during the Nazi period, Hitler preferred to pervert the traditional Christian forms of worship to enhance his own mass appeal. Indeed he was able to redefine Nazism successfully in semi-sacral terms, as a faith (*Glauben*) which transcended intellect and understanding.[11] This secular political faith was predicated on an unshakable belief in the laws of race, the manifest destiny of the Reich in the eastern territories, the destruction of Bolshevism and the negation of liberal, humanistic Western culture. On the other hand, Christianity and above all its root, Judaism, were the embodiment of those universalistic, pacifist and rationalist values which were perceived by Hitler and the Nazis as completely antithetical to their own creed. Hence the annihilation of the Jews could be seen as a profoundly symbolic as well as an ideological-political action. It seemed both to affirm and negate the Christian tradition.

It was from Christian theology that the Nazis had ultimately inherited their demonological view of Jews and Judaism as a satanic force and the embodiment of universal evil.[12] On the other hand, in contrast to the Church, Nazism allowed no escape from Jewishness into conversion. The satanic evil was metamorphosed from a theological into an unchangeable racial essence. Biology had become destiny and with it a policy of genocide which had never been accepted or implemented by the churches at the height of their authority in the Middle Ages. In that specific sense Auschwitz was not built into the logic of Christianity itself but rather was the work of a heretical movement which in order to spiritually *dejudaize* Christendom aimed to make it physically *judenrein* (free of Jews). Yet the 'Final Solution', it must not be forgotten, was carved out by a people who belonged to the mainstream of Western Christian civilization; many Nazis may have been ideologically anti-Christian (e.g. Himmler's SS practised neo-paganism in its most radical form),[13] but they were virtually all the baptized children of Christians. They had grown out of a Christian culture which over centuries had nourished the anti-Jewish virus and was now unable to provide antigens when the disease broke out in its most rabid anti-Christian form. The hard truth is that, for all its underlying hostility to the established churches, National Socialism could not dialectically have existed *without* Christianity and especially without its anti-Jewish stereotypes.

This was particularly true in Catholic Bavaria which became the cradle of the Nazi movement after the ill-fated Munich Soviet of 1919. Religious anti-Jewish traditions, especially strong in the countryside and typified by such popular festivals as the Oberammergau Passion Play, converged with the Nazi onslaught on Weimar democracy, the Left and the Jews. It was in this climate that Hitler's early speeches could utilize Jesus Christ's so-called 'struggle against the Jews' as a model for his own war on the materialistic 'Jewish spirit'. It was 'as a Christian', Hitler insisted, that he had a duty to see that society did not suffer the same collapse as the civilization of Antiquity 'which was driven to its ruin through this same Jewish people'.[14] On 12 April 1922 in Munich he had declared: 'I would be no Christian . . . if I did not, as did our Lord 2000 years ago, turn against those by whom today this poor people is plundered and exploited.'[15] Adopting the mask of militant Christianity, Hitler told his Bavarian audience: 'In boundless love, as a Christian and a human being, I read the passage which tells us how the Lord at last rose in his might and seized the scourge to drive out of the Temple the brood of vipers and adders. How terrific was His fight against the Jewish poison. I realize more profoundly than ever before the fact that it was for this that He had to shed His blood upon the Cross.'[16]

The image of the stern Christ who 'drove the enemies of every form of humanity out of the Temple of the Lord',[17] of Jesus 'the scourge', 'the fist and the sword' appears frequently enough in these early Munich speeches;[18] similarly prominent is the deicidal motif of the 'Jewish hucksterers' who killed 'the great Nazarene'.[19] In a speech in Munich in December 1926, Hitler even claimed Jesus as the first National Socialist. 'The birth of The Man, which is celebrated at Christmas, has the greatest significance for National Socialists. Christ has been the greatest pioneer in the struggle against the Jewish world enemy. Christ was the greatest fighting nature, which ever lived on the Earth. . . . The struggle against the power of capital was his life's work and his teaching, for which he was nailed to the Cross by his arch-enemy the Jew. The task which Christ began but did not finish I will complete.'[20] Four years earlier he had sharply answered Count Lerchenfeld, a former Prime Minister of Bavaria, who had recently stated in a Landtag session that his feeling 'as a man and a Christian' prevented him from being an antisemite. Hitler's reply was based on the opposite premise. Precisely as a Christian he was *obliged* to be an antisemite. 'I say my feeling as a Christian points me to my Lord and Saviour as a fighter. It points me to the man who once in loneliness, surrounded only by a few followers, recognized those Jews for what they were and summoned men to fight against them and who, God's truth! was greatest not as a sufferer, but as a fighter.'[21]

Hitler's image of Jesus was essentially that of a Germanic warrior, transfigured psychologically into a wielder of the sword rather than the wearer of a crown of thorns. With this stereotype, doubtless familiar to him from the 'Aryan Jesus' myth of late nineteenth-century German Christianity and the writings of Houston S. Chamberlain, Hitler could readily identify. In April 1921 he had spoken of 'the tragedy of the Germanic world that . . . Jesus was judaized, distorted, falsified, and an alien Asiatic spirit was forced on us. That is a crime we must repair.'[22] In his wartime table talk he was to return to the motif of the Aryan Jesus. On 21 October 1941, for example, he described Christ as 'a popular leader who took up his position against Jewry'. The Galilean, Hitler insisted, was not a Jew. His object was 'to liberate His country from Jewish oppression. He set Himself against Jewish capitalism, and that's why the Jews liquidated Him.'[23] On 13 December 1941 in the presence of Ribbentrop, Rosenberg, Goebbels, Terboren and Reichsleiter Bouhler, Hitler reaffirmed: 'Christ was an Aryan, and St Paul used his doctrine to mobilise the criminal underworld and thus organise a proto-Bolshevism.'[24] Three years later, Hitler repeated a favourite thesis of H. S. Chamberlain and the German theorists of the Aryan Christ. 'Jesus was most certainly not a Jew. The Jews would never have handed one of their own people to the Roman courts; they would have condemned Him themselves. It is quite probable that a large number of the descendants of the Roman legionaries, mostly Gauls, were living in Galilee, and Jesus was probably one of them. His mother may well have been a Jewess. Jesus fought against the materialism of His age, and, therefore, against the Jews.'[25]

Hitler's identification with the myth of a militant anti-Jewish Jesus survived even the sharp change which occurred in the 1930s in his attitude to Christianity and the established churches. So too, though to a much lesser extent, the Führer retained a certain respect for the Catholic Church. Hitler's Austrian origins, his early upbringing in Catholic schools and his boyhood impressions of the Mass had undoubtedly had a deep effect on his adult mind. From this South German Catholic ethos, so different to the austerity of Prussian Protestant Christianity, Hitler acquired much of his feeling for ritual and liturgy.[26] Like his fellow Catholics, Goebbels and Himmler, he had an intuitive sense for the importance of outward forms, for dogma, hierarchy and organization, which was used to powerful effect in the Nazi movement. The party created its own 'Messiah', Bible, martyrs and dogma in imitation of the Catholic Church just as Himmler would look to the Jesuit order as inspiration for his SS elite. In that sense National Socialism could indeed be described as a kind of 'Catholicism without Christianity'.[27]

In *Mein Kampf* Hitler recalled the influence on him of the 'mysterious artificial dimness of the Catholic churches', the burning candles and incense. He perceived the Church as a past master in the arts of mass psychology and persuasion, gifts he had also discerned in Karl Lueger and the Catholic populist party of late Habsburg Austria. It was in pre-war Austria that he had first been convinced of the folly of any open confrontation with the Catholic Church – even when it ostensibly favoured Slavic over German interests.[28] Significantly, he did not share the Pan-German hostility to Catholicism as a supra-national religion nor did he attack the Roman church for its universalism, in sharp contrast to the anticlerical *völkisch* movement in Hohenzollern and Weimar Germany. Indeed, he pointed out that in Catholic nations like Ireland, Poland and France there was no conflict between nationalism and religion.[29] The key to overcoming the historic schism between Catholics and Protestants in Germany lay in a *political* rather than a religious reformation.

Hitler accepted the typically Catholic view of the 'greatness of the visible organization before our eyes' as being far more significant than the failings of the flesh in individual priests.[30] For every unworthy cleric 'there are a thousand and more honourable ones, shepherds most loyally devoted to their mission, who, in our present false and decadent period, stand out of the general morass like little islands'.[31] The devotion of the lower clergy to the poor was one of the qualities he had most admired in the popular Catholicism of his native Austria where the church served as a vehicle for the social mobility of many able individuals from the ranks of the people. In these and other positive assessments by Hitler of Catholic Christianity, the criterion was never religious but invariably political. In contrast to Protestant racist antisemites like Houston S. Chamberlain, Theodor Fritsch and Alfred Rosenberg who equated Catholicism with Roman dogma and intolerance, Hitler clearly regarded the hierarchical structure and authoritarian discipline of his own boyhood faith with considerable admiration.[32] In the 1930s he told Rauschning that Bismarck's *Kulturkampf* against German Catholics sixty years earlier had been a typically Protestant act of folly. Protestants did not even understand the meaning of a church, their pastors were insignificant little people and they did not have a great position to defend like Rome.[33] 'The Catholic Church is a really big thing. Why, what an organization! It's something to have lasted nearly two thousand years. We must learn from it.'[34] National Socialism was in his eyes the heir of Catholicism. 'We, too, are a Church', Hitler insisted.[35]

This conscious identification did not, however, directly affect Nazi policy, which was primarily determined by racial ideology and before 1933, above all, by electoral considerations. In the years of the *Kampfzeit*, Hitler had been primarily concerned to avoid any involvement in religious disputes which might affect his own image and the unity of the Nazi Party. In *Mein Kampf* he had presented the dissension between Catholics and Protestants in *völkisch* circles as a purely 'Jewish' interest. 'Catholics and Protestants wage a merry war with one another, and the mortal enemy of Aryan humanity and all Christendom laughs up his sleeve.'[36] In Germany this denominational warfare was far more dangerous than in countries like France, Spain or Italy where there was a much greater degree of national and religious cohesion. Moreover, in Germany, both Christian denominations failed to grasp the acuteness of the Jewish peril – especially the mortal threat of the contamination of 'Aryan' blood. 'Both, yes, both Christian denominations look on indifferently at this desecration and destruction of a noble and unique living creature, given to earth by God's grace. The significance of this for the future of the earth does not lie in whether the Protestants defeat the Catholics or the Catholics the Protestants, but in whether the Aryan man is preserved for the earth or dies out. Nevertheless, the two denominations do not fight today against the destroyer of this man, but strive mutually to annihilate one another.'[37]

Hitler angrily insisted that the fight against Ultramontanism waged by former comrades like General Erich von Ludendorff, the bitterly anti-Catholic hero of the *völkisch* Right, was an act of national betrayal. Those who introduced religious quarrels into the Nazi movement were 'consciously or unconsciously' fighting for Jewish interests and were worse traitors to their people 'than any international Communist',[38] for while Germans devoured themselves in religious quarrels, 'the Jew destroys the racial foundation of our existence and thus destroys our people for all time'.[39] Hitler constantly warned that the religious issue was therefore a dangerous diversion. The Jews themselves had never even constituted a religion but had always been 'a people with definite racial characteristics'.[40] Lacking idealism and hence any belief in a hereafter (an idea he may have picked up from Arthur Schopenhauer, one of his favourite philosophers), the Jews, according to Hitler, were inherently incapable of religious faith. Economic not ethical problems, the profitable life in this world and not the hereafter, was the essence of Talmudic teaching.

Moreover the 'religious' doctrine of Jewry consisted primarily in 'prescriptions for keeping the blood of Jewry pure and regulating the relation of Jews among themselves, but even more with the rest of the world; in other words, with non-Jews'.[41] The orientation of the Jew was therefore entirely materialist and *this-worldly* 'and his spirit is inwardly as alien to true Christianity as his nature two thousand years previous was to the great founder of the new doctrine'.[42] Jesus had, of course, 'made no secret of his attitude toward the Jewish people', since the Jew always saw in religion 'nothing but an instrument for his business existence'. In return, Christ had been nailed to the Cross 'while our present-day party Christians debase themselves to begging for Jewish votes at elections and later try to arrange political swindles with atheistic Jewish parties – and this against their own nation'.[43]

Hitler's views on Judaism and Christianity in the early 1920s were strongly influenced by his spiritual mentor, the Bavarian Catholic poet and antisemite, Dietrich Eckart.[44] From Eckart he had learned to see the world in terms of an all-pervasive Gnostic dualism, as a permanent battle between the forces of Light and Darkness, the spirit and the flesh, Aryan and Jew. Eckart's conviction that 'the Jewish question is the chief problem of humanity, in which, indeed, every one of its other problems is contained'[45] undoubtedly reinforced Hitler's antisemitism and gave it a more cosmic dimension; perhaps more than any other *völkisch* publicist in post-war Munich, Eckart saw the Jewish menace as *the* key problem of German regeneration. Hitler, who looked up to him as a mystic, a seer, 'an outstanding writer and thinker', was to take up many of his ideas and sayings, expressing them in his own more direct and brutal manner.[46] In particular, he may have been influenced by Eckart's combination of *völkisch* racism with Catholic mysticism.

The Bavarian poet had argued that Christ was the incarnate revelation. His message had, however, been overlaid and distorted by St Paul with Jewish Old Testament teaching, from which all evils proceeded. Whereas the Jew had deprived mankind of its soul through cold materialism, the 'Aryan' Christian continually aspired to the immortality of the soul, to absolute idealism and

eternal values.[47] Building in autodidactic fashion on the German philosophical heritage of Kant, Feuerbach, Schopenhauer and the writings of the
Viennese Jewish antisemite, Otto Weininger, Eckart presented the God of the
Jews as 'nothing but the projection of their innate essence'.[48] This jealous,
vindictive, egoistic and cruel God had promised the Israelites that 'you shall
devour all peoples' – a phrase that constantly recurs in Hitler's speeches and
was almost certainly taken from Eckart. Jehovah was 'the absolute master on
earth, and they too have that in mind. . . .'

Eckart regarded the spiritual *Verjudung* (judaization) of the German people
as the central problem of the age. Capitalism, Bolshevism and freemasonry
were merely outward manifestations of this curse. He compared the situation
of post-1918 Germany to that of the declining Roman Empire, whose collapse
had been brought about by Judaism under the 'cover' of Christianity.[49] At the
same time he saw in a positive German Christianity mixed with national and
socialist components the only salvation for the German *Volk*.[50] According to
Eckart, early Christianity was built on the true communist principle of the
*Volksgemeinschaft*, the supremacy of the community over egoistic individualism;
the theory of *laissez-faire* liberalism was fundamentally 'Jewish' in origin. The
impact of these ideas on the early Hitler is self-evident, even though Eckart
never quite embraced the biological-racist antisemitism that was to characterize fully-fledged Nazism.

The convergences between master and pupil are also apparent in *Der
Bolschevismus von Moses bis Lenin*, a posthumously published record by Dietrich
Eckart of his conversations with Hitler, which appeared in Munich in 1924. In
particular, one can see here the outlines of Hitler's primitive philosophy of
history, derived in part from Eckart's inspiration and pseudo-scientific
references. In this dialogue Moses appears as the first leader of Bolshevism,
which is presented in wholly ahistorical terms as the most recent form of an
age-old Jewish conspiracy. Its origins went back to the Old Testament and the
exodus from Egypt.[51] According to Eckart and Hitler, the mass exodus of the
Children of Israel as recounted in the Bible was the result of a revolutionary,
terrorist assault on the Egyptian ruling classes, in which 'Jewish-Bolshevik'
agitators had mobilized the Egyptian rabble. The slaying of the first-born was
supposedly part of this terror campaign which was aborted by 'nationalist'
Egyptians at the last minute and led to the expulsion of the Jews together with
the 'rabble' (*Pöbelvolk*).[52]

The conversations also dealt at length with the problem of Christianity –
Eckart and Hitler denouncing St Paul for his proto-Bolshevism. 'He goes to
the Greeks, to the Romans. And he takes them *his* 'Christianity'. Something
which can unhinge the Roman Empire. All men are equal! Fraternity!

Pacifism! No more dignity! And the Jew triumphed.'[53] The lesson of early Christianity was that every revolution had ultimately developed under conspiratorial Jewish leadership. The Protestant Reformation, too, had essentially been a Judeophile movement which *weakened* the German people by creating a denominational split in its ranks. Luther's fight against Rome had been a truly fateful blunder – on this the nominal Catholics, Eckart and Hitler, could readily agree. Martin Luther had prepared the way for Jewry, instead of seizing the historic opportunity of unifying the German people. He had therefore become the victim of the Jews, who, as in ancient Egypt, once again successfully encouraged fratricidal wars amongst the Gentiles. For this reason, according to Hitler, the Jews had naturally celebrated the great Reformer while ignoring his later antisemitism.[54] Luther's translation of the Old Testament into German had in fact been a disastrous action; it gave a Christian religious halo to the Jewish *Satansbibel* and thereby falsified completely the meaning of the Scriptures.

Too late, Luther had grasped the full magnitude of his error and reversed his earlier call for tolerance. If, instead of attacking Catholicism and Rome, Luther had only concentrated his fire from the beginning against Jewry, the history of Germany would have been quite different.[55] Thus while Eckart and Hitler recognized in Luther a great German and at the end of his life a 'powerful opponent of Jewry', his career as a whole was in their eyes a terrible tragedy. The 'substitute Lutherism' (*Lutherersatztum*) of the Puritans, the Anabaptists, Calvinists, Jehovah's Witnesses and other revolutionary Protestant sects was nothing but a product of the same subversive 'Jewish spirit' which had contaminated Christendom since its origins.[56] Nor was Luther's final solution to the 'Jewish question' (evoked by Eckart) – i.e. to burn their synagogues, schools and houses – of any help.[57] 'Burning them down would do us precious little good', Hitler claimed. 'Even if there had never been a synagogue or a Jewish school or the Old Testament, the Jewish spirit would still exist and exert its influence. It has been there from the beginning, and there is no Jew, not a single one, who does not personify it' (*der ihn nicht verkörperte*).[58] The 'Jewish spirit' (*der jüdische Geist*) had always been a symbol for the Austrian Catholic, Adolf Hitler, of intellectual subversion and revolutionary upheaval. The Exodus from Egypt, early Christianity, the Reformation and Bolshevism were simply some of its more pernicious fruits. On the other hand, Rome stood for Empire, hierarchy, civilization and a will-to-power which Catholicism had inherited.

In the 1920s Hitler could not have openly proclaimed that Christianity itself was an early prototype of Jewish Bolshevism without committing political suicide. Not only were there many Catholics and Protestants in the Nazi movement who would have been deeply offended, but the party would have alienated most of its potential electorate. By emphasizing, instead, fervent nationalism, anti-Communism and an opposition to Jewry still tinted with a Christian colouring, the Nazis could, however, be sure of attracting broad inter-denominational support. Hitler himself was well aware of this tactical consideration, telling General Ludendorff: '. . . I need, for the building up of a great political movement, the Catholics of Bavaria just as the Protestants of Prussia. The rest can come later.'[59] Indeed it was his sensitivity to this factor which partly led to the break with General Ludendorff, whose fanatical anti-Romanism infuriated Hitler, and to the expulsion of the Thuringian Nazi leader, Arthur Dinter, for founding a Protestant religious reform group called the *Geistchristliche Religionsgemeinschaft*. Equally significant was the fact that NSDAP policy in Bavaria deliberately sought to counter the negative image of Nazi atheism by emphasizing the slogan of 'positive Christianity', written into the party's official platform of 1920.[60] The Nazis even tried to present themselves (with some success) as defenders of traditional religious values in Bavaria and as the main barrier against godless Marxism.[61] Hitler's self-projection as a deeply religious figure and the conscious use of his Catholic background by the image-makers did much to offset the anticlerical reputation of the Nazi Party itself. Though his own views on Christianity did not ultimately differ from the hard-core anticlericalism of Rosenberg, Goebbels, Himmler and Bormann, the Führer managed to preserve his quasi-sacral image almost until the end of the Third Reich.

This was especially important given the negative attitudes, above all in Catholic circles, to the scurrilous attacks on Christianity by the NSDAP's chief ideologist, Alfred Rosenberg. Rosenberg's *The Myth of the Twentieth Century*, which was first published in October 1930, had advocated the abolition of the Old Testament, expurgation of the New Testament and the creation of a new German faith based on Nordic mysticism. The book was considered second only to *Mein Kampf* as a 'Bible' of the Nazi movement. The myths which it fostered, including blood-purity, Aryan-Nordic racial superiority and the neo-pagan cults of the swastika, Wotan worship, the old Norse gods and runes, stood in open contradiction to church teachings.

Christianity itself was denounced by Rosenberg as a race-destroying doctrine invented by Jews. The Roman Catholic Church, in particular, was singled out by this Protestant Balt for its 'Semitic-Latin' spirit, and for its pernicious 'internationalism' which had supposedly sprung from the 'oriental races' in Judea and Syria; Christianity as much as, if not more than, Judaism was depicted as the mortal enemy of the Teutonic master-race, poisoning its soul and negating its central values of honour, nobility, independence and freedom. Rosenberg's assault aroused the Catholic Church to an unusually energetic counter-attack led by Cardinal Faulhaber of Munich in 1934. But from the moment of its publication, Rosenberg's book had aroused a degree of Catholic antipathy which not even Hitler's reassuring remarks could altogether calm. The Nazi leader's embarrassment was evident.[62] Though he insisted that the *Myth* was Rosenberg's private work and did not represent official party policy, the chief NSDAP ideologue was allowed to retain his high position despite the book. In his *Table Talk*, Hitler later confessed that he had not read Rosenberg's opus, but 'like most of the Gauleiters, I have myself merely glanced cursorily at it'.[63]

Whatever annoyance Hitler may have personally felt at Rosenberg's lack of tactical finesse, there is no evidence to suggest that he profoundly disagreed with his anti-Christian theses. Shortly after the seizure of power he had confided to Julius Streicher that 'the religions are all alike' – they had no future. 'Fascism, if it likes, may come to terms with the Church. So shall I. Why not? That will not prevent me from tearing up Christianity root and branch, and annihilating it in Germany.'[64] The Germans were altogether more serious people than the Italians and French who could be 'heathens and Christians at the same time'. For the German people it *was* a matter of decisive significance 'whether they acknowledge the Jewish Christ-creed with its effeminate pity-ethics, or a strong, heroic belief in God in Nature, God in our own people, in our destiny, in our blood'.[65] Both the Old and New Testaments, Hitler informed Streicher, represented 'the same old Jewish swindle'; it was therefore impossible to clean up Christianity completely, but it was also unnecessary and harmful to confront it directly. The best strategy was to allow the churches to continue losing ground and to trap the priests eventually by exploiting 'their notorious greed and self-indulgence'. At the appropriate moment one could brand the monks and nuns as common criminals in the eyes of the masses. The sexual immorality and currency trials of 1936 and 1937 and the sustained campaign of vilification by the Nazi regime against monasteries and convents demonstrated that these were not idle threats.[66]

While Hitler was privately convinced that Christianity was already finished, he did not believe – unlike Rosenberg and Himmler – in the founding of a new Nordic religion. He favoured instead preserving traditional beliefs but changing their meaning. Christmas and Easter would eventually become symbols of the 'eternal renewal of our people' and the spirit of heroism and national freedom. Instead of worshipping the blood of the saviour, the masses would learn to 'worship the pure blood of our people'.[67] They would receive the fruits of the German soil as a 'divine gift'; the peasants would go back to their ancient, inherited beliefs and values which had been superficially overlaid by Christian mythology. 'The peasant will be told what the Church has destroyed for him: the whole of the secret knowledge of nature, of the divine, the shapeless, the daemonic. The peasant shall learn to hate the Church on that basis. Gradually he will be taught by what wiles the soul of the German has been raped. We shall wash off the Christian veneer and bring out a religion peculiar to our race.'[68]

In this passage Hitler came closest, perhaps, to the romantic, *völkisch* ideal of a return to the pre-Christian (and therefore pre-Judaic) roots of German history – to a non-alienated sense of wholeness in the union of nature, blood and soil.[69] Christianity was inevitably perceived as alien to this Nazi dream of a timeless communitarian utopia rooted in racial homogeneity. It was also profoundly alien to Hitler's belief that 'God' or 'Providence' were identical with the laws of nature – according to which the strong must prevail over the weak and power guarantees right. A vulgar Nietzscheanism allied to his own combative temperament led Hitler to utterly despise the Christian values of charity, meekness and humility, which he saw as part of the 'slave-revolt' in morals first championed by Judaism. Such Judeo-Christian values were clearly incompatible with the Nazi vision of a *Herrenvolk* based on the natural rights of a superior race to dominion.

It was probably no accident that Himmler, Rosenberg, Goebbels and Martin Bormann, the most committed among the other top Nazi leaders to race theory, also fully shared this aspect of Hitler's *Christenhass*. The central difference between them was that Hitler for tactical reasons preferred publicly to disguise his antipathy to Christianity. He had not yet abandoned the hope that the Christian churches might still join him in a joint anti-Jewish struggle. In April 1933, in his first conversation as Reich Chancellor with the Catholic Bishop Berning from Osnabrück, Hitler had for example explained that his *Judenpolitik* was based on the principles pursued for 1,500 years by the Catholic Church. Only in the modern liberal era had the Church no longer correctly perceived the Jewish danger.[70] Clearly, at this time Hitler still expected to win support from the churches for his anti-Jewish legislation. But in a three-hour discussion in Novemebr 1936 with Cardinal Faulhaber, Hitler was already more critical, demanding that the Catholic Church abandon its opposition to racial legislation. If National Socialism did not triumph over Bolshevism, he warned the Cardinal, then it was all over for Christianity and the Roman Church in Europe.[71]

The decisive shift in Hitler's attitude to the churches appears to have come in 1937–8, which significantly coincided with the growing radicalization of Nazi policy towards the Jews. Increasingly it seemed to the Nazi leadership that the Christian churches were 'allies' of Judaism rather than of National Socialism.[72] The churches still persisted, for example, in regarding the Old Testament as a major source of Christian revelation; they had rejected the cult of the 'Aryan' Jesus; in Protestant circles a militant opposition had emerged to the Nazi-sponsored *Deutsche Christen*; moreover, in 1937 the Vatican had released the papal encyclical *Mit Brennender Sorge* (With Deep Anxiety) which sharply protested at Nazi violations of the Concordat with the Holy See. Though German Catholic and Protestant leaders avoided expressing any sympathy for persecuted Jews, they did by and large oppose the assault on the Jewish origins of Christianity and condemn certain manifestations of Nazi neo-paganism. Even such mealy-mouthed and passive opposition was sufficient to convince Hitler that Christianity had been infiltrated by 'Jewish' influences and that there was no hope for co-operation, let alone an 'Aryan' renewal of Christianity.[73]

Hitler's growing antagonism to the churches found its full expression, however, only during the war years, in particular once the 'Final Solution' had already begun to be implemented. On the night of 11–12 July 1941, shortly after the invasion of Russia, he declared that the coming of Christianity had been 'the heaviest blow that ever struck humanity'.[74] It had been responsible for the extinction of the Roman Empire and of fifteen centuries of civilization at a stroke. Sounding like a caricature of the great eighteenth-century English historian Edward Gibbon, Hitler liked to pontificate on how the ancient world had been enlightened by the idea of tolerance. Christianity, on the other hand, was 'the first creed in the world to exterminate its adversaries in the name of love'.[75] Worst of all, 'Bolshevism is Christianity's illegitimate child'. Both were 'inventions of the Jew'. The deliberate lie of religion had been first introduced into the world by Christianity. 'Bolshevism practises a lie of the same nature, when it claims to bring liberty to men, whereas in reality it seeks only to enslave them.'[76]

Hitler increasingly emphasized the parallels between Christianity and Bolshevism as subversive doctrines which were destructive of culture – both deriving their origin from the same tainted Jewish 'ferment of decomposition'. Thus on 21 October 1941 he observed: 'Whilst Roman society proved hostile to the new doctrine, Christianity in its pure state stirred the population to revolt. Rome was Bolshevized, and Bolshevism produced exactly the same results in Rome as later in Russia.'[77] Under the influence of the Germanic spirit, Christianity had subsequently lost its 'openly Bolshevistic character' and became almost tolerable, but with its contemporary collapse 'the Jew restores to pride of place Christianity in its Bolshevistic form'.[78] The objective was to destroy nations by 'vitiating their racial integrity'. Under Jewish rule in

Russia, hundreds of thousands of men were deported and their women delivered 'to males imported from other regions'. Race-mixing, in Hitler's feverish imagination, had now become a synonym for Christianity as well as Jewish Bolshevism!

The Judeo-Christian-Bolshevik assault on civilization was itself one of the ostensible reasons given by Hitler for the 'Final Solution' – incredible as the amalgam may sound to a contemporary ear. 'In the old days, as now, destruction of art and civilization. The Bolsheviks of their day, what didn't they destroy in Rome, in Greece and elsewhere? They've behaved in the same way amongst us and in Russia. One must compare the art and civilization of the Romans – their temples, their houses – with the art and civilization represented at the same period by the abject rabble of the catacombs. In the old days, the destruction of the libraries. Isn't that what happened in Russia? The result: a frightful levelling-down. Didn't the world see, carried on right into the Middle Ages, the same old system of martyrs, tortures, faggots? Of old, it was in the name of Christianity. Today, it's in the name of Bolshevism. Yesterday, the instigator was Saul: the instigator today, Mordochai. Saul has changed into St. Paul, and Mordochai into Karl Marx. By exterminating this pest, we shall do humanity a service of which our soldiers can have no idea.'[79]

Hitler's obsession with the crypto-Marxist St Paul while the *Einsatzgruppen* were busy massacring countless Jews in the Russian steppes indicated the depths of his hysterical Christophobia. Following his old mentor, Dietrich Eckart, he saw in Paul 'the first man to take account of the possible advantages of using a religion as a means of propaganda'. The Jews had basically destroyed the Roman Empire from the moment that 'St Paul transformed a local movement of Aryan opposition to Jewry into a supra-temporal religion, which postulates the equality of all men among themselves, and their obedience to an only God'.[80] Pauline Christianity and its offshoots in the Reformation and modern Bolshevism meant the death of all empires. Unlike Athens, where the tradition of Greek philosophy was far superior 'to this poverty-stricken rubbish', decadent Rome had been an ideal terrain for St Paul. 'His egalitarian theories had what was needed to win over a mass composed of innumerable uprooted people.'[81]

In the tradition of late nineteenth-century German anti-Christian racialism, Hitler sharply distinguished between Jesus and Paul. The latter had simply inverted the 'anti-Jewish' teachings of the Nazarene and turned them against Rome. Whereas 'the Romans were tolerance itself', allowing every man to pray to the god of his choice and even reserving a place in the temples for the unknown god, St Paul had concocted the insane idea of a universal god over and above the State. 'On the road to Damascus, St Paul discovered that he could succeed in ruining the Roman State by causing the principle to triumph of the equality of all men before a single God – and by putting beyond the reach of the law his private notions, which he alleged to be divinely inspired. If, into the bargain, one succeeded in imposing one man as the representative on earth of the only God, that man would possess boundless power.'[82] In other words, St Paul's egalitarian monotheism was a political tool to incite the masses against the Roman state. But the real gods of the Jews remained, as always, money and power. The Jew continued to worship, 'then and now, nothing but the golden calf'. In Antiquity, as in the modern world, he was simultaneously capitalist and Bolshevik.

St Paul's proto-Bolshevism had marked the end for Hitler of the reign of 'the clear Graeco-Latin genius'.[83] In place of the peace and harmony of the natural order with its 'hierarchy amongst nations', the Jews through the cover of Christianity had introduced the mad conception of a Beyond! Life here below thereby became negligible – since it would only 'flourish later, when it no longer exists'.[84] Under the mask of religion, the Jew had as a consequence 'introduced intolerance in a sphere in which tolerance formerly prevailed'. Even worse, Judeo-Christianity had deliberately subverted the natural order. 'It constantly provokes the revolt of the weak against the strong, of bestiality against intelligence, of quantity against quality. It took fourteen centuries for Christianity to reach the peak of savagery and stupidity. We would therefore be wrong to sin by excess of confidence and proclaim our definite victory over Bolshevism. The more we render the Jew incapable of harming us, the more we shall protect ourselves from this danger. The Jew plays in nature the role of a catalysing element. A people that is rid of its Jews returns spontaneously to the natural order.'[85]

In such passages Hitler echoed the central themes of anti-Christian antisemitism in Germany, which for sixty years had denounced Judeo-Christian morality as antithetical to nature, to the life-force and the human instinct for survival. Not surprisingly, then, Hitler showed a clear preference for classical Antiquity and for the Far Eastern cultures which believed in the perpetual renewal of living beings – especially for the Japanese, whom Hitler admired above all for their sharp racial instincts.[86] When adopting his philosophical pose, Hitler could occasionally sound like a man of the Enlightenment – a latter-day Voltaire combining belief in 'toleration' and science with hatred of superstition, of Jewry and the Church. On the night of 20–21 February 1942, for example, he fantasized about building an observatory in his boyhood hometown of Linz, where Johann Kepler had once lived. 'To open the eyes of simple people, there's no better method of instruction than the picture. Put a small telescope in a village, and you destroy a world of superstitions.'[87] The Church, on the other hand, had always exploited 'poverty of spirit', the ignorance of the masses and their credulity. 'Christianity is the worst of the regressions that mankind can ever have undergone', Hitler insisted, 'and it's the Jew who, thanks to this diabolic invention, has thrown him back fifteen centuries. The only thing that would still be worse would be victory for the Jew through Bolshevism. If Bolshevism triumphed, mankind would lose the gift of laughter and joy.'[88]

Christianity, however, fared little better in Hitler's eyes – a religion of 'intolerance and persecution', which was the 'bloodiest conceivable'.[89] It had denied all the joys of the senses, the primacy of the beautiful and the riches of nature. Calvinist Protestantism, which had all 'the warmth of an iceberg', was especially stifling in its hypocrisy.[90] The Catholic Church was admittedly more adroit, though it, too, had not lost contact with its Jewish origins. But Catholic priests did at least recognize human weakness, which made life more endurable in Catholic regions. The Roman Church, as always, earned her living from the sins of the faithful and declared herself satisfied with confession. 'Indulgence, at a tariff', Hitler observed, 'supplies the Church with her daily bread.' But the laxity of Catholicism could not change the fundamentally subversive character of Christianity which, according to Hitler, had not only destroyed the libraries of Antiquity but was even responsible for the burning of Rome![91] The collapse of Rome, which had led to 'a night that lasted for centuries', remained the most potent historical analogy in Hitler's arsenal. He would endlessly evoke it in his *Table Talk* to explain his own twentieth-century crusade against Judeo-Christianity and Bolshevism. However paradoxical it may sound, this eschatological war had an explicitly *anti-messianic* character. For the wartime monologues present religion as a form of collective madness, a long history of interminable atrocities, including the burning of heretics, witches and free-thinkers, climaxing above all in the Inquisition.

Naturally Hitler had Christianity in mind as the archetype of such a persecutory religion. 'One cannot succeed in conceiving how much cruelty, ignominy and falsehood the intrusion of Christianity has spelt for this world of ours', he announced on the night of 3 February 1942.[92] This collective madness had been exclusively due to the Jews, who had deliberately fixed the attention of non-Jews on that which *did not exist*, in order to blind them to what was material and real. This 'diabolic stratagem' was an 'excellent calculation' which had enabled the Jews to exploit Gentiles for centuries. If the victims had only realized what was going on, then 'all Jews would be exterminated'. 'But, this time, the Jews will disappear from Europe', Hitler assured his small circle of listeners. 'The world will breathe freely and recover its sense of joy, when this weight is no longer crushing its shoulders.'[93]

The disappearance of the Jews, however, would not be enough by itself. The 'Jewish spirit', too, as he had warned Dietrich Eckart twenty years earlier, would have to be eradicated. That meant destroying the hold of 'the Jewish pettyfoggery of the Old Testament' and especially of Christianity on the popular mind.[94] The only Divine Commandment in Hitler's New Order would be the preservation of the species. 'Thou shalt not kill', the ancient Mosaic commandment which for three millennia had laid the normative basis for human civilization, would be consigned to dust. In its place would come the Darwinian law of nature which Hitler regarded as the beginning of wisdom – that all living creatures devour each other and the strongest survive. To act against this law was to revolt against Heaven itself.[95] This, then, was the return to the natural order which Hitler had always preached and which inevitably brought Nazism on to a confrontation course with Christianity.

National Socialism, in spite of its agnosticism, did not, however, emerge as a simple antithesis of Christian faith and culture, for its conviction that the world was dominated by an 'evil, tyrannous power of boundless destructiveness', symbolized by the demonic Jews, came straight out of medieval Christian chiliasm.[96] Like the apocalyptic movements of the late Middle Ages, Nazism endowed social conflicts with transcendental significance and dreamed of a last decisive struggle of the 'chosen people' (metamorphosed into a *Herrenvolk*) for victory. Its dreams of a thousand-year-Reich recalled the medieval prophecies derived from Joachitic speculation. In their obsessive fear of annihilation, imminent ontological disaster and ultimate redemption through violent action, the Nazis also followed an established pattern of Christian millenarianism.[97]

Nevertheless these parallels were not conscious and they do not change the essentially secular political character of the Nazi phenomenon, which unquestionably sought to root out Christianity once the war was over.[98] To move from Christian to Nazi antisemitism was to make a fateful step from an uncomfortable to a lethal fever, as Milton Himmelfarb recently put it. The 'Final Solution' did not, after all, have any Christian precedent. Indeed, it was arguably the weakening of Christian morality and its ultimate collapse in most of Europe which permitted the anti-Jewish mythology of Christendom to find its horrible consummation in the death camps.[99]

The real chasm between National Socialism and Christianity was perhaps best summed up by the most sinister and mysterious figure in Hitler's immediate entourage, Martin Bormann. The head of the Party Chancellery and private secretary of the Führer, Bormann acquired extraordinary power during the Second World War, controlling all questions concerning the security of the regime, party affairs, appointments and promotions. A fierce guardian of Nazi orthodoxy, Bormann was an arch-fanatic on racial policy and prime advocate of the *Kirchenkampf* (war against the churches). In a confidential memo to *Gauleiters* in 1942 he had written that the power of the churches 'must absolutely and finally be broken'. The sharpest anticlerical in the Nazi leadership (he collected all the files of cases against the clergy that he could lay his hands on), Bormann almost certainly contributed something to radicalizing Hitler's hostility to Christianity.

On the night of 29 November 1944, during the course of one of the Führer's familiar diatribes against the Jews, St Paul and Christianity, Bormann suddenly broke out of his sinister anonymity, to expound the essence of Nazi antisemitism and *Christenhass.* Hitler had repeated his by now classic theme that 'the religion fabricated by Paul of Tarsus, which was later called Christianity, is nothing but the Communism of today'.[100] According to the protocol, Bormann then summed up: 'Jewish methods, he said, have never varied in their essentials. Everywhere they have stirred up the *plebs* against the ruling classes. Everywhere they have fostered discontent against the established power. For these are the crops which produce the crop they hope later to gather. Everywhere they fan the flames of hatred between people of the same blood. It is they who invented class-warfare, and the repudiation of this theory must therefore always be an anti-Jewish measure. In the same way any doctrine which is anti-Communist, any doctrine which is anti-Christian must *ipso facto*, be anti-Jewish as well. The National Socialist doctrine is therefore anti-Jewish in *excelsis*, for it is both anti-Communist and anti-Christian.'[101]

CHAPTER EIGHT

# Swastika,
# Crescent and Star of David

Adolf Hitler had first encountered Zionism as a young man in Vienna. Only three years before his arrival in the Habsburg capital, the founder of political Zionism, Theodor Herzl, had been laid to rest in the hills surrounding Vienna. The prophet of the Jewish state had in his youth been an ardent apostle of *Deutschtum* in its liberal pan-German form, like many assimilated Jews in Austria. Subsequently, Herzl had become convinced by the rise of political antisemitism that Jews would never be fully accepted in non-Jewish environments. His awakening is generally attributed by historians to the impact on him of the Dreyfus Affair in France. But Viennese antisemitism, which Herzl knew at first hand, was a much more dynamic and significant electoral phenomenon in the 1890s than its French counterpart.[1]

Both Herzl and Hitler in their opposite ways were products of the same antisemitic maelstrom of *fin de siècle* Austria-Hungary, exacerbated as it was by endless racial conflicts. Both came to recognize the Jews as a *single* people rather than a mere confession and to reject the viability of liberal emancipation as a 'solution' to the Jewish problem. Several European antisemites, especially in France, Hungary and the German-speaking countries, initially even welcomed Herzl's *Der Judenstaat* for precisely this reason. They were attracted by his proposal for an orderly exodus of Jews from Europe to a state of their own.[2] The convergence was not surprising, for both antisemites and Zionists could readily agree that the assimilation of Jews was undesirable, even if for different reasons; both regarded the influx of too many Jews into a given society as bound to produce a hostile backlash; both deplored the over-concentration of Jews in certain professions, their excessive wealth and at the same time the prominent participation of Jews in revolutionary movements. On the face of things here was a promising basis for 'collaboration'.[3] *Fin de siècle* antisemites like Dühring in Germany, von Schoenerer in Austria, von Istoczy in Hungary or Drumont in France wished simply enough to rid their countries of 'alien intruders'; Herzl and the Zionist movement wished, on the other hand, to save Jews. But both camps agreed that Jews should leave

Europe, if the elements of friction with Gentile society were not to lead to catastrophic consequences.

Herzl had convinced himself that it was both possible and desirable to do business with such Jew-haters, on the basis of national self-interest. Antisemitism could be 'used' to solve the Jewish question in a mutually satisfactory manner for both parties – a legacy which he handed down to the Zionist movement.[4] This strategy had one major flaw – it failed to see that radical antisemitism would ultimately *deny the right of Jewish existence per se*, including that of a Jewish state.[5] Zionism itself in the course of time would come to be perceived as an integral part of the perennial Jewish 'conspiracy', for many radical antisemites genuinely believed that the Jews were doomed by their 'parasitic' nature to live in exile at the expense of their host nations; since the Jews were congenitally incapable of creating an independent state, the only possible purpose of Zionism in their eyes was to provide a mask for the secret Jewish aim of world-power by subverting other nations. It was exactly in this spirit of the 'Protocols of Zion' that Alfred Rosenberg had interpreted the Jewish national movement. Hitler, too, regarded Zionism in a similar light, writing in *Mein Kampf*: 'The Jew's domination in the state seems so assured that now not only can he call himself a Jew again, but he ruthlessly admits his ultimate national and political designs. A section of this race openly owns itself to be a foreign people, yet even here they lie. For while the Zionists try to make the rest of the world believe that the national consciousness of the Jew finds its satisfaction in the creation of a Palestinian state, the Jews again slyly dupe the dumb Goyim. It doesn't even enter their heads to build up a Jewish state in Palestine for the purpose of living there; all they want is a central organization for their international world swindle, endowed with sovereign rights and removed from the intervention of other states: a haven for convicted scoundrels and a university for budding crooks. It is a sign of their rising confidence and sense of security that at a time when one section is still playing the German, the Frenchman or Englishman, the other with open effrontery comes out as the Jewish race.'[6]

For Hitler, Zionism clinched his thesis that Jews were intrinsically all of one piece, even though, as he recalled, in pre-war Vienna 'the great majority condemned and inwardly rejected such a formulation'. But, examined more closely, Jewish anti-Zionist pretensions dissolved 'into an unsavoury vapour of pretexts advanced for mere reasons of expedience, not to say lies',[7] for the so-called liberal Jews simply regarded Zionists 'as Jews with an impractical, perhaps even dangerous, way of publicly avowing their Jewishness'.[8] This pseudo-struggle between Zionist and anti-Zionist Jews disgusted Hitler, 'for it was false through and through, founded on lies and scarcely in keeping with the moral elevation and purity always claimed by this people'.[9]

Hitler's wholly negative view of Zionism had been influenced both by his mentor Dietrich Eckart and by the foremost Nazi philosopher, Alfred Rosenberg, whose *Die Spur des Juden im Wandel der Zeiten* (The Trace of the Jews in the Wanderings of Time) (1919) had presented the movement as an international conspiracy designed to protect Jewish intrigues and promote crooked dealings. In a lengthy pamphlet, first published in 1922 and significantly entitled *Der Staatsfeindliche Zionismus*, Rosenberg had expounded further on the domestic and foreign danger represented by Zionism.[10] In the first place it was an *international* rather than a genuine national movement, which aimed to unify world Jewry on a political basis. It had aligned itself with the enemies of the German Reich during the First World War and controlled the financial strings of British policy, as the Balfour Declaration of November 1917 had decisively proved.[11] Behind Zionism stood the occult conspiracy between big Jewish bankers like Rothschild and Jewish revolutionaries like Trotsky, Zinoviev and Radek who had overthrown Tsarism.[12] Both had acted in close liaison with British interests in order to weaken Germany and subject it to the dictates of the Entente. At the same time the Zionists had transformed the Arab majority in Palestine into second-class citizens in the service of British imperialism.[13] Zionism was therefore in no sense a *völkisch* movement of national renaissance but one more manifestation of a voracious Jewish imperialism, seeking to accumulate money and power at the expense of non-Jews. It bore a close affinity to Bolshevism, for it threatened all states with its subversive designs.[14] At the same time, while supporting Bolshevism, the Zionists had cunningly linked their future with the United States, the nerve-centre of world Jewry, which was already being used to pressure the British Empire to meet its demands. As part of its global strategy Zionism sought to unite together all strands of Jewry – liberal, national, orthodox or left-wing – in a pan-Jewish movement which was invariably hostile to German national interests.[15]

More importantly, from an ideological viewpoint, it was clear to both Rosenberg and Hitler that the creation of a Jewish state in Palestine would be a contradiction in terms.[16] Since Jewry was *a priori* defined as a usurious international race, incapable of creative endeavour in the fields of art, science and politics, all the efforts by Zionists to productivize this nation were doomed to failure.[17] In *Mein Kampf* Hitler had pontificated that 'the Jewish State' was completely unlimited as to territory. This resulted not so much from the dispersion of the Jews as from the lack of 'an idealistic attitude' and especially of 'a correct interpretation of the concept of work'. Without these prerequisites, neither 'a spatially delimited State' nor a true culture could arise.[18] The Jews, deprived of these virtues, were the archetype of a *parasitic* cosmopolitan people, lacking all the qualities of state-building displayed by Aryan nations. Their diasporic existence inevitably resulted from the perpetual need to find 'a new feeding ground' for the race. At all times the Jew had lived 'in the states of other peoples, and there formed his own state, which to be sure, habitually sailed under the disguise of "religious community" as long as outward circumstances made a complete revelation of his nature seem inadvisable'.[19]

Thus, for Hitler, Zionism was in the nature of things a *non sequitur* which stood in fundamental contradiction to the racial characteristics (*Eigenart*) of Jewry. This race without roots which aspired to world domination had never seriously tried to establish an independent state because this would conflict with its unnatural mode of existence.[20] The Jew was in any case no more capable of building such a state than he was of founding an art, a culture or an army of his own. He neither could nor wished to farm the land, clear the forests, or build his own temples. How could a Jewish state be constructed by such a race of middlemen and exploiters? The best illustration of what would happen if such a 'State' ever came into being was Soviet Russia, which had been reduced to the level of 'a ruined civilisation, a colony ripe for development through alien capital'.[21] Whereas the state-building Nordic races had always recognized the creative value of labour and the supremacy of the collective over the individual, Jewry could only function through parasitic exploitation and the triumph of anarchic egoism.

Hence Zionism was 'nothing but a comedy', so much dust in the eyes of the Gentiles.[22] At any time in the past, the Jews, if they had so desired, could have established a state of their own but they had preferred to remain 'a state within the state', corrupting and subjugating the nations through banking and usury.[23] Hence, as Hitler sarcastically suggested in a speech in Munich on 13 August 1920, the only conceivable purpose of a Zionist state would be to grant Jewish crooks and swindlers immunity from prosecution in their countries of residence.[24] The real power of Jewry, as Hitler never tired of stating, lay in their control of international finance. For this purpose a nerve-centre in Jerusalem would undoubtedly be useful; but the mass of Jews could have no interest in toiling to establish a desert kingdom that possessed none of the raw materials necessary for the making of a modern nation.[25] The new Zion might perhaps strengthen the 'political backbone' of the Jews, as Hitler admitted to Dietrich Eckart; but he had no illusions about their readiness to leave the fleshpots of the Diaspora voluntarily.[26] Tiny Palestine could, in any case, scarcely provide for the masses of Jewry, still continuing their parasitic existence in the pores of non-Jewish society. Moreover,

Zionism would never be able to alter the unchangeable Jewish character, as
the Viennese Jewish philosopher, Otto Weininger, had already warned at the
turn of the century.[27] On this point, Weininger, Eckart and Hitler, in spite of
the many differences in emphasis between them, could agree. The Zionist
'revolution' would be unable to overcome the Diasporic essence of Judaism.

The ideology of racial determinism underlying the Nazi view of Zionism
did not have to confront reality until 1933. Only after coming into office did
Hitler fully realize that overseas Jewish retaliation against the Third Reich
might seriously undermine his efforts to rebuild the German economy; he
became increasingly worried by the effects of a Jewish-inspired anti-Nazi
boycott which could damage the exports of the Reich, its foreign currency
reserves and the war on unemployment.[28] The advice he received from his
Economics Minister Hjalmar Schacht, and the pressure exerted by German
exporters who feared the loss of foreign markets and millions of Reichsmarks,
forced him to seek a way of breaking the boycott.[29] Zionism offered such an
opportunity, the prospect of opening up a breach in the world-wide Jewish
resistance to the Reich which appeared to threaten Germany's economic
recovery.[30] The German Zionist leader Kurt Blumenfeld had already told
Goering in March 1933 that only the Zionist movement possessed the
international organization to call a halt to the anti-German boycott.[31] He
had indicated that Palestine was the obvious haven for German Jewry, as the
Zionists had always maintained, provided that Jewish middle-class and
professional people could leave with part of their property and assets intact.
This was the basic *quid pro quo* demanded by the Zionists, who looked not
only to Jewish immigration but to an influx of German Jewish investment
capital to help build up the *Yishuv* in Palestine.

It seemed a small price for the Nazis to pay in 1933, obsessed as they were
by expelling as many Jews as possible, reconstituting the Treasury and
finding employment for masses of Germans. The 200,000 Jews in far-off
Palestine, scattered in unconnected enclaves across the mandated territory,
did not constitute any obvious danger to the Reich. Perhaps it was preferable
to have Jewish refugees there than in neighbouring countries like France,
Belgium, Holland, Czechoslovakia or Britain where they could whip up
anti-German propaganda.[32] Palestine looked like an even more convenient
dumping-ground, given that the British controlled the country and the Arab
majority could be counted on to cause trouble for them and to check any
excessive Jewish ambitions. At the same time Hitler could even pose in
October 1933 as Jewry's benefactor as against his British critics. The
mandatory power's immigration restrictions permitted only wealthy Jewish
capitalists into Palestine, over and above the rather narrow established

quotas. 'In England people assert that their arms are open to welcome all the oppressed, especially the Jews who have left Germany . . .', Hitler sarcastically observed. 'But it would be still finer if England did not make her great gesture dependent on the possession of £1,000. . . .'[33] While the British restricted Jewish entry into the National Home, 'we wild folk have once more proved ourselves better humans', the Führer added, with a cynical eye to the propaganda benefits of his policy.

Palestine's economic importance to Germany at the time of the Great Depression was by no means negligible.[34] If, as happened under the Transfer Agreement, the purchase of German goods was linked to settling Jews in Palestine, this would further the economy of the Reich at a critical moment and provide a possible gateway for German exports into the Middle East market. From the Zionist point of view, the benefit was equally obvious. The new immigrants brought with them an influx of money, equipment and technical know-how as well as increased employment for the *Yishuv*. Zionism had in any case always preached the need for a permanent solution to the problem of anti-Jewish persecution. The Transfer Agreement (*Ha'avara*) signed in the summer of 1933 therefore seemed a perfect bargain, even if it was struck with the self-proclaimed Enemy No. 1 of the Jewish people. In essence, German Jews would be exchanged for the purchase of German goods by the *Yishuv*. A momentary convergence of interests had led to a situation in which, as Edwin Black has recently put it, 'the national aspirations of both Nazis and Zionists hinged on the successful removal of Jews from Germany to Palestine'.[35] The Nazis between 1933 and 1937 desired above all to strengthen the economy and to rid Germany of its Jews, and for the sake of this priority they temporarily ignored their own ideological opposition to Zionism. The Zionist movement, on the other hand, was prepared to override the international Jewish boycott and a natural reluctance to give legitimacy to the Hitler regime, for the sake of building a Jewish homeland in Palestine.[36] Both sides hoped to use each other to obtain their economic and political goals, regarding the relationship as above all a practical one.

Nevertheless, for a few years a degree of ideological détente arising from the *de facto* co-operation prevailed in certain circles within both camps. On the Nazi side, the most interesting case was that of Baron Leopold von Mildenstein, who in the summer of 1935 became the head of the Security Service's (SD) Jewish department. He had travelled to Palestine in the spring of 1933 at the invitation of Kurt Tuchler, of the German Zionist Federation. Though a member of the NSDAP and of the SS, von Mildenstein, who came from an aristocratic Austro-Hungarian background, was an ardent 'Zionist' who believed that Jewish national aspirations should be encouraged as a matter of practical policy. His very positive impressions of Jewish Palestine were recorded in an illustrated series for Joseph Goebbels' *Der Angriff* which ran from 26 September to 9 October 1934. Entitled 'Ein Nazi fahrt nach Palästina' (A Nazi Travels to Palestine), the series captured something of the vitality and exuberance of Jewish life in Palestine in the 1930s.[37] It depicted a hard-working, self-confident new breed of Jew who had finally kicked off the middle-class existence of the Diaspora. Von Mildenstein had obviously been impressed by Zionist achievements in the areas of agriculture, education and colonization, by the *Kvutzot* (small collective settlements) and *Kibbutzim*; in Palestine he encountered for the first time Jews who were rooted in the soil. 'This new Jew', he concluded, 'will be a new people.'[38] While not ignoring the intensity of Arab opposition to British rule and to the Jewish National Home, he was nonetheless convinced that the presence of 250,000 Jews in Palestine was a reality which could no longer be denied.

As a liberal Nazi, von Mildenstein could still display some sympathy for the Zionist section of Jewry, in those early years of the Hitler regime. Moreover, his ideas found an echo in the SS, ironically enough the most 'pro-Zionist' wing of the NSDAP in the mid-1930s. The intelligence arm of the SS, under Reinhard Heydrich, genuinely believed at that time that mass emigration to Palestine was the only practical way to make Germany *judenrein*. Therefore, the position of the Zionists within German Jewry had to be strengthened, their cultural activities were encouraged and certain 'privileges' provided for Zionist functionaries, youth groups and vocational training centres.[39] In May 1935, Heydrich, in an article for the official SS organ *Das Schwarze Korps*, remarked on the importance of distinguishing between Zionists and assimilationists. 'The Zionists adhere to a strict racial position', he wrote, 'and by emigrating to Palestine they are helping to build their own Jewish state.'[40] Hence there seemed to be no reason for the SS to oppose the Zionist movement, especially at a time when most of German Jewry was still tenaciously trying to cling to a foothold in the Third Reich. Under the Nuremberg Laws of 15 September 1935, the regime even gave official recognition to the blue and white Star of David as the one flag that Jews were permitted to fly.

It was during this period of Nazi–Zionist détente that Adolf Eichmann first entered the SD's Jewish department at von Mildenstein's invitation.[41] Eichmann described his mentor to the Israeli police in 1960 as 'an open-minded, friendly sort, a native of Austria' who was the only man at Central SD Headquarters 'capable of providing me with reliable and thorough information about Jews'.[42] It was von Mildenstein who gave Eichmann a copy of Herzl's *Der Judenstaat* for study and he soon became an 'authority' on Zionism. According to Eichmann, the SS was still searching in 1935 for a 'political solution' and sharply opposed the vulgar *Stürmer* method of attacking Jews.[43] The contacts with Zionists were generally courteous and Eichmann was actually instructed by Heydrich to accept an invitation to visit Palestine in 1937. This brief trip came to nothing and the report on the journey by Eichmann and Herbert Hagen presented an extremely negative picture of Palestine from the economic and moral angle. Moreover, the report openly opposed the further transfer of Jewish capital abroad as a loss to the German Reich of sources of hard currency; even more important, Eichmann and Hagen noted that 'since the above-said annual emigration would primarily strengthen the Jews in Palestine, this plan must be rejected in view of the fact that German national policy opposes the establishment of an independent state in Palestine'.[44] In other words, Eichmann's 'Zionism' was no more than a temporary reflection of the prevailing climate in SS circles and the orientation of German foreign policy in general.

Once this began to change in 1937 with the realization by the German Foreign Office that the creation of a Jewish state in Palestine would be inimical to the interests of the Reich, Eichmann quickly readjusted his views.[45] Nevertheless, just as the Transfer Agreement continued until the outbreak of the Second World War, so too did some limited degree of co-operation between Zionist emissaries from Palestine and the SS. For example, Eichmann, who had been transferred to Vienna after the *Anschluss*, was helpful in providing facilities for Zionist vocational training camps; Gestapo officials unofficially encouraged the illegal immigration of Jews into British Mandatory Palestine. The Nazis even in 1939 were still primarily interested in forcing out as many Jews as possible from German-controlled territories; the Zionist organizations, for their part, could only welcome the reality that every new Jewish immigrant strengthened the *Yishuv* in Palestine.

The extraordinary fact is that this brutal Nazi emigration policy inadvertently contributed to saving at least 60,000 German Jews from the Holocaust which was shortly to descend on the European continent. An even more astounding irony is that those officials like Heydrich and Eichmann who were later most directly involved in implementing the mass murder of European Jews should in the 1930s have been active in encouraging their emigration to Palestine. There seems little doubt that their directives came from the very top and were part of the Reich's cat-and-mouse game with the Jews, the Arabs and the Western democracies. Possibly, for a few months in the second half of 1937, the Führer had wavered, uncertain of the wisdom of the Transfer Agreement. But in early 1938 the German career diplomat Otto von Hentig, who was sympathetic to Zionism, told Ernest Marcus (the Berlin representative for *Ha'avara*) that the matter had been settled: 'The Führer had made an affirmative decision and all obstacles in the way of emigration to Palestine had been removed.'[46]

This decision was all the more notable in view of the sudden panic engendered in the German government and Nazi Party by the Peel partition plan of June 1937 which had proposed the establishment of a tiny Jewish state alongside an Arab state and a British mandatory enclave in Palestine. This official report by a British Royal Commission had considerable prestige behind it and could not be lightly dismissed. Though far from satisfying Zionist aspirations in full, its proposals were eventually accepted by Weizmann, Ben-Gurion and the mainstream Zionist leadership. Its recommendations were in fact never to be implemented by the British government, partly as a result of Arab pressure and in part through fear of the consequences for imperial defence in the eventuality of a new world war. Nevertheless for the first time the prospect of a Jewish state in the Middle East appeared as a real possibility which the Nazi regime had to take into account. As a consequence it must have become apparent to Hitler that he might unintentionally be financing the development of a Jewish homeland through the mechanism of the Transfer Agreement.

Within only a few years a commercial-industrial infrastructure had indeed been established in Palestine, paid for largely out of the assets of German Jews. The trade agreement which had been conceived in the *interests of the Reich* was now producing undesirable economic and political consequences; the population of Jewish Palestine had doubled by 1936, its economy was rapidly expanding and, most important of all, the British government had recognized the reality of its aspirations for national independence. The foundations of what is called in Zionist historiography the *Medina ba-derech* (the state in the making) had been laid, in part thanks to the blind hatred and greed of the Nazis themselves. If Hitler had perhaps hoped to embarrass the British government by encouraging an Arab backlash to this Jewish influx into Palestine, then the manoeuvre seemed to have boomeranged. It is more plausible to assume that he had simply been motivated by a mixture of pragmatic considerations relating to the need to break the anti-Nazi boycott, to reinforce the German economy, and by the unchanged ideological imperative of clearing the Reich of Jews, in preparation for another world war.

At no time, not even between 1933 and 1939, did Hitler support the idea of a Jewish territorial state in Palestine. According to von Hentig, 'he saw in such a state a second Vatican which might become a spiritual centre for the international Jewish conspiracy, in which view he was being strengthened by Goebbels'.[47] He had anxiously interrogated Lord Halifax about the matter during the visit of the British statesman to Berlin on a special mission.[48] On 22 June 1937 a circular letter of the Foreign Office was sent out to all German posts abroad which expressed the underlying anti-Zionist orientation of Nazi policy. Signed by Bülow-Schwante, it stated that it was in the interests of Nazi Germany to keep the Jews dispersed since they were permanent enemies of the Reich. 'For when no member of the Jewish race is settled on German soil any longer, the Jewish question will still not be solved for Germany. Rather, the developments of recent years have shown that international Jewry will of necessity always be the ideological and therefore the political enemy of National Socialist Germany.'[49] Territorial concentration in Palestine or elsewhere could only strengthen this irreconcilable enemy. The British government was therefore informed of the negative attitude of the Reich towards the establishment of a Jewish state.

The Bülow-Schwante memorandum represented the views of *Referat Deutschland*, the 'Nazi' section of the Foreign Office, which, like the German Templar colonists in Palestine, the Ribbentrop Bureau, the Propaganda Ministry and the NSDAP *Auslandsorganisation* (the organization of expatriate Germans), strongly opposed the Transfer Agreement.[50] Against this 'anti-Zionist' lobby stood a curious alignment of forces favouring the continuation of *Ha'avara*. They included the Ministry of the Interior, the Ministry of Economics, the SD and Gestapo and individuals like von Hentig, the head of the Middle East division in the Foreign Office. This alignment was sufficiently influential to persuade Hitler that a continuation of the transfer arrangements was still desirable on pragmatic grounds; at the same time the ideological opposition to the principle of Jewish sovereignty in Palestine was virtually common ground by the summer of 1937 to all policy-making bodies in the Third Reich.[51] Rosenberg, von Ribbentrop, von Weiszacker and Foreign Minister von Neurath all warned against the creation of a Zionist state; not only would it offer a new operational base for Jewry, it might also be able to provide special protection for Jewish minorities in every European country, including Nazi Germany.[52] Von Neurath's telegram of 1 June 1937 to the German Embassy in London, the legation in Baghdad and the Consulate-General in Jerusalem summed up official German policy on the Palestine question. Echoing Hitler's preoccupations, von Neurath rejected the proposal for a Jewish state as providing 'a new power-base for World Jewry' which was not in the German interest.[53] It would represent a nodal-point similar to the role that Moscow played for the Communist International or the Vatican on behalf of political Catholicism. It was therefore to the Reich's advantage to contribute to the reinforcement of the Arab world as a counterweight, in case of need, to the potentially increased power of world Jewry.[54]

The Germans had not hitherto been in any hurry to establish contact with the Arabs, in spite of the feverish efforts of the Palestinian leader, Haj Amin el-Husseini, Grand Mufti of Jerusalem, to win their support. It was indeed a striking fact that in the 1930s a growing number of Arab nationalist and Islamic leaders came to admire the Reich for its discipline and order, its challenge to Britain and France, and not least for its war on the Jews. Nowhere was this more apparent than in Palestine. In this particular case the antisemitism of the Palestine Arabs proved even stronger than their anti-Zionism. For they were well aware that the *Ha'avara* agreement had seriously damaged their position. Yet such was their antisemitism that they were prepared to forgive the Nazis who were daily augmenting the Jewish population and fortifying the Jewish economy of Palestine, while at the same time they engaged from 1936 to 1939 in an armed revolt against the British, who were trying as hard as they could to restrict Jewish immigration! Hitler's occasional platonic declarations of sympathy for the Arab cause and allusions to the lack of democracy in Palestine were taken at face value; his *deeds*, in particular the lack of any military assistance to the Palestinian Arab revolt against the British, were ignored.[55]

The Arabs disregarded Hitler's global strategy at this time, which was still based on a desire to *preserve* rather than destroy the British Empire. In the 1930s Hitler saw British imperial rule as a shining example of the superiority of the white race in action. Thus he could no more contemplate offering real support for Arab liberation before 1939 than he could approve of Indian independence from the British Raj.[56] Both for pragmatic and racial reasons, Hitler simply did not take the Arabs seriously as partners.[57] The two individual exceptions to this rule were Haj Amin el-Husseini, whom the Führer came to respect as a 'sly old fox', and Rashid Ali, the leader of the wartime anti-British *coup* in Iraq. In his *Table Talk* Hitler typically enough attributed the Grand Mufti's 'quite exceptional wisdom' to the probability of 'Aryan' blood. 'With his blond hair and blue eyes', Hitler speculated, 'he gives the impression that he is, in spite of his sharp and mouse-like countenance, a man with more than one Aryan among his ancestors and one who may well be descended from the best Roman stock.'[58] But in neither case was substantial German military support forthcoming, even in wartime conditions, when an Arab rising in the Middle East might have seriously embarrassed the Allies.[59]

Until 1939 the main German argument against supporting the Palestine Arabs had been the need to maintain good relations with the mandatory power, Great Britain. Hitler's desire for a British alliance clearly excluded broad commitments to the Arabs. So, too, did his close relations with Mussolini whose imperial ambitions in the Middle East and North Africa had aroused the deepest Arab mistrust. Italy ultimately hoped to supplant both Britain and France as the dominant power in the region, and Hitler was prepared to encourage this ambition within certain limits. Since his own interest in the Middle East was marginal and the immediate focus of German *Lebensraum* lay in Russia, Eastern Europe and the Balkans, the Reich had everything to gain by allowing Italy a free hand in the Mediterranean.[60] The Near East was informally designated, therefore, as an Italian sphere of influence, though the Germans undertook no major actions to undermine British power in the region before 1939.

These considerations of *Realpolitik* clearly mitigated against any response to Haj Amin el-Husseini's constant appeals to the Reich authorities to form a common anti-British and anti-Jewish alliance. The Arab demands also conflicted with Hitler's domestic interest in a *judenrein* Germany. As long as Palestine appeared to offer the most promising dumping-ground for German Jewish refugees, it would be self-defeating to back the Arab revolt. These considerations were reinforced by Hitler's basic contempt for the Arabs as a 'mongrel' race, by the warnings of some of his advisers concerning the inherent instability of Arab politics and the prevailing evaluation of their chronic unreliability as allies.[61] The delay of the Arab states in adopting a unified position on the British partition plan of 1937 appeared to confirm this negative impression. Thus, while opposed to the Jewish National Home, the Nazis saw no reason to risk the broader interests of the Reich as a great power by providing anything more than token verbal support for Arab aspirations.[62] Why, after all, should the Third Reich make a public declaration in favour of the Palestine Arabs when even the Arab states themselves had not dared to challenge British policy over the issue openly?

Until the outbreak of the Second World War the Reich continued to broadly accept Anglo-French domination of the Middle East, and in spite of some small arms shipments to Iraq and Saudi Arabia in 1939 had not actively sought to undermine the status quo in the area. During the war, circumstances changed sharply but Hitler developed no coherent strategic or political concept for the Middle East nor did he abandon his underlying attitude of contempt for the anti-colonialist movements of the 'lower races'. Admiral Raeder's suggestions for weakening British sea communications by striking at her colonies and bases in the Mediterranean and Middle East were ignored; Hitler persisted in a classic continental strategy built around Operation Barbarossa, neglecting the Mediterranean theatre.[63] Even Rommel's spectacular successes in North Africa in the spring of 1941 did not fundamentally change German policy. In Berlin, the North African campaign was seen as a sideshow in comparison with the massive resources concentrated on the Russian front. Only with regard to Iraq did a German strategy develop to assist the Rashīd Alī revolt, but even here military help was hesitant, limited and came too late to do serious damage to British positions in the Middle East.[64]

Hitler and the German High Command had evidently concluded that Arab diplomatic and military activity in the Middle East would be more of a hindrance than a help to their objectives. They had decided that the Middle East would be conquered from the north by the progress of German forces, which by the summer of 1942 were advancing on the Caucasus. From here they would descend southward on Iraq and Iran. Though Rommel had already penetrated into Egypt, this was to be no more than an auxiliary to the main thrust via Russia into the Middle East.[65] This basic German strategy was made clear in the record of the conversation between the Führer and the Grand Mufti of Jerusalem, held in Berlin on 28 November 1941. Also present were the Reich Foreign Minister and the Arab expert Fritz Grobba, former German emissary to Iraq, who wrote up minutes of the meeting in German.[66] The Mufti began by conveying 'to the Fuhrer of the Greater German Reich, admired by the entire Arab world, his thanks for the sympathy which he had always shown for the Arab, and especially the Palestinian cause, and to which he had given clear expression in his public speeches'.[67] The Arabs, he insisted, were 'Germany's natural friends because they had the same enemies as had Germany, namely the English, the Jews, and the Communists'.[68] Hence the Arabs would co-operate 'with all their hearts' on the side of the Reich not only in acts of sabotage and revolt but also in creating an Arab legion. The Mufti would use his 'close relations with all Muslim nations' for the common cause.

The Mufti's proclaimed objective was a united, independent Arab state encompassing Palestine, Transjordan, Syria and Iraq. His confidence in the Führer had been enhanced by the fact that Germany was holding no Arab territories and that she had recognized Arab national aspirations 'just as she supported the elimination of the Jewish national home'.[69] A public German declaration on this issue would, however, rouse the Arabs 'from their momentary lethargy' and help rally them to Germany's side. The Mufti then sought to persuade Hitler that there was no ground for fearing the negative reactions of the Turks and the French to his unification plan (since 1939 this had been an additional factor in German objections to pan-Arab and pan-Islamic ambitions). Finally, the Mufti warned that excessive German delay in issuing a declaration could only benefit the British.

Hitler's reply, with the crucial exception of the 'Jewish question', must have been disappointing to the Palestinian leader. 'Germany stood for uncompromising war against the Jews' (*Deutschland trete für einen kompromiss-losen Kampf gegen die Juden ein*),[70] the Führer immediately affirmed. 'That naturally included active opposition to the Jewish national home in Palestine, which was nothing other than a center, in the form of a state, [*ein staatlicher Mittelpunkt*] for the exercise of destructive influence by Jewish interests. Germany was also aware that the assertion that the Jews were carrying out the function of economic pioneers in Palestine was a lie. The work there was done only by Arabs, not by the Jews. Germany was resolved, step by step, to ask one European nation after the other to solve its Jewish problem, and at the proper time to direct a similar appeal to non-European nations as well' (*Deutschland sei entschlossen, Zug um Zug eine europäische Nation nach der anderen zur Lösung des Judenproblems aufzufordern und sich im gegebenen Augenblick auch an aussereuropäischen Völker zu wenden*).[71]

In this part of his answer, Hitler, in appropriately guarded language, was in fact revealing to the Mufti the secret of the 'Final Solution' which was being formalized at precisely this time. For five months, indeed, the *Einsatzgruppen* had been massacring Jews in Russia; four months earlier Goering had on the Führer's orders commissioned Heydrich to prepare the organizational guidelines for the *Endlösung* of the European Jewish question; plans for the gassing of Polish Jews in the Generalgouvernement were already under way and the Wannsee Conference was scheduled to be held in only ten days' time (the original date of 8 December). All these facts were known to Hitler though presumably not to his guest. The minutes note, however, that the Führer told the Mufti that 'he would carry on the battle to the total destruction [*Zerstörung*] of the Judeo-Communist empire in Europe', a statement which he enjoined the Palestinian leader to lock 'in the uttermost depths of his heart'.[72]

Hitler also stressed the centrality of the ideological dimension of the world war in terms that were perhaps sharper than in any other German diplomatic document. 'Germany was at the present time engaged in a life and death struggle with two citadels of Jewish power: Great Britain and Soviet Russia.'[73] Hitler admitted that 'theoretically there was a difference between England's capitalism and Soviet Russia's communism'; but in practice 'the Jews in both countries were pursuing a common goal'.[74] For the Führer, the hour of reckoning with the Jews was fast approaching. 'This was the decisive struggle; on the political level, it presented itself in the main as a conflict between Germany and England, but ideologically it was a battle between National Socialism and the Jews' (*weltanschaulich sei es ein Kampf zwischen dem Nationalsozialismus und dem Judentum*).[75] It was self-evident, Hitler declared, that 'Germany would furnish positive and practical aid to the Arabs involved in the same struggle' because this was a war of survival 'in which the Jews were able to mobilize all of England's power for their ends'.[76]

Hitler had thus made it crystal clear that his fanatical struggle against the Jews lay at the very core of the military offensive which the Third Reich was currently waging against the British Empire and Russia (the United States had not yet entered the war). This exterminatory war against the Jews would also be carried on *beyond* the European continent once the German armies had reached the southern exit of the Caucasus.[77] 'As soon as this had happened, the Führer would on his own give the Arab world the assurance that its hour of liberation had arrived. Germany's objective would then be solely the destruction of the Jewish element residing in the Arab sphere under the protection of British power' (... *die Vernichtung des in arabischen Raum unter der Protektion der britischen Macht lebenden Judentums sein*).[78] In other words, the Nazis would take upon themselves the wiping out of the Jewish National Home in Eretz Israel and also of the predominantly Sephardi Jewish communities in the Arab lands.

Beyond this commitment Hitler was very cautious. He spoke 'as a rational man and primarily as a soldier, as the leader of the German and allied armies'.[79] The fate of the Arab world would be decided by the 'very severe battles' going on in the Soviet Union. To raise the Arab problem before Germany had forced open the road to Iran and Iraq would be premature and merely produce unnecessary difficulties for the Reich. In particular Hitler openly admitted his concern that 'those elements in France which were under de Gaulle's influence would receive new strength'. They would interpret a pro-Arab declaration regarding Syria 'as an intention to break up France's colonial Empire and appeal to their fellow countrymen that they should rather make common cause with the English to try and save what still could be saved'.[80] The only result would be 'that a portion of the German armed forces would be immobilized in the west and no longer be available for the campaign in the east'.[81] Clearly Hitler and his advisers valued highly the strategic importance of the status quo maintained by the Vichy regime in France and her colonies (including Syria and Lebanon as well as North Africa) – which they were not prepared to risk for the sake of pan-Arab daydreams.[82] Moreover, given their conviction that the fate of the Middle East would be decided in the Caucasus rather than in the Western desert of

Egypt, the Nazis logically enough preferred to back the Iraqi leader, Rashīd Alī, rather than Haj Amin el-Husseini.

Mussolini, on the other hand, was much more prone to recognize the Mufti's leadership of the Arab world and to support an Arab army under his control which would co-operate in North Africa with the Axis powers.[83] German scepticism and the victory of the British Eighth Army at El Alamein aborted these plans. The Mufti's hopes of leading a broad Islamic-Arab national movement to liberate Palestine in the wake of the Axis armies faded. Henceforth the focus of his wartime activities would be in the Balkans where he mobilized Muslim volunteers for the Axis forces and in preventing the rescue of Jews from the Nazi Holocaust in Europe. He wrote assiduously to the German, Italian, Hungarian and Rumanian Foreign Ministries and to the Bulgarian King, and intervened in Croatia to prevent Jewish refugees, mainly orphaned children, from reaching Palestine.[84] During the last two years of the war his fanatical determination to prevent European Jews from escaping the gas chambers even brought him into close collaboration with the SS and its head, Heinrich Himmler. It had become apparent to the Palestinian leader that the shortest road to a post-war Arab Palestine ran over the corpses of European Jewry.

Haj Amin's propagandist activities in the Reich capital also revealed a remarkable degree of ideological *rapprochement* between Islamic antisemitism and National Socialism. At the opening of the Islamic Central Institute in Berlin on 18 December 1942 the Grand Mufti launched into a vicious attack on the 'bitterest enemies' of the Muslims, the 'Jews and their lackeys', the British, Americans and Bolsheviks. World Jewry, which controlled godless Communism, had supposedly unleashed the war. The Jews had always been a 'disintegrative element' in history, provoking wars between the nations, he declared, in language which was barely distinguishable from that of Hitler.[85] In another speech in the summer of 1943 before the Imams of the Bosnian SS division, the Mufti proudly emphasized the parallels between Nazism and Islam. The National Socialist *Führerprinzip*, its cult of obedience, discipline, *Volksgemeinschaft* and readiness to struggle, were essentially Islamic virtues. So, too, was the high value placed on the family, on labour and the community.

Above all Islam taught the Muslims to fight against Jews, ever since the prophet Muhammed had been 'obliged' to drive them out of the Arabian peninsula.[86] On 2 November 1943, the twenty-sixth anniversary of the Balfour Declaration, the Mufti put forward the classic Islamic fundamentalist position. There could be no toleration of Jews – it was the duty of all Muslims and especially of the Arabs to expel these heretics from their lands.

This had been the teaching of the Prophet 1,300 years earlier. The Jews had always been the enemies of the Arabs and of Islam ever since its foundation. They were the bloodsuckers of the nations and corrupters of morality, incapable either of loyalty or of genuine assimilation.[87] Their boundless egoism and perverse belief that they were the 'chosen people' had led them to expropriate the indigenous inhabitants wherever they settled. National Socialism had fully grasped the nature of the 'Jewish peril' and resolved to find 'a final solution' (*eine endgültige Lösung*) which would liberate the world from this danger.[88] There was every likelihood that Haj Amin el-Husseini, who by now enjoyed close access to Himmler and Eichmann, was referring to the death camps. His 'final solution' to the Palestinian question was clearly Auschwitz. Indeed, according to Simon Wiesenthal, the Grand Mufti had actually visited both Auschwitz and Majdanek where 'he paid close attention to the efficiency of the crematoria, spoke to the leading personnel and was generous in his praise for those who were reported as particularly conscientious in their work'.[89]

Whether or not the leader of the Palestine Arabs was ever *physically* present during the extermination process we may never know, but there is no doubt at all concerning his close practical and ideological identification with the Nazi genocide. As late as 21 January 1944, he was still stressing the need for all Muslims to collaborate with Hitler to destroy 'World Jewry' and the British Empire. Once more he underlined the uncompromising struggle of the Nazis against the people whom the Koran had defined as 'the worst enemies of the Muslims'.[90] Again, he reaffirmed that 'there are considerable similarities between Islamic principles and those of National Socialism. . . . All this brings our ideologies close together and facilitates co-operation.'[91]

The collaboration of the Mufti of Jerusalem with the Nazis was an extreme but by no means an isolated phenomenon in the Arab world. Ever since 1933 the Third Reich had also aroused considerable enthusiasm among Arab leaders *outside* Palestine who were impressed by its nationalist fervour, its militarism and opposition to the Versailles post-war settlement. The German Consulate in Beirut and the Baghdad Embassy received many admiring letters from Syrian and Iraqi citizens, expressing their approval of Hitler and support for the German Reich.[92] The Ministry of Propaganda was told, for example, by one of its sources that throughout the Middle East 'all of the inhabitants with the exception of the Jews are following events in the new Germany with great sympathy and enthusiasm'.[93] This sympathy may have been, in part, based on the illusory hope that Nazi Germany would help the Arabs to achieve their national liberation from the Anglo-French colonial yoke; but, as in Palestine, radical Arab nationalists were no less impressed by

Hitler's anti-Jewish policies, which appeared to them as a model worthy of imitation.

Antisemitism and anti-British sentiment rather than strategic factors were the best potential building blocks of German–Arab friendship, though these were assets never fully exploited by the policy-makers of the Nazi regime. On the German side, Arabists in the Third Reich, beginning with Fritz Grobba, who recognized the parallels and ideological affinities between Nazism and Arab nationalism, were never to achieve a decisive say in the formulation of Middle East policy.[94] But if the Nazis were reticent, the pro-German tendencies on the Arab side were far stronger and more lasting in their impact. Apart from the actions of highly influential pro-German politicians like Rashīd Alī in Iraq and 'Aziz 'Ali al-Misri in Egypt, the ideologically inclined members of the younger generation in the Arab world increasingly looked to Nazi and fascist models as a solution to their social and national problems. Several movements in Syria, including the Parti Populaire Syrien (PPS), the League of Nationalist Action and the Nationalist Youth Movement, belonged to this category.[95] Much of their emotional inspiration came from Nazi Germany, and according to a former Syrian Baathist leader, Sami al-Jundi, this reflected a widespread generational mood. 'We were fascinated by Nazism, reading its books and the sources of its thinking and particularly Nietzsche, Fichte and Chamberlain. And we were the first who thought about translating *Mein Kampf*. He, who lived in Damascus, would appreciate the tendency of the Arab people to Nazism which was the power which appealed to it.'[96]

This fascination of Arab youth and radical movements in Syria with the illiberal, militant nationalism of Hitler had important consequences, for, as Itamar Rabinovich has pointed out, it was 'in these movements that some of the major political figures in Syrian politics of the 1950s and 1960s were schooled'.[97] A similar situation prevailed in Iraq where the nationalist press hailed Nazi Germany as the Arabs' patron in the struggle against Britain and World Jewry.[98] The 'anti-Zionism' of Iraqi Pan-Arab nationalists in the 1940s was invariably a mask for their antisemitism. The arrival of the Mufti of Jerusalem in Baghdad shortly after the outbreak of the Second World War further exacerbated the situation. German influence was therefore able to penetrate into Iraq on the wings of an already existing anti-British and antisemitic mood. The result was that in the dying hours of the pro-Nazi regime of Rashīd Alī al-Gailani in Iraq (1–2 June 1941) the Jews of Baghdad suffered a devastating pogrom.[99] Several hundred Jews were killed, many more wounded, numerous houses destroyed and business premises ransacked. Even after the British reconquest of Iraq, antisemitic invective continued unchecked and some nationalist intellectual leaders like Dr Sami Shawkat and Fadhil al-Jamali were prominent in efforts to Nazify the state school system.[100] At every level of Iraqi society, but especially among the youth, there was open sympathy for the Reich and its anti-Jewish policies.

In Egypt, too, there was a growing sympathy in the 1930s and 1940s for Nazism, which seemed to offer the most promising alternative to the boredom of constitutional liberalism and parliamentary democracy. The successes of the Reich enhanced its appeal to those Egyptians who idealized power and the omnipotence of the state and had visions of resurrected national grandeur. At the same time, the radical movements of the 1930s – from Islamic revivalism to the Green Shirts of Young Egypt (*misr al-fatāh*) – also adopted much of the social demagogy and paramilitary organization of European fascism. Hassan al-Banna's Muslim Brotherhood was officially too anti-Western to admit to borrowing from foreign models, but its leader-cult, its militarism and xenophobic antisemitism recalled Nazi and fascist examples.[101] The Young Men's Muslim Association was more openly pro-Nazi, as was the Young Egypt society founded by Ahmad Husayn, whose credo was consciously borrowed from Nazi ideology.[102] Husayn believed in the fascist values of discipline, struggle, order, aggressiveness, militarism and sacrifice. His cohorts were drilled in the paramilitary style and the movement cultivated the *Führerprinzip* associated with Hitler and Mussolini. Radical Egyptian nationalism was combined with a strong Islamic, anti-Western colouring. *Lebensraum*, too, was part of its programme, as was the racist antisemitism associated with the Nazis. Ahmad Husayn, for example, wrote in July 1939 that 'they [the Jews] are the secret of this moral desolation which has become prevalent in the Arab and Islamic worlds. They are the secret of this cultural squalor and these filthy arts. They are the secret of this religious and moral decay, to the point where it has become correct to say "search for the Jew behind every depravity".'[103] This language, analogous to that of German Nazi antisemitism, was becoming more common in Egypt by the eve of the Second World War.

Young Egypt's influence extended far beyond the ranks of its own militants. It had close links with the pro-German circle of politicians around Prime Minister 'Ali Maher and with the military officers led by General 'Aziz 'Ali al-Misri who formed a spy ring to help German intelligence. A number of members of the Free Officers *junta* who came to power in the Egyptian Revolution of 1952, in particular the dominant figures of Gamal Abdel Nasser and Anwar el-Sadat, were strongly influenced by the Nazi-inspired radical nationalist movements of the 1930s and 1940s. The desire to rid themselves of British imperialism clearly played an important role in this pro-German orientation, which was indeed shared by the court of King Farouk. But Hitler's genocidal war against the Jews also left its unmistakable imprint in Egypt, as it had in Iraq, Syria, Palestine and other parts of the Arab and Islamic world. It was not an accident that nowhere else would the antisemitic legacy of the Nazis be more fervently seized upon to nourish the Islamic Holy War against Israel after 1948.

# CHAPTER NINE

# Militant Islam
# and Arab Nationalism

Modern Arab nationalism was in many respects the heir of Islam and like its prototype developed a fundamental intolerance towards minorities who tried to resist its claim to hegemony. To a considerable degree the Islamic and pan-Arab visions of the world overlapped so that the traditional Muslim ideology of *jihad* (Holy War) against non-believers had continued to be a central driving-force in contemporary Arab history.[1] Such an anomaly has been made possible by the fact that in the world of Islam there had never been equality between believers and non-believers, between Muslims and non-Muslims; Christians and Jews as 'people of the book' were granted the status of *dhimmis* (protected persons) which made them at best second-class citizens.[2] Though there were periods in the past of relative toleration and even cultural symbiosis under Islamic rule, to belong to the despised category of the *dhimmis* had in practice meant, for the mass of Jews and Christians, long centuries of persecution, discrimination and humiliation in the Muslim world.[3] The sense of superiority of Islam as the final prophetic revelation reinforced the self-righteousness that underlay this unequal treatment of the *dhimmis*. But in spite of episodes like the Crusades, it was only in the eighteenth and nineteenth centuries that European domination of the Arab-Muslim world produced a truly lasting and traumatic shock that affected the traditional world of Islam to its foundations.

The anti-Western orientation of Islamic revivalism and modern Arab nationalism were in large measure a consequence of this shattering experience.[4] The Jewish national revival in Eretz Israel (Palestine), sponsored initially by Great Britain and coinciding with betrayed Arab hopes of independence, intensified the bitter feelings of resentment to the West. But the success of Zionism represented a far more devastating blow to Muslim and Arab morale than the earlier subjection to Western colonialism. For the achievement of a *dhimmi* people in exercising sovereignty over an area (Palestine) located in the very centre of the Arab world was inevitably perceived by Muslims as an intolerable affront to their sense of chosenness and pride. In 1948 the Arab world promptly launched its first Holy War to prevent the creation of Israel. Its failure and that of four successive *jihads*, which merely expanded the borders of the Jewish state, made the wound deeper than ever, for worldly material success has always been the vindication of the *Ummah Muslimah* (the Muslim Community) and the decisive affirmation of the superiority of the Islamic faith. Failure in war and political struggle, by the same token, implied a shocking subversion of Allah's plan in history.[5] The inexplicable subjection of God's 'chosen' people (i.e. the Muslims) could only be due to alien, fiendish powers of which Jewish Zionism was perhaps the most obvious though not the only manifestation. Thus both militant Islam and 'secular' Arab nationalism, in their abortive attempts to wrestle with the broader challenge of modernity, increasingly sidetracked most of their emotional energy into the *jihad* against Israel. The existence of a Jewish state since 1948 in the heart of the Arab East seemed to symbolize for them in a unique and special way the deep malaise of the Muslim world; for Israel was perceived not only as a Western outpost but more specifically as the collective representation of Islam's oldest antagonist, the Jews.

But if the Islamic component has remained the most authentically Middle Eastern inspiration in modern Arab ideologies,[6] the connection between the Nazi 'Final Solution' and post-war efforts to liquidate the state of Israel should not be overlooked. On the one hand, there is the obvious historical connection between Nazi tyranny and the Jewish exodus to Palestine, which in the wake of Israel's War of Independence led after 1948 to the Palestinian Arab refugee problem. At the same time the Arab-Israeli conflict and renewed Muslim persecution provoked an exodus of Sephardi Jews from Islamic countries to Israel after 1948. This vicious circle of tragedy and oppression was in large measure an unintended result of the Nazi earthquake in Europe.

But a more sinister nexus also bound Auschwitz with the war on the newly-born Jewish state undertaken in May 1948 by five Arab armies. For was it not the case that Hitler's genocide against the Jews had actually encouraged the Arabs to try and complete his work?[7] Was this hope not implied in the prophecy of Azzam Pasha, Secretary-General of the Arab League, quoted by the BBC on 15 May 1948? 'This will be a momentous war of extermination, which will be spoken of in history like the Mongolian massacres and the Crusades'.[8]

The abortive Arab war against Israel may well have further reinforced the conscious sense of identification with Hitler and the German Reich which had already been apparent in radical Arab nationalist circles since the 1930s. One symptom of this persistent feeling was the revealing reply of Anwar el-Sadat to the Cairo weekly *Al Musawar* in September 1953, following reports in the press that Adolf Hitler was still alive. 'My dear Hitler, I congratulate you from the bottom of my heart', Sadat declared. 'Even if you appear to have been defeated, in reality you are the victor. You succeeded in creating dissensions between Churchill, the old man, and his allies, the Sons of Satan. Germany will win because her existence is necessary to preserve the world balance. . . . You may be proud of becoming the immortal leader of Germany. We will not be surprised if you appear again in Germany or if a new Hitler rises up in your wake'.[9]

In Nasser's Egypt, in Iraq, Syria or Jordan, such statements were commonplace enough and it was no accident that the Free Officers' Junta in the 1950s welcomed with open arms the old German Nazis who now came flooding into the country.[10] Their qualifications as experts on 'Jewish Affairs' probably made them seem like valuable adjuncts to Arab antisemitic propaganda which increasingly bore their trademark after the mid-1950s. The most prominent of these former collaborators of Hitler and Goebbels was the notorious antisemite Johann von Leers, invited to Cairo by Haj Amin el-Husseini. Von Leers had initially settled after the war in the Argentine where he edited the neo-Nazi monthly *Der Weg*. The Grand Mufti had repeatedly sent messages of encouragement to von Leers and his fellow Nazis in Buenos Aires and in August 1956 he had publicly complimented *Der Weg* for having 'always championed the Arabs' righteous cause against the powers of darkness embodied in World Jewry'.[11] An exalted figure in Nasser's entourage, the ex-Mufti of Jerusalem obtained a post for von Leers as political adviser in the Egyptian Information Department, where, according to the *Manchester Guardian*, he exercised 'considerable influence on the nature of the current anti-Jewish measures'.[12] Von Leers continued to be active as an antisemitic propagandist in Cairo under his Muslim name, Omar Amin, until his death in 1965.

Other prominent Nazi converts to Islam included ex-SS officer Leopold Gleim, one of the propagandists behind the vicious antisemitic pamphlet *Complotto contra la Chiesa* (Conspiracy against the Church), designed to thwart Vatican Council II's determination in 1963 to remove traditional anti-semitism from the Catholic Church. This rehash of Nazi conspiracy theories was enthusiastically encouraged and backed by the Arabs.[13] Another ex-Nazi, Louis Heiden (el Haj), was responsible for a new translation into Arabic of Hitler's *Mein Kampf*, copies of which were found in the kit of Egyptian officers captured by the Israelis during the Sinai campaign.[14]

There was nothing surprising in this fact, for as the organ of the Muslim Brotherhood in Damascus explained in October 1956: 'It must not be forgotten that in contrast to Europe, Hitler occupies a respected place in the Arab world. His name arouses in the hearts of our movement sympathy and enthusiasm.'[15] This latent pro-Nazi feeling probably accounted for the remarkable popularity of Germans in Arab countries at a time when such sentiments were comparatively rare in Europe.

Much more significant even than *Mein Kampf* in its immediate impact in the Middle East was *The Protocols of the Elders of Zion* which influenced such key Arab leaders as Gamal Abdel Nasser of Egypt and King Feisal of Saudi Arabia. Widely quoted in Arab anti-Israel literature and repeatedly translated into Arabic from European languages, the *Protocols* were seen as the most important of all 'secret' Zionist documents. In the *Protocols*, the power of world Jewry and its bid for global domination were supposedly unmasked; they appeared to provide the key to the true nature of Israel and a blueprint for future Zionist expansionism.[16] Above all, the *Protocols* suggested the nightmare of a shadowy world Jewish conspiracy against which only the unity and total mobilization of Arab resources could prevail. Behind Israel stood occult, sinister forces which endangered the very existence of Islam and the Arab nation. As in Nazi mythology, the *Protocols* provided a Manichean, eschatological dimension to the Arab conflict with the Jews, which seemed to lift the armed struggle from the level of a local national conflict to a universal plane.[17]

This was not, however, the only element of continuity. Significantly, Egyptian editions of the *Protocols* contained numerous references to Nazi sources (including quotations from Adolf Hitler, Alfred Rosenberg and the German antisemitic news agency, *Weltdienst*) which respectfully referred to them as authorities.[18] President Nasser himself attached considerable importance to the *Protocols*, telling R. K. Karanjia, the Indian editor of a Bombay English-language illustrated magazine, *Blitz*, in 1957: 'It is very important that you should read it. I will give you a copy. It proves beyond a shadow of a doubt that three hundred Zionists, each of whom knows all the others, govern the fate of the European Continent and that they elect their successors from their entourage.'[19] Nasser was in fact embellishing a classic theme of early Nazi antisemitism. The Nazis had distorted an article of Walther Rathenau in 1909 in which the German-Jewish financier had claimed that three hundred bankers and industrialists determined the economic destiny of Europe. Since Rathenau, who in 1921 became the ill-fated Foreign Minister of the Weimar Republic, was a favourite *bête-noire* of the antisemites in Germany, his reference to three hundred financiers quickly became transformed into 'Jewish bankers'.[20] In Nasser's hands, the Jewish bankers simply became 'Zionists'.

This was not the only example of the Egyptian President's high regard for the *Protocols*. He also wrote a letter of praise incorporated into a blatantly antisemitic work, *Palestine and the Conscience of Mankind*, published in Cairo in 1964, which presented the *Protocols* as the link between the 'capitalist Jew' of the West and the 'communist Jew' in the East.[21] Like King Feisal, Nasser had frequently alleged in the early years of his rule that Zionism and Communism were two sides of the same coin – a favourite theme of the neo-Nazis and the post-war radical Right in Germany and numerous Western countries.

The fascination of Arab leaders with the *Protocols* cannot be divorced from their consistent efforts to liquidate the Jewish state. Knowing as they did of the link between the myth of the 'Elders of Zion' and the Nazi 'Final Solution', the Jewish conspiracy theory which it embodies must have provided them with a source of inspiration for their own politicidal objectives.[22] In Arab eyes the *Protocols* might justify the most extreme measures to fend off what was depicted as a satanic Jewish plot against Christianity and Islam. As Salih Jawdat wrote in *Al Musawar* on 6 October 1967: 'It is the duty of every Arab government to publish these *Protocols* and to disseminate them among the people so that they become aware of the danger of the Zionist plan. And it is the duty of every Arab to read these *Protocols*. The truth which every Arab ought to know is that the power of the Jews surpasses their numerical strength, their armed forces and their scheming.'[23] Evidently only by postulating a sinister conspiracy of the forces of evil could the successive defeats of 1948, 1956 and 1967 become explicable to many bewildered and confused Arabs.

The *Protocols* have also been extremely attractive to those Islamic anti-semites obsessed with the supposed Jewish threat to disintegrate the Muslim *Ummah* (community) and to frustrate the revival of Islam. A Pakistani edition of the *Protocols* published in February 1967, for example, claimed that the only remaining obstacle to Jewish world domination lay in the realm of Islam.[24] The Muslim Brotherhood had traditionally been the group in the Middle East most opposed to Israel on fundamentalist grounds (i.e. denying the very possibility of a Jewish state on 'Muslim' soil) but they had been repressed by Nasser. This proved to the Pakistani editor that the Egyptian leader was a 'Zionist agent'. Indeed, secular Arab nationalism itself was, according to this version, a conspiracy against Islam initiated by Christians and Jews.[25]

Such seemingly bizarre offshoots of the *Protocols* mythology have become increasingly familiar in recent years with the emergence of the Islamic revolution in Iran and its palpable threat to neighbouring Arab regimes. The Ayatollah Khomeini's Holy War against the 'infidel' dictator of Iraq, Saddam Hussein, was, for example, presented to the Iranian masses as the beginning of the 'final war' against Israel. But to liberate Jerusalem (*Al Quds*) the Iranian Revolution had first to defeat the Iraqi 'Zionist agent' Hussein and to overthrow by subversion the corrupt Wahhabi Kingdom of Saudi Arabi and the Sunni Muslim sheikhdoms of the Persian Gulf.[26] Not only 'Westernization' in general but above all the conservative Arab rulers from Egypt's Sadat to King Fahd of Saudi Arabia, from King Hussein of Jordan to King Hassan of Morocco, are considered traitors and mortal enemies of the Islamic revolution.[27]

The Khomeinist turmoil with its predominantly religious fundamentalist inspiration is, of course, an indigenous Middle Eastern phenomenon which has owed relatively little to foreign sources. The antisemitism of the Khomeini regime derives mainly from Islamic Shia traditions, but in its more demonological aspects it does clearly recall some features of Nazism. For Khomeini, as for other Islamic bigots, the Jews are 'enemies of God' who have distorted the reputation of Islam and slandered it from the beginning of its history. They have always tampered (and continued to do so) with the Koran, publishing distorted editions of the work in the Israeli 'occupied' territories. In his treatise on *Islamic Government* Khomeini wrote that Muslims '. . . must shout at the top of our voices so that we may make the people realise that the Jews and their foreign masters seek to snare Islam and pave the way for Jews to dominate the entire world'.[28] Khomeini, in a series of lectures published in 1970, claimed that it was Israel which had systematically tried during the Shah's rule to de-Islamize the country and was responsible for all its social, economic and religious problems.

Zionism in his mind was identified not only with the United States and with Western colonialism but with the broader menace of atheistic materialism *within* Iran and the Muslim world. 'Israel does not wish that the Koran exist in this kingdom: Israel does not wish that the mullahs of Islam exist in this country. . . .'[29] With the help of the 'Great Satan', the United States, Israel had sought to force its evil values on Iran and 'turn Muslim Arabs into vagrants'. As for Palestine, Khomeini took the classic fundamentalist view that it 'belongs to the Islamic space and must be returned to Muslims'.[30] It is not surprising, therefore, that Yasser Arafat, leader of the Palestine Liberation Organization, should have sent an unambiguous message of support on 11 February 1979 to the Ayatollah Khomeini: '. . . I pray Allah to guide your steps on the road of faith and *jihad* in Iran, which will continue the struggle until we reach the walls of Jerusalem where we will raise the flags of our two revolutions.'[31]

In recent years, however, the 'anti-Zionist' propaganda of the Islamic revolutionary Republic has been, more often than not, no more than a thin cover for the dissemination of a fanatical antisemitism based on the *Protocols of the Elders of Zion*.[32] A case in point is the journal *Imam*, published by the press and information department of the Iranian Embassy in London, which reproduced parts of the *Protocols* in a series of articles from February to May 1984 In its introduction to short extracts from this tainted source the publication began by pointing out: 'All through history, Zionism has been the perpetual enemy to Islam. According to the Holy Quran the religion of man is to be Islam, then as Imam Khomeini says, Zionism is an enemy of humanity.'[33] The Prophet Muhammed from the outset of his mission 'was up against the Jews who were behind all sorts of conspiracies designed to threat [*sic*] his life, to intimdate Muslims and denounce Islam altogether'.[34] Although no place in the world was immune from Zionist aggression, the Islamic Revolution was especially exposed, for it is 'a threat to these children of evil and the contemporary exploiters'. This was the reason for American and European economic sanctions against Iran and for the 'atmosphere of emotional blindness with regard to our Islamic Revolution' nourished by the world's media; this explained why 'the Zionist regime of Iraq has invaded Iran' and why Israel 'created a bloodbath in Lebanon'.

The key to all these contemporary events lay in the guidelines set by the 'learned Elders of Zion' in 1895. 'The outcome of the Israeli as well as the West's governmental policies, particularly that of the US, and judging by the results of their decision making prove the fact that the Protocols of the Elders of Zion are being adhered to word by word, by the Jewish influenced Western governments.'[35] According to *Imam*, the Israelis are 'the true descendants of the Elders of Zion' and following instructions they 'occupied Palestine and took over Quds', employing in their conquest the recommended tactics of brutality and ferocity.[36] The 'pogrom' against Muslims in Lebanon was also carried out on the orders of the Elders of Zion.

In its March 1984 issue, *Imam* explained more clearly the connection between the *Protocols* and Israel. 'The illegal state of "Israel" is only the tip of the iceberg which brought about the shameful existence of this entity in the first place. The invisible hand of "Zionism" seems to have been at work for centuries everywhere, perpetrating crimes of unbelievable magnitude against human societies and values.'[37] (A *Stürmer*-like Jew, replete with hooked nose and skullcap, encircling the globe in serpentine fashion makes it visually explicit that for *Imam*, as for most Islamic and Arab antisemites, there is no distinction at all between 'Zionist' and Jew.) Once the *Protocols* which laid bare their age-old strategy had unfortunately leaked out, the Zionists did everything in their power to prevent their wider distribution, buying up copies so as to suppress the 'Book of Shame'. But the fulfilment of the 'prophecies' in the *Protocols* had irrefutably proved their reality for the commentators of *Imam*, as it had in the past for Hitler and the Nazis. The desire for a 'National Home' in Palestine was 'only camouflage and an infinitesimal part of the *Zionist World Plot*'.[38] As if echoing *Mein Kampf*, the Khomeinist publication emphasized that 'the Zionists of the world have no intention of settling in Palestine'. The annual Jewish prayer 'Next Year in Jerusalem' was merely a piece of 'characteristic make-believe'. It was up to Muslims, therefore, to draw the correct conclusions. The governmental and administrative structures of Islamic states would have to be totally purged of Zionist infiltration, and preparations made for 'an all-out confrontation with the Zionist nonentity, the Occupiers of Palestine'.[39]

At the same time, 'Zionism' is presented by these sources not merely as a threat to Muslims but to all existing human societies. Its spirit has utterly demoralized the West, creating vice and immorality wherever it penetrates. According to the Khomeinists, whenever 'the masses realize that their beliefs are being disregarded by their government, they can be sure that theirs is a Zionist government'.[40] Following the advice of the Elders, the ruling 'Zionists' in the West have allegedly encouraged trivialization, the dissemination of mindless luxuries, the disregard of traditions and faith; they have legalized prostitution, homosexual and lesbian demonstrations, and mass pornography, and brought about the death of 'spiritual personality'. Even such marginal activities as dog-exhibitions or the existence of societies for the prevention of cruelty to animals are depicted as symptoms of 'Zionist societies'. From an Iranian revolutionary perspective it would appear indeed that 'Zionism' has taken over most of the major capital cities of the world![41]

In May 1984 *Imam* reached a peak of grimly Hitlerian hysteria, accusing the British task force that reconquered the Falkland Islands of committing atrocities on the 'recommendations of the Elders of Zion'. Indeed, from the atom bombs dropped on Hiroshima and Nagasaki to the wars in Korea, Vietnam, Afghanistan, Lebanon and the Persian Gulf, all the massacres in post-1945 history have supposedly been inspired by 'the Zionists' and their beastly methods.[42] Both superpowers were themselves enslaved to this inhuman force which intervened everywhere on the globe, inflicting countless atrocities on innocent people. The secret source of the Zionists' strength lay in their deliberate undermining of the moral fabric of society through alcoholism and sexual immorality.[43] According to the mouthpiece of Islamic militancy, 'the Jews admit that it is they who, through many means at their disposal, encourage the non-Jews; particularly the youth . . . to an "early immorality" to grow "stupid" by consuming alcohol. By means of exploiting women in suggestive and cunning advertisements, calling to mind prurient thoughts, the Zionists lead the ignorant people to an ultimate self-destruction for their own ends.'[44] Only by studying the *Protocols*, the London publication of the Iranian Embassy concludes, can one 'rediscover some horrifying realities of the corrupted Human Society as trademarks of Zionism. Zionism is a plague which must be destroyed.'[45]

Most of these wild Khomeinist aspersions against Zionism and Jewry have in fact long been part of the arsenal of Arab war propaganda, though the militancy of the Iranian variant gives it perhaps a special virulence. Nonetheless one has only to examine the contents of the Fourth Conference of the Academy of Islamic Research (held at Al Azhar in Cairo between 27 September and 24 October 1968) to see the consistency of the Islamic approach.[46] None of the distinguished Muslim *ulemas* at that gathering, sponsored by the Egyptian government, differentiated between 'Zionists' and Jews. The authority of the Koran was constantly invoked to brand all Jews as the 'deadly enemies' of God and Islam and their wickedness as being beyond redemption.[47] The venom of the Al Azhar denunciations and their view of Jewish history as a continuing series of acts of robbery, sedition and intrigue were so many variations on one of Hitler's choicest themes.

In a manner reminiscent of the Nazis, these Muslim Arab theologians and academics presented the Jewish character as eternally tainted;[48] the Jews as controlling the world's media and poisoning public opinion; as hostile to all human values, as 'carriers of diseases and pests' and as a plague of the nations. In the words of Professor Abdul Sattar El Sayed, the Mufti of Tursos (Syria), the Jews were branded for ever by the Koran as 'a pest or a plague that is cursed like Satan who was expelled by God from the realm of His mercy'.[49] According to Hassan Khaled, Mufti of the Lebanese Republic, the Jews were 'dogs of humanity' and 'the most atrocious enemies to Islam and the Muslims', while Zionism represented 'a very perilous cancer, aiming at domineering the Arab countries and the whole Islamic world'.[50] Using the Jewish weapons of treachery, cunning and deceit, Zionism had done everything to undermine the character of contemporary Muslim society which was 'one of disconnected limbs, shattered body and dissolved character'. Alcoholic drinks, usury, indecency and rape, the violation of holy sanctities were so many symptoms of this corruption and malaise which only a successful *jihad* could cure.[51]

Repeatedly the Arab theologians denounced the immutable and permanent evil embodied by the Jews, by their bloodthirsty creed of Judaism and by the Zionist world-conspiracy. The Old Testament was depicted by one speaker after another as a compendium of bloodshed, sex perversion and evil deeds, proving that the Jews' wickedness 'is incurable unless they are subdued by force'.[52] The doctrines of the Bible were a blueprint for extermination – 'you will find nothing but murder, arson, destruction and genocide', according to Kamal Ahmad Own.[53] But the Jews' Holy Books were not just historical documents, for 'their nature, habits and customs have remained unchanged since the dawn of their history'.[54]

This perfidy and constantly evil nature of the Jews explained why they had suffered persecutions and calamities throughout history, culminating in the Nazi Holocaust. They had always stirred up sedition, corrupted the peoples among whom they lived and sought to undermine their sacred beliefs.[55] According to Muhammad Azzah Darwaza, they had 'rightfully deserved the wrath and curse of Allah', hence 'the Muslims should spare no effort to exterminate their state and deliver every place of the Muslims' homeland from the Jews' desecration and keep it under the control of the Islamic authorities'.[56] His Eminence, Sheikh Abdul-Hamid 'Attiyah al-Dibani (Rector of the Libyan Islamic University), similarly believed that there could be no treating for peace with 'a mere gang of robbers and criminals'.[57] According to the Arab theologians, the state of Israel was the culmination of the historical and cultural depravity of the Jews, and only by destroying it could the congenital, immutable evil which it incarnated be finally removed.[58]

The frenzy of hatred behind such declarations was by no means confined to Muslim *ulemas*. It has continued to be part of the standard indoctrination in the newspapers, radio, television and textbooks of all kinds in the Arab world. Teaching material captured by Israeli forces after the Six-Day War had already confirmed what had long been evident from the *Stürmer*-like caricatures of Jews in the pre-1967 Arab press; full of hatred and driven by the will-to-exterminate, the Syrian, Jordanian and Egyptian textbooks presented Jews as barely human creatures – 'as puny, miserable scarecrows facing Arab 'Superman'-type heroes'.[59] This Arab antisemitic propaganda, with its visions of strangling Israel and throwing her into the sea, displayed an obvious affinity with Nazism. Repeatedly, the Jewish state had been presented as a 'malignant cancer' infecting the Arab homeland, a nest of wicked criminals which had to be purged and cleansed for the sake of humanity as a whole. It was in this spirit of eradicating the 'cancer' of Israel that Ahmad Shukeiry, head of the PLO, had declared on the eve of the Six-Day War that hardly a Jew would survive to be repatriated to Europe. The fact that the Nazi legacy of extermination was now dressed up in a *gharbya* and *kaffiah* did not make it any less racist than its earlier model.

Nor should the continuity between Shukeiry's radical 'solution' of the Palestine Question and that of his successor Yasser Arafat be overlooked, in spite of some cosmetic changes in rhetoric designed for Western consumption. For the 'Liberation of Palestine' in the literature of Al Fatah has always meant the annihilation of Israel and the 'elimination of the Zionist institutions'. In its Arabic texts the intention of the PLO to destroy Israeli society and all its institutions, its means of livelihood and cultural identity, is clearly expressed. A Fatah Arab pamphlet of 1968 on the liberation of the occupied territories underlined the point: 'The liberation action is not only the removal of an armed imperialist base; but, more important – it is the *destruction of a* society. . . . In addition to the destruction of the military force of the Zionist occupying state, it will also be turned towards *the destruction of the means of life* of Zionist society in all their forms – industrial, agricultural and financial. The armed violence must seek *to destroy the military, political, economic, financial and ideological institutions* of the Zionist occupying state, so as to prevent all possibility of the growth of a new Zionist society. The aim of the Palestine Liberation War is not only to inflict a military defeat but also *to destroy* the Zionist character of the occupied land, *whether it is human or social.*'[60] At the same time, the authors were uneasily aware of the need to 'supply to public opinion a solution which will satisfy it or will be acceptable to it, even marginally'. Conciliating world opinion did not, however, mean changing 'the *character* of the solution to the Palestinian problem, but [only] the *method* we shall adopt in solving it'.[61] It was, in other words, a question of tactics which did not affect the overall strategy of liquidation. 'World public opinion has no right to argue with us about the need to solve this problem. But it has a right to know the *way* of the solution, so that it will not imprint us with fascism, antisemitism. . . .'

It was precisely for this purpose that the PLO under Yasser Arafat cunningly came to accept the formula of a secular democratic Palestinian state supposedly guaranteeing equality for Muslims, Jews and Christians. Having learned that world opinion was allergic to explicit language concerning 'the destruction of Israel', the PLO invested major efforts in masking its true intentions under a cloud of 'progressive' verbiage.[62] The endless calls for a 'just solution' to the Palestine problem or for a 'democratic Palestine' were so many euphemisms for the liquidation of the state of Israel and its Jewish majority. A symposium among the representatives of six Palestinian organizations published in a Lebanese newspaper in March 1970 revealed the purely *tactical* character of the 'Democratic Palestine' slogan.[63] The so-called 'Democratic' state would in practice be overwhelmingly Arab in composition and there was no question of co-existing with any form of Israeli 'entity'. The basic premise shared by the PLO and all Arab states that there was no room in the Middle East for Jewish nationalism or a Jewish state was to remain unchanged.

As the 1971 edition of the PLO *Handbook to the Palestine Question*, published in Beirut, put it, quoting the well-known Arab publicist Fayez Sayegh: 'The call for a compromise solution in the case of the Palestine problem is not permissible. . . .' Virtually every article in the Palestinian National Covenant makes this crystal clear, from the opening assertion that 'Palestine is the homeland of the Palestinian Arab people and an integral part of the great Arab homeland . . .' to the insistence that only Jews who were physically present in the territory before 1917 could be considered as 'Palestinians'.[64] In other words, the great bulk of Israeli Jews, if they survived an Arab reconquest, would in fact be regarded as aliens and at best expelled. Only a tiny number might be allowed to exist as a religious minority in the new 'democratic' state – a fact which reveals how closely the PLO continues to share the fundamentalist Islamic view which rejects genuine equality or national independence for Jews.

Moreover, as Yehoshofat Harkabi has pointed out, the PLO's consistent refusal to recognize Israel's right to exist has always been a tacit admission of its destructive intentions.[65] While generally avoiding explicit genocidal threats, Fatah and PLO literature has continued to stress its aim of liquidating the Zionist 'entity' in all its aspects. The premise for this intransigent position is, to quote Harkabi, that 'the evil in Israel is deeply rooted, inherent in the people who founded it, their history and culture'.[66] This intransigent outlook, shared by extremist Islamic and Pan-Arab radicals like Colonel Qadhafi of Libya, still regards the destruction of Israel as the prime aim of the Arab revolution. As Arafat admitted in an unusually frank interview given to the Venezuelan paper, *El Mundo*, and published on 11 February 1980: 'Peace for us means the destruction of Israel. We are preparing for an all-out war, a war which will last for generations. . . . The destruction of Israel is the goal of our struggle and the guidelines of the struggle have remained firm since the establishment of Fatah.'[67] Less than four months later the Al-Fatah Congress in Damascus issued a communiqué confirming its aim as 'the complete liberation of Palestine and the liquidation of the Zionist entity economically, politically, militarily, culturally and ideologically'.[68]

The PLO has been unique among modern liberation movements in its single-minded determination to destroy a whole society and expel (if not exterminate) its inhabitants as part of its 'freedom' struggle. It has, moreover, operated in an Arab environment where the state of Israel has been presented for years as the symbol of a nation that is the very incarnation of evil and deserving of the final death-sentence. As Professor Harkabi has put it: 'The volume of anti-Semitic literature published in the Arab world has had no parallel in modern history since the demise of Nazi Germany. What makes this literature even more significant is that it has been put out by official government publishing houses – not from the fringes of Arab society but from its very center.'[69] Where else could *The Protocols of the Elders of Zion* appear (as they did in Arabic translation) at the top of the best-seller list of a Beirut newspaper? Where else in the post-war world could a leading intellectual and confidante of his country's rulers openly refer to Jews using human blood at Easter and describe them as 'wild beasts in human form'?[70] Where else could the Jews be simultaneously accused of being 'ever zealous to spread wars and antagonism' *and* of being the first victims of wars and revolts – this being the proof of their 'historic Jewish self-destruction'?[71] Yet the tone for such vicious antisemitism had been set by none other than the late President Sadat. In a speech of 25 April 1972 at the El Hussein Mosque, celebrating the birthday of Muhammed, he remarked that 'the most splendid thing that the Prophet . . . did was to drive them [the Jews] out of the whole Arabian peninsula. . . . They are a nation of liars and traitors, contrivers of plots, a people born for deeds of treachery.'[72] Quoting the Koranic teaching that they shall be 'condemned to humiliation and misery', Sadat promised the Egyptian people that 'we shall send them back to their former status'.[73]

His Chief of Staff, Lieutenant-General Said Shazli, in an introduction to the orientation manual *Our Faith – Our Way to Victory*, published in a million copies by the supreme command of the Egyptian Armed Forces on the eve of the Yom Kippur War, quoted another Koranic injunction: 'Kill them wherever you find them, and take heed that they do not deceive you, for they are a treacherous people.'[74] The Head of the Academy of Islamic Research and Rector of Al Azhar, Dr Abdul Halim Mahmoud, in his *Al Jihad wa al-Nasr* (Holy War and Victory), published in 1974, was not to be outdone by General Shazli. 'Allah commands the Muslims to fight the friends of Satan wherever they are found. Among the friends of Satan – indeed, among the foremost friends of Satan in our present age – are the Jews.'[75] The Jews, according to this learned Egyptian, had developed 'a programme for the destruction of humanity' by subverting religion, falsifying knowledge and literary truth, and controlling the mass media through their money and propaganda. 'But Allah – praise be to Him – will wreck the edifice the Jews have built and eliminate their destructive machinations and double-dealing.'[76] The Peace Treaty with Egypt did not, unfortunately, change this strain of rabid antisemitism which to the present day depicts Israel as a threat not only to the Arabs but to all of humanity. Although Egypt entered into direct negotiations with the Israelis, it has abandoned neither its view of the fundamental illegitimacy of Jewish sovereignty and statehood in the Middle East nor its demonic image of Zionism and the Jewish people.[77] The revolutionary breakthrough of Anwar el-Sadat was to try to seek the gradual dissolution of the Jewish state through peaceful rather than violent means. This has not, however, led to any revision of Egyptian antisemitic propaganda and popular prejudices.[78]

It has, of course, sometimes been argued that Arab hostility to Israel is essentially political and has nothing to do with antisemitism,[79] except perhaps among Christian Arabs who historically played a leading part in introducing European Judeophobia into the Middle East. Similarly it has been suggested that Muslim Arab antisemitism 'does not rest on any real popular feeling, and has no roots in the past', that its contemporary manifestations are 'overwhelmingly foreign in content and style'.[80] This assumption is extremely questionable, though the influence of German and Russian stereotypes on Arab antisemitic cartoons, for example, is undeniable. For many in the Arab world the enemy remains *al-Yahud* (the Jews) even when great efforts are invested in raising them to the more abstract level of 'the Zionist entity'. The same antisemitic myths propagated (though not invented) by the Nazis of a secret Jewish world-power have in the past forty years been eagerly absorbed in parts of the Arab and Muslim world. Moreover, nowhere is there a greater readiness to sympathize with Adolf Hitler and Nazism, even when hurling the 'Nazi' epithet of his old victims. Unlike most Europeans and Americans, Arabs have often shown themselves to be unmoved by the magnitude of Nazi crimes against the Jewish people, thereby creating the impression that they harbour similar dreams.

Reactions to the Eichmann trial in the Arab world were a case in point. In the Egyptian National Assembly a few weeks before the trial, Deputy Foreign Minister Hussain Zulficar Sabri declared that Hitler was innocent of the slaughter of Jews. He had been the victim of Zionists who had 'compelled him to perpetrate crimes that would eventually enable them to achieve their aim – the creation of the State of Israel'.[81] The *Jerusalem Times*, an English-language Jordanian daily, published an open letter of sympathy to Eichmann on 24 April 1961 in which it congratulated the Nazi mass murderer for having 'conferred a real blessing on humanity' by liquidating six million Jews. It promised that 'this trial will one day culminate in the liquidation of the remaining six million to avenge your blood. . . .'[82] A senator in the Jordanian senate (and former commander of the Arab Legion in 1948),

Abdallah al-Tall, wrote of Eichmann as a 'martyr' and in 1964 attacked the Jewish 'slander' of Hitler and the Nazis. The Führer only 'did to the Jews as has been done unto them throughout the generations – killing, burning, and expulsion from the countries which they betrayed and whose peoples they deceived'.[83] Hitler was no worse than Pharaoh, Nebuchadnezzar, Titus, Muhammed and the European peoples who had slaughtered the Jews through the centuries. The evil character of the Jews was to blame for these continuous massacres and Hitler had merely taken preventive measures, once he realized that Jewish treason was responsible for the German defeat during the First World War. A similar viewpoint was expressed by the Egyptian publicist Muhammad Ali 'Aluba in 1964, when he depicted Hitler as saving his people 'from this malignant evil that had permeated the Christian peoples, and the poison that flowed in the bodies of the non-Jews'.[84]

Such justifications of Nazi crimes, as Professor Harkabi long ago pointed out, have been commonplace in Arab 'anti-Zionist' literature. Far from regarding Hitler as a mass murderer, many Arabs were inclined to see in his antisemitism a model to be studied and emulated. Thus Dr Muhammad Abd al-Mu'izz Naṣr in his book, *Zionism in International Affairs* (1957), could write: 'The truth is that the study of what Hitler wrote on World Zionism has become a vital matter for anyone who lives in the Arab countries after 1948.'[85] Dr Naṣr was clearly using the term 'World Zionism' interchangeably for 'World Jewry', since Hitler, having died three years too early, had never written a line about the state of Israel.

Arabs were also among those who sought to minimize or even to deny the Holocaust, even as they regretted that the Nazis had not finished the job. President Nasser of Egypt in a notorious interview with the editor of the neo-Nazi *Deutsche Soldaten und National Zeitung*, published on 1 May 1964, insisted that no one '. . . takes seriously the lie about six million Jews who were murdered'.[86] The then Jordanian Prime Minister, Sa'ad Jum'a, echoed this theme of the 'hoax' of the six million in a book published in Beirut in 1968.[87] It would appear that, as with the 'so-called revisionists' in the West who deny that the Holocaust ever occurred, antisemitic logic can reconcile all contradictions. Hitler's crimes could be denied by some Arabs in the same breath as they praised and justified his massacre of the Jews. According to Anis Mansour, a leading Egyptian intellectual and adviser of the late President Sadat, writing in the semi-government daily *Al-Akhbar* on 19 August 1973: 'The world is becoming aware of the fact that Hitler was right and that the cremation ovens were the appropriate means of punishing such contempt of human values, principles of religion and law.'[88] Since Anis

Mansour has frequently described Jews either as 'the enemies of mankind', as racist fanatics or as ritual murderers, perhaps this outburst was not surprising.

Another Muslim admirer of Hitler's genocide was the bloodthirsty former President of Uganda, Idi Amin, who proved by the butchery of his own people and his racist expulsion of Uganda Asians how much he personally owed to the Führer's inspiration. On 12 September 1972 in a message to the United Nations Secretary-General, Idi Amin had enthusiastically recalled: 'Germany is the right place where, when Hitler was Prime Minister and supreme commander, he burned over six million Jews.'[89] Disappointed that no statues had been erected in West Germany to honour the dead Führer, Amin pledged himself to build one in Uganda. In a rambling review of world events before the General Assembly of the United Nations in October 1975, he called for 'the expulsion of Israel from the UN and the extinction of Israel as a state' – no doubt this was *his* way of honouring Hitler's memory. During this same visit to New York he also sought to whip up antisemitism among the local black population, claiming that the poverty in Harlem was part of the 'damage' which the Zionist movement had done by extorting money for Israel from innocent Americans over the years.[90]

The Idi Amin brand of antisemitism has its counterpart in Muslim nations like Pakistan and in Turkey among the Islamic right-wing organizations. The bi-weekly, *Yageen International*, for example, which purportedly presents Islam in its pristine purity, is published in Pakistan and specializes in the most rabid anti-Jewish slander. This has been paralleled by a number of Black Muslim sects in the United States. Both anti-Zionism and a raw, primitive Judeophobia have been the policy of the Chicago-based Nation of Islam which spontaneously identifies with the Arab world and, like other Black nationalist groups, has a deep, abiding hatred of Caucasian 'blue-eyed white devils'.[91] In the last few years the fundamentalist factor in these sectarian movements has grown, encouraged by Libyan funding. A recent case in point was the vicious antisemitic outburst by black Muslim leader Louis Farrakhan, a political ally of the Reverend Jesse Jackson during the last Democratic primary campaign in the United States. In a radio broadcast on 11 March 1984 Farrakhan claimed *inter alia* that 'Hitler was a very great man. He wasn't great for me as a black person but he was a very great German. . . . He rose Germany up from nothing. Well, in a sense you could say there's a similarity in that we are raising our people up from nothing.'[92] In another broadcast in June 1984 Farrakhan repeated that 'Hitler was great, but wickedly great', adding that the Zionists had made a deal with him, which enabled them 'to take the land away from the Palestinian people'.[93] The bulk of the black Muslim preacher's remarks were, however, directed against Israel and the so-called 'chosenness' of the Jews. Judaism was a 'gutter religion' and the only true 'chosen people of God' were the black Muslim people in America. The Jews had, as the Holy Koran charged, falsified the Scriptures and fathered false religions. The state of Israel was the product of their 'old naked scheming, plotting and planning against the lives of a people there in Palestine'.[94] They had been aided in this 'criminal conspiracy' by America, England and the nations. As a punishment for backing Israel, America and its allies were now 'being drawn into the heat of the third world war, which is called Armageddon'.

This hate-filled black Muslim rhetoric echoes in its primitive way some of the basic themes of Arab and Muslim propaganda. In practice the latter makes no distinction between Zionism as a political movement and Jewry, which is regarded as its fifth column all over the world. Since Israelis are mainly Jews, the hostility against the Israeli state easily flows over into generalized physical and verbal attacks on Diaspora Jewry, just as traditional Islamic prejudices continue to nourish and support Arab 'anti-Zionism'. From the prophet Muhammed's confrontation with Jews 1,300 years ago to the present day, the Islamic element in this antisemitism is presented by its own protagonists as one unchanging continuum. Superimposed on this deep substratum are the more modern stereotypes derived from the *Protocols of the Elders of Zion*, from Nazi conspiracy theories and anti-imperialist ideological rationalizations of the Arab–Israeli conflict.[95] Hence the terrible trio of Israel, Zionism and Jewry frequently appear as a monolithic demonic entity implanted in the Middle East by the satanic forces of Western imperialism. But the Zionist Monster, as pointed out by the 'International Conference on Zionism' opened by Colonel Qaddafi in Tripoli in July 1976, is a threat not just to the Middle East but to the whole world. This satanic force is constantly wreaking misery and calamity upon all of humanity, fomenting disorder on a global scale and carrying out inhuman atrocities. The infinitely corrupt nature of Zionism can only be explained by the evil characteristics of Jews, genetically transmitted from one generation to another. Nevertheless, these traits have not prevented Jews from attaining positions of great power and influence in world politics and international economic affairs.

It should not be forgotten that such rabidly bigoted views are openly expressed at the United Nations by the various Arab and Iranian representatives. For example, the then Permanent Representative of Jordan, Mr Hazem Nuseibah, told the General Assembly on 15 December 1980 that there was a Jewish cabal 'which controls, manipulates and exploits the rest of humanity by controlling the money and wealth of the world'.[96] In the same blatantly antisemitic vein, which recalled the choicest rhetoric of the Nazi era, Nuseibah remarked that it was a well-known fact that 'the Zionists are the richest people in the world and control much of its destiny. People like Lord Rothschild every day, in ironclad secrecy, decide and flash round the world how high the price of gold should be each particular day. And there is Mr Oppenheimer of South Africa, who holds 15 million blacks in bondage in order to exploit and monopolize the diamonds, the uranium, and other precious resources which rightfully belong to the struggling African people of South Africa and Namibia.'[97] The Jordanian representative was, moreover, concerned that 'while millions of hard-working God-fearing Americans are unemployed, the Zionists own a lion's share of that great abundance'.[98]

Syrian and Iraqi representatives have also made similarly anti-Jewish statements in recent years, but for sheer Hitlerian virulence they must cede pride of place to the representatives of Iran and Libya. On 30 September 1983 the Iranian Foreign Minister, Mr Velayati, had flatly stated: 'There is no cure for the cancerous growth of Zionism but surgery.'[99] On 2 November 1983 Mr Ragaie-Khorassani, the Permanent Representative of Iran, had urgently expressed his hope, with reference to Israel, 'that the Moslem countries in the area will soon consider the final solution'.[100] On 19 December 1983 Mr Hosein Latify returned to the medical metaphor so favoured by Adolf Hitler: 'The Zionist entity . . . should be removed like a cancerous tumour.'[101] The Libyan representative, Mr Treiki, had shown himself to be no less frank in a statement of 8 December 1983, of which Hitler, too, might have been proud. 'It is high time for the United Nations and the United States, in particular, to realize that the Jewish Zionists here in the United States attempt to destroy Americans. Look around New York, who are the owners of pornographic film operations and houses? Is it not the Jews who are exploiting the American people and trying to debase them? If we succeed in eliminating that entity, we shall by the same token save the American and European peoples. We hope that the day will soon come when we can eradicate this affront, this aberration of history which we committed when we accepted within our Organization this band of criminals, mercenaries and terrorists.'[102]

Sadly, it is not only the Arab Rejection Front that believes in such Nazi-like fantasies of eradicating a satanic Jewish world power. The Egyptian media, in spite of President Sadat's historic visit to Jerusalem and the resulting peace treaty, continue to publish no less virulently antisemitic diatribes. These anti-Jewish outbursts are prevalent not solely on the Muslim Right and Socialist Left but even in mainstream Egyptian journalism. Not only the denigration of the Talmud but even the blood libel have now made their reappearance, demonstrating once more the fact that the most traditional Christian themes can always resurface even in a Muslim culture. The eclectic nature of Arab antisemitism should not, however, be allowed to obscure its intensity and the genocidal passions that have thus far underpinned its endless *jihad* against Israel.

This hatred remains rooted in the age-old Islamic negation of Jewish equality and the consequent denial of the legitimacy of Jewish statehood in Palestine. Contemporary Islam, as we have seen, still looks upon Israel as the nucleus of a conspiratorial Jewish power seeking to undermine and destroy cherished Muslim values and institutions. It regards the struggle against the Jews and Israel in *global* terms as a fight for Islam: both for the internal purging of alien and anti-Islamic forces which have infiltrated into the Middle East and as part of the continuous external *jihad* against the infidel West. In this war against an insidious and permanent enemy which from the days of Muhammed until the present has always sought to undermine Islam, no compromise is possible. The struggle against Jewish machinations and against the 'agents of Zionism' is decreed by fate. It is a doctrinal, ideological war of destiny for the soul of Islam, a life-and-death struggle to throw back the diabolical conspiracy sapping the foundations of the true faith. As the elect of God, the Muslim *Ummah* is called to conquer the unbelievers (Jews and Christians) whose heresy contradicts the cosmic order. For the present, the Jews of Israel remain the prime targets of this *jihad*, just as the Jews of Europe were the main objects of Hitler's earlier apocalyptic struggle for world hegemony.

Yet as the assassination of President Sadat showed, the real objectives of Islamic fundamentalism reach much deeper and its aspirations necessitate the sweeping away not only of Israel but also of all Zionist lackeys within the Arab leadership. In the eyes of integral Islam, a peace initiative such as that pursued by the late President Sadat (who, ironically enough, had frequently played the Islamic card in the past) was ultimately a confession of the weakness and decadence of Islam. As the spiritual leader of the Muslim Brotherhood in Egypt, Umar al-Tilmisani, summed it up: 'Normalization of relations with Israel is the most dangerous cancer eating away at all the life cells in our bodies.' For the fundamentalists, as Ronald Nettler has recently pointed out, Israel and the Jews do threaten the very 'lifeblood of Islam' and they are perceived as the central symptom of the Islamic malaise.[103] But the eradication of Israel only represents one aspect of the ultimate fundamentalist goal of a *reconquista* of the Muslim-Arab world in the name of Islam. With the defeat of the forces of westernization and modernization within the

Arab and Muslim worlds, the road would then finally be clear for the decisive *jihad* against the infidel West.

# CHAPTER TEN

# The Soviet Protocols

Ever since the late 1930s many similarities between Stalinism and Hitlerism as political systems have been recognized by perceptive observers of comparative politics. Not only did Soviet Russia and Nazi Germany share such features as the *Führerprinzip*, one-party dictatorships, an aggressive ideology and policy of foreign expansionism, centralized control of the mass media and the invasion of the omnipotent state into all areas of private life; both systems were built on the use of internal terror against potential as well as real adversaries of the regime and an extensive system of concentration camps.[1] It should also be remembered that Stalin had preceded Hitler in achieving power, having established a totalitarian dictatorship by 1929, and the total number of victims during the admittedly much longer period of his autocratic rule approached 20 million, far exceeding that of the German dictator.[2] Furthermore, the personality and politics of Stalin were to leave an enormous and continuing imprint not only on the ideology and internal life of his country but also on the foreign policy of the Soviet Union.[3]

No less than the Führer, Stalin was driven by a pathological fear of what he perceived as insidious conspiratorial forces operating at home and abroad to undermine the Soviet system. The ideological rationale for this paranoid outlook was that the Soviet Union lived under conditions of permanently hostile capitalist encirclement. The state terrorism that accompanied the forced collectivization and industrialization programme between 1929 and 1933, followed by the Great Purges of 1936–8, were the terrifying consequences. As in the case of Nazism, the dictates of a fanatical ideology, the resolve to crush all opposition and the logic of an omnipotent bureaucratic state apparatus fused together in the Stalinist terror. But in the last analysis the 'holocaust' inflicted by Stalin on Soviet society was as much the will of a single all-powerful dictator as Hitler's inflexible resolve to destroy European Jewry.

Though Stalin as an 'Old Bolshevik' was the heir of an ideology which on the surface appeared to be the very antithesis of Nazism, it was his historic role to gradually blur the distinction. In his successful campaign against Leon

Trotsky in the late 1920s under the slogan of 'Socialism in One Country', Stalin had already appealed to ancient Russian reflexes of national messianism tinged with antisemitism.[4] Between 1928 and 1933 Stalin's policies also substantially contributed to the Nazi rise to power. It was under his instructions that the Communists in Germany (KPD) became passive and at times even active auxiliaries of Hitler's assault on the Weimar Republic.[5] They concentrated their fire less at the Nazis than against the German Social Democrats who were officially described as representing 'Fascism in its currently most dangerous form'.[6] All distinctions between fascists and democrats, between liberals, socialists and Nazis, were deliberately obscured by the Comintern at the very time when Stalin in 1929 began to unleash his internal Russian policy of 'exterminating the kulaks as a class'. In 1930 the KPD even published a 'Programme for the National and Social Liberation of the German Nation' which sought to outbid the Nazis in nationalist demagogy. In 1932 the Communists openly campaigned with the Nazis to remove the SPD-led government in Prussia; a few months earlier they had called on NSDAP supporters to join with them in a common struggle against the Versailles Treaty, the American Young Plan and the 'government of finance-capital'.[7] The Stalinist strategy of the Comintern, which minimized the Nazi danger, daily denounced the 'social fascism' of the SPD and claimed that fascism itself already ruled under the Catholic Chancellor Bruening, in effect ensured the victory of Hitler in Germany.[8]

For the Stalinists, National Socialism was merely an instrument of the capitalist bourgeoisie and the Reichswehr. They had no insight at all into the racialist antisemitic ideology which largely determined Hitler's domestic and foreign policy and the dire threat which Nazism would eventually pose to the Soviet Union.[9] On the contrary, Stalin sought from the beginning of Nazi rule to come to an accommodation with the Third Reich. At the Seventeenth Party Congress of 1934, he declared: 'Of course, we are far from enthusiastic about the fascist regime in Germany. But fascism is beside the point, if only because fascism in Italy, for example, has not kept the USSR from establishing the best of relations with that country.'[10] As early as 1934, then, he did not preclude a *rapprochement* with Berlin if a more pro-Eastern orientation were to prevail within the Nazi regime. The Show Trials and terrible Purges of 1936–8 can be seen *inter alia* as Stalin's way of signalling to Hitler that he was ready to do business.[11] For the totally fictitious charges against the Trotskyist and Bukharinist oppositions, of secretly negotiating a deal with the Nazis and being pro-fascist agents of the Third Reich, were clearly known in Berlin to be spurious. The defendants in the Moscow Show Trials included leading anti-fascist Communists, many of them Jews. Why then was Stalin striking them down? Significantly, no less an authority than Mussolini, writing in *Popolo d'Italia* (15 March 1938) on the Bukharin trial, wondered if Stalin had not secretly become a fascist.[12]

Hitler, too, was impressed by the Great Purges, subsequently seeing in them a signal that Stalin had abandoned international Communism and was determined to liquidate the 'Jewish' intelligentsia. The Purges evidently served an important foreign policy goal for Stalin of smoothing the way for the Nazi–Soviet pact. By liquidating its most obvious opponents in advance and at the same time implicitly undermining the idea that Communism stood for anti-fascism, Stalin somewhat lessened the shock that was to be engendered by his imminent bargain with Hitler. His goals, moreover, were by no means confined to securing a breathing-space for the Soviet Union and buying time to strengthen Russian defences. As the 1939–41 alliance with Hitler clearly demonstrated, he envisaged a policy of Soviet imperialist expansion *in collaboration with* the Nazis but based on a division of spheres of influence in Eastern Europe, the Balkans and the Persian Gulf. Only the German invasion of the USSR in June 1941, which completely stunned Stalin, who had ignored all advance warnings, put an end to this policy of dynamic collaboration.[13]

The Nazi–Soviet pact had also signified the extent of the Soviet dictator's latent antisemitism, which became increasingly more open and pathological during and immediately after the war years. He began to repeat standard antisemitic stereotypes about Jews shirking military service, and at the time of the 'anti-cosmopolitan' campaign (1948–9) told his daughter Svetlana Alliluyeva that 'the entire older generation is contaminated with Zionism and now they are teaching the young people too'.[14] These deeply-rooted prejudices had not, however, prevented him after the German invasion in June 1941 from utilizing to the full the complete dedication of Soviet Jewry to the war effort of the Red Army.[15] Nor did he hesitate to encourage the creation of a Jewish Anti-Fascist Committee at a time when the Soviet Union was in mortal danger of collapse. A degree of latitude was even allowed for the stimulation of Soviet Jewish national feelings, and contacts with Jews in America and Britain were actually encouraged in order to obtain vital financial support and political goodwill for the USSR.[16] Soviet policy towards the Palestinian Jewish *Yishuv* also showed signs of positive change in this period which foreshadowed Stalin's temporary shift of 1947–8 to support for a Jewish state.

Nonetheless the Soviet authorities carefully avoided mentioning during the war years that Jews were being singled out for destruction in German-occupied areas of the USSR and invariably sought to show that Nazi terror was equally directed at the entire Soviet population. In part this may have been due to the awareness that, as a result of Nazi propaganda, antisemitism had already spread widely among different Soviet nationalities and in Red Army ranks during the war; above all, though, it expressed Soviet fears of strengthening Jewish nationalism. Almost immediately after the war, a bitter campaign began against 'nationalist deviations' (in particular the Jewish variant), one of whose main features was the attack on Jewish writers for 'harping' on the theme of the Holocaust. The result of this crusade was the liquidation of Jewish culture in the Soviet Union. The final offensive began towards the end of 1948 and soon fused with the so-called 'anti-cosmo-politan' campaign that ran its course between 1949 and 1953.[17] A leading theme of Nazi antisemitism – the accusation of *rootless* cosmopolitanism – was now for the first time adapted for use in the Soviet Union against the assimilated Russian-Jewish intelligentsia. The 'cosmopolites' were invari-ably described in the Soviet press as persons without backbone or identity, knowing and worshipping everything foreign, and were assailed for behaving like passportless wanderers. They were accused of defaming the Russian nation and Great Russian man, of lacking loyalty to their socialist fatherland and of boundless servility towards Western imperialism. The Jewish names of the offenders were prominently displayed in an obvious effort to incite popular sentiment against them.

The 'Doctors' Plot' of early 1953 was the culmination of this ugly campaign. It created a morbidly anti-Jewish atmosphere in the USSR and most probably would have been the prelude to a Stalinist 'Final Solution' of the Jewish question. The six Jews among the nine physicians accused of seeking to poison Stalin and the top Soviet leadership were significantly charged with being in league with 'Zionist spies' as well as American and British agents. Only Stalin's death on 5 March 1953 prevented a large-scale pogrom and the intended deportation *en bloc* of Soviet Jewry to Siberia.[18] The legacy of this last phase of Stalinist rule was indeed a grim one. During the 'Black Years' of Soviet Jewry (launched by the murder of the great actor and President of the Jewish Anti-Fascist Committee, Solomon Mikhoels, in January 1948), which lasted until Stalin's death in 1953, the remnants of a living Jewish culture in the USSR were totally extirpated. Most of the leading Yiddish artists were arrested and imprisoned and all remaining Jewish institutions except for a few synagogues were closed down. On 12 August 1952 the cream of the surviving Soviet Yiddish writers, including Perets Markish, Itzik Fefer and Dovid Bergelson, had been executed on Stalin's orders, thus completing the work of physical and cultural destruction begun by Hitler.

At just this time, Stalin was to choose Czechoslovakia as the laboratory experiment for his first attempt to extend antisemitism outside the borders of the Soviet Union, presumably as a means of ideologically cementing together the satellite nations of the Communist bloc. Czechoslovakia, with its pre-war democratic system, its more Western outlook and its popular-based Communist Party which had a genuinely internationalist tradition, might have seemed a surprising choice, especially since Czechoslovak antisemitism, though by no means negligible, was rather less militant than the variants prevailing in some neighbouring East European nations. On the other hand, it was Czechoslovakia which had sent desperately needed arms to Israel in 1948 on Stalin's own instructions. The 'Zionist' connection was therefore more easily established. This suggests that the trial against Rudolf Slansky, the Jewish-born General Secretary of the Czechoslovak Communist Party, and thirteen other leading party and state functionaries, which began on 20 November 1952, may have been intended among other purposes to signal a change in Moscow's Middle East policy. Eleven of the fourteen defendants were of Jewish origin, as the prosecutors constantly stressed, and the Israel connection featured prominently in the indictment as a central part of the so-called 'Trotskyite-Titoist-Zionist' conspiracy to overthrow the socialist order in Czechoslovakia.[19]

The antisemitic tone of the proceedings had unquestionably been the direct result of orders transmitted to the Czech security organs by Soviet 'advisers'. Moreover, Major Smola, a rabidly antisemitic admirer of Hitler, had been put in charge of the Slansky case. Artur London, the Deputy Foreign Minister, who had been interrogated earlier by the major, recalled in his memoirs (*L'Aveu*, Paris, 1968): 'Major Smola took me by the throat and in a voice shaking with hatred shouted, "You and your dirty race, we shall exterminate it. Not everything Hitler did was right; but he exterminated the Jews and that was a good thing. Far too many of them managed to avoid the gas chamber but we shall finish where he left off." '[20] Another victim of the Slansky purge also noted the similarity between the Soviet security advisers and the Gestapo 'both by their marked antisemitism and by their methods of interrogation'.[21] The chief Russian adviser was particularly eager to demonstrate the 'dangers inherent in the world Zionist movement' and persuaded Klement Gottwald, head of the Czech Communist Party and Government, to establish a special 'anti-Zionist' department in the Ministry of Home Security.

At the time of the Slansky trial, the Czech Communist press began on Soviet instructions to openly identify 'Zionism' with fascism, as well as with American imperialism. *Rudé Právo* venomously wrote on 24 November 1952, for example, that 'the Zionist organizations with which Slansky was associated were nothing but Fascist shock troops. It is, moreover, self-evident that any bourgeois nationalism, including of course its Jewish variant, must inevitably produce fascism.'[22] Such open incitement soon led to a revival of wartime Nazi-type antisemitism in Czechoslovakia, with remarks like 'Hitler ought to have finished them all off' becoming increasingly common. The Stalinist antisemites at the top of the party apparatus openly encouraged this mood, spreading views that were redolent of Hitler's propaganda machine, down through every level of 'public opinion' to the masses. Klement Gottwald gave this Judeophobia an official blessing at the December 1952 Czech Communist Party Conference. Turning the truth on its head, he accused 'Zionists' of using Gentile sympathy for their sufferings under Nazism to penetrate and subvert the workers' movement and communist parties. 'The Zionist organizations and their American masters were thus able to exploit shamelessly the sufferings Hitler and the other Fascists inflicted on the Jews. It could almost be said that they were quite willing to make capital out of Auschwitz and Maidanek. Normally, former bankers, industrialists, estate owners or Kulaks would hardly have been accepted into a Communist Party, let alone allowed to rise to leading positions.'[23] Gottwald here reiterated the spurious claim that 'Jewish' leaders of the Czech party were middle-class traitors to the working masses, brought up in 'a spirit of Jewish nationalism' – though it was a well-known fact that they had all been militantly anti-Zionist and long since estranged from their Jewish origins.

The Slansky trial retrospectively proved that Hitler and von Ribbentrop were correct in 1939 in their feeling that Stalin was indeed a radical antisemite. It had, however, taken the Soviet dictator another decade to fully embrace the Nazi version of the 'Jewish world conspiracy', which even in the early 1950s was still disguised under the mask of bourgeois 'Zionism', 'rootless cosmopolitanism' and other Stalinist euphemisms. Moreover, with a Machiavellian cunning that surpassed his German mentors, Stalin had known how to utilize Jewish Communists to consolidate the deeply unpopular post-war Communist regimes in Poland, Hungary and Rumania as well as exploiting their services in Stalinizing Czechoslovakia. He realized that he could rely on their unconditional loyalty, precisely because their own security amidst endemically antisemitic populations (whose hostile predisposition the Holocaust had aggravated rather than diminished) depended on the strength of Communist power.[24] The very fact that Jews loyal to Moscow had emerged in the top ranks of the new post-war Stalinist regimes in Eastern Europe at a moment of national catastrophe for these countries was bound to increase popular Judeophobic resentment and hatred. The Communist Jews were roundly detested by the local masses as servants of an alien 'colonial' yoke of Soviet power: none of this, of course, was unknown to Stalin and the Soviet leadership. When he decided therefore on large-scale purges in Eastern Europe at the end of the 1940s, in order to accelerate the process of satellization, Stalin could all the more easily divert popular wrath against the Jews; he was thereby satisfying endemic East European nationalism and encouraging the careerist ambitions of the younger generation of more manipulable home-grown Communists.

The removal of Jews from key positions in the Communist Party hierarchy under the mask of a struggle against 'Zionism' had been accomplished only in the Soviet Union, Rumania and Czechoslovakia (where it was temporarily reversed in 1968) by the time of Stalin's death.[25] It would take another fifteen years to complete the task in Poland, even though only a tiny remnant remained from what had once been the largest Jewish community in Europe. The surviving Jews who remained in Poland after 1948 were mostly convinced Communists and had provided an indispensable reservoir of cadres for imposing Stalinism on a recalcitrant population in the most inflammable of Moscow's satellites. Though Poland had been spared the post-war Show Trials that occurred in Hungary, Bulgaria and Czechoslovakia, the repercussions of the Doctors' Plot soon revealed the uses of the new 'anti-Zionist' conspiracy theories forged in Moscow.

Thus in January 1953 the theoretical review of the Polish Communist Party published an article accusing the 'Zionists' of collaborating with the Hitlerites in the 'extermination' of Jews during the Second World War and of concealing the truth of the Holocaust from the Jewish masses on the orders of the American State Department.[26] According to this fantastic concoction, American imperialist circles wished above all to delay the opening of a second front in Europe and had therefore deliberately sought to paralyse all mass movements of resistance on the Continent which might embarrass the Western Allies. At the same time Ben-Gurion was accused, with American connivance, of unleashing 'a real campaign of extermination of the Arab population living in the State of Israel' – a policy supposedly identical to that of the Hitlerites during the world war. Furthermore, Ben-Gurion and Nahum Goldmann were alleged to be in collusion with Federal Chancellor Konrad Adenauer in order 'to revive Hitlerism in West Germany'.[27] Thus the essentials of the Nazi–Zionist 'collaboration' myth had already appeared by the end of 1952 in the Stalinist media, several months before the death of the Soviet tyrant.

Ironically enough, however, it was de-Stalinization which produced a veritable irruption of political antisemitism during the Polish October of 1956. Communist Jews who had been denounced by Russian Stalinists in 1949 as pro-Western 'cosmopolites' were now accused in Poland of pro-Stalinism! Anti-Soviet riots, as in Poznan, quickly degenerated into anti-semitic demonstrations, and following Gomulka's return to power everything was done to stimulate an exodus of the remnant of Polish Jewry.[28] The role of Soviet political and police agents in encouraging the purge of Jewish Stalinists in 1956 was central.[29] It was part of Nikita Khrushchev's 'liberal' de-Stalinization policy to spread the idea that Jews were responsible for all the crimes of Stalinism in Poland, a myth that was in any case widely believed by Poles, but not immediately acted upon in 1956. Within four years, however, Jews began to be systematically removed from the civilian and military security apparatus as well as from high positions in the state and party administration – initially on Polish rather than Soviet initiative.[30]

In the early 1960s orders were given by Gomulka to strictly watch all senior officials of Jewish origin, and a full card index for Polish Jews was prepared with Soviet blessing. By 1965 a Polish Politburo plan for the complete purge of Jews from all positions of influence was operationally ready.[31] Simultaneously, antisemitic pressure was building from the lower party echelons. A younger generation of careerists, who resented both Great-Russian domination and the influence of those Communist Jews who had returned to Poland from abroad after 1945, looked to the former Partisan leader General Moczar (the then Minister of the Interior) and to his ultra-nationalist brand of Polish Communism to advance their material interests. The power-struggle between the Gomulka and Moczar cliques, both of whom were antisemitic in varying degrees, provided the background to the 'anti-Zionist' crusade of 1967–8, as a result of which Poland was made virtually *judenrein*. The campaign was ostensibly sparked by the Six-Day War of June 1967 and by the student unrest in Polish universities in March 1968, caused by the banning of a nineteenth-century patriotic drama, *Dziady*, by Poland's national poet Adam Mickiewicz. The regime blamed the internal unrest on a conspiracy between Marxist 'revisionists', 'Zionists' in Poland, the Israelis, the West German *revanchists* and American imperialists, designed to separate Poland from the Soviet Union and restore bourgeois democracy.[32] A book by Tadeusz Walichnowski, *Israel a NRF* (Israel and the German Federal Republic), published in Warsaw in 1967, tried to sub-stantiate the thesis. A speech of Gomulka in June 1967 accusing Polish Jewry of being a 'fifth column' of Israel and Western imperialists had made it clear that this was also *official* policy.

In an even more notorious speech on 19 March 1968 Gomulka publicly divided Polish Jews into those who served Israel, 'cosmopolitans' who were neither Jews nor Poles, and those who saw themselves as loyal Poles. For the first time in the history of Communism, Jews *qua* Jews were *openly* made the scapegoats for the failures of the regime rather than trying to rely on the more devious methods of Stalinist Russian antisemitism. It was now publicly made clear by Gomulka that even the most loyal Polish Jews could not hope to hold posts of national responsibility again. Once the signal had been given from the top, the 'anti-Zionist' purge soon swept through all layers of Polish society. The official party newspaper openly blamed the 'Zionists' on 16 June 1968 for the student riots; it demanded the removal of persons of 'Jewish origin' from the universities, from the government, party and security organs on the grounds of their 'inner cosmopolitanism', their 'privileged' positions and links with Zionism.

A frankly racist article by the head of the Cultural Section of the Polish Communist Central Committee, Andrzej Werblan, published in June 1968, inscribed the antisemitic principle of the *numerus clausus* into Marxist theory for the first time. In the past, he claimed, the 'ethnic composition' of the Polish Communist Party had 'not been correctly balanced'. The disproportionate number of Jewish militants in the post-war party had led to the sins of 'sectarianism' and 'dogmatism', just as before 1939 it had produced an excessively 'cosmopolitan' interpretation of internationalism. Thus both Stalinism and its antitheses (Trotskyism/Luxemburgism) were equated with a Jewish ethnic background! Moreover, no society, according to Werblan, 'would be willing to tolerate an excessive representation of a national minority in the leading councils of the nation, particularly in departments concerned with national defence, security, propaganda and diplomacy. . . . Every society rejects such privileges with disgust.'[33] Jewish cadres were not only incapable for ethnic reasons of correctly harmonizing Polish national interests with internationalism; they were now assumed to be inherently prone to the deviationist sins of 'revisionism' and Zionism.[34]

For the less sophisticated, a speech on 11 April 1968 by Gomulka's supporter, Communist Party First Secretary in the Gdansk region Stanislaw Kociolek, presented the 'anti-Zionist' crusade as a way of 'throwing off the humpback of the nationalist [i.e. Jewish] misrepresentation of internationalism, and of the nationalist defence of group interests. . . . There can be no philosophy of humility towards any *Herrenvolk* thrown up by history.'[35] In other words, Jews had become a *Herrenvolk* in the new Communist dispensation and Poles were merely defending their national honour against 'alien' domination. This return of leading Polish Communists to the pre-war rhetoric of the Polish antisemitic fascists ('Jews to Palestine!' etc.) and the imitation of suitably adapted Hitlerian themes to justify a purge of non-existent 'Zionists' in a country where barely 30,000 Jews (0.1 per cent of the population) still remained, after the Holocaust, was obviously not spontaneous. It did not correspond, in contrast to pre-war Poland, to any identifiable Jewish minority problem, but rather to inner-party conflicts in which antisemitism had become integral to the nationalist type of Communism espoused by General Moczar and his 'partisans'; the latter favoured eradicating all trends towards liberalization, dissent and social democracy and encouraged an eastward, pro-Moscow, orientation of Polish policy. The veteran Gomulka played the same fascist and racialist game, partly out of conviction and partly to remain in power, in a situation where encouraging antisemitic hysteria seemed to be an effective diversion from the regime's own socio-economic failures.[36] There was, moreover, strong pressure from the Russian big brother and the internal security organs to stage show-trials of Jews in 1968 (which was resisted by Gomulka) as well as to 'Aryanize' completely the Polish Army, which was duly carried out.[37]

Antisemitic 'anti-Zionism' in Poland, as in Czechoslovakia after the Soviet invasion of August 1968, had thus proved itself an effective temporary method of *re-Stalinizing* a system in which too many liberal-democratic cracks had begun to appear. The crushing of the intelligentsia and all manifestations of dissent in both countries was the direct result of this neo-Stalinist war on 'Zionism' and the true measure of its demoralizing effect. Here, too, the Communist rulers of Poland and Czechoslovakia, under Soviet prodding, had clearly taken a leaf out of Hitler's book. Like the dead Führer, they well understood that a 'final solution of the Jewish question' was simultaneously a blow struck at free criticism, intellectual independence, the aspirations for greater personal freedom and a more representative popular democracy. By raising the spectre of the abstract, demonic Jew in 'Zionist' disguise, responsible for subverting the socialist system, the Polish and Czech Stalinist leaders repressed the legitimate aspirations of their own peoples at the price of plunging them into economic backwardness and political stagnation. Perhaps it is no accident that since 1956 a more liberal East European Communist regime like Hungary (though its leadership had until the 1956 revolution been predominantly Jewish) has prospered economically and managed to avoid the internal 'anti-Zionist' witch-hunts of Poland and Czechoslovakia;[38] or that the extremely nationalist Communism practised in President Ceausescu's Rumania in accordance with its *independent* foreign policy line has steadfastly resisted any imitation of Moscow's untiring efforts to demonologize Israel, Zionism and the Jewish people.[39]

In the Soviet Union itself, the post-war antisemitic policy had been continued, though at a lower level of intensity in spite of Khrushchev's bold de-Stalinization programme.[40] It had received a new dimension with the increasing orientation of Soviet foreign policy towards anti-Western Arab nationalism and Third World liberation movements – a change which took place under Khrushchev.[41] The menacing warning of Soviet Premier Bulganin to the Israeli government during the Sinai campaign (5 November 1956), which asserted that the 'very existence of Israel as a state was in jeopardy', had signified the final wreckage of the brief post-1948 honeymoon in Russian–Israeli relations.[42] That *rapprochement* had been primarily intended to drive the British out of Palestine and to establish a pro-Soviet foothold in the Middle East. But the closer Moscow drew to its so-called 'progressive' allies in the Arab world, the more consistently Israel was now portrayed as a mere reactionary puppet of Western imperialism.[43] Meanwhile, domestic antisemitic propaganda continued unabated. It tended, however, to be more focused under Khrushchev on the Jewish role in 'economic crimes' or else engaged in vilifications of Judaism in the context of the atheist campaigns against religion. A proto-Nazi work such as Trofim Kichko's *Judaism without Embellishment* (1963), which alleged a universal Jewish conspiracy involving Judaism, Jewish bankers, Zionism and Western capitalism, was still something of an exception. Even the hard-line French Communist daily *L'Humanité* felt obliged to denounce the vile caricatures in Kichko's opus and the book was withdrawn from circulation a year later.[44]

It was the Six-Day War which literally overnight transformed the situation, leading to the longest and most expensive antisemitic campaign not only in the history of the Soviet Union but in the twentieth century as a whole.[45] As a result, ever since 1967 a mighty superpower has been flooding the world with a never-ending flow of 'anti-Zionist' propaganda whose intensity far exceeds all its past campaigns against such ideological heresies as Trotskyism, Titoism or Maoism. Only the Nazis in their twelve years of power succeeded in producing a similarly sustained campaign of anti-semitism and using it in a comparable way as a major ideological tool of domestic and foreign policy. In the guise of anti-Zionism, the men in the Kremlin had discovered a new form and an unexpectedly effective justi-fication for the antisemitism which was officially proscribed by Marxist-Leninist ideology.[46] The Russian national counter-revolution begun by Stalin in the 1930s could now gradually reconnect with the pogrom traditions of the autocratic Tsarist state;[47] while still using the hollow shell of Marxist verbiage to conceal the sea-change which the official ruling ideology had undergone, the Soviet regime was able to invent a new form of Russian National Communism. In this bastard form of socialism, rampant antisemitism has largely swallowed up the residues of Marxist international-ism.[48] During the last seventeen years Brezhnev, Andropov and Chernenko have as a consequence inadvertently proved to the world that they were the heirs of Hitler no less than of Stalin.

The systematic Russian campaign of vilification had begun on the morrow of Israel's lightning victory over Moscow's Arab allies, a severe blow to her great-power prestige and the reputation of her armaments. Soviet inter-national representatives and the domestic media immediately accused the Israelis of 'behaving like Nazis' and on 5 July 1967 CPSU General Secretary Leonid Brezhnev, speaking to graduates of the military academies gathered at the Kremlin, stated that 'in their atrocities it seems they [the Israelis] want to copy the crimes of the Hitler invaders'.[49] It now became *de rigueur* to slander the state of Israel and its Jewish inhabitants as imitators of the Nazis, ardent advocates of 'racism', 'barbarians', 'pirates', 'vandals' and 'practi-tioners of genocide'. All the clichés, images and trigger-words like *Blitzkrieg*, *Herrenvolk*, *Gauleiters*, concentration camps, SS uniforms, etc., were mobilized on a truly massive scale for the benefit of an overseas as well as a Soviet domestic audience.

Around 1969 the Nazi metaphor was elaborated to include the charge of 'Zionist racism', which became a central prong in the Soviet effort to defame and delegitimize Israel, Zionism and the Jewish people. Yuri Ivanov, one of the new breed of 'Jewish experts' at the higher levels of the party apparatus, in his *Beware! Zionism!* (1969) presented Zionism as being no less racialist than Nazism, for allegedly speaking of the 'outstanding' abilities of the Jews as compared to other nationalities. The Zionists perhaps relied less on brute force than on the weapons of money, corruption, control of the media and distortion of news on a global scale to achieve their ends. But their ideology and methods made them sworn enemies of the Soviet Union and the Communist movement. Ivanov, one of the founders of the new pseudo-science of anti-Zionism, further 'enriched' Soviet Marxism with a by now classic definition of Zionism as 'the ideology, the ramified system of organization and the political practice of the big Jewish bourgeoisie that has merged with the monopolistic circles of the USA and other imperialist powers. Its basic content is militant chauvinism and anti-communism.'[50]

Yuri Ivanov, Trofim Kichko, Yevgeny Yevseyev (author of *Fascism under the Blue Star*), Vladimir Bolshavkov, Vladimir Begun, Dmitri Zhukov, Lev Korneyev and other Soviet dragon-slayers of 'Zionism' now surreptitiously set to work to revise the classic Marx–Lenin interpretation of the workings of the capitalist system and Western imperialism. According to the neo-Marxist antisemitic world-view, the villainy of the big Jewish bourgeoisie was actually unequalled in history. Their tool, 'Zionism', resembled a great invisible power whose octopus-like tentacles extend into every sphere of politics, finance, religion and the communications media in capitalist countries. This international Mafia, controlled by big Jewish bankers and financiers, also had a vast intelligence service at its disposal. The 'Zionists' themselves were often depicted as including many non-Jews – according to Yevgeny Yevseyev, writing in *Komsomolskaya Pravda* (4 October 1967), they numbered as many as 20–25 million people in the United States, where they owned most of the news agencies (80 per cent) and much of the industry (43 per cent), and exerted a decisive influence over banking, law, journalism and the professions. In other words, the old antisemitic myth much diffused by the Nazis of a Western world controlled and manipulated by Jewish high finance had resurfaced with a vengeance in contemporary Soviet propaganda.

Thus according to Vladimir Kiselev, writing in 1977, Zionism was merely a convenient cover for the Jewish bourgeoisie 'to enhance its positions in the economy of the largest capitalist states . . . and in the capitalist system as a whole'.[51] The ultimate objective of Jewish capital was to exploit its special kinship relations to achieve world domination through control of the international banking system – an old-new version of the *Protocols of the Elders of Zion* in pseudo-Leninist disguise. In Lev Korneyev's more apocalyptic view, the Jewish capitalists were already well on the way to achieving this aim, for the military-industrial monopolies in the United States were to a large degree 'controlled or belong to the big pro-Zionist bourgeoisie'.[52] Many of the oil companies also allegedly fell into this category. So, too, did Lockheed Aircraft, 'controlled' by Lazard Frères, a finance empire 'founded . . . by bankers of Jewish origin'[53] – and even McDonnell-Douglas. The latter, according to Korneyev, was controlled by the Rockefeller Chase Manhattan Bank, one of the major financial institutions which has been consistently (and quite absurdly) depicted in Soviet propaganda as crypto-Zionist. Korneyev has also repeatedly alleged that Zionism 'controls and directly owns 158 of the 165 largest death corporations in the West'[54] – thereby identifying the Jews with the 'war-mongering' industrial-military complex.

In line with the theory of the *Protocols*, the superprofits of the big Jewish bourgeoisie derived from such sinister activities are intended to bring about a super-government under its control. Israel is merely one connecting link in this vast design of the Rothchilds, Rockefellers, Lehmanns, Lazard Frères, etc. For the 'Zionist Corporation', in Soviet as in Western neo-Nazi mythology, is a complex network of interlocking parts with tentacles in every single area of business, politics, the media, culture and religion. What ultimately motivates the evil machine and provides the cement for this cosmopolitan Mafia is another theme much emphasized in the *Protocols*, one belonging to the millennial traditions of antisemitism: the Judaic concept of the 'chosen people'.[55] In the Soviet version (as also in some Nazi variations) this feature of Judaism is perceived as an ideological-religious mask for the Jewish power-lust and desire for world-domination. No less common, however, is the Soviet Marxist attempt to present Jewish 'chosenness' as a rabidly racist doctrine of *anti-goyism* which demands that the Jew ruthlessly exploit, humiliate and kill non-Jews.

In his *Judaism and Zionism* (1968) Kichko had denounced the 'chauvinistic idea of the God-chosenness [*bogoiz brannost*] of the Jewish people, the propaganda of messianism and the idea of ruling over the peoples of the world'.[56] This 'dogma', according to Kichko and other Soviet antisemitic ideologues, had provided the justification for Zionist 'criminality', for the 'extermination' of Palestinian Arabs and 'hatred towards other peoples'. Vladimir Begun's *Creeping Counter-Revolution* (1974) developed this by now standard hate-theme in Soviet propaganda, in classical anti-Judaic language. Describing the Bible as 'an unsurpassed textbook of bloodthirstiness, hypocrisy, treason, perfidy and moral degeneracy', Begun wrote that Zionist 'gangsterism', too, had 'its ideological roots in the scrolls of the "holy" Torah and the precepts of the Talmud'.[57] Judaic messianism was nothing but 'a specific version of ultra-imperialism, an international trust of capitalists exploiting the world'.[58]

In the light of such widely diffused views it is not surprising to find Vladimir Begun and others of his ilk also revising the traditional Marxist-Leninist interpretation of antisemitism as a reactionary tool of the ruling classes. In the new dispensation, the pre-revolutionary Judeophobia of Polish, Ukrainian and Byelorussian peasants and the Tsarist pogroms themselves become metamorphosed into a populist class-struggle against merciless Jewish usurers.[59] Dmitri Zhukov, reviewing Begun's work in the mass circulation *Ogonyok*, fully agreed with the proposition that antisemitism was a spontaneous reaction of the oppressed classes to 'barbarous exploitation by the Jewish bourgeoisie'.[60] Thus the *pogromshchiks* of moribund Tsarism have been belatedly rehabilitated by some Soviet ideologues into heralds of a new and better socialist order.

No less indicative of the transformation of recent decades was the fact that in 1972 the journal of the Soviet Embassy in Paris, *URSS*, could reproduce, without acknowledgement, whole extracts from a pamphlet first published in 1906 by the pogromist Black Hundred, *Soyuz Russkii Narod*, merely substituting the code-word 'Zionist' for 'Jew'. The original brochure was revealingly called *The Jewish Question or the Impossibility of Granting Rights to Russian Jews*. The Embassy article, entitled 'The School of Obscurantism', consisted of various fabricated quotations from such Tsarist sources designed to prove that 'Zionist' society was based on a goy-hating religion, which claimed divine sanction to massacre Gentiles.[61] On 24 April 1973 a Paris court found the French publisher of *URSS* (the Communist Deputy Mayor of Nanterre) guilty of public slander and incitement to racial discrimination, hatred and violence. During the trial a Catholic witness, Father Braun, had aptly commented: 'Unfortunately the text we are studying today is reminiscent of the worst fabricated theories of *Der Stürmer* and other sheets distributed by Nazi propaganda. It stupefied me, for in it I found the identical falsifications which have been exploited in all antisemitic publications, whether recent or old.'[62]

In fact the propaganda contained in the *URSS* journal is standard fare in the Soviet Union where it has for years been repeated daily in all the communications media. Its indigenous sources derive, indeed, from the ultra-reactionary chauvinist Black Hundreds and the *Protocols of the Elders of Zion* – itself a Russian secret police (*Okhrana*) fabrication. Thus the made-in-Russia theory of a secret and well-organized Jewish drive for world supremacy, which was then taken over by Hitler and the Nazis in the 1920s, has returned home with a vengeance.[63] Moscow has once more become the fountain head of a new antisemitic International. The imaginary national conflict between Russians and Jews, a confrontation between cosmic forces of good and evil in the eyes of the old-new Soviet antisemites, thereby assumes an apocalyptic significance, exactly as it did for Hitler.[64] Demonological superstitions derived from the traditions of Holy Russia and Russian Orthodox Christianity, from the scurrilous anti-Talmudic literature of the eighteenth and nineteenth centuries and Pan-Slavic nationalism, have openly resurfaced; this time they are backed by the massive military might of a major superpower and the unlimited resources of a vast totalitarian propaganda machine. The age-old suspicion of Jews as a malevolent power, rooted in *muzhik* popular traditions, in Slavophile sentiment and Russian Orthodoxy, has been reactivated on an unprecedented scale to do battle with the forces of 'international Zionism'.[65] Revolutionary unrest in the satellite states, attempted subversion in the USSR, liberalism, freemasonry and dissent are once again all attributable, as in Tsarist Russia, to the same monolithic destructive force.

In this atmosphere, even fanatical neo-Nazi antisemites like Valery Emelianov, an 'Arabist' lecturer from the Oriental Institute of the Academy of Sciences in Moscow, could become *salonfähig* in the eyes of the Soviet

Establishment. In a memorandum of 10 January 1977 submitted to the CPSU Central Committee, Emelianov claimed that the United States was in the hands of a Zionist–Masonic government led by President Carter, who was himself under the thumb of the B'nai Brith 'Gestapo', which engaged in world-wide espionage rather than in anti-defamation work. Nearly three years earlier, in a notorious lecture on 19 February 1974 to the Scientific Research Institute of the Soviet Rubber Industry, Emelianov had warned his audience of a deadly Zionist–Masonic plot to achieve world mastery by the year 2000.[66] This obsession with a vast network of secret Masonic Lodges aiming at the destruction of the socialist system by penetrating party, government and ideological institutes was to be Emelianov's major contribution to Soviet 'Marxism', providing another link to the *Protocols* and the Nazi past. According to Emelianov, the 'Zionists penetrate into the goy's midst through the Masons'. Every Mason is 'an active informer of the Zionists'. Since the mid-1970s this motif of the Zionist–Masonic conspiracy, hitherto restricted to the fringes, began to appear more widely in official Soviet publications.

In Emelianov's version, 'Goyish' freemasonry provided the vital fifth column for Jewry in a world where they were decidedly short on manpower;[67] kits task was to pave the way for Zionism, which already dominated the Western economy. 'The Zionists base themselves on the Judaic-Masonic pyramid, as well as on 80 per cent of the economy in the capitalist countries and 90–95 per cent of the information media.'[68] The apocalyptic struggle against 'the Zionist–Masonic danger' threatening the Soviet Union required a 'merciless struggle', as the subversion of Czechoslovakia in 1968 had already proved. In his memorandum to the Soviet Communist Party Central Committee of January 1977, Emelianov suggested deportation to remote areas of the Soviet Union or possibly even sterner measures in the event of a new war. He argued that the mass emigration of Soviet Jews had removed all Russian illusions about their loyalties. 'They have emigrated from Socialism to Fascism under the blue star of David. Is this not a threatening warning of the possibility of an even greater mass betrayal . . . if a new military situation arises?'[69] Among various concrete measures, he also urged the creation of a world-wide anti-Zionist and anti-Masonic front, wide diffusion of the *Shulkhan Arukh* (Judaism's 'cannibal book'), the outlawing of 'Zionist Masonry' and war on its organized manifestations, including especially human-rights groups and Soviet dissidents. This call was also echoed by other Soviet publicists such as Rayevsky and Polezhaev who condemned 'Zionist' Masonry as being behind Western campaigns for human rights. Such 'non-political' American elitist organizations as the Rand Corporation or the Bilderberg Club ('created according to the Masonic model') were part of the same Zionist–Masonic front for conspiratorial capitalist interests. Freemasonry, according to Polezhaev, served as a 'screen for the "chosen ones" and as a convenient instrument for the representatives of finance capital who seek unrestricted mastery in the "free world" '.[70]

These and numerous articles of a similar hue published in recent years in the Soviet press give public expression to the existence of a Russian neo-Nazi right, far more influential than its counterparts in the West; its counter-slogan to Marxism might have been taken directly from Hitler's early speeches: 'Gentiles of the world unite – against the Judeo-Masonic peril.' Emelianov's last work, *De-Zionization*, published by the Palestine Free Press in Paris, explicitly revealed the weight of the Nazi influence and showed the same underlying irrationality. The Christianization of Russia was presented as part of 'an international Zionist plot' and the root cause of her troubles in history, for it had undermined the Slav race, 'the backbone of the Aryans' and the 'greatest creative force' in Antiquity. Christianity had been nothing but a Jewish secret weapon for weakening the *Slav* master-race – Emelianov's only significant change from the familiar Hitlerian schema. As for the Jews, they were a 'criminal genotype of a hybrid character', the result of crossbreeding 'of the criminal world of the black, yellow and white races'.[71]

Emelianov's Russian neo-Nazism has remained influential even after his own downfall, for it seems probable that a considerable number of Soviet leaders have become victims of their own mythology and genuinely believe in the world Jewish conspiracy.[72] Moreover, in the armed forces this phantas-magoria has virtually been official doctrine for a number of years, with the imperialist world perceived as being ruled by 'Zionists'. In Army circles, as on the New Right within the party (and in dissident circles of an openly fascist character centred around the *Samizdat* publication *Veche*), hatred of the West, Great-Russian nationalism and a quasi-Hitlerian antisemitism fuse together in an unholy trinity. The ex-naval officer Ivan Shevtsov's two very popular antisemitic novels, published in 1970 and compulsory reading for the armed forces, *In the Name of the Father and the Son* and *Love and Hate*, also enjoyed official Politburo backing. They provide an insight into the under-lying flavour of the new Soviet neo-Nazism. In the first novel, world Jewry led by Zionists already controls American imperialism and is busy 'secretly infiltrating all the life cells of all the countries in the world, undermining from within all that is strong, healthy and patriotic'. Agents of Zionism like 'Judas Trotsky' and his followers are shown to be part of the same subversive strategy. So, too, with the penetration of liberal ideas, modernist art and pornography from the West into the Soviet Union.[73] In Shevtsov's second novel, the Jewish villain Nahum Hotzer is depicted as a sadistic pervert, drug-peddler and murderer who kills his own mother for money and dismembers the body of a beautiful 'Ayran' teenager, after first seducing her and turning her into a dope addict. Other characters in this popular novel include treacherous Jewish scientists ready to sell Soviet nuclear weapon secrets to the United States and a Russian hero murdered by Jewish colleagues for wishing to reveal that Albert Einstein had plagiarized the theory of relativity. Shevtsov's 'aesthetic' division of humanity into racially pure, blue-eyed, fair-haired Russians and diabolical dark-haired Jews is one more indication of how deeply the Nazi antisemitic poison has infiltrated Soviet Communism.

Russian television programmes like the notorious 'Traders of Souls' (*Skupshchki dush*), first shown on 22 January 1977, which branded persecuted Jewish activists as 'soldiers of Zionism within the Soviet Union', or other overtly antisemitic novels and films which denigrate Jews as congenital traitors, deliberately appeal to the basest instincts of the population, continually whipping up suspicion and hatred of Soviet Jews.[74] Pseudo-historical works, in which all the activities of Jews in Russian and Soviet history (including that of the *Evsektsiia* in the 1920s and the Jewish Anti-Fascist Committee) are depicted as maliciously subversive, simply represent more academic versions of the same genre. Throughout the Soviet media the motif of 'Zionist' ideological subversion of the Communist system, of Jews as a 'fifth column', and of international Zionism as a vast intelligence-gathering apparatus threatening the Socialist fatherland, is daily being hammered home.[75] Zionism is the 'enemy of the Soviet people' and it actively seeks to overthrow Soviet power.[76] The struggle against it is even placed on a par with the total war waged by the Soviet Union against Nazi Germany between 1941 and 1945.

What emerges from this vast chorus of defamation and vituperation against Zionism is the enormity of the power and evil with which it is credited. In William Korey's words: 'Its power, as in the "Protocols", is cosmic, bordering on the Divine, although a Divine that is Satanic in character. Diabolical and displaying trascendent conspiratorial and perfidious talents, Zionism strives for domination over all other peoples and nations in keeping with the Biblical "Chosen People" concept. That concept, whether consciously or unconsciously distorted, is the centerpiece of the virulent propaganda drive.'[77]

The roots of Zionist satanism, according to the contemporary Soviet horsemen of the Apocalypse, do indeed lie in the Jewish religion and its 'racist' postulates. Another Soviet neo-Nazi propagandist, V. Skurlatov, for example, has even claimed that 'the racist concept of Judaism served as a prototype of European racism'.[78] According to Skurlatov, the preservation 'of the purity of their blood was proclaimed as the most sacred obligation of Jewry' while 'the despised goyim were useful only as "speaking tools", as slaves'.[79] The ultimate aim of this doctrine, as in the case of Nazism, was supposedly 'to realize world domination'.[80] But 'Zionist racism', according to the Soviet neo-antisemites, also serves to ideologically justify Israeli aggression in the entire Middle East and the constant oppression of Arabs in the Jewish state.[81] According to Moscow Radio, 'everyone who believes in Zionism admits that a non-Jew in the Jewish State is a sub-human'.[82]

As part of its disinformation offensive directed at Africa, Moscow Radio told its listeners on 4 October 1967: 'It is known that the ruling circles of Tel Aviv justify their aggressive policy by the policy of the "chosen people" – which in plain words means racism. It would seem that a people who suffered from Hitler's Nazi theory should hate racism, but the leaders of Israel have adopted racism, this extremely reactionary ideology of imperialism as their own. The theory of the Israelites being the chosen people is now being energetically spread. . . . It is well known that the Israeli extremists despise the people of Africa . . . consider them to be a second-class people.'[83]

This type of insidious myth-making, exported to Africa, Asia and the Arab countries, has obviously been intended to build up support for Soviet Middle Eastern policies and accentuate Israel's isolation. The constant comparisons in the Soviet media, both visual and verbal, between Israel and South Africa serve the same purpose and have found many echoes in the West, where they are taken up by a motley spectrum of anti-Zionists. According to 'Radio Peace and Progress' on 15 October 1975, for example, it was monopoly circles representing Zionist organizations who 'invest their capital in the economy of the South African Republic and together with the local businessmen, control various branches of industry and agriculture'.[84] The South African Zionists, it was alleged, were 'highly interested in preserving the regime of exploitation in the South of the continent. . . .'[85] The South African diamond billionaire, Harry Oppenheimer, has been a favoured target of this Soviet-style antisemitism for export to the Third World. Thus the Moscow-based *Asia and Africa Today* described this 'uncrowned king of South Africa' as 'a secret patron of the Zionist community in South Africa'.[86] Repeatedly, the point is made that behind the Pretoria-Tel Aviv nexus lie the interests of 'the rich 120,000 strong Jewish community of South Africa, which has amassed huge capital by exploiting the native population'.[87] The 'pious' among them have assumed 'the key positions in economy and trade and obtain great profits from the system of racial inequality that reigns in that country'.[88]

Emphasizing the South African connection has been an integral part of an extensive Soviet propaganda drive to portray 'Zionism' as a Trojan horse of imperialism and racism in the Third World.[89] The basic function of Israel is said to be the subversion of Afro-Asian and Arab liberation movements, as part of the neo-colonialist role assigned to it by world imperialism. Thus Zionism acts to mask American infiltration and exploitation in Africa, though at the same time it also has its own plans for neo-colonialist expansion.[90] Naturally, only the most corrupt methods are employed by the money-grabbing Zionists. Thus Israelis in Africa have been accused by Moscow of 'selling untested and unproven vaccines . . . having the effect not so much of curing the patient's ailments as of emptying his pockets'.[91] Far from being harmless experts, Israeli technicians and advisers are constantly presented as engaging in subversive activities against African countries. The Soviets have been particularly eager to stress the desire of Israelis to sow dissension between Africans and Arabs as part of the broader imperialist conspiracy.[92]

Russian and Arab efforts to persuade more African states to break off relations with Israel finally bore fruit at the end of 1973, and Moscow now further intensified its campaign against the 'close military co-operation' between Pretoria and Tel Aviv. According to Moscow, both countries pursued 'racist policies' and had a common ideological outlook; both favoured territorial expansionism and together fought Third World national-liberation movements; both were jointly developing nuclear and chemical weapons. The constant twinning of apartheid and Zionism in this manner by Moscow has in fact been one of its main methods of infiltrating Africa, and this propaganda weapon has also been rather effective in those Western countries where the anti-apartheid movement is strong.

The greatest international success of Soviet antisemitism, the November 1975 UN resolution condemning Zionism as racism, was the fruit of the patient Russian offensive to blacken and defame Israel in the eyes of the Third World. The historic meaning of the debate of the UN resolution in the Third Committee was not lost on a number of more perceptive Western journalists. Two comments deserve more extensive quotation. The first came from the British literary critic, the late Goronwy Rees, in *Encounter*. 'There were ghosts haunting the Third Committee that day; the ghosts of Hitler and Goebbels . . . grinning with delight to hear, not only Israel, but Jews denounced in language which would have provoked hysterical applause at any Nuremberg rally. . . . And there were other ghosts also at the debate; the ghosts of the 6,000,000 dead in Dachau and Sachsenhausen and other extermination camps, listening to the same voices which had cheered and jeered and abused them as they made their way to the gas chambers. For the fundamental thesis advanced by the supporters of the resolution, and approved by the majority of the Third Committee, was that to be a Jew, and to be proud of it, and to be determined to preserve the right to be a Jew, is to be an enemy of the human race.'[93]

Writing in the 'Observer' column of the *International Herald Tribune*, Russell Baker wrote in a similarly ironic, if more jaunty, vein: 'Hitler must have had a good laugh down in hell last week when the United Nations General Assembly formally endorsed anti-Semitism by a large majority. After thirty years in odious repute the old dictator's theory of what made the world go wrong has finally been declared the collective wisdom of the higher-minded nations of the planet. The sweet irony of it, of course, was that the Soviet Union was right out in front there with Himmler. . . . The last time Russia embraced Hitler was in the non-aggression pact on the eve of World War II. By signing it, Stalin gave the Nazis the security they needed to march into Poland, a march that eventually led to the deaths of 20 million Russians. . . . The Soviet government has been so helplessly mired in political cynicism for so long that one has come to take it for granted. . . . But rehabilitating Hitlerism – surely there were some things they wouldn't do. There weren't.'[94]

But the Soviet Union has not been content just to breathe new life into its own variant of Nazi antisemitism at home and abroad. It had also prepared a perfect alibi during the previous decade, whose resonance has proved to be unexpectedly powerful in recent years: not only was Zionism officially declared by the United Nations to be 'racism' in 1975 – the Soviet Union has since then been assiduously at work to further blacken Israel's reputation as *the* contemporary home of Nazism. Not only does the Jewish state continue to be defamed on every conceivable occasion by the Soviets as a 'Nazi' power pursuing a policy of undisguised 'extermination' towards the Arabs in the occupied territories; Soviet rewriting of history, Orwellian style, has retrospectively made the Zionists into the foremost 'collaborators' of the Nazis in the mass destruction of Jews during the Holocaust. In the words of its most prolific contemporary Jew-baiter Lev Korneyev, 'the blood of millions of victims is on their [i.e. the Zionists] hands and on their conscience'.[95] According to current Soviet mythology, both in Europe and in the Middle East, Zionists shamefully colluded with the Nazi murder-machine while millions of oppressed victims gave their lives in the fight against fascism.[96] The reason for the alliance was that 'top-echelon Zionists and Hitlerites were drawn together by their common social nature'.[97]

In the latest cycle of 'anti-Zionist' vituperation in the Soviet Union, the Nazi–Israeli parallel has been drummed into public consciousness with unprecedented intensity and viciousness. The extremism of this Judeophobia may doubtless have been exacerbated by the Lebanon war, but its deeper causes lie in the resurgence of the Russian Black Hundred tradition and its uses in the ongoing power-struggle within the Soviet Union.[98] The neo-Stalinists and the neo-Nazi Right in the USSR, who continue to promote an image of the Great Russian nation as representing the forces of Light combating the dark powers of 'international Zionism', would appear to be preparing the ground for their own Soviet-style 'Final Solution' of the Jewish question. Under the banner of 'Zionism is Fascism', they have revealed the final bankruptcy of Marxism-Leninism.

# CHAPTER ELEVEN

# Inversions of History

The Soviet myth of 'Jewish Nazism' is probably equalled in its mendacity only by the Nazi spectre of 'Jewish Bolshevism', of which it is both the exact mirror-opposite and faithful replica. For the Nazis, 'Jewish Bolshevism' was part of an international Jewish conspiracy, linking Moscow with Wall Street and the City of London. For the Stalinists, 'Zionist Nazism' is the agent of a world Zionist cabal of international financiers seeking to subvert the Soviet Union and the socialist camp. Both mythologies found a broad echo in their respective periods, though the Stalinist formula, unlike its predecessor, is still very much alive. Indeed its spread into the Western world during the past few years suggests that it may also have a promising future. Nowhere in the West, however, has the twinning of the Nazi Swastika and the Star of David as symbols of genocidal fascism been so insistently promoted as in the Soviet Union, in no other state has his campaign been so carefully orchestrated from above, so remorseless and intense.[1] It appeared for the first time during the Slansky trial, which depicted leading Czech Communists of Jewish origin not only as crypto-Zionist traitors but as fascist shock-troops for the subversion of the 'popular democracies'. Joseph Stalin, the inventor of this post-Holocaust 'anti-Zionist' phantasmagoria, had learned from Hitler the importance of euphemisms and the indispensability of the corporate Jew as an invisible, omnipotent enemy to justify eternal vigilance and internal repression. What better method of disguising the source of his inspiration and providing an acceptable mask for his own Judeophobia than the equation of 'Zionism' with Nazism?

Stalin's heirs at first used the theme rather sparingly, with the Soviet press sometimes charging Zionist leaders (though not Zionism itself) with having had contacts with Nazi officials in German-occupied Europe.[2] Soviet hostility to the growing links between the Federal German Republic and the state of Israel led in the late 1950s to an escalation, with attacks on Ben-Gurion as 'a tool of the Bonn revanchists'. The price of West German economic aid to the Jewish state had, according to Moscow, been an Israeli government promise of silence concerning the presence of former Nazis in Chancellor Adenauer's government and civil service.[3] The absurdity of this charge of collusion was shortly to be exposed with the capture of Adolf Eichmann by Israeli secret agents and his public trial in Jerusalem for crimes against the Jewish people. If Israel's leadership wished to cover up Nazi crimes, why expose Eichmann to the view of the whole world and allow him to state his case? Moscow's explanation of this riddle was to fabricate an even more complicated conspiracy theory which it maintains to this day. The real purpose of the Eichmann trial was to remove from circulation 'the principal witness of world Zionism's deals with the Gestapo'.[4] In this way, his silence over the secret dealings between Zionists and 'Hitlerites' during the Second World War could be ensured. Why, then, did the Israelis not execute Eichmann at once, to avoid the complications of a trial? The explanation, as Lev Korneyev put it seven years ago, was that the Zionists wanted '. . . to pull off a big political *coup* by presenting aggressive and racist Israel in the eyes of world public opinion as a "fighter for justice" and "chastiser of war criminals" '.[5]

The Eichmann Affair was in the main used by the Soviets as a means of insinuating that in the 1930s there had been close collaboration between Nazi and Zionist secret services.[6] Eichmann's brief visit to the Middle East in 1937, according to Soviet and other fabrications, was primarily 'to secure an agreement on the creation there of a pro-Nazi Jewish State of "Palestine" and the strengthening of reciprocity between Hitlerite Germany's special services and the Tel Aviv Jewish Agency'.[7] But it was in conjunction with the earlier Kastner case (which had shaken Israeli public opinion in the mid-1950s) that Eichmann's activities were of particular interest for Soviet disinformation efforts. As a Tass foreign broadcast on 1 February 1978 put it: 'In 1944 Eichmann and one of the Zionist leaders, Kastner, signed an agreement on Hungarian Jews. The agreement guaranteed the lives of 600 "prominent" Jews, while condemning to death 800,000 Jews without sufficient money to pay for their lives. The Zionists' collaboration with the Nazis . . . led to a catastrophe which cost the lives of nearly 6,000,000 Jews. This shatters the myth that the Zionists defend and express the interests of the Jewish people.'[8]

Whatever the inadequacies of Zionist rescue efforts during the Second World War and Kastner's own admittedly dubious role in trying to save at least a remnant of Hungarian Jewry in 1944, the motive behind the tissue of lies contained in such anti-Zionist propaganda is made transparent in the implications behind the final sentence of the Tass statement. The Zionists failed to defend the Jewish people during the Holocaust – therefore they were and still are traitors. But this so-called betrayal by the Zionists must be given the semblance of ideological truth by showing that in Marxist terms it corresponded to their so-called 'class interests'. Thus in Soviet demonology, the Jewish millionaires and the Zionist leaders who had allegedly helped rear the monster of Hitlerism had not the slightest interest in the fate of the Jewish masses. In a review of the Soviet antisemitic film 'The Secret and the Overt', *Kino* wrote in August 1975 that it was no accident that 'the leaders of Zionism and the big Jewish bourgeoisie were in collusion with the Hitlerites. . . . It is no longer a secret today that Zionist capital helped to strengthen the Hitler regime in Germany and the fascists' preparations to attack the Soviet Union. And notwithstanding the fact that the Hitlerites had murdered and burned in gas chambers hundreds of thousands of Jewish workers and poor people, the Zionist leaders continued to collaborate with the fascists. The leaders of Zionism took care only of chosen persons of the rich families.'[9]

According to Tsezar Solodar, one of a select group of self-hating Jewish anti-Zionists employed by the Soviet regime in this field, the Zionist leadership regarded the millions of Jews in Eastern Europe as 'economic and moral dust' whom it was inexpedient to save from Hitler.[10] Even more incredibly, Solodar singled out 'the Nazi accomplice' Chaim Weizmann (perhaps the most sensitive of all Zionist leaders to the plight of East European Jewry and filled with grim foreboding at what lay in store for them) as the arch-criminal. Six million Jews in Europe were 'considered useless for Israel's future'. All that the Zionists were interested in were 'young people filled with the poison of fanatical nationalism and fit for armed attacks on the native population of Palestine'.[11]

Having written off the poor and defenceless Jewish masses to the mercy of fate, the Zionists had even tried to ensure the defeat of the anti-Hitler coalition, to 'block the advance of the Soviet armies and save the fascist regime from complete rout . . .' – criminal plans which, according to the Russian antisemite Semenyuk, were frustrated by the Red Army.[12] In their boundless treachery and villainy towards their own people, the Zionists actually 'took part in the mass extermination of Jews', singling out and surrendering their brethren to the fascists. 'The Zionists doomed the Jews, including children, to death in the gas chambers whereas Soviet soldiers rescued the children who were threatened with death.'[13] The *Judenräte* (in this Soviet smear literature completely identified with Zionists) did not touch the rich, but they 'sent the poor to their deaths'. The 'chosen' ones were removed from the transports to the death camps in order to save 'the cream of the nation'.[14] Driven by boundless rapacity and cold-blooded cruelty, the Zionist millionaires, wrote Yuri Ivanov in 1970, 'in accordance with an agreement with the Hitlerites, helped the latter herd Jews either into the ovens of the concentration camps or the Kibbutzes in the 'Land of Canaan'.[15]

During the orchestrated Soviet anti-Zionist campaign of 1970 these vile falsehoods were echoed in hundreds of letters from 'loyal' Jews to the Soviet press, all written in the same frantic, semi-hysterical tone of righteous indignation. Even the tragedy of Babi Yar (whose Jewish content was deliberately erased by the Soviet authorities) was described in *Pravda Ukrainy* not only as a symbol of 'Hitlerite cannibalism' but also of 'the indelible disgrace of their accomplices and followers, the Zionists'.[16] In the Soviet Ukraine, where real collaboration of the local population with the Nazi invaders, especially in anti-Jewish *Aktionen*, had been extensive, such macabre falsehoods have a particularly hollow ring. From a Communist viewpoint, there was, however, much to be gained by 'exposing' the anti-Soviet alliance of Zionists and Ukranian bourgeois nationalists and their 'joint' collaboration with the Nazis.[17] R. M. Brodsky's Ukrainian-language pamphlet *Zionism and its Class Essence* (1973) was an excellent example of the genre; pointing to Zionist dealings with the pogromist Ukrainian Petlyurites and the Makhnovites during the Russian Civil War, with the fascist regimes in Poland, Rumania and Italy and also to their 'common language with the Hitlerites', Brodsky asserted: 'It has been established that many fascist criminals avoided the punishment they deserved only thanks to their Zionist protectors'.[18]

In Soviet hate-literature there is a clear link between the historical myth of Nazi–Zionist 'collaboration' and the parallel slanders against contemporary Israel as a 'Nazi' state. For if, as *Pravda* pointed out at the beginning of 1984, the Zionists had helped the Nazis send their co-religionists to the gas ovens and Zionist agents had joined hands with the Gestapo, then it was hardly surprising if Menachem Begin and Yitzhak Shamir were using 'Hitlerite methods' to massacre 'sub-human Arabs' in Lebanon.[19] Was it not logical that the allies of Hitler in the past should also be his foremost imitators, successors and heirs in the present?

The link had already been made twenty years ago in Soviet cartoons juxtaposing Zionism and Nazism. In an *Izvestia* drawing (12 November 1964) depicting West German arms sales to Israel, the Star of David had been metamorphosed into a symbol of death and destruction. Two Nazi officers are shown selling arms to an Israeli. The caption reads: 'I recommend these first-class weapons. They have been tried and tested and used in Auschwitz and the Warsaw Ghetto.'[20] More significant still was the stance taken by the Soviet Union in the Third Committee of the United Nations on 14 October 1965 in which it demanded that Zionism, Nazism and neo-Nazism, *in that order*, should be classified as 'racial crimes'.[21] The Soviet amalgam came in response to a motion by the United States and Brazil proposing that the UN Charter of Human Rights contain a clause banning antisemitism. Clearly afraid that such a clause might be used against itself and ready to pander to the Arab states' resolve to uproot Israel from the Middle East, the Soviets countered with what can retrospectively be seen as the opening gambit in their war of defamation against Israel.

The outbreak of the Six-Day War and the crushing defeat by Israel of Moscow's allies proved, however, to be the event which triggered the Russian Communist slander-machine into action. The Soviet Permanent Delegate to the UN, N. T. Fedorenko, echoed the Arab delegates who had pointed to the similarity between Israel's policies and methods and those of the Nazis. According to the representative of Jordan, for example, both Israelis and Nazis 'have the concept of race, both have the concept of force, of acquiring lands by invasion and the use of force, and both have fifth columns'. Fedorenko, however, was much more explicit: 'The overweening aggressors have taken over the notorious Nazi theories of geopolitics, of *Lebensraum*, of establishing a "new order" and "vital frontiers" in the Middle East. The peoples are familiar with these ultimatums, these insensate theories, this talk of a "new order" and of recarving the political map. It was the Nazi conquistadors that set out to recarve the map of Europe and the world, and attempted by armed force to impose what they called a "new order".... How monstrous that these devices of the Nazi brigands, condemned by the International Military Tribunal in 1946, have now been revived by a government claiming to represent a people which suffered so bitterly at the Nazi butchers' hands!'[22]

Fedorenko's charges were repeated by Moscow Radio and on 6 June 1967 *Izvestia* deceptively informed its readers that 'even the western correspondents compare these crimes with those the Nazis perpetrated in the occupied countries during World War II'. A leading article in *Pravda* on 17 June 1967 made clear what was now the official Soviet Communist Party line on Israel's war of survival and self-defence – 'This is Genocide'. For the next few years, Moshe Dayan, Israel's Defence Minister, complete with eye-patch, was to be a favoured symbol of Soviet cartoonists – a pupil of Hitler's *Lebensraum* theories and Rommel's *Blitzkrieg* methods. A notorious cartoon in *Kazakhstanskaya Pravda* (21 June 1967) showed a subdued Adolf Hitler cringing before a superior, sinister-looking Dayan who orders him to 'Move On!'[23] Repeatedly, Dayan was accused of following in the footsteps of the SS and the 'mad Führer', sowing death and destruction in the Middle East. Labour Prime Minister Golda Meir, the 'fascist-imitating protectress of the Jews', received similar treatment, being denounced by *Sovetskaya Moldavia* (10 March 1970) for having 'proclaimed the nightmare idea of "Greater Israel" and for bringing back the "rotten theory of racial superiority" '. Even the more dovish Foreign Minister, Abba Eban, was compared to Hitler and attacked by *Radianska Ukraina* (3 March 1970) for 'meeting near the walls of Dachau with the ideological heirs of Eichmann'.

Not only was Israel presented as a 'successor state' of the Third Reich, but, as we have seen, a direct line of continuity had been traced between fictive Zionist 'collaborators' with the Gestapo and the no less imaginary 'genocide' of the Arabs. But within this witches' brew of mendacity it became increasingly unclear who were the masters and who the disciples. As one of the leading Soviet antisemitic publicists, Yevgeny Yevseyev, pointed out in October 1967, the roles had been reversed: 'Now it is the German revanchists and militarists who are performing services for Zionism in practical affairs.'[24] It was the same Yevseyev who wrote in May 1970: 'The Zionists should put up a memorial to Hitler. After all, it was the raving Führer in his *Mein Kampf* who asserted the basic dogma of Zionism – the existence of a "world-wide Jewish people" and of the "Jewish race".'[25] Increasingly, the Nazis found themselves demoted to the position of anticipating or even borrowing from Zionists rather than the other way round. Thus an article in *Sovetskaya Belorussia* (April 1970) produced the following startling innovation in historical research: 'When Hitler proclaimed his hate policies of the war for "living space", for a "Greater Germany" in which only Aryans would live, then in this particular case he was simply repeating the idea of the Father of Zionism, T. Herzl, on the need for a colonial struggle against barbarism.'[26] A cartoon in *Bakinsky rabochy* (22 December 1971), entitled 'Champions Among Professionals', in more familiar agitprop style has Himmler raising the blood-stained left arm of a Dayan-like Israeli in victory; the 'champion' is holding a napalm rocket and barbed wire in his right hand.[27]

Again and again, Soviet visual media have merged the Star of David and the Swastika. Sometimes a resurrected Nazi is shown offering plans for a gas chamber to a militaristic Israeli while Arabs in the background resignedly await their fate;[28] sometimes the Israelis are offered neo-Nazi mercenaries; at other times as in *Vechernayaya Moskva* (11 March 1970) the Nazi is shown as simply destroying, while the ugly Israeli builds new concentration camps. The caption on this cartoon read: 'The rulers of Israel operate today with Fascist methods. Israeli Zionists wipe out Arab houses, settlements and cities in occupied territory, throw people into concentration camps and apply terrorist methods towards Communists.'[29]

This campaign has been maintained unchanged, with occasional ups and downs, from 1967 until the present. Long before the advent of Mr Begin and the Lebanese war, Israel was daily being accused of bombing and wiping out Arab villages, just as the Nazis had flattened Lidice and Oradour during the Second World War, murdering their defenceless inhabitants.[30] Prime Minister Golda Meir's speeches were already compared in the Army newspaper *Krasnaya Zvezda* as far back as 1970 with the rantings of the Führer, and 'the pure blooded warriors of Israel' were likened to the 'executioners of Hitler in the last war' and 'the American aggressors in Vietnam'.[31] As the visual media reveal, no effort has been spared to make sure that the belligerent Israelis are endowed with certain classic 'Jewish' traits such as a pot-belly, bow legs, flat feet and sometimes a protruding *Stürmer*-like nose. The cartoons invariably show the 'Zionists' either as potential 'destroyers' of the world, rabid militarists, Satanic figures, money-grubbing parasites, serpentine or spider-like figures, clasping Arab lands; or else in even more overtly Nazi fashion, either as poisonous mushrooms taking root in occupied territories or as the tentacles of a giant octopus seeking to encompass the globe.

At the more theoretical level some effort is periodically made to provide a pseudo-Marxist gloss on this vicious Judeophobia. Thus Hitlerism is at times presented, not so much as a 'Jewish' characteristic but as 'the outcome and product of the organic and regular features of imperialism'. It is occasionally pointed out that Israeli 'Hitlerism' is merely the logical result of its alliance with 'the most reactionary and aggressive force in the world today – US imperialism'. Since Soviet propaganda treats 'colonial oppression' in Africa, Asia and Latin America as 'essentially the same thing as Hitlerism', it is perhaps not surprising that Zionism should be categorized in this way. But even these superficially more restrained analyses invariably slide into outright antisemitism by dredging up such Nazi-like fictions as 'the old ties of Jewish financiers and Zionist leaders with big monopoly capital, with the Rothschilds and Kuhn-Loebs'.[32]

Moreover, the Soviet media do not in practice relate to Zionism as just one more manifestation of Nazism in the contemporary world. They insist that Zionist terror and repression of Arabs results 'in a policy of genuine genocide', and that the racist doctrine of Judaism leads to 'direct extermination'.[33] They point out that just as the false theory of the Hitlerites concerning the 'racial superiority of the Aryans' led to the gas chambers, so too Zionist racism must result in mass genocide. S. Astakhov, writing in the Moscow daily, *Selskaya Zhizn* (16 November 1975), claimed indeed that genocide had been practised in Israel 'from the first days of the establishment of the State', which must have left a few Soviet citizens wondering why the USSR had been so precipitate in granting it *de jure* recognition. Vladimir Bolshakov, a veteran Soviet antisemite, writing in *Pravda* (1 August 1982), also stressed the historical continuity of Zionist 'genocide' policy. Menachem Begin and Arik Sharon were in no sense departing from Israeli norms. 'The policy of genocide being carried out at this time by the Zionists in Lebanon', he observed, 'is inseparable from Zionism as an ideology and the criminal practices of the Jewish bourgeoisie.'

There was in fact relatively little that was novel in the content of Soviet rhetoric during the Lebanon war, with the same atrocity stories, false quotations, antisemitic imagery and Nazi–Zionist parallels being drawn on as in the past. However, the press and media campaign reached an intensity that can only be compared with Soviet propaganda against Nazi Germany during the Second World War when the USSR was fighting for its very existence against a ruthless enemy that did indeed deliberately practise a genocide policy. The very fact that the small state of Israel, in no sense a direct threat to a mighty superpower like the Soviet Union, could be compared with the Nazi danger reveals the frighteningly irrational depths of contemporary Russian antisemitism.

At the same time, as in the case of Hitler, this demonological Russian image of Jews is linked to a coldly calculated *Realpolitik* backed by the unlimited propaganda resources of a totalitarian state. It must be realized that the onslaught against Israel and against Jewish nationalism serves multiple purposes in Soviet domestic and foreign policy, not all of which are in fact connected with Jews. Internally it continues to be a weapon in the ongoing power-struggle within the Soviet elite; a means of demoralizing and crushing all forms of dissidence and dissent; of controlling unresolved social tensions and national passions seething beneath the surface of Soviet society; and, last but not least, of diverting the masses from their real problems. Externally, it is a major tool for promoting Soviet influence in the Third World, for destabilizing Western democracies and undermining American policy in the Middle East. This last function was particularly apparent in the wake of Israel's invasion of Lebanon.[34]

Moscow blasted the invasion as part of 'a global offensive on the "Third World" liberation forces' sponsored by Washington.[35] The USA was consistently presented not only as Israel's mentor and manipulator, but as the supporter of 'fascists' and 'exploiters' all over the world. As Moscow's domestic TV service announced on 18 July 1982: 'Serving as the supports for this bridge have been McCarthyism, the American aggression against Vietnam, the crimes there by American soldiers, the killing of Martin Luther King, Hitlerite criminals taken into the service of the United States, the

Hitlerite saboteurs who have been training their Israeli counterparts and Washington's direct support for fascist forces and dictators throughout the entire world.'[36] The 'extermination' of Palestinians and 'enslaving' of Arab states was an integral part of the strategic alliance between the US and Israel in which the latter was blindly 'carrying out the will of American hegemonism'.[37] The Israeli aggression was, of all things, allegedly performed at the behest of the American 'monopolies', in order to impose their *diktat* not only on the Arab world but also on Western Europe. '. . . By destroying Beirut, and Lebanon in general, Israel and the United States hope to destroy the advanced post of West European capital in the Near East.'[38]

However, while remorselessly emphasizing American responsibilities, Moscow has not for one moment let up on the Nazi–Zionist parallel in the past two or three years. A cartoon in *Pravda* on 5 August 1982 entitled 'Familiar Handwriting' had Tel Aviv goosestepping arm in arm with Hitler's skeleton over a field strewn with Arab bodies. In the left hand of the Israeli was an axe and in the right a rocket labelled 'Made in the USA'. Viktor Mikhayev, in a Moscow broadcast two days later, stated that according to 'the basic cannibalistic theory of Zionism, the chosen people of Israel must prosper even at the expense of the death of the lower races'.[39] Tass claimed that Tel Aviv had embarked on its plan 'for a physical destruction of the Arab people of Palestine, for a giant Holocaust'. On 5 August 1982 it asserted that 'concentration camps and prisons staffed by sadists, who are drawing on the experience of Nazi criminals, have been set up for them. The number of Lebanese and Palestinians sent to these "death factories" is growing with every day.'[40] A *Vremiya* newscast on 7 August 1982 described Israel's then Prime Minister, Menachem Begin, as 'a maniac and fanatic like Hitler, and probably no less a racist than the Führer. . . .'

This campaign has continued unabated into 1984, well after Begin's resignation and the drastic scaling down of Israel's involvement in Lebanon. Thus, on 17 January 1984 Vladimir Bolshakov published an authoritative article in *Pravda* equating Zionism with fascism, which echoed most of the tired clichés of Soviet propaganda. It argued that Zionism, like fascism, was the lackey of imperialism and big capital; that both shared common features including deliberate 'genocide' (as in Lebanon) and an ideology of racial purity; that Zionists had always collaborated with Nazis and, like their prototype, recruited Jews from all over the world to support the Fatherland. This last comparison suggested the ominous implication that world Jewry constituted a Nazi-like 'fifth column' in the Diaspora, owing loyalty to Israel alone.[41] Subsequent developments indicate that this suggestion may well prove to have been a trial-balloon for the implementation of a more drastic policy of restricting the emigration of Soviet Jews and crushing all forms of 'activism' or dissent.

Although the USSR has not been the only source for the dissemination of the legend of 'Zionist Nazism' and some of its antisemitic offshoots, there can be little doubt that its role has been of decisive importance. While the Arab world has in recent decades taken up this fabrication with great relish and used its own manifold channels of petro-dollar influence in the West and the Third World to spread a similar message, the Holocaust theme has never assumed the same centrality in its war on Israel. In the first place, many Arabs continue to admire Hitler and hope to emulate his actions, thereby undermining the persuasiveness of any 'anti-Nazi' stance; secondly, according to certain Islamic conceptions, the Holocaust was a just punishment for the inherently tainted and corrupt nature of the Jewish people which throughout history had inspired persecution. Arab propaganda has, moreover, tried over the years to limit natural sympathy for the Jewish survivors of the *Shoah*, by subsidizing and encouraging the belief that the Holocaust was a Zionist 'hoax' to win Western support for the state of Israel.[42]

In this endeavour Arabs and neo-Nazis have shared a common objective, both regarding public sensitivity in the West to the Jewish tragedy as a major obstacle to their political aims. To overcome this barrier, a major thrust of Arab public reactions has been the effort over the past fifteen years to substitute the Palestinians for the Jews as *the* supreme victims of contemporary history. By appropriating Holocaust terminology so that the Palestinians become the 'new Jews' and the Israelis are transformed into genocidal Nazis, the Arabs evidently hoped that the West might be freed of its so-called guilt complex.[43] The Lebanon war offered in this regard a golden opportunity for Arab and Soviet propaganda in the West, which had hitherto not made really substantial dents in mainstream public opinion. This earlier failure may require some explanation.

The ideological antisemitism so prevalent in the Soviet, Islamic and Arab worlds had been largely confined in the West, after the Second World War, to small groups on the extreme Right and to a lesser extent on the far Left. The National Socialist slaughter of the Jews had in fact acted in the aftermath of the war as a deterrent against the resurgence of racist antisemitism in liberal-democratic Western societies. The feelings of shame, guilt and horror at the magnitude of Hitler's crimes appeared for the moment to discredit racist doctrines and make open political antisemitism taboo in Western Europe and North America.[44] With the exception of a few countries like Argentina, the Jews of the free world seemed to be secure from attack until the end of the 1960s. During these first two post-war decades, Western

Jewry experienced, indeed, an unprecedented degree of upward mobility in the socio-economic spheres and acceptance into political elites which had previously rejected them.[45] While post-war Communist and Arab governments were sponsoring a venomous political antisemitism, old stereotypes in the West seemed to be giving way to a public mood of 'philosemitism', connected in part with remorse at the horrors of the Nazi mass murder. The sincere efforts of the Christian churches to revise traditional teachings of contempt toward Jews and Judaism was one important sign of this change.[46] Western sympathies with the young state of Israel also expressed in a different way an earnest desire to atone for past crimes against Jewry as well as admiration for its pioneering ethos and achievements.

After the mid-1960s, with the rise of an increasing number of radical Right and Left extremist groups in Western Europe, Latin America and the United States, the picture slowly began to change.[47] Neo-fascism and neo-Nazism particularly flourished in those European societies where there was a significant coloured or Third World immigration problem, high unemployment, inflation and social tensions. But with the exception of Italy, these extremist groups of the Right were never to win significant electoral strength.[48] The overtly Hitlerian type of antisemitism which these radical Right movements still advocate has proved to have little appeal to post-war Western public opinion, and not even the severe economic depression that followed the Arab oil embargo has changed this trend. While anti-black and anti-immigrant racism has certainly been rampant in Western society, the classic forms of antisemitism preached by the Nazis and the pre-war radical Right have been unable to generate mass appeal.[49]

Only in the murky area of so-called historical 'revisionism', with its grotesque claim that there was no mass murder of Jews by the Hitler regime, have the neo-Nazis enjoyed a kind of publicity breakthrough in recent years. Publications like Richard Harwood's *Did Six Million Really Die?* (1974) and Arthur Butz's *The Hoax of the Twentieth Century* (1977) which peddled sensational assertions that the gas chambers were 'a Jewish invention' or that 'the Jews conjured up the idea of the Holocaust to establish Israel and get money from the Germans' did achieve a certain notoriety.[50] The brazen denial of Nazi crimes was transparently intended to lift the burden of guilt from fascism in general and to win greater social acceptance and political legitimacy for right-wing radicalism in the West. The theory behind this so-called 'revisionism' is, however, no less clearly, an updated version of the *Protocols* tradition. Its central thesis is that the cunning forces of 'international Zionism' have been able to hoax, deceive and manipulate naive Gentiles into believing that millions of Jews were murdered in gas chambers.[51] In this ultra-right literature, all the stereotyped attributes which Nazis and antisemites traditionally applied to Jews are now transferred to 'Zionists' or unnamed shadowy cosmopolitan conspirators. As with so much of Soviet and left-wing propaganda, the Judeophobe content is fairly transparent beneath the thin veneer of 'anti-Zionist' verbiage,[52] for if there was indeed no Holocaust, then Jewish power and influence must really be boundless, to have successfully carried out such a monumental fraud.[53] The news media and the financial and political institutions of the West must really have been reduced to total subservience to accept this so-called 'atrocity propaganda'; for in neo-Nazi terms the sole purpose of the Holocaust myth was to steal millions of Western taxpayers' money to further a Communist-Zionist (i.e. a Jewish) conspiracy whose geo-political centre lies in Israel.[54]

Not all post-war 'anti-Zionist' inversions of history have been inspired by such undisguised antisemitism. Even before 1967 a small but influential section of Western public opinion was driven primarily by its pro-Arab proclivities to delegitimate Israel and at the same time to deform the Holocaust experience. A classic example of this syndrome can be found in the writings of the British historian, Arnold J. Toynbee, who had a considerable intellectual influence during the 1950s in reinforcing Arab intransigence toward Israel. Toynbee had already assigned the Jews the unattractive role of being the fossilized relic of an extinct Syriac civilization in his monumental *Study of History*.[55] Moreover, he held Judaism responsible for the religious fanaticism and tribal nationalism in Christian civilization, which he insistently regarded as its original sin. It was, however, Toynbee's chapter headed 'The Fate of the European Jews and the Palestinian Arabs, A.D. 1933–48' which provided the most controversial and shocking equation in his philosophy of history, one which nevertheless took two more decades to become fashionable in the Western world. Toynbee, while declaring himself profoundly shocked by the extent of German apostasy from Western civilization[56] and the 'maniacal sadism' of the Nazis, permitted himself the reflection that 'the Nazi Gentiles' fall from grace was less tragic than the Zionist Jews'.

According to the British historian, 'on the morrow of a persecution in Europe in which they had been the victims of the worst atrocities ever suffered by Jews or indeed by any other human beings, the Jews' immediate reaction to their experience was to become persecutors in their turn for the first time since A.D. 135. . . .' Toynbee denounced the fact that the Israelis had taken the first opportunity presented to them to take revenge on the Arabs and to inflict upon them 'some of the wrongs and sufferings that had been inflicted on the Jews'.[57] Not only did Toynbee thereby ignore completely the brutal aggression of the Arab states, who in 1948 had sought to strangle the infant state of Israel at birth and complete Hitler's genocide;[58] he implied that the Israelis in a bloodthirsty and unprovoked frenzy had either murdered or expelled peaceful, law-abiding Arabs in a fashion analogous to the Nazis.[59]

The tiny, overcrowded Jewish state of 1948, with its survivors and refugees from the European Holocaust, was saddled by the eminent British historian with responsibility for a crime no less dastardly than that which had made its creation a moral imperative for humanity. 'On the Day of Judgement the gravest crime to the German Nationalists' account', Toynbee sanctimoniously wrote, 'might not be that they had exterminated a majority of Western [sic] Jews but that they had caused the surviving remnant of Jewry to stumble.'[60] Over twenty-five years ago, Toynbee had already seen 'in the Jewish Zionists ... disciples of the Nazis',[61] prompting another British historian, Professor Trevor-Roper, to describe him in turn as an 'unconscious ally of Hitler in the non-Nazi world'.[62] In fact, the Zionists were worse than the German Gentiles, in Toynbee's view, for rather than learning from their bitter experience they had knowingly chosen 'to imitate some of the evil deeds that the Nazis had committed against the Jews'.[63]

For example, the massacre of some 250 Arabs at Deir Yassin on 9 April 1948 was to be ranked, according to Toynbee, on a par with Nazi crimes – similar Arab atrocities during the Israeli War of Independence were of course ignored. Zionism was totally condemned as an imitation of Western nationalism, but the poisonous chauvinism at the root of many Arab anti-Jewish attitudes and actions was completely disregarded. The nation-state was for Toynbee an unmitigated catastrophe, especially when adopted by Zionist Jews as an instrument of survival in a hostile world; in Arab hands, however, it became progressive and anti-colonialist. Toynbee's litany of double standards was admittedly ahead of its time, as was his sophisticated inversion of the tragedy of the Holocaust and his dialectical twisting of its meaning against the Jews.[64] It was only in the aftermath of the Six-Day War that such views were gradually to acquire greater resonance, especially in Western Europe.

This partial reversal of Western attitudes after 1967 had much to do with the crushing quality of the Israeli military victory and the changed perception of the essence of the Middle East conflict. The Jews no longer appeared in their traditional role of sacrificial victim but rather in General de Gaulle's words on the morrow of victory as 'un peuple d'élite, dominateur et sûr de lui-même'.[65] Suddenly, they found themselves widely stigmatized as militarists, as 'Prussians of the Middle East', colonial occupiers and oppressors of the Palestine Arabs. A bizarre amalgam of Christian, Marxist and Third Worldist myths began to coalesce in the Western consciousness, especially among the younger post-Holocaust generation of radical students. The rise of a militant *gauchisme* in Western society, whose heroes like Mao Tse-tung, Ho Chi Minh, Franz Fanon, Che Guevara and Fidel Castro belonged to the Third World, led to an instinctive identification with the Palestinians rather than Israel. This new generation, while concentrating its fire on American imperialism, was not generally enamoured of the Soviet system. But it had ceased to believe in the picture of a tiny embattled Jewish state surrounded by bellicose enemies intent on its destruction. The Holocaust seemed little more than an abstraction to many on the new Left, one which could, however, be readily appropriated for more contemporary and fashionable causes. At the same time, the more Israel radiated an image of self-confident, coldly efficient power and expanded its hold over conquered territories, the easier it became to project against it the fashionable hate-symbol of historic fascism while identifying with the homeless, abandoned Palestinians as the 'Jews' of the Middle East.

To this post-war generation both racism and fascism were indeed the ultimate crimes against humanity, but in the framework of their Third World ideology they tended to be seen as exclusively 'Western' colonialist sins. Thus the more Israel was depicted as the inheritor of Europe's colonial heritage, the more readily it could be saddled with metaphors from this same Western past such as the image of an all-conquering *Herrenvolk*.[66] On the radical Left, especially its Trotskyist and Maoist wings, a militant anti-Zionism appeared, which openly called for the violent overthrow and dismantling of the Jewish state. In its methods, argumentation and aims this anti-Zionism closely resembled both Soviet and radical Arab propaganda, denouncing Israel as a rascist, 'Nazi' state whose destruction was the *sine qua non* for socialist revolution in the Middle East.

Unconditional solidarity with the PLO increasingly led the extreme Left in Western societies to equate 'the struggle against racism and antisemitism' with the destruction of Israel as a 'progressive' goal.[67] In West Germany, the radical Left was driven by its fanatical anti-Zionism and descent into terrorism into particularly macabre actions. A leaflet signed by the anarcho-communist 'Black Rats' in November 1969 attempted to justify the bombing of the communal hall (*Gemeindehaus*) of West Berlin's Jewish congregation, on the anniversary of the *Kristallnacht* pogrom, by denouncing German guilt-feelings.[68] It declared that the time had come to stop doing penance for the gassing of Jews in the Second World War. 'This kind of neurotic, backward-looking anti-Fascism, obsessed as it is by past history, totally disregards the non-justifiability of the State of Israel. True anti-Fascism consists in an explicit and unequivocal identification with the fighting *Fedayin*. Our solidarity with them will no longer be satisfied by purely verbal protests of the Vietnam variety, but will pitilessly combat the combination of Fascism and Israeli Zionism. . . .'[69]

The smearing of Jewish memorials with the words 'El Fatah' and 'Shalom/Napalm' were now deemed to be expressions of international socialist solidarity and liberation from bourgeois Germany's *Judenkomplex*.[70] A leaflet distributed by *internationale solidarität* at this time closed with the slogan, *Schlagt die Zionisten tot, macht den Nahen Osten rot* (Beat the Zionists dead, make the Near East red) – evoking more than an echo of pre-war Nazi hate-mongering.[71] The Berlin trial in December 1972 of Horst Mahler, a lawyer involved in the Baader–Meinhof terrorist movement, brought to the surface some of the latent antisemitism in this extreme Left 'anti-Fascism'.[72] Mahler read in court a polemical declaration of the Red Army Faction (RAF), justifying the murder of Israeli athletes at the Munich Olympic Games by Palestinian terrorists. The action was 'anti-fascist . . . because it was in memory of the 1936 Olympics'. It was a blow against the strategy of imperialism and the Federal Republic's law-and-order state. 'Israel weeps crocodile tears. It had burned up its sportsmen like the Nazis did the Jews – incendiary material for the imperialist extermination policy.'[73]

Ulrike Meinhof, who gave evidence for Mahler, insisted for her part that unless the German people were pronounced 'not guilty' of fascism, they could not be mobilized for the revolution. The Left and the Communists had failed to explain Auschwitz properly to the German masses. In reality, antisemitism was anti-capitalism; it expressed the unconscious longing of the people for Communism. Their justified hatred of finance-capital and the banks had been diverted by the Nazis on to the Jews. 'Auschwitz means that six million Jews were murdered and carted on to the rubbish dumps of Europe for being that which was maintained of them – Money-Jews' (*Auschwitz heisst, das sechs Millionen Juden ermordet und auf die Müllkippen Europas gekarrt wurden als das, als was man sie ausgab – als Geldjuden*).[74] By implication, there was therefore nothing wrong with their murder as *Geldjuden*, which was not an act of racism but of class-hatred. Hence the German people could be pronounced 'not guilty' of genocide and mobilized in the future for their apocalyptic mission of destroying capitalism. Not content with standing the history of the Third Reich on its head and whitewashing the German masses in such convoluted fashion, Ulrike Meinhof also felt compelled to express a 'historical identity' with the Jews of the Warsaw ghetto; for her terrorist group was supposedly suffering from the same treatment at the hands of the

West German authorities as the Jews had experienced under the Third Reich.[75]

The concrete meaning of this 'anti-fascist' identification would soon be revealed, however, in the Entebbe hijack. A member of Ulrike Meinhof's gang, Wilfried Böse, was directly involved on 27 June 1976 in the hijack of the Air France airbus flying from Tel Aviv to Paris. He and his comrades forced the plane to land at Entebbe in Idi Amin's Uganda as part of a terrorist operation masterminded by the notorious 'Carlos'. The Jewish passengers were separated by Böse and his colleagues from the non-Jews, who alone were released. Some of the Entebbe hostages were survivors of Nazi concentration camps. One of the captives even showed Böse the camp number indelibly branded on his arm and told his captor that he found it difficult to see the difference between the new German generation and that of the Nazis. Once again, Jews were being *selected* by Germans to die, even though the Baader–Meinhof group claimed that they were fighting for world-revolution.[76] The real difference, as the spectacular Entebbe rescue of the hostages by Israeli paratroops shortly revealed, was the existence of a Jewish state capable of the speedy action which alone could prevent a tragic repetition in miniature of the Nazi past.

This lesson has, however, been lost on the contemporary far Left which has continued to talk emptily about itself, or about women, students, homosexuals and other 'oppressed' groups as 'the Jews of today'. In the suspended limbo of its historical false consciousness, radical German youth insists that it has no connection with the Nazi past; yet, as Heinrich Broder, a former member of the German new Left, has recently pointed out in an open letter, 'there still is the Super-Jew – the State of Israel' with which to stubbornly preoccupy oneself.[77] This state is judged by altogether different standards from non-Jewish states. It alone is depicted as the living incarnation of what the Third Reich once represented – namely racism-in-action.[78] Broder has well described the diversionary tactics underlying the historical and psychological campaign of self-delusion practised by his ex-comrades. 'So you make it easier for yourselves by projecting on your parents' victims, the debates and the arguments you never had with your parents. And it works: the Jews are the Nazis, the Palestinians are the victims of the Jews – and your parents are out of the picture (and you, too). You don't have any more problems. At last, you can look them in the face, because you now know where the Nazis, who were never here [i.e. in Germany] really are.'[79]

In reality, just as Hitler needed 'the Jew' to explain away capitalism, Communism, inflation, pornography, war and the humiliating Versailles

Peace Treaty, so, too, sections of the contemporary Left need Zionism and the state of Israel as their scapegoat for world problems. Without the Jews, there would be no strife in the Middle East, no more obstacles to peace and socialism in their idyllic utopia. It is ultimately a matter of principle – 'the Jewish State must not be'.[80] Similar attitudes can be found throughout those myriad radical Left groups in the Western world which have accepted the destruction of Zionism as a cardinal point in their programmes.[81] They reject not only the national dimension of Jewry, its historical continuity, religion and cultural traditions, but also the right to self-determination of three and a half million Israelis who almost alone among the nations of the world are seen as an *organic* obstacle to revolution, peace and progress. Inverting Hitler's slogans, it is in the name of 'anti-racism' and a universalist revolutionary utopia that they negate the contemporary national framework of Jewish existence – and arrive at a similar result: *Israel delenda est!* Since in its essence and existence the Jewish state *a priori* represents the principle of absolute injustice, it therefore *deserves* to be destroyed.

This leftist anti-Zionist ideology does not, of course, identify with the brutal, violent antisemitism of the Nazis and the pre-war radical Right who had openly sought to undermine the civic equality of Jews in bourgeois society, to confiscate their property, expel them from the country or in the last extreme physically to extirpate the biological foundations of Jewry.[82] The Holocaust discredited this type of *racial* antisemitism. But it did so, only to give birth to a new anti-Jewish ideology focused against Israel, the central expression of collective Jewish identity in the post-war era. To paraphrase the noted French sociologist Annie Kriegel: anti-Zionism has come to fulfil the same role in the 1970s and 1980s for Communism and for the Left as did antisemitism for the Nazis and the Right in the 1930s and 1940s.[83] The essence of the Hitlerian project *and* of its post-war successors remains the physical uprooting of the Jewish collectivity as a people and its disappearance from the face of the planet. The slogan of the Nazis was *Judah Verrecke!* (Perish Judah), that of radical anti-Zionism is the destruction of Israel. As far as the Jewish people are concerned, the consequences would in practice be similar, for there can be no physical elimination of the Jewish state without mass destruction. Most Jews who somehow survived a successful Arab war against Israel would again be turned into homeless wanderers, dependent on the mercy of the nations; and the position of the Diaspora would be seriously undermined.

Theoretically, of course, it is true that militant anti-Zionism claims only to reject the *national* expression of Jewish identity, and strongly denies any genocidal intentions towards Jewry. But apart from Hitler and the Nazis who candidly admitted to hating *all* Jews without exception and seeking their extinction, genocide has scarcely been the predominant mode of anti-Judaism and antisemitism throughout the ages.[84] Post-1945 antisemitism, having been placed on the defensive by the unique extent of the Nazi horror, has had to adapt itself to the contemporary *Zeitgeist*. In the 'post-Holocaust' age it has become increasingly necessary for rabid Jew-baiters to mask their true feelings and intentions. It is in many ways an age of 'antisemitism without antisemites',[85] where not only the radical Left but even the neo-Nazis assert that they have nothing against Jews, but oppose only 'Zionists';[86] an era where Communists promote national liberation movements in the Third World but denounce the Jewish national movement as the 'fascism of our time'; where pseudo-liberals applaud the 'progressive' content of Palestinian terror organizations while disapproving of the 're-actionary' and ghetto-like character of Zionist Jewry. Though no other people in modern times became nationalist under the pressure of such desperate adversity as the Jews, even 'enlightened' anti-Zionists frequently continue to express astonishment at the refusal of the Jewish people to assimilate and disappear. This negation of the national dimension in Jewish existence has become in the post-Holocaust era the focal point for attacks on Jewry as a whole.[87] For the fact is that the centrality of Israel in Jewish life makes it virtually impossible to differentiate between anti-Zionism and antisemitism. Thus, whether intended or not, the 'anti-Zionist' campaign strikes in practice not only at Israel but at the security and standing of all Jews.[88]

Diaspora Jews find themselves willy-nilly accused by radical organizations of complicity in 'crimes' allegedly committed by Israel, and the object of Arab terrorist attacks. For in the militant anti-Zionist conception, the Jews of the Diaspora are readily metamorphosed into a fifth column, the reservoir of a vast tentacular organization whose geo-political centre is the state of Israel.[89] Every Jew can thereby become transformed into a potential *enemy*, unless he overtly opposes Zionism. The Dispersion itself becomes the object of suspicion, the visible manifestation of an intangible yet omnipresent secret empire.[90] Bomb attacks in Paris, London, Brussels, Berlin or Vienna against Jewish targets appear as the natural extension of the anti-Zionist crusade, to its more vulnerable hinterland. The Arab Holy War against Israel is turned, with the active complicity and assistance of neo-Nazi and Left-wing extremists in the West, into an assault on the very principle of Jewish solidarity.

This terrorist war which began in the 1970s under the mask of 'anti-fascism' has revealed its macabre reality in outrages like the attack on the synagogue in Rue Copernic in October 1980 and the machine-gun assault on the Goldenberg restaurant in the Rue des Rosiers on 9 August 1982. The Middle East background to these murderous crimes was only too apparent. Less obvious at first sight is the ideological inversion of history that permits such terrorist actions to be considered expressions of resistance to imperialism and Zionism; for if Jews really are Nazis then it might become as natural and 'moral' to kill them as it would be to assassinate Hitler and his henchmen. All that is required is for modern Jewish history to be rewritten in the light of the so-called Israeli 'Final Solution' of the Palestinian problem, in order to justify bloody acts of revenge that can then be glorified as 'resistance to Nazism'. The Jewish tragedy of yesterday becomes the pretext for Arab retribution in the present and the herald of a future apocalypse in which Israel will finally be extinguished.[91]

Such notions, it might plausibly be argued, have little chance of gaining acceptance beyond the lunatic fringe of politics in the Western world. Yet by the beginning of the 1980s the mood of public opinion had significantly changed with regard to the Jewish state. The steady trivialization of the German mass murders, the radical chic ideology which has confused forms of social discrimination with outright fascism and eagerly transformed every victim of oppression into a Holocaust 'Jew', the cumulative impact of Communist and PLO propaganda, the weight of Arab petro-dollar influence, the continuous European slide into appeasement and Israel's own incompetent public relations have had a cumulative impact.[92] Beyond the powerful economic and political factors which have led to the erosion of Israel's image there are also certain intangibles which the war in Lebanon thrust to the surface: the inability of many Gentiles to come to terms with the real meaning of Hitler's murder of the Jews, the persistence of unconscious Christian stereotypes concerning the status of the Jewish state and the paralysing Western guilt-complex *vis-à-vis* the history of European colonialism and the Third World.

There is finally the reality of Israel's own behaviour: its questionable use of military power in reprisals that have sometimes appeared disproportionate to the provocation from the other side; the implanting of new settlements in Judea and Samaria regardless of world opinion; the rise of a narrow, integral nationalism with a strong particularist and religious colouring which has underlined the withering of much of Israel's original socialist pioneering ethos. Moreover, an aggressive Israel, recreated in the image of Mr Begin and Mr Sharon, consciously flexing its muscles and abrasively radiating an image of unrestrained power, was not guaranteed to inspire excessive sympathy in the West. The disastrous Lebanon war launched by Begin and

Sharon, with its accompanying stark images of death and destruction, of innocent men and women being blown to smithereens, underlined the instinctive distrust which many people in the Western world who were neither anti-Zionist nor antisemitic felt for the right-wing Israeli leadership. It was against this tragic background that the myth of Zionist 'Nazism' could for the first time find a responsive echo in the West.

# CHAPTER TWELVE

# From Berlin to Beirut

Menachem Begin, Israel's Prime Minister at the time of the invasion of Lebanon, was a man traumatized by the Holocaust, the indelible imprint of which had profoundly shaped his political psychology. In an interview on 3 November 1977, shortly after taking office, he had summed up the lessons of the Second World War in classical Zionist terms. 'The defencelessness of the Jews was the real scourge of our life, for centuries, but mainly in our generation. That must never happen again. Therefore, we decided to take up arms and fight for liberation. In order to have a State, an army, a means of national defence. That was the prime mover. And to make sure that the Jewish State is secure, that the borders are unbreakable, that the land is un-conquerable. That is the second prime mover of all our actions. . . .'[1] The Jewish state was conceived in his mind, therefore, as the answer to the endemic powerlessness of the Diaspora which had been so starkly exposed by the Holocaust. For Menachem Begin, who had grown up in inter-war Poland, the genocide of six million Jews in Europe (including his own parents and brother) had also left in him an uncompromising hatred not only of Nazism but of all things German. For instance, as leader of the Herut opposition party he had at the beginning of the 1950s militantly opposed the reparations agreement with West Germany, condemning it as a terrible stain on Jewish honour. Addressing a crowd in Jerusalem on 7 January 1952 he shouted: '. . . There is not one German who did not murder our parents. Every German is a Nazi. Every German is a murderer. Adenauer is a murderer. All his aides are murderers. But their reckoning is money, money, money. This abomination will be perpetrated for a few million dollars.'[2]

Begin, as a survivor of murdered Polish Jewry, could never reconcile himself to the 'new' Germany and even opposed the establishment of diplomatic relations between Israel and the Federal Republic in 1965. So deep was his Germanophobia that it led him in office to make a diplomatically damaging and rather unfair personal attack on West German Chancellor Helmut Schmidt and to repeatedly identify *all* of Israel's many enemies with the Nazis. In particular, Yasser Arafat, the PLO leader, who had indeed frequently sworn to destroy Israel, was perceived in Begin's mind as a reborn Hitler. During the Lebanon war, Israel's Prime Minister was to send a somewhat grotesque letter to American President Ronald Reagan in which he described himself as the head of a valiant army flushing out Arafat-Hitler from his bunker at the gates of Berlin-Beirut. The gross unreality of this comparison between the PLO guerrilla forces and the powerful armies of the Third Reich at Hitler's disposal during the Second World War must have been embarrassingly apparent even to some of Mr Begin's most uncritical admirers. The 2½ million Palestinians, dispersed over the Middle East, without land or a national economic base, could hardly be evoked in the same breath as the military and industrial powerhouse that was Nazi Germany. Nor was Israel, a technologically and militarily developed state which had decisively defeated the combined armies of the Arab world, about to be decimated by the PLO. Could it have been on the basis of these hallucinations that Beirut was mercilessly pounded into submission in the summer of 1982?[3] Was it because of the staggering horror of 1½ million Jewish children murdered by the Nazis that PLO terror had to be inflated by Begin to the level of another potential Holocaust?[4] Were the Palestinian guerrilla forces, and the miserable refugee camps from which they sprang, seriously comparable to the superbly drilled and equipped Nazi hordes who fell upon a defenceless Jewish and Gentile civilian population in Eastern Europe?

Even to pose these questions is to suggest the latent paranoia behind Begin's equation; one can recognize this reality without for a moment denying the fact that the Palestinian National Covenant almost invites exposure as a thinly disguised warrant for genocide. The problem with the Beginist equation lies less in its reading of ultimate Palestinian *intentions* than in its lack of all proportion with regard to the *means* at the enemy's disposal. For Israel, in spite of its economic and political vulnerability, remains the dominant Middle Eastern power, with a well-trained, highly mechanized army more than capable of dealing with the Arab threat. The comparison of Arafat with Hitler was therefore demagogic and grossly exaggerated in real operational terms, even if it was less so at the level of PLO ideology and declared objectives with regard to Israel. Furthermore, Begin's blatant misuse of the Holocaust for political ends gave Israel's enemies an all too convenient pretext for throwing the imagery of the 'Final Solution' back in his face.[5] Not every act of aggression against Israel, as many critics have pointed out, is a continuation of the Holocaust.[6] Not every condemnation of Zionism is an expression of latent or manifest antisemitism.

Some of the wrath aroused in the televisual and news media by Israel's incursion into Lebanon can, furthermore, be better explained by other factors; for instance, by the constant need of the media to juxtapose heroes and villains, by its general tendency to sentimentalize the underdog and by the simple, stark story which the tele-images themselves conveyed of Israeli bombing raids and destroyed Lebanese cities.[7] Even the obsessive use by the Western media of the linguistic débris of Nazism to convey the horrors of war might have been partially excusable; for as Michael Marrus has argued, every era 'operates in the shadow of its historical past, and it is inevitable that the great reference points of our own time – particularly Hitler and the Nazi genocide against Jews – will be used and misused to describe what people think and feel about momentous political upheavals'.[8]

Yet such explanations are ultimately only half-truths, for the selectivity of journalists also obeys deeper historical patterns which crises like Lebanon tend to bring into the foreground. The constant flurry of statements and cartoons in the Western media comparing Begin to Hitler, the Israel Defence Forces to the Wehrmacht or the siege of Beirut to the Warsaw ghetto cannot really be described as innocent analogies; nor can the invention of a figure of '600,000 homeless civilians' in Lebanon, first issued by PLO sources and then endlessly repeated in the Western media until it was finally realized that the *entire* Lebanese population under Israeli control constituted less than half a million inhabitants![9] But then 600,000 refugees must have sounded beguilingly reminiscent of six million Holocaust victims, a fact which could not have escaped the attention of those determined to transform Palestinian Arabs into 'Jews' and Lebanese camps into replicas of Dachau.[10] Such analogies were not surprising when they originated from Arab capitals or from Moscow. Nor was any great sophistication required to explain why the Western Communist press published lurid editorials and headlines demanding 'a stop to the genocide';[11] the fact that left-wing Social Democratic statesmen like Bruno Kreisky, Olaf Palme and Andreas Papandreou, known for their antagonism to Israel, indulged in similar demagogy was also less than astounding.[12] Had not Chancellor Kreisky, for example, consistently savaged Mr Begin and the 'fascist mentality' of the partisans of Greater Israel? Had he not attacked Zionist ideology as a 'posthumous assumption of Nazi ideas in reverse' and helped to make Yasser Arafat *salonfähig* in the chancelleries of Europe?[13]

But when newspapers in far-off exotic places like the Malaysian capital, Kuala Lumpur, which had no direct historical experience of Nazis and Jews, parroted the same formulas, one appeared to be in the presence of a universal epidemic.[14] Malaysia was, admittedly, a hard-line Islamic country, a fact which reflected in its ban on Jewish songs and the creations of Jewish composers. But neither such petty-minded antisemitism nor all the verbal expressions of Third World 'solidarity' could help the PLO, any more than the self-deceptions of those many European politicians who had failed to warn the Palestinians adequately 'against dreaming of the liquidation of a state whose power these politicians knew only too well'.[15] Even more impotent was the hyperbole of the many pro-Palestinian scholars, academics and fashionable leftists who had rather recklessly encouraged the illusions of the PLO. All their fantasies about 'Israeli Nazism' and the epic of the Resistance could not wash away their own irresponsibility in egging the Palestinians on towards disaster. Jacobo Timerman, whom no one can accuse of partiality to the Begin–Sharon government, summed it up eloquently. 'To speak of a Palestinian Holocaust, to compare Beirut with Stalingrad or with the Warsaw Ghetto, will move no one. . . . Jews know what genocide is, a Holocaust, a Nazi. We don't need, nobody needs, to resort to truculent comparisons to be desperate for the victims of Lebanon, for the homes destroyed, for the massacre committed by the Begin government.'[16]

Yet many Western correspondents, whether driven by passion or bias, seemed unable to free themselves from the temptations of literary overkill. In the London *Spectator* (19 June 1982) Nicholas von Hoffmann, writing from the United States, openly compared the Israelis to Nazis and Lebanon to Lidice: 'Incident by incident, atrocity by atrocity, Americans are coming to see the Israeli Government as pounding the Star of David into a swastika.'[17] Respectable British newspapers like the *Guardian* printed obnoxious letters from readers which suggested that the day would come 'when an increasing number of non-Jews in Europe and America say that perhaps Hitler had a point'. Another *Guardian* letter-writer asserted that every Jew would have 'to accept some responsibility for the Israeli Army's attempted genocide of the Palestinian people'.[18]

These antisemitic flourishes prompted the former editor of *The Observer* newspaper, Conor Cruise O'Brien, to remark that 'the notion that Israel behaves towards the Arabs as Nazi Germany did to the Jews is a fantasy, and to my mind a peculiarly odious one'.[19] Israel's armed forces had gone into the Lebanon 'in pursuit of armed enemies of their people, pledged to the destruction of their State'.[20] They had caused some heavy casualties among the Lebanese and Palestinian population, because the PLO had deliberately entrenched themselves in civilian positions. The Israeli reaction was arguably disproportionate to the threat, but what did this have to do with 'the systematic murder of six million entirely unarmed people, who had represented no threat at all to Germany'?[21] Was the outraged reaction really due to compassion for suffering Arabs? Why then was the Western press virtually indifferent to the contemporaneous massacre of 20,000 Sunni Muslim Arabs by Syrian President Assad's ruling Alawite regime in the city of Hama? Why were there no comparisons between Hafez el-Assad and Adolf Hitler? Could it have been because President Assad was not a Jew? O'Brien's rhetorical questions pointed perhaps to the reappearance of a classical Christian tradition of antisemitism in the West, though in a relatively mild form. Jews were being reminded once more of their collective guilt and 'collectively *warned* of its possible consequences for themselves'. Jews, it would seem, have no right to complain about the Holocaust because they were behaving as badly as the Germans themselves. While they were being feverishly turned by the media into Nazis, Arabs suddenly enjoyed the doubtful halo of martyrdom hitherto reserved for Jews.

These insipid projections of the Holocaust onto the Lebanese tragedy in order morally to delegitimize Israel ignored the yawning chasm between the events. There were no Palestinians in Lebanon wearing the Yellow Star; no men, women and children condemned to hard labour by the Israelis, to the slow death of forced ghettoization, to mass murder by mobile firing-squads or assembly-line death in gas chambers. Far from having been abandoned by the world like the European Jews during the Holocaust, the Palestinians enjoyed unprecedented media coverage. Their leaders received red-carpet treatment in many capitals of the world; they enjoyed the backing of the mighty Soviet Union and its Communist satellites, of their Arab brethren and most of the Third World; Yasser Arafat was even received by His Holiness the Pope after his highly publicized exit from Beirut with the rest of his guerrilla force.[22] When Mordechai Anielewicz and his comrades had made *their* last stand in the Warsaw ghetto, the world was emphatically not listening, the Allies were preoccupied with purely military matters and the Vatican was deafeningly silent. At best, the Jewish Resistance could count on a few primitive weapons smuggled into the ghetto – certainly nothing to compare with the vast quantities of arms accumulated by the PLO, undoubtedly the wealthiest terrorist organization in history.[23]

But the comparison with Nazism was not the only form of the mythologizing of Israel which surfaced during the war in Lebanon. The comparison, so beloved of Soviet ideologues, between Zionism and the 'bloodthirsty fanaticism' of the Old Testament also found buyers in the West. Even a generally sober and balanced British weekly like *The Economist* (whose reporting of the war was by and large notable for its objectivity) could not resist seeking biblical roots for ruthless Israeli behaviour and confusing the Book of Joshua with twentieth-century military professionalism.[24] Suddenly it appeared even to *The Economist* that the Israeli bombardment of Beirut was fundamentally alien to Christian morality, though not of course to the anachronistic, vengeful people of Jehovah.[25] A recent poem by Peter Reading in the prestigious *Times Literary Supplement*, purporting to be an eye-witness account of an incident in the Lebanon war, underlines the ease with which fashionable anti-Israelism can slide into the muddy waters of antisemitism. A boy spatters 'a fat juicy jeep of Israelis' with machine-gun fire: 'windscreen-glass frosted and one of the front seat occupants oozed red, / there was a crackle of fire, ten or so seconds, and then, / as from a colander, into the pavement streamed out the juices / of the assailant, a slight soldier / homunculus. Well, / nobody looks for a *motive* from these Old Testament shitters – / thick hate is still in the genes; I learned the boy was aged 12.'[26]

The Israelis appear in the poem merely as 'Old Testament shitters' and *their* hatred presumably is 'still in the genes'. As Roger Scruton concluded in *The Times*, the logical implication in this poem was that since 'the duty of such vermin is to be fired on and patiently accept their extinction, they had no motive to retaliate'.[27] In the England of the 1980s, as he has suggested, 'the legitimizing of "anti-Zionism" has cast a shadow of antisemitic feeling, so that belligerent or questionable actions by the state of Israel are condemned as expressions of this or that quintessentially "Jewish" characteristic'.[28] This has been most obviously the case in recent years in parts of the British left-wing press, which has become almost as venomous as Moscow in its 'anti-Zionist' mudslinging. The Nazi–Zionist parallels and the onslaught against 'Zionist racism' are repeated with the kind of deadening uniformity more normally associated with totalitarian Communist productions.[29]

The Trotskyist press, especially in Great Britain, has for many years been in the forefront of this propaganda barrage against the 'racist', fascist ideology of Zionism, held to be responsible for carrying out the 'final solution' of the Palestinian question.[30] In its reports on Lebanon, for example, the Trotskyist *News Line* successively accused the Israeli Zionists of employing 'horrendous gas weapons which were once used against the Jewish people by the Nazis'; of planning to turn West Beirut into a gas chamber for the PLO; of herding civilians into concentration camps and trying to systematically murder 4 million Palestinians.[31] The *Young Socialist* wrote on 21 August 1982 that 'Begin's and Sharon's bombing of Beirut today has some parallels with Stroop's bombardment of the Warsaw ghetto. Inside courageous freedom fighters, outside military representatives of a racist regime slaughtering women and children to impose their will'.[32] In the *Socialist Worker*, veteran Trotskyist leader Tony Cliff (himself a former Israeli and son of pioneering Russian Zionists) wrote that the Israelis were acting 'as if they were copying the Nazis' and recalled the 1930s in Palestine when the Irgun 'used the Hitler salute and wore the brown shirts'.[33] *Socialist Review*, for its part, parroted the official Soviet propaganda line in October 1982 that the racist ideology of Zionism 'leads directly to the concentration camps'. *Labour Review*, the monthly magazine of the Workers Revolutionary Party (a sectarian Trotskyist organization, one of whose leaders is actress Vanessa Redgrave), fulminated in July 1982 against 'Israel's genocidal strike against the Palestinian people'; it was Begin's 'Nazi-like doctrine of superior and inferior races' which supposedly underlay 'his decision to wipe out the Palestinians'.[34]

Vanessa Redgrave told a Hyde Park rally in July 1982 that the Palestine revolution 'will march to triumph over the Nazi-style barbarism of Zionism and imperialism'.[35] She referred to the Israeli operation as having included the 'most barbarous and ferocious acts committed since the days of the Nazi terror' and described the mind-set of the pro-Israeli Reagan administration as 'the mentality of the Auschwitz torturers, the thinking and policies of Auschwitz and Dachau'.[36] Even such wild hyberbole was to be outdone, however, when some Trotskyist leaders claimed to have discovered a 'Jewish conspiracy' at the heart of British cabinet politics and of the BBC, after their own funding by Libyan petro-dollars was exposed in a television programme. This hysterically antisemitic overreaction prompted *Socialist Organiser* to chide Vanessa Redgrave's Workers Revolutionary Party (WRP) for being 'uncomfortably close to marching under the portrait of Adolf Hitler'.[37] Sean Matgamna ironically commented on the WRP that 'they can't even disavow antisemitism without linking the Zionists to Hitler, saying that Hitler consciously and deliberately made forcible conversions to Zionism'.[38]

Significantly, the neo-Nazi National Front, for all its loathing of Trotsky-ism, found some common ground with the far Left's onslaught on 'world Zionism'. It praised a malevolent anti-Zionist Labour Briefing pamphlet written by a Jewish militant, Tony Greenstein, for its 'excellent and painstaking researches into the murky relationship between Hitlerism and Beginism'.[39] This study, according to a review in a National Front publication, was as important in its own way as Richard Harwood's 'revisionist' polemic *Did Six Million Really Die?* As this neo-Nazi accolade revealed, the rhetoric of the far Right and the far Left joined hands when it came to the 'anti-Zionist' witch-hunt. Both have consistently referred to Israel as a capitalist 'bandit state', openly called for its destruction and proclaimed their unconditional solidarity with the Palestinian people. The only detectable difference is that for the neo-Nazis, the Holocaust remains a 'fairy tale', cynically exploited by Zionists to 'justify' the liquidation of the Palestinian people. As Derek Holland's vilely repugnant National Front tract, *Israel – The Hate State*, chose to phrase it: '. . . a mythical Jewish Holocaust does not justify a horribly real Arab Holocaust'.[40]

At the other end of the spectrum, sections of Britain's ethnic press representing those coloured immigrants whom the National Front wishes to expel have also found solace in the popular sport of Israel-bashing. The *Caribbean Times* on 1 October 1982, for example, carried a cartoon comparing an Auschwtiz Jew ('I was the victim of a Genocide') with a Beirut Arab ('Me too'). A few months earlier, an editorial in the same paper (which is reputed to enjoy Libyan subsidies), entitled 'Israel's Racism', saw 'little to differentiate in brutality and disregard for human life between Israel's astounding onslaught on the Palestinians and Lebanese people and the psychopathic crimes the Nazis had perpetrated on the Jews during the last war. It was the intention of the Nazis to exterminate the Jews whom they considered to be a threat to the pure aryans. Similarly, the Israelis have not made any bones about their determination to exterminate the Palestinian fighters. . . .'[41]

This myth of 'extermination' was by and large confined to the margins of the British political spectrum. On the other hand, the *Labour Herald*, a paper co-edited by left-wing Lambeth Labour leader Ted Knight and the popular head of the Greater London Council, Ken Livingstone, did carry a rather sinister and repulsive cartoon on 23 June 1982, of which *Pravda*'s caricaturists might have been proud. A bespectacled, Jewish-looking Begin dressed in Nazi jackboots and uniform, complete with the Death's Head insignia and a Star of David armband, is to be seen raising his right arm in a *Sieg Heil* salute over a mountain of skullbones. There he stands impassively, left hand on hip in a conqueror's pose, while a bleeding Lebanon lies sprawling at his feet. The headline in Gothic script inevitably reads, 'The Final Solution'; the caption sneers; 'Shalom? Who needs Shalom with Reagan behind you?'[42] This macabre symbolism doubtless represented the views only of the *Labour Herald* and not necessarily of the trade union movement or the entire left wing of the Labour Party. The fact that Ted Knight (who publicly demanded an international inquiry into Israel's 'war crimes' in Lebanon) could openly describe Israel as 'a bandit capitalist state, created on stolen land and totally dependent on the US' faithfully reflected the extremist trend.[43] So, too, did the remarks of Labour MP Ernie Ross, chairman of the emergency committee against the invasion of Lebanon, who publicly accused Begin of 'resorting to the tactics employed against the Warsaw ghetto' in his siege of Beirut.[44] How far such utterances were merely the outpourings of a small and unrepresentative minority within the Labour Party must, however, remain an open question.

As in Soviet propaganda, the efforts of the far Left press in Britain and other Western countries have been no less intensive in trying to prove the grotesque historical thesis of Nazi–Zionist 'collaboration'. On 19 March 1982, for example, *Labour Herald* carried a review of some recent literature in this field, which ranged from the lunatic fringe of ultra-orthodox Judaism (Reb Moshe Schonfield's *The Holocaust Victims Accuse*) to special pamphlets produced by the pro-PLO and anti-Jewish BAZO (British Anti-Zionist Organization). The reviewer claimed after reading these books that Israel was 'a state entirely built on the blood of Europe's Jews, whom the Zionists deserted in their hour of greatest need'; that the Zionist leaders deliberately hindered rescue of Jews out of love of property ('namely the land of Palestine') rather than of humanity; that they hypocritically exploited 'the sympathy stirred up for Jews after the Holocaust for their own devious ends'.[45] Such charges have been standard fare for some years in the Trotskyist and far Left press of Great Britain, which has been no less energetic than Moscow or the PLO in rewriting modern Jewish history as a catalogue of Zionist 'crimes against humanity'.[46] In *The News Line* of 8 September 1978, for instance, the Zionist leaders were typically decribed as the 'most blatant collaborators with the Nazis. They actively sought to prevent any ghetto revolts and were involved in selecting those poor Jews who were to go to their deaths in the camps while the rich were allowed to go to Palestine.'

But it was the fortuitous combination of Yitzhak Shamir's emergence in 1983 as Israel's Prime Minister and the publication of an obviously tendentious book by an American-Jewish anti-Zionist, Lenni Brenner, which momentarily gave newsworthiness to this miserable charade. Brenner's account contained nothing novel, least of all in its Trotskyist illusion that had the Jews of Europe joined the ranks of the sectarian Left's pre-war 'struggle against Fascism', the Holocaust might somehow have been averted. Not even Brenner's reproduction of a Stern Gang document dated January 1941, showing that this tiny fringe-group of Zionist extremists still hoped it might obtain German support to transfer the Jews from Europe and oust the British from Palestine, was in any way new.[47] (It had been published nearly ten years earlier by an Israeli historian, but at the time did not attract any attention.[48]) Brenner typically misused the fact of Shamir's membership of the Stern Gang forty years earlier to brand him as 'a would-be ally of Adolf Hitler'. There was 'no better proof', so he suggested, 'that the heritage of Zionist collusion with the Fascists and the Nazis and the philosophies underlying it, carries through to contemporary Israel'.[49]

The radical left-wing press in Britain eagerly seized on Brenner's sensation-mongering to proclaim that Shamir was Israel's first 'Nazi Prime

Minister'.[50] The Communist *Morning Star*, which had in the past shown no interest in Anwar el-Sadat's *actual* links with the Germans, was far more concerned about the hypothetical possibility of Shamir's connection. Was it possible, the Communist daily asked, that 'Israel will re-elect . . . a politician who once tried to shake hands with the Nazis?'[51] The socialist *Labour Herald* typically headlined its review of Brenner's book, 'Shamir and the Nazis'; the reviewer commented about the Stern Gang that 'these same fascist admirers' of Hitler 'are the government of Israel'.[52]

Such fashionable modes of anti-Zionism are by no means confined to the British Isles. One can find parallel phenomena in virtually every Western country. While ostensibly devoted to the Palestinian cause, this unreal discourse of the Left has demonized 'Zionism' to the point where it becomes metamorphosed not only into a synonym for Nazism but into the essential *cause* of the Holocaust itself.[53] Contemporary Israel, too, is fictionalized into a monstrous replay of the Nazi past; the unsuspecting reader might never realize that Israel still enjoys a free parliament, a free press, a democratic opposition, an independent judiciary and a powerful trade-union movement, not generally considered to be attributes of a 'fascist' or National Socialist system. Nor, if he had to rely on the dogmatic, pseudo-Marxist ravings of left 'revisionists', would he understand anything of the tragic reality of the Holocaust, in which 'collaboration' was the one option the murdered Jews of Europe were never given. Least of all could he grasp that the Holocaust represented a devastating demographic, cultural and political amputation of that great reservoir of manpower and talent which was embedded in East European Jewry; a vibrant Jewish community of millions, which by its culture, ideology and social structure was perhaps the best equipped to have realized the Zionist dream in Palestine.

But the fictionalizing of the Holocaust and the classification of Zionism as a form of Nazism are trends by no means confined to the militant Left in Western societies. A famous children's author, Roald Dahl, reviewing a pictorial book on the Lebanese conflict for the London-based *Literary Review*, also chose to stigmatize the Jewish people collectively for actions in Lebanon undertaken by the state of Israel. 'Never before in the history of Mankind', wrote Mr Dahl, 'has a race of people switched so rapidly from being much pitied victims to barbarous murderers.' In his eyes, 'Mr Begin and Mr Sharon are almost the exact carbon copies in miniature of Mr Hitler and Mr Goering. They are equally shortsighted and no less bloodthirsty. We had the Nuremberg Trials after the Hitler war. It is tragic and ironic that now, only thirty-seven years later, Begin and Sharon and a number of other Israeli leaders should themselves be qualifying for the same treatment. . . .'[54] Not content with this broadside, Mr Dahl continued: '... is it not rather wonderful that the German nation, once so hated, has today succeeded in rehabilitating itself and becoming anti-Nazi? Now is the time for the Jews of the world to follow the example of the Germans and become anti-Israeli. But do they have the conscience? And do they, I wonder, have the guts? Or must Israel, like Germany, be brought to her knees before she learns how to behave in this world?'[55] Later, when asked to explain, Dahl did not hesitate to develop his implicitly antisemitic line of thought, asserting that Jews were 'cowards' in the Second World War and 'even a stinker like Hitler didn't just pick on them for no reason'.[56]

It would be tempting to dismiss such remarks simply as bad taste or the expression of British eccentricity. But whether or not they represent a significant current in Western society today, in the long term they are probably more dangerous than the marginal ravings of outmoded Jew-baiters who might dream of a second coming for Hitler and his jackbooted Nazis. Anti-Zionism, it should be realized, has provided the intellectual framework for often latent anti-Jewish feelings to re-emerge among people who may subjectively consider themselves as liberals, 'progressives', humanitarians or democrats.[57] Such 'enlightened' circles will generally disclaim all racist motivation in their criticism of Israel and express their horror of Hitler and Nazism in no uncertain terms. On the other hand, they do at times exploit public revulsion in the West against racism and Nazism as a stick with which to beat contemporary Israel, or to suggest that Zionists in their prejudices, passions and behaviour are a new version of the old antisemitic European Right. This has been one of the more sophisticated techniques of quality newspapers like the influential French daily, *Le Monde*, which for many years has excelled in pillorying Israel behind a high-minded mask of mandarin objectivity and 'anti-fascist' solidarity. During the Lebanese war it opened its columns to regular outpourings against '*le fascisme, aujourd'hui aux couleurs d'Israel*' and the so-called 'Nazi war-crimes' perpetrated by the Israeli army; to be fair, at the same time it also published occasional articles which exposed the gross hyberbole and exaggeration behind these odious comparisons.[58]

By the summer of 1982, the climate in France and West Germany was as ripe as in England for a reversal of the post-war trends of 'philosemitism'. Against the background of the Sabra and Shatilla massacres (blamed, of course, far more on Israel than on the Christian Phalangist perpetrators) anti-Zionist authors like the ex-Stalinist and ex-Catholic convert to Islam, Roger Garaudy, could more plausibly present Nazism and Zionism as identical. Garaudy's assault on the 'Chosen People' myth and the tribal 'racism' of the Jews returned to the classic anti-Judaic themes of the French Enlightenment. Jewish 'racism' with its biblical roots was depicted as deeper and more dangerous than the pagan Nazi myth of race.[59] Garaudy's diatribe was only the tip of the iceberg. In the left-wing Paris daily *Libération*, the Israelis were predictably compared to the Polish Generals, the South African racists and, of course, the Nazis.[60] Throughout much of the French press the impression was created that Israel had deliberately set about massacring innocent civilians and children in Lebanon; a troubled former Prime Minister, Pierre Mendès-France, commented shortly before he died: 'On parle des Juifs tueurs d'enfants, de génocide, d'holocauste'.[61]

The French press during the summer and autumn of 1982 allowed words and images to run riot, as if the destruction of the entire Palestinian nation was about to take place. Even before the invasion, as Alain Finkielkraut pointed out, the Israeli–Palestinian conflict had been increasingly treated in France as a Hitlerian tragedy rather than on its own terms; the present was feverishly being converted into the past, history into mythology, and the Middle East was all too frequently seen through the distorting prism of a superficial anti-fascist consensus.[62] After the Israeli campaign in Lebanon began, nothing therefore seemed more natural than to castigate the state of Israel as a living reincarnation of the ferocity of Nazism. Above all, the French televisual media created a climate of disinformation and unprecedented hostility towards Israel with its ceaseless use of emotionally charged Holocaustal terminology, which undoubtedly intensified latent antisemitic sentiment that had never altogether disappeared in France.[63] The French Communist Party, through its manifold channels of influence, added its own Soviet-inspired legends of fascism and Zionism as inseparable 'Siamese twins';[64] to this motley chorus one would have to add the left-wing Catholics of *Témoignage Chrétien*, a section of the French Socialist Party, the various Franco-Arab and Franco-Palestinian associations and the myriad promoters of anti-American Third World ideologies in France.[65]

French Jewry thus found itself unexpectedly confronted, in the summer of 1982, with the borrowed language of the Hitlerian apocalypse; directed this time at the Jewish state which Theodor Herzl had dreamed would finally liberate the Jewish people and the Gentiles from the savage yoke of antisemitism. It was this 'bloodthirsty' Middle Eastern state which now seemed to symbolize, in the eyes of its opponents, not the promised redemption but a diabolical curse; not the end of the 'Jewish question' but its resurgence in a paroxysm of resentment and bitterness. Israel was no longer Europe's guilt-ridden gift and belated compensation to the Jewish people but an unwanted beachhead of Western imperialism in the Middle East, to be unceremoniously rejected by its former patrons and sponsors. Worse still, it was being identified as the heir of Nazism – Europe's most suicidal creation – only this time not as its victim but as a *successor state*. 'Greater Israel' in its efforts to secure borders more defensible than the pre-1967 armistice lines (at points a mere 9–15 miles wide) was being more and more frequently compared in the West, and not only in Moscow, to an expansionist superpower hungry for *Lebensraum*! It was as if Israel, the last refuge for many of the survivors of the Holocaust, had finally unveiled to the world its hidden face – that of an inhuman occupying power, ruthlessly scattering to the winds the victims of its own nationalist delirium. Israel, sometimes idealized as the historical superego of Western civilization, the moral conscience of the unredeemed world and a self-appointed 'holy nation of priests', had finally sunk to the level of profane imperialism and the cruel politics of the mailed fist. These symbolic substitutions, to quote Alain Finkielkraut, 'levait le tabou qui, depuis Auschwitz, pesait sur l'antisémitisme'.[66] The guilt-ridden collective unconscious of Europe could breathe freely at last; the time of shame and the 'philosemitic interlude in European history' was finally over.[67]

The *Schadenfreude* was particularly striking in West Germany, where a spontaneous outpouring of wrath against Menachem Begin's Israel cathartically released long-suppressed feelings of resentment.[68] As in England and France, images of Old Testamentarian cruelty and Judaic pretensions of 'chosenness' were simplistically equated in some circles with Nazi notions of a 'master race'. No longer was Israel perceived as a plucky David facing the Arab Goliath but rather as a regional superpower pitilessly crushing all resistance to its expansion. The editor of *Der Spiegel*, for example, convinced himself that just as the Jews had once been the victims of German Nazis, so 'now the Arabs are the victims of the Jews'.[69] The West German media, with some honourable exceptions, echoed the comparison and a Bundestag deputy publicly demanded that Mr Begin be tried as a 'war criminal' before an international tribunal.[70] Allusions to the post-war Nuremberg trials became more frequent as did the references to Begin's 'final solution of the Palestinian question'. The Lebanese invasion was even turned by some theologians into a Holocaust of biblical dimensions, an act of merciless cruelty and blind revenge, worthy perhaps of the Judaic God, but not of Christian charity. Theology, political and ancestral prejudices fused in an unholy trinity of self-righteous indignation; exacerbated perhaps by the latent German fear that Israel might be a divine (or satanic?) sword of vengeance capable of plunging the world into a third and final world war. An Israel that seemed to embody not only the wiles of Satan and the logic of power but the terror of Armageddon was guaranteed to resuscitate the most archaic obsessions of Christian myth.[71]

This phantasmagoria of confusion and hatred against the Jewish state did not emerge in a vacuum, nor was it wholly unconnected with Israeli actions. However exaggerated, it should not blind one to those mutations within Zionism that do provide grounds for legitimate concern. It is undeniable that Israel has steadily moved to the Right in the past fifteen years and that its innovative pioneering ethos and robust secularism have been replaced by a religious messianism of very different complexion. The rise of a militant Israeli nationalism with a strong ethnocentric orientation, that came into its own during seven years of Likud rule, has coincided with a visible increase in 'clerical' influence and a growing reliance on military power alone to solve complex political problems. The 'occupation' of the territories has taken its toll in creating for the first time something akin to a 'colonial' mentality in Israel and in intensifying hostility and contempt toward Arabs: while there may be no more 'racism' in Israel than in any other Western democracy, there *are* institutionalized double standards in official behaviour towards Jews and Arabs.[72] The discrimination which exists in housing, jobs, education and health may have some of its origins in Israel's permanent security problems, but it cannot be explained by these alone.

Nor can the militant anti-Arab racism of Meir Kahane's tiny *Kach* party be dismissed on the basis of its minimal electoral support. As is the case with the various racist and neo-fascist movements in Europe and the Americas, the popular, xenophobic prejudices to which 'Rabbi' Kahane appeals are far more widespread than the number of votes he may obtain. What prevents Kahanism for the moment from making a greater electoral impact is the consensus that still exists over the rights of Israel's Arabs and other minorities to free speech, participation in the democratic system and equality before the law. The unresolved problem of the territories and the existence of 1.2 million Palestinians who live in a suspended limbo, deprived of some of their basic civil rights, obviously casts a cloud over Israeli democracy and its future. It is from this source and the deepening economic crisis that the seeds of the fascist cancer may grow in Israel, as the recent rise of anti-Arab terror groups within the country indicates.

The emergence of Gush Emunim (Bloc of the Faithful) after 1973 as a militant elite committed to defending the sacredness of the land of Israel and its messianic redemption as an *absolute* value presents a different though related danger. The radical insistence of the Gush on the idea of reconquest and resettlement of the territories contains within itself not only an exclusivist vision of Israel's 'manifest destiny' but the roots of intolerance. The ideology of the Bloc presupposes a 'metahistorical' bond between the people and the soil deriving from divine election, which transcends all pragmatic considerations.[73] The right to use force, even against the decisions of a democratically elected Israeli government, is *a priori* justified by the vision of the messianic process shared by members of the Bloc and some of their right-wing allies in the Tehiya (Rebirth) party. This type of messianic nationalism, in theory at least, regards the relinquishing of even one square kilometre of sacred soil as forbidden. Moreover it tends to consider secular Western values as a threat to the integrity of Israel and to its vision of the coming redemption.

The parallels with some contemporary forms of Islamic fundamentalism are perhaps more striking than those with the traditions of European integral nationalism, of which Begin's Likud party might be seen as a more legitimate heir. Nevertheless, as the late Professor Uriel Tal pointed out, there is still some common ground between the European nationalisms of the nineteenth century and the ideologues of Gush Emunim, even though the former did not generally regard themselves as religious in inspiration. The European nationalisms developed 'a yearning for the mythic and romantic strata of their distant past'; German nationalism, in particular, nurtured a cult of historic sites, of blood and soil (*Blut und Boden*), as well as sanctifying history 'as an absolute source for socio-political values, aspirations and policies'.[74] In contemporary Israeli messianic nationalism, symbols have also turned into substance; in Professor Tal's words, 'a particular stone; the Wall, the Tombs of the Patriarchs, and historical places no longer serve as mere symbols, but have become for Gush Emunim the sanctified reality itself'.[75]

This post-1967 ultra-nationalist ideology ultimately based on a religious foundation should be distinguished from the secular nationalism of the pre-war 'Revisionist' movement led by Vladimir Jabotinsky, on which the Likud (more specifically Begin's Herut party) is based. Though both camps favour annexation of Judea and Samaria and are committed to the belief that Israel's survival demands on an aggressive military posture, 'Revisionism' historically tended to reject traditional Judaism as a relic of *galut* (exile) mentality.[76] Jabotinsky's pre-war vision of a Jewish state comprising both banks of the Jordan was primarily based on the need to absorb millions of Jewish immigrants from Eastern Europe and not at all on biblical fundamentalism. He did not ground Israel's territorial claims in biblical promises or argue that settlement of the whole land of Israel was a divine commandment, as the post-1967 ultra-nationalists have consistently done. His right-wing nationalism was built not on divine election but on the centrality to the Zionist movement of such secular attributes as the state, army, territory and political sovereignty.[77]

Militaristic symbolism and emphasis on armed struggle were especially important to the Revisionists and it was this which led their Labour Zionist opponents in the 1930s to brand them polemically as 'Jewish fascists'. Though some Palestinian-Jewish revisionists like Abba Achimeir did indeed admire Mussolini and briefly even found some positive features in National Socialism, Jabotinsky thoroughly detested the totalitarian *Polizei-Staat* and the robot-like servitude of the masses which it induced. It is true that there were elements of racial thinking in his early writings on national problems (which included a surprising degree of empathy for xenophobic Ukrainian nationalism) – at a time when Nazism had barely appeared on the horizon.[78] But racial ideology *per se* was never part of his political thought, any more than it featured in the outlook of any prominent Zionist leaders. Where the 'revisionism' of Jabotinsky and his disciples (including Menachem Begin) came closest to fascism was in their emphasis on military discipline, parades, para-military uniforms, the cult of force and a violent anti-Marxism.[79] The hatred of the labour movement was particularly intense because it had successfully achieved an unprecedented hegemony in the Palestine *Yishuv* by the 1930s and did not hesitate to use this position to isolate and weaken the 'Revisionists'.

Of greater long-term significance has been the attitude of the 'Revisionist' movement to the Arab question. Both Jabotinsky and Begin after him consistently maintained support for the idea that the Arabs of Palestine should enjoy equal civil rights as *individuals* but not as a national group in the Jewish state – in many ways an echo of European liberalism and its position on Jewish rights since 1789.[80] In his evidence to the British Royal Commission on Palestine in 1937, Jabotinsky denied that this would impose a major hardship on the Palestine Arabs.[81] The claims of the Jewish nation, landless, impoverished and threatened by raging antisemitism in Central and Eastern Europe, were urgent and imperative. Without mass evacuation from Europe they faced calamity. For the Palestine Arabs who would eventually be reduced to minority status with Israel, this would not be a major human tragedy. The Arabs possessed many national states whereas the Jews had only one Palestine – 'it is like the claims of appetite versus the claims of starvation'.[82]

Jabotinsky and his followers could not, however, free themselves of a certain disdain for Arab and Muslim culture, which reflected the classic European colonial stereotypes of the time. They believed wholeheartedly in the superiority of the West over the East, of European over Middle Eastern civilization.[83] The Islamic world was stagnant and backward in their eyes – a view by no means confined to the political Right and one which was deeply embedded in both Western and Zionist Marxism. The difference was that such views have served to strengthen 'Revisionist' refusals to compromise with any Arab demands either in principle or for tactical reasons. Ben-Gurion despised 'Levantinism' no less deeply than Jabotinsky, but this did not lead him to the same political conclusions about Arab nationalism. The Revisionist rejection of the East was not, however, racial but *cultural*. The Islamic spirit had to be swept from Eretz Israel because it represented political despotism, theocratic rule, social decay, the oppression of women and a fatalistic psychology. Zionism, on the other hand, was a daughter of the West and of European Jewry – dynamic, imbued with the spirit of liberty, enlightenment and individualism.[84]

But if Jabotinskian revisionism despised Islam and radically deromanticized the Levant, it was certainly not unaware of the existence of an Arab nationality in Palestine, whose national consciousness and vitality posed a serious challenge to Zionism.[85] The Zionist Right, like the Labour movement, initially sought to protect the *Yishuv* by a policy of socio-economic segregation (e.g. preventing the inroads of Arab labour in the Jewish economy) and by reliance on armed might, if possible in alliance with Great Britain. Against the rising tide of Arab nationalism (manifested in the Palestine Arab revolt of 1936–9 against British rule) it held that an 'iron wall' of Jewish power was essential. The breakaway of the Irgun Zvai Leumi (National Military Organization) from Jabotinsky's control in the late 1930s was based on their assessment that Britain could no longer be relied upon to provide such a wall. Only an activist national policy (which included terrorism) could prevent the Palestine Arabs from seizing control of Eretz Israel.[86] The Irgun and its successor, the Herut party of Menachem Begin, shared, however, the confident premise of Zionist Revisionism – that Jewish nationalism was inherently superior in quality and motivation to its Arab counterpart. With sufficient national determination, willpower and military training it was in the power of Zionism to establish the territorial integrity of Eretz Israel and to radically change the shape of the Middle East.[87]

This unrestrained cult of force and power has indeed been the one constant feature of 'revisionist' Zionism which brings it closest to the traditions of European fascism. Nevertheless polemical anti-Zionist efforts to transpose this historic past to the contemporary Israeli reality are misleading. This is not only for the obvious reason that Menachem Begin throughout his polical career behaved as an impeccable parliamentarian and his party played strictly by the rules of Israeli democracy. Nor is it solely because, for forty years, the Labour movement dominated the politics of the *Yishuv* and the

Israeli state, successfully reducing the Zionist Right for decades to a position of virtual impotence. For, as the past decade has proved, the Likud is now solidly rooted in a working-class Oriental Jewish constituency as well as in those bourgeois social strata to which Herut appealed in the past. There are, however, deeper structural reasons connected with Israel's centrality for the Jewish people and its links with the West (especially the United States) which have hitherto restrained any trends towards the growth of indigenous fascist-style movements. The constant need for internal unity in the face of the Arab threat and of mounting international pressures have also acted to brake the internecine class-war on which fascism traditionally thrives. The control of the class-struggle through the centralized power of the *Histadrut*, the decisive role of the state and of unilateral transfers from abroad on the economy, have been further inhibiting factors.[88]

For these and other reasons the scarecrow of fascism (and even more of Nazism) remains largely irrelevant to Israel, where there is no imminent danger either of acute class-struggle or of a socialist revolution to galvanize the radical Right.[89] Moreover, no foreseeable Israeli government which wishes to maintain its support in American public opinion and in the Jewish Diaspora could readily afford to throw the democratic system overboard. Nor could it risk the danger of public disaffection, collapse of morale in the Army and massive emigration, if it resorted to the brutal authoritarian methods common enough elsewhere in the Middle East and the Third World. An Israel which even began to approximate to the demonic image of itself spread abroad by its enemies would very soon forfeit its *raison d'être*, not only as the political nerve-centre of the Jewish people but also as its spiritual inspiration.

But if the 'Nazi' and fascist scenarios are unconvincing to any fair-minded critic, the potential dangers to democracy are serious enough. As things stand, Israel is virtually unique in the world in thus far living with an 800 per cent inflation rate without undergoing collapse or resorting to an authoritarian dictatorship. Its electoral system and political regime are obviously far less stable than before, in particular after the series of shocks which the country has undergone since the Lebanese war. An ideological as well as an economic and political crisis, which concerns not only the future of the territories but the soul of Zionism itself, continues to rend the nation. International isolation strengthens the xenophobic, obscurantist and narrowly chauvinist elements within Israeli society, and the link between class and internal ethnic divisions (Ashkenazim/Sephardim) remains a potentially explosive issue. Extremist and anti-Arab opinions, as well as disdain for humanist and democratic values among Israeli youth, are on the upsurge. Moreover, the Lebanon war and the problem of the occupied territories have exacerbated internal divisions and encouraged a significant growth in the violence within Israeli society. The present National Unity government, which is unlikely to last for long, may temporarily check the slide into further chaos, factionalism and dissonance. But the dire prospect of a collapse of Israeli democracy cannot be ruled out.

Particularly disturbing are the evil spirits that continue to haunt the land of Israel from within, the emotions, fears and prejudices which perhaps only the hand of the artist can fully decipher. For in a more subtle way that transcends the ceaseless war of ideologies and the phony propaganda, Israel still stands suspended, in the words of Amos Oz, 'between Hitler and the Messiah'. One can sometimes feel it in Jerusalem's ultra-orthodox Meah Shearim with the angry slogans calling for 'Death to Zionist Hitlerites', or in the graffiti sprayed by lower-class Sephardi hooligans on the walls of smart Tel-Aviv suburbs, stressing the last syllable in 'Ashkenazi', or in the verbal violence of internal Israeli debates where accusations of 'Nazi' and 'fascist' are flung to and fro with breathtaking disregard for truth or historical reality. Such wild rhetoric can be paralleled in other democracies, but in Israel it has a specially emotional and bitter edge. Because of Hitler's evil work of destruction, a whole world of European Jewish creativity which would have infinitely enriched Israel was cut off in its prime; because of Hitler's apocalypse, a stream of imitators, both great and small, continue to dream of completing his less than 'final solution'; because and even in spite of Adolf Hitler, something of his malignant nationalist venom continues to infect Israel itself, as it does the Arab world and a large part of late twentieth-century humanity.

The ghosts of the past have not even spared those who once dreamed of turning their backs on a decadent Europe and building a pure socialist utopia in far-off Palestine. Amos Oz, in his moving and poignant *In the Land of Israel*, devotes a whole chapter to the kind of bigoted Jewish nationalist whom the Holocaust has irredeemably poisoned beyond all repair. 'As far as I'm concerned you can call the State of Israel by any pejorative you like. Call it Judeo-Nazi, the way Professor Leibowitz did. Why not? How does the saying go – "Better a live Judeo-Nazi than a dead saint"? Me, I don't mind being Qaddafi. I'm not looking to the gentiles for admiration and I don't need their love. But I don't need it from your kind of Jew, either. I want to survive.'[90] The message is a Hitlerian one. Kill or be killed! Destroy the existence of the nice, clean little *Zhids* in the Diaspora, spit on brotherhood, morality, human dignity; return mankind to its pristine state of aggression in the name of a sick, self-hating Judeo-Nazism. 'That's right: Judeo-Nazis,

Leibowitz was right. And why not? Why the hell not? Listen friend, a people that let itself be slaughtered and destroyed, a people that let its children be made into soap and its women into lampshades, is a worse criminal than its tormentors. Worse than the Nazis. To live without fists, without fangs and claws, in a world of wolves is a crime worse than murder. Fact: Himmler and Heydrich and Eichmann's grandchildren live well, on the fat of the land, and even preach to us while they're at it, and the grandchildren of the sainted *rebbes* of Eastern Europe and those humanistic, pacifistic Jews who philosophized so prettily in Prague and Berlin – they can't preach to anyone. They've gone, never to come back.'[91] Amos Oz's Israeli *Zhid*-hater is not, unfortunately, just a literary figment of the imagination. He is a parochial and sectarian legacy of the Hitlerian apocalypse which has yet to be fully overcome in contemporary Israel.

The Holocaust was unique in both Jewish and world history.[92] Its transposition to the Middle East or other contemporary conflicts can only confuse and envenom a struggle which is intractable enough without the highly toxic infusions of the Hitlerian nightmare. It is therefore important to recognize and expose the ways in which the trauma of mass extermination can lead to false perceptions, to the blurring of past and present, symbol and substance, metaphor and reality.[93] Beirut was not Berlin but neither was it the Warsaw Ghetto; neither the Israeli army nor the Palestinian 'terrorists' are reincarnations of the Nazis. But in a century where hatred of Jews could lead to a devastating world war and planned mass murder, eternal vigilance is unfortunately the price of survival. Moreover, as we have extensively documented in this book, antisemitism is far from being a mere relic of the Hitler era. Its continuing vitality underlines the truth of Emil Fackenheim's dictum that 'all historically post-Holocaust forms of anti-Jewishness are posthumous victories for Hitler and witting or unwitting continuations of his work.'[94]

# Notes

*The following àbbreviations are used in the Notes:*

*DGFP – Documents on German Foreign Policy, 1918–1945*, Series C, 1933–1937 (Washington, United States Government Printing Office, 1957–66); *Documents on German Foreign Policy, 1918–1954*, Series D, 1937–1945 (Washington, United States Government Printing Office, 1949–64).

*Documents on Nazism* – Jeremy Noakes and Geoffrey Pridham (eds.), *Documents on Nazism, 1919–1945* (London, 1974).

*Goebbels Diaries* – Louis P. Lochner (ed.), *The Goebbels Diaries, 1942–43* (New York, 1948).

*IMT* – International Military Tribunal, *Trial of the Major War Criminals Before the International Military Tribunal*, 42 vols. (Nuremberg, 1947–9, Blue Series).

Jäckel/Kuhn – Eberhard Jäckel and Axel Kuhn (eds.), *Hitler Sämtliche Aufzeichnungen 1905–1924* (Stuttgart, 1980).

*Letters* – Werner Maser (ed.), *Hitler's Letters and Notes* (New York, 1974).

*Mein Kampf* – Adolf Hitler, *Mein Kampf*, trans. Ralph Mannheim (Boston, 1943).

*Speeches* – Norman H. Baynes (ed.), *The Speeches of Adolf Hitler* (London, 1942).

*Table Talk* – H. R. Trevor-Roper (ed.), *Hitler's Table Talk, 1941–1944* (London, 1973).

*Testament* – H. R. Trevor-Roper (ed.), *The Testament of Adolf Hitler: The Hitler-Bormann Documents, February–April 1945* (London, 1961).

*WLB – The Wiener Library Bulletin.* Old Series I–XIX (1946–65); Kraus reprint 1978; New Series XX–XXXV (1965–83).

*Zweites Buch* – Gerhard L. Weinberg (ed.), *Hitler's Zweites Buch: Ein Dokument aus dem Jahre 1928* (Stuttgart, 1961).


## INTRODUCTION

1 'Hitler in His Own Defence', *Newsweek*, 29 March 1982.
2 See *Jerusalem Post Magazine*, 2 April 1982, p. 9.
3 George Steiner, *The Portage to San Cristobal of A. H.* (London, 1981), p. 120.
4 Ibid, p. 121.
5 Ibid, p. 122.
6 Ibid, p. 126.
7 'Das politische Testament Julius Streichers' (Dokument), *Vierteljahrshefte für Zeitgeschichte*, 26, (1978), pp. 670–93.
8 Ibid, pp. 674–5.

NOTES

9 Ibid, pp. 677–8.
10 Ibid, pp. 691–2.
11 Ibid, p. 693.
12 J. F. Pilat, 'Euroright Extremism', *The Wiener Library Bulletin*, Vol. XXXIV, new series, Nos 53/54, (1981), pp. 48–63.
13 Ibid, p. 50.
14 See D. Edgar, *Racism, Fascism and the Politics of the National Front* (London, 1977); Martin Walker, *The National Front* (London, 1977); J. Bloch-Michel, 'Anti-Semitism and the French "New Right" ', *Dissent* (Summer 1980), p. 27; and F. Weil, 'The Imperfectly Mastered Past: Antisemitism in West Germany since the Holocaust', *New German Critique* (Spring/Summer 1980), p. 20.
15 See Saul Friedländer, *Reflections of Nazism* (New York, 1984).
16 Regine Friedman, 'Le juif et les camps dans le cinéma "rétro" ', *Les Nouveaux Cahiers*, No. 58 (Autumn 1979), pp. 10–14.
17 Ibid, p. 13.
18 'Was ist am Faschismus so sexy?', *Der Spiegel*, No. 8, 17 Feb. 1975.
19 Susan Sontag, 'Im Zeichen des Saturn' (Fischer Taschenbuch 1983), pp. 122 ff.
20 Ibid, pp. 148–75.
21 Leon Wieseltier, 'Syberberg's Hitler', *The New Republic*, 8 March 1980.
22 Ibid, p. 28.
23 Henry Pachter, 'Unser Hitler – oder seiner?', *Frankfurter Allgemeine Zeitung*, 1 August 1980.
24 See Alvin Rosenfeld, *Imagining Hitler* (Bloomington, 1985), which appeared too late to be considered here but underlines my point.
25 Nicolaus Sombart, 'Wir sind mit Hitler noch lange nicht fertig', *Frankfurter Allgemeine Zeitung*, 19 November 1977.
26 Karl-Heinz Bohrer, 'Hitler, der Held der siebziger Jahre?', Ibid, 29 June 1977.
27 Eberhard Jäckel, 'Hitler und der Mord an den europäischen Juden', in *Jüdischer Presse Dienst*, No. 5/6 (1977), pp. 12ff.
28 Hyam Maccoby, 'Christianity's Break with Judaism', *Commentary* (August 1984), Vol. 78, No. 2, pp. 38–42, describes the Gnostic vision of *this world*, as having been captured by the powers of Darkness, in terms readily applicable to Nazism.
29 See Heiko A. Oberman, *The Roots of Anti-Semitism* (Philadelphia, 1984) for an excellent account of the relation between Luther's antisemitism and his apocalyptic expectations of 'the end of time'.
30 Norman Cohn, *The Pursuit of the Millennium* (London, 1970), revised edn, pp. 68–80, 102–4.
31 L. Poliakov and J. Wulf, *Das Dritte Reich und die Juden* (Berlin, 1955), pp. 91–2. Also N. Cohn, *Warrant for Genocide* (London, 1970) pp. 198–9.
32 Cohn, ibid.
33 Robert S. Wistrich, 'Antisemitism as a "Radical Ideology" in the Nineteenth Century', *The Jerusalem Quarterly* (Summer 1983), No. 28, pp. 83–95.
34 See Bat Ye'or, 'Holy War or Peace?', *Jewish Chronicle*, 28 May 1982, p. 22.
35 Ronald Nettler, 'Muslim Scholars on the Peace with Israel', *Midstream* (November 1980), Vol. XXVI, No. 9, pp. 15–19.
36 Ronald Nettler, 'Islam vs. Israel', *Commentary* (December 1984), pp. 26–30.
37 Robert Wistrich, 'The New War against the Jews', *Commentary* (May 1985), pp. 35–40.
38 Yehuda Bauer, 'Anti-Semitism Today – A Fiction or a Fact?', *Midstream* (October 1984), pp. 24–31.

## 1 LABORATORY OF WORLD DESTRUCTION

1 Norman H. Baynes (ed.), *The Speeches of Adolf Hitler* (London, 1942), Vol. II, pp. 1456–7.

2 Adolf Hitler, *Mein Kampf* (Boston, 1943), translated by Ralph Mannheim, p. 124.

3 Friedrich Herr, *Der Glaube des Adolf Hitler. Anatomie einer politischen Religiosität* (Munich, 1968), pp. 12ff.

4 Kurt Tweraser, 'Carl Beurle and the Triumph of German Nationalism in Austria', *German Studies Review*, 4 (October 1981), pp. 403–26; and F. L. Carsten, *Fascist Movements in Austria: From Schoenerer to Hitler* (London, 1977), pp. 9–30.

5 *Mein Kampf*, p. 52. Hitler observed that the only discernible difference lay in their 'strange religion'.

6 See August Kubizek, *Adolf Hitler, Mein Jugendfreund* (Graz, 1953), pp. 112–13.

7 *Mein Kampf*, pp. 95, 141, 148.

8 Ibid, p. 11.

9 Ibid, p. 16.

10 See Gerd-Klaus Kaltenbrunner, 'Houston Stewart Chamberlain – The Most Germanic of Germans', *WLB* (1967/8), Vol. XXII, No. 1, new series, No. 10, pp. 9ff. Also Geoffrey G. Field, *Evangelist of Race. The Germanic Vision of Houston S. Chamberlain* (New York, 1981), p. 111.

11 *Mein Kampf*, p. 123.

12 Ibid.

13 Hermann Rauschning, *The Voice of Destruction* (New York, 1940), p. 87.

14 Ibid, pp. 87–8.

15 See H. R. Trevor-Roper, *Jewish and Other Nationalism* (London, 1962), pp. 12–13, 20–1. Also Andrew G. Whiteside, *Austrian National Socialism before 1918* (The Hague, 1962), for the social background to the German–Czech conflict.

16 William J. McGrath, *Dionysian Art and Populist Politics in Austria* (New Haven, 1974). Also by the same author, 'Student Radicalism in Vienna', *Journal of Contemporary History*, 2(3) (July 1967), pp. 183–202.

17 See now Marsha L. Rosenblit, *The Jews of Vienna 1867–1914. Assimilation and Identity* (Albany, New York, 1983), on the immigration of Galician Jews.

18 On the development of the *Ostjude* stereotype, see Steven E. Aschheim, *Brothers and Strangers. The East European Jew in German and German Jewish Consciousness 1800–1923* (Wisconsin, 1982), pp. 58–79.

19 *Mein Kampf*, p. 55.

20 Ibid.

21 Ibid, pp. 59ff.

22 Ibid, p. 59.

23 Ibid.

24 Edward Bristow, *Prostitution and Prejudice. The Jewish Fight against White Slavery* (Oxford University Press, 1982).

25 See Theodor Fritsch, *Handbuch der Jüdenfrage: Die Wichtigsten Tatsachen zur Beurteilung des jüdischen Volkes* (Leipzig, 1933). The catechism first published in 1887 had already gone through 26 printings by 1907. Also Robert G. L. Waite, *Hitler, The Psychopathic God* (New York, 1977), pp. 97–8.

26 Quoted in Paul Massing, *Rehearsal for Destruction* (New York, 1949), p. 306.

27 *Mein Kampf*, p. 338.

28 Ibid, p. 512.

29 *Die Rede Adolf Hitlers in der ersten grossen Massenversammlung bei Wiederaufrichtung der NSDAP* (Munich, 1925), p. 10.

30  *Mein Kampf*, pp. 250ff.

31  On the occult background, see James Webb, *The Occult Establishment* (1976) and Jeffrey A. Goldstein, 'On Racism and Anti-Semitism in Occultism and Nazism', *Yad Vashem Studies*, XIII (Jerusalem, 1979), pp. 53–72.

32  See Michael Biddiss, *Father of Racist Ideology* (London, 1970) for a discussion of de Gobineau's theories. Hitler and the Nazis did not share the aristocratic Frenchman's pessimism.

33  *Ostara: Briefbücherei der Blonden und Mannesrechtler*, ed. Adolf Lanz (Rodau bei Wien, 1905–18).

34  A. Lanz, 'Rasse und Weib und seine Vorliebe für den Mann der niederen Artung', *Ostara*, 21 (March 1908), pp. 1–17. Also 'Revolution oder Evolution? Eine freikonservative Osterpredigt für das Herrentum europäischer Rasse', ibid (3 April 1906), pp. 3–15.

35  See Wilfried Daim, *Der Mann, der Hitler die Ideen gab: Von den religiösen Verirrungen einer Sektierers zum Rassenwahn des Diktators* (Munich, 1958). Also Friedrich Heer, *Der politische Glaube des Adolf Hitler. Anatomie einer politischen Religiosität* (Munich 1968), pp. 709–18.

36  Goldstein, op. cit.

37  *Mein Kampf*, p. 64.

38  Ibid, p. 55.

39  Letter dated 29 November 1921. Quoted in Werner Maser (ed.), *Hitler's Letters and Notes* (New York, 1974), p. 107.

40  On Hitler's material circumstances at this time, see Bradley F. Smith, *Adolf Hitler: His Family, Childhood and Youth* (Stanford, 1967), pp. 111–12. Also the lively account by J. Sydney-Jones, *Hitler in Vienna 1907–1913* (New York, 1983).

41  *Mein Kampf*, pp. 60–2.

42  Ibid, p. 21.

43  Ibid, p. 51 See also J. L. Talmon, *The Myth of the Nation and the Vision of Revolution* (Cambridge University Press, 1981), pp. 516–23.

44  *Mein Kampf*, p. 320.

45  Robert S. Wistrich, *Revolutionary Jews from Marx to Trotsky* (London, 1976), pp. 94–114.

46  For further details, Robert S. Wistrich, *Socialism and the Jews. The Dilemmas of Assimilation in Germany and Austria-Hungary* (London, 1982).

47  *Mein Kampf*, p. 65.

48  Ibid, pp. 445–8.

49  Ibid, pp. 382, 391.

50  Robert S. Wistrich, 'Karl Lueger and the ambiguities of Viennese antisemitism', *Jewish Social Studies* (Summer–Autumn 1983), Vol. XLV, Nos 3–4, pp. 251–62.

51  *Mein Kampf*, p. 98. Also H. R. Trevor-Roper (ed.), *Hitler's Table Talk 1941–1944* (London, 1973), 17 February 1941, p. 146; 'When I arrived in Vienna I was a fanatical opponent of Lueger.'

52  *Mein Kampf*, p. 99. See also E. Pichl, *Georg von Schoenerer und die Entwicklung des Alldeutschtums in der Ostmark* (Oldenburg, 1938); Andrew G. Whiteside, *The Socialism of Fools, Georg Ritter von Schoenerer and Austrian Pan-Germanism* (Berkeley/ Los Angeles, 1975); and Robert S. Wistrich, 'Georg von Schoenerer and the genesis of Austrian antisemitism', *WLB* 29 (1976). Nos 39/40, pp. 20–9.

53  *Mein Kampf*, p. 108.

54  Ibid.

55  *Table Talk*, p. 147.

56  *Mein Kampf*, p. 124.
57  Pichl, op. cit., Vol. III, p. 267.
58  Ibid, pp. 332–5.
59  See Oskar Karbach, 'Georg von Schoenerer. The Founder of Modern Political Antisemitism', *Jewish Social Studies*, 8 (1) (January 1945), pp. 12–13.
60  Robert S. Wistrich, 'Karl Lueger . . .', op. cit., pp. 251–61.
61  Sigmund Mayer, *Die Wiener Juden. Kommerz Kultur, Politik 1700–1900* (Vienna and Berlin, 1917), p. 475.
62  *Mein Kampf*, p. 120.
63  Ibid.
64  Ibid.
65  *Table Talk*, p. 146.
66  *Mein Kampf*, pp. 55, 69.
67  *Table Talk*, p. 147.
68  On Lueger's political style, see Carl. E. Schorske, 'Politics in a New Key – An Austrian Triptych', *Journal of Modern History*, 4 (December 1967), pp. 343–86; John W. Boyer, *Political Radicalism in Late Imperial Vienna* (Chicago, 1981); and Robert S. Wistrich, 'Karl Lueger . . .', op. cit., pp. 251–60.
69  *Mein Kampf*, p. 100.
70  Ibid.

## 2  THE POLITICS OF EITHER-OR

1  *Hitler. Sämtliche Aufzeichnungen 1905–1924*, Eberhard Jäckel and Axel Kuhn (eds.) (Stuttgart, 1980), p. 69. Also *Letters*, p. 107.
2  *Mein Kampf*, pp. 161, 163–4. Also 'Positiver Antisemitismus', *Völkischer Beobachter*, 4 November 1922, pp. 1ff.
3  *Mein Kampf*, pp. 157–9.
4  *Letters*, p. 107.
5  R. H. Phelps, 'Before Hitler Came: Thule Society and Germanen Orden', *Journal of Modern History*, Vol. 35, No. 3 (September 1963), pp. 247–52.
6  Goldstein, op. cit., pp. 65–72.
7  See George L. Mosse, *The Crisis of German Ideology: Intellectual Origins of the Third Reich* (New York, 1964), for the best general account of the *völkisch* idea.
8  *Mein Kampf*, p. 360.
9  See *Hitlers Zweites Buch*, introduced and edited by Gerhard L. Weinberg (Stuttgart, 1961), for a sustained polemic against the *völkisch* nationalists, on the issue of *Lebensraum*, the South Tyrol and the policy of 'Germanizing' non-German peoples, which Hitler categorically opposed.
10  *Speeches*, Vol. I, p. 15 (12 April 1922). See J. P. Stern, *Hitler. The Führer and the People* (London, 1975) for a perceptive discussion of Hitler as 'the representative individual' of his age and the connection between language, ideology and the notion of authentic experience.
11  See James M. Rhodes, *The Hitler Movement. A Modern Millenarian Revolution* (Stanford, 1980) for elaboration of this hypothesis.
12  *Mein Kampf*, p. 206.
13  *Die Rede Adolf Hitlers in der ersten grossen Massenversammlung* (Munich, 1925), p. 8.
14  Ernst Boepple (ed.), *Adolf Hitlers Reden* (Munich, 1933), pp. 55–6.
15  See Geoffrey Barraclough, 'Farewell to Hitler', *New York Review of Books* (3 April

1975), pp. 11–16, who in my view quite mistakenly regards Hitler's antisemitism in the 1920s as 'entirely conventional' and no different from that of bourgeois conservative leaders in Germany at the time.

16 Helmut Krausnick *et al.*, *Anatomy of the SS State* (London, 1973), p. 38; *Letters*, p. 215.

17 A speech of 6 April 1920 in Munich at NSDAP meeting, in Jäckel/Kuhn, Dokument 91, pp. 119–20.

18 'Warum sind wir Antisemiten?' Rede Auf einer NSDAP Versammlung, in: Jäckel/Kuhn, ibid, p. 201.

19 Ibid.

20 Ibid, pp. 176–7.

21 Quoted in Joachim Fest, *Hitler* (London, 1973), p. 212.

22 *Mein Kampf*, p. 772 (1962 ed.). See also Rudolph Binion, *Hitler and the Germans* (1976), for a controversial and completely ahistorical psychoanalytic interpretation of the link between his mother's death from cancer, Hitler's own gas-poisoning at the front in 1918 and the Holocaust.

23 See *Völkischer Beobachter*, 11 June 1920, 30 January 1921, 17 and 28 April 1921. Also Binion, op. cit., p. 29.

24 Major Hell's notes of his conversation with Hitler are deposited in the *Institut für Zeitgeschichte*, Munich. See John Toland, *Adolf Hitler* (New York, 1977), p. 157. Also Nathaniel Weyl, 'The Marx-Hitler-Holocaust Enigma', *Midstream* (November 1983), pp. 12–13.

25 Weyl, ibid.

26 Quoted in Weyl, op. cit., p. 13.

27 See Jäckel/Kuhn, op. cit., p. 105. Speech of 16 January 1920.

28 Ibid, pp. 122–3, 'Der Weltkrieg und seine Macher', 17 April 1920.

29 Ibid, pp. 136–9, 'Das deutsche Volk, die Judenfrage und unsere Zukunft', speech in Munich, 31 May 1920.

30 Speech of 28 July 1922 on 'Free State or Slavery', in *Speeches*, Vol. I, p. 29.

31 'Einige Fragen an den deutschen Arbeiter', *Völkische Beobachter*, 22 May 1921, p. 2. Also 'The Stock Exchange Revolution of 1918', in *Speeches*, I, pp. 42ff.

32 *Speeches*, p. 29.

33 Ibid, p. 9; speech of 12 April 1922.

34 Jäckel/Kuhn, op. cit., pp. 794–5. Munich, 18 January 1923, 'Zwei Fronten in Deutschland'.

35 'Versammlung im Zirkus Krone', ibid, pp. 795–6.

36 See Klaus Scholder, 'Die Kirchen im Dritten Reich' (The Churches in the Third Reich), *Das Parlament*, 10 April 1971 (Beilage zur Wochenzeitung).

37 See Hans Staudinger, *The Inner Nazi. A Critical Analysis of 'Mein Kampf'* (Baton Rouge, 1981), pp. 53–84. The original text was written in 1944.

38 See Jäckel/Kuhn, op. cit., pp. 136–139. Speech in Munich on 31 May 1920, 'Das deutsche Volk, die Judenfrage und unsere Zukunft'.

39 Ibid. Hitler blames the Jews for the denationalization of the peoples and the subjugation of Germany in the interests of international Jewish loan-capital. At the same time he describes 'Der Jude als nationalste Rasse aller Zeiten'. Also *Mein Kampf*, p. 306.

40 Jäckel/Kuhn, pp. 774–5. 'Gesprach mit Eduard August Scharrer' (end of December 1922). 'Sie sind geboren zum Zerstören des Bestehenden, sie sind der Geist der stets verneint . . . Sie besitzen keine Kultur, wie sie auch keine eigene Kunst besitzen.'

41 See for example 'Positiver Antisemitismus', *Völkischer Beobachter*, 4 November 1922, pp. 1ff. Also Jäckel/Kuhn, op. cit., pp. 718–20 for Hitler's references to the Book of Esther – a favourite theme of Nazi antisemitism.

42 *Mein Kampf*, p. 206. Also Nuremberg speech, 3 January 1923, in Jäckel/Kuhn, op. cit., pp. 776ff. Hitler stressed that 'international' capital was in reality 'national' and Jewish.

43 *Mein Kampf*, p. 655.

44 Ibid. Also *Speeches*, Vol. I, pp. 37–9, on 'Bolshevist Judaism' preparing for the decisive battle in Germany.

45 Lucy Dawidowicz, *The War against the Jews 1933–45* (Pelican Books, 1983), p. 208.

46 Rauschning, op. cit., p. 237.

47 Ibid, p. 241.

48 Ibid, pp. 241–2.

49 Ibid, p. 238.

50 Ibid.

51 Ibid, p. 235.

52 Dawidowicz's view that 'generations of antisemitism had prepared the Germans to accept Hitler as their redeemer', op. cit., p. 209, seems to me misleading, as does the claim that racial doctrine was the most popular part of the Nazi appeal. This is not supported by studies such as William S. Allen, *The Nazi Seizure of Power* (Chicago, 1965) or, more recently, Ian Kershaw, *Popular Opinion and Political Dissent in the Third Reich: Bavaria 1933–1945* (Oxford University Press, 1983), pp. 226ff.

53 Mosse, op. cit.

54 Rauschning, op. cit., p. 236.

55 Ibid.

56 *Table Talk*, p. 7.

57 Uriel Tal, *'Political Faith' of Nazism prior to the Holocaust* (Tel Aviv University, 1978), p. 35.

58 Ibid, p. 31.

59 *Mein Kampf*, p. 307.

60 *Speeches*, Vol. I, p. 42; speech of 10 April 1923.

61 Jäckel/Kuhn, op. cit., p. 137, 'Das deutsche Volk, die Judenfrage und unsere Zukunft.'

62 'Hitler the German Explosive', *The American Monthly* (New York, October 1923), interview with Georg Sylvester Viereck, in Jäckel/Kuhn, ibid, pp. 1023–6.

63 'Das verratene Deutschland', *Völkischer Beobachter*, 26 May 1921, p. 2.

64 Jäckel/Kuhn, op. cit., p. 166. Speech in Munich on 27 July 1920 in which Hitler declared *inter alia*: 'Ich bin Arbeiter und aus Arbeiter-fleisch-und-blut.' A police report pointed out that he was in fact an architect.

65 *Speeches*, Vol. I, p. 26 (28 July 1922).

66 'Die Wahlen und unser Kampf', 11 June 1920, ibid, pp. 142–3.

67 'Der Jude als Arbeiterführer', Jäckel/Kuhn, op. cit., pp. 152ff (speech of 24 June 1920).

68 *Mein Kampf*, pp. 557ff, where Hitler describes how 'the international Jew Kurt Eisner began to play Bavaria against Prussia' and the attempts of the 'Jews' to sow discord between Protestants and Catholics.

69 Ibid, p. 561.

70 *Speeches*, Vol. I, pp. 12ff; speech of 12 April 1922.

71 Ibid, p. 13.

72 Ibid, p. 15.
73 Ibid, p. 13.
74 Max Domarus (ed.), *Hitler: Reden und Proklamationen, 1932–1945* (Würzburg, 1962), Vol. 2, pp. 1828–9.
75 Ibid, pp. 1920, 1937.
76 The point has been forcefully made by Lucy Dawidowicz, op. cit., p. 201.
77 *Mein Kampf*, p. 326.
78 See Robert Cecil, *The Myth of the Master Race. Alfred Rosenberg and Nazi Ideology* (London, 1972).
79 Alfred Rosenberg, *Die Spur des Juden* (Munich, 1920), pp. 151–8.
80 See Walter Laqueur, *Russia and Germany. A Century of Conflict* (London, 1965).
81 *Völkischer Beobachter*, 15/16 April 1923, p. 1.
82 'Der Klassenkampf ein Börsenbetrug', ibid, 4 March 1922, p. 3.
83 Boepple, op. cit., pp. 14–15.
84 Ibid, p. 71.
85 R. H. Phelps, 'Hitler als Parteiredner', *Vierteljahreshefte für Zeitgeschichte*, 11 (1963), p. 308; speech of 27 July 1920.
86 *Völkischer Beobachter*, 26 April 1922.
87 See Geoffrey Stokes, 'The Evolution of Hitler's Ideas on Foreign Policy, 1919–1925', in Peter D. Stachura, *The Shaping of the Nazi State* (London and New York, 1978), pp. 22–48.
88 *Mein Kampf*, p. 660.
89 Ibid, p. 661.
90 Ibid.
91 *Speeches*, I, p. 697; Hitler's closing speech at the 1937 Nuremberg Party rally.
92 *Zweites Buch*, p. 222.
93 Ibid, pp. 222–3.
94 See 'Parteipolitik und Judenfrage', 8 December 1920, Jäckel/Kuhn, op. cit., p. 274.
95 *Hitlers Zweites Buch*, p. 158.
96 Ibid.
97 Edward Calic (ed.), *Secret Conversations with Hitler* (New York, 1971), p. 58.
98 *Mein Kampf*, p. 654.
99 *Zweites Buch*, p. 159.
100 Ibid, pp. 128–9.
101 *Mein Kampf*, p. 662.
102 Domarus, op. cit., Vol. I, p. 729.
103 *Frankfurter Zeitung*, 14/15 September 1937.
104 *Speeches*, II, p. 1396.
105 Ibid, p. 1380.
106 Ibid, p. 1396.
107 Ibid, p. 1601.
108 'Memorandum by Adolf Hitler on the Tasks of a Four-Year-Plan' (Obersalzberg, August 1936), *DGFP*, Series C, Vol. 5, No. 490, pp. 853–62. The document was handed personally to Albert Speer in 1944 and found in his files after the war.
109 Ibid, p. 855.
110 Ibid.
111 See Meir Michaelis, 'The Third Reich and Russian "National Socialism"; 1933. A Documentary Note,' *Soviet Jewish Affairs* (1975), Vol. 5, No. 1, pp. 88–95. Also

his 'Rosenberg's Foreign Policy and "Jewish Influence" in the Soviet Union, 1940: A Documentary Note.' (1974), ibid Vol. 4, No. 1, pp. 66–72.
112 Hitler-Chvalkovsky, 21 January 1939, in *Documents on German Foreign Policy 1918–1954*, Series D, pp. 190–5 (Washington, 1949–64).

## 3 A NEW ORDER

1 *Speeches*, II, p. 1329.
2 Ibid, pp. 1218ff; Reichstag speech, 21 May 1935.
3 *Mein Kampf*, p. 654.
4 MacGregor Knox, 'Conquest, Foreign and Domestic, in Fascist Italy and Nazi Germany', *The Journal of Modern History*, Vol. 56, No. 1 (March 1984), pp. 1–57.
5 *Table Talk*, pp. 24–5 (8–11 August 1941).
6 Ibid, p. 69 (17 October 1941).
7 See John J. Stephan, *The Russian Fascists. Tragedy and Farce in Exile, 1925–1945* (New York, 1978).
8 Axel Kuhn, 'Das nationalsozialistische Deutschland und die Sowjetunion', in Manfred Funke (ed.), *Hitler, Deutschland und die Mächte* (Düsseldorf, 1977), pp. 639–53.
9 *Table Talk*, pp. 24–5 (8–11 August 1941); 'What India was for England, the territories of Russia will be for us.'
10 Ibid, p. 562 (5 July 1942).
11 See Milan Hauner, 'Did Hitler Want a World Dominion?', *Journal of Contemporary History*, Vol. 13 (1978), pp. 15–32.
12 Andreas Hillgruber, 'England's Place in Hitler's plan for world dominion', *Journal of Contemporary History*, Vol. 9, No. 1 (January 1974), pp. 5–22.
13 Josef Henke 'Hitlers England-Konzeption . . .', in Funke, op. cit., p. 592.
14 *Mein Kampf*, p. 720.
15 Ibid, pp. 622, 638.
16 *Zweites Buch*, pp. 167–73.
17 Domarus, op. cit., Vol. II, p. 1342.
18 *Table Talk*, p. 678 (31 August 1942).
19 Ibid, pp. 394–6.
20 Ibid, pp. 264–5 (31 January 1942).
21 Ibid, p. 202 (12–13 January 1942).
22 Ibid, p. 117 (5 November 1941).
23 'British Antisemitism was Hitler's Hope', *WLB* (1962), Vol. VXI, No. 1, p. 17, for extracts from the despatch of the German ambassador in London, von Dirksen, dated 19 July 1939, on the growth of antisemitism in Great Britain. Von Dirksen wrote, *inter alia*: 'It goes without saying that antisemitic circles adopt a more or less positive attitude towards the new Germany, and an increase of antisemitism goes hand in hand with a growing appreciation of our cause.'
24 Louis P. Lochner (ed.), *The Goebbels Diaries 1942–43* (New York, 1948), p. 377.
25 *Goebbels Diaries*, p. 334 (18 April 1943).
26 Ibid, p. 241 (13 December 1942).
27 Ibid, p. 251. See also ibid, p. 377 (13 May 1943): 'Because of their thoroughly materialistic attitude, the English act very much like Jews. In fact, they are the Aryans who have acquired most of the Jewish characteristics.'
28 See Shlomo Aronson, 'Hitler's Judenpolitik, die Alliierten und die Juden',

*Vierteljahreshefte für Zeitgeschichte*, 32 (January 1984), pp. 29–66 (esp. pp. 38–41) on Hitler's perception of the relationship between British policy and the Jews. Aronson suggests that massive Allied bombing of Germany was attributed by Hitler to a Jewish will to annihilate Germany and in turn reinforced his determination to wipe out all Jews in his grasp. This seems to me a plausible hypothesis, though the decision to carry out the 'Final Solution' had, in my opinion, nothing to do with the Anglo-American bombing.

29 H. R. Trevor-Roper (ed.), *The Testament of Adolf Hitler. The Hitler–Bormann Documents*, (London, 1961), 1–4 February 1945, pp. 30–5.

30 Ibid, pp. 32–3.

31 Ibid, p. 30.

32 Ibid, p. 35.

33 Ibid, p. 31.

34 *Zweites Buch*, p. 218.

35 Ernst Hanfstaengl, *Unheard Witness* (London, 1953), p. 42.

36 Gerhard L. Weinberg, 'Hitler's Image of the United States', *American Historical Review*, 69 (July 1964), pp. 1006–21.

37 Hitler-Mussolini, 25 August 1941, in: *DGFP*, Series D, XIII (Washington 1949–62), p. 383.

38 See remarks of Hitler to the Spanish ambassador Espinosa, on 12 August 1941, quoted in Saul Friedländer, *Prelude to Downfall, Hitler and the United States 1939–1941* (London, 1967), p. 266.

39 See Edwin Black, *The Transfer Agreement* (New York, 1984) for an interesting recent account that discusses the reactions of Nazi leaders in 1933 to the boycott of German goods inspired by American Jewry.

40 *DGFP*, Series D, IV, p. 335 (18 November 1938).

41 Saul Friedländer, *Prelude to Downfall. Hitler and the United States 1939–1941* (London, 1967), p. 266.

42 Hitler-Mussolini, 25 August 1941, *DGFP*, Series D, XIII, p. 383.

43 See Sandor A. Diamond, *The Nazi Movement in the United States* (Ithaca and London, 1974).

44 *Testament*, 19 February 1945, p. 77.

45 Ibid, p. 78.

46 Ibid, pp. 88–9 (24 February 1945).

47 Ibid, p. 89.

48 Ibid.

49 Ibid, p. 90.

50 Eberhard Jäckel, *Frankreich in Hitlers Europa* (Stuttgart, 1966).

51 *Mein Kampf*, p. 624.

52 Ibid.

53 Franz Kipping, 'Frankreich in Hitlers Aussenpolitik 1933–1939', in Funke, op. cit., pp. 612–27.

54 Alan Mitchell, 'Nazi Occupation Policies and the Response of Polish, Dutch, and French Elites', *WLB* (1979), Vol. XXXII, new series, Nos 49/50, pp. 34–40.

55 See Michael R. Marrus and Robert O. Paxton, *Vichy France and the Jews* (New York, 1981), p. 358: '. . . in Nazi eyes, to be allowed to join Germany among the *judenfrei* peoples was too good a fate for the defeated and racially inferior French'. This was especially true in the first phase of Nazi occupation when the Germans tried to use France as a dumping-ground for German-Jewish refugees.

56 Ciano minutes of 18 December 1942. Quoted in F. W. Deakin, *The Brutal*

*Friendship: Mussolini, Hitler, and the Fall of Italian Fascism* (London, 1962), p. 114.

57 Ibid, p. 118.

58 *Table Talk*, pp. 264–5 (31 January 1942).

59 *Testament*, p. 106 (2 April 1945).

60 Ibid, p. 107.

61 Ibid, p. 60 (14 February 1945).

62 Ibid, p. 61.

63 Ibid, pp. 70–1 (17 February 1945).

64 Ibid, p. 71.

65 Deakin, op. cit., p. 7.

66 *Speeches*, Vol. II, 361–4 (speech on the Maifeld, 28 September 1937).

67 Ibid.

68 Walter Werner Pese, 'Hitler und Italien 1920–1926', *Vierteljahrshefte für Zeitgeschichte*, III (1955), pp. 113ff.

69 Ibid, pp. 121ff.

70 *Zweites Buch*, pp. 191–209, 223.

71 *Mein Kampf*, p. 637.

72 A. Rosenberg, 'Deutschland und Italien', *Völkischer Beobachter*, 17–18 June 1923.

73 See 'Mussolini Kapituliert!', ibid, 7 July 1925.

74 R. Kühnl, *Die nationalsozialistische Linke* (Meisenheim, 1966), pp. 203–6.

75 See Meir Michaelis, *Mussolini and the Jews. German-Italian Relations and the Jewish Question in Italy 1922–1945* (Oxford University Press, 1978), p. 356. This is probably the definitive study of the subject.

76 Ibid, p. 69. See also E. R. von Starhemberg, *Between Hitler and Mussolini* (London, 1942), pp. 92–3.

77 M. A. Ledeen, 'The Evolution of Italian Fascist Antisemitism', *Jewish Social Studies*, XXXVII (January 1975), pp. 3–17.

78 Michaelis, op. cit., pp. 322ff.

79 *Goebbels Diaries*, p. 241.

80 Ibid, pp. 335–6.

81 A. J. Gregor, *The Ideology of Fascism* (London, 1969), pp. 266–7.

82 *Table Talk*, p. 33.

83 On the question of continuity in foreign policy, see Andreas Hillgruber, *Germany and the Two World Wars* (Cambridge, Mass., 1981), pp. 54–5.

84 Ernst Nolte, *Three Faces of Fascism* (1971), pp. 408ff.

85 *Mein Kampf*, pp. 136–7.

86 Eberhard Jäckel, *Hitler's Weltanschauung. A Blueprint for Power* (Middletown, Conn., 1972), p. 93.

87 *Zweites Buch*, p. 62.

88 Ibid, pp. 64–6.

89 Ibid, p. 64.

90 See Fred Weinstein, *The Dynamics of Nazism. Leadership, Ideology and the Holocaust* (London, 1980), pp. 139–40, for some interesting observations on the Nazi search for timelessness.

91 *Zweites Buch*, p. 220.

92 Ibid, pp. 220–1.

93 Andreas Hillgruber, 'Die "Endlösung" und das Deutsche Ostimperium als Kernstück des Rassenideologischen Programms des Nationalsozialismus', *Vierteljahrshefte für Zeitgeschichte*, 20 (1972), pp. 133–55.

## 4 NAZIS AND JEWS

1 *Mein Kampf*, p. 640.
2 Ibid.
3 *Speeches*, Vol. I, p. 60; speech in Munich on 20 April 1923.
4 Alan Bullock, *Hitler, A Study in Tyranny* (London, 1962), p. 407. Curiously enough, Bullock never really followed up his own insight.
5 *The Times*, 10 July 1933.
6 Kurt G. W. Ludecke, *I Knew Hitler* (London, 1938), p. 432.
7 *New York Times*, 10 July 1933.
8 *Völkischer Beobachter*, 28 November 1935. Also *Speeches*, Vol. I, pp. 733–4.
9 Ibid.
10 Hermann Rauschning, *The Voice of Destruction* (New York, 1940), p. 89.
11 Ibid, pp. 88–9.
12 Ibid, p. 89.
13 Jeremy Noakes and Geoffrey Pridham (eds), *Documents on Nazism 1919–1945* (London, 1974), p. 467.
14 'Hitler versus Mussolini', *WLB*, Vol. XVIII (October 1964), No. 4, p. 50.
15 Lucy S. Dawidowicz, *The War Against the Jews 1933–45* (Pelican Books, 1983), pp. 202ff., for a good overview.
16 Hjalmar Schacht, *Abrechnung mit Hitler* (Hamburg, 1949), pp. 59ff. Also his *76 Jahre meines Lebens* (1953), pp. 445ff.
17 See Helmut Genschel, *Die Verdrängung der Juden aus der Wirtschaft im Dritten Reich* (Göttingen, 1966), pp. 112–13.
18 *Dokumente der deutschen Politik und Geschichte*, Vol. 4 (Berlin, n.d.), pp. 147–8.
19 Ibid, pp. 148–9.
20 *Völkischer Beobachter*, 7 April 1933. See also *Speeches*, Vol. I, pp. 128–9.
21 *Speeches*, ibid.
22 See Fritz Seidler, *The Bloodless Pogrom* (London, 1934). Also *Speeches*, I, pp. 727–8.
23 Joseph Goebbels, *My Part in Germany's Fight* (London, 1935), pp. 236–7.
24 Ibid, pp. 237–8.
25 John L. Heinemann, *Hitler's First Foreign Minister: Constantin Freiherr von Neurath, Diplomat and Statesman* (Berkeley, 1979), p. 275.
26 See Edwin Black, *The Transfer Agreement* (New York, 1984) for a comprehensive account of the boycott movement in 1933.
27 George L. Mosse, *The Crisis of German Ideology: Intellectual Origins of the Third Reich* (New York, 1964) p. 249.
28 See Irving Fetscher, 'Zur Entstehung des politischen Antisemitismus in Deutschland', in H. Huss and A. Schroder (eds), *Antisemitismus. Zur Pathologie der bürgerlichen Gesellschaft* (Frankfurt-am-Main, 1965), p. 23.
29 Avraham Barkai, *Das Wirtschaftssystem des Nationalsozialismus. Der historische und ideologische Hintergrund 1933–1936* (Köln, 1977).
30 Karl Schleunes, *The Twisted Road to Auschwitz. Nazi Policy toward German Jews 1933–1939* (Urbana, Chicago and London, 1970), pp. 148–9.
31 *Documents on Nazism*, p. 232.
32 Ibid, p. 462.
33 Ibid.
34 See, for example, William S. Allen, *The Nazi Seizure of Power* (Chicago, 1965). Also Ian Kershaw, 'The Persecution of the Jews and German Popular Opinion in the Third Reich', *Leo Baeck Institute Yearbook* (LBIYB) (1981), pp. 261–91.
35 T. Abel, *Why Hitler came to Power?* (Prentice Hall, 1938), p. 164.

36  Schleunes, op. cit., p. 90.
37  Uwe Dietrich Adam, *Judenpolitik im Dritten Reich* (Düsseldorf, 1972), p. 96, deals extensively and often convincingly with the connection between *Kompetenzen-Anarchie* in the power-structure and legislation on the Jewish question, but in my view derives somewhat exaggerated conclusions from his research.
38  David Irving, *The War Path. Hitler's Germany 1933-9* (London, 1978), p. xv, claims that Hitler used antisemitism as a vote-catcher until 1933, and thereafter merely paid lip-service to it. This absurd statement, which flies in the face of all the known evidence, is designed to bolster Irving's sensational but even less founded suggestion (p. xvi) that Hitler did not *know* of the 'Final Solution'.
39  Randall T. Bywerk, 'Julius Streicher and the impact of Der Stürmer', in Robert S. Wistrich (ed.), *European Antisemitism 1890-1945* (special issue of *The Wiener Library Bulletin*, 1976, Vol. XXIX, new series, Nos 39/40, pp. 41-6).
40  Ibid, p. 42.
41  *Table Talk*, p. 154 (28-29 December 1941).
42  Domarus, op. cit., I, pp. 537-8.
43  See Uwe Adam, op. cit., pp. 330ff. Also Bernhard Losener, 'Als Rassereferat im Reichsministerium des Innern', *Vierteljahrshefte für Zeitgeschichte* (9 July 1961), pp. 264-313, on the different drafts which had to be prepared at short notice for the Party Congress. Half-Jews, quarter-Jews and Jews living in so-called 'privileged' mixed marriages were protected and exempted from many of the further legal restrictions imposed on full-blooded Jews.
44  Domarus, op. cit., I, p. 537. See also *Speeches*, I, pp. 732-4.
45  Domarus, ibid, p. 537.
46  Quoted in Abraham Margaliot, 'The Reaction of the Jewish Public in Germany to the Nuremberg Laws', *Essays in Holocaust History* (Hebrew University, Jerusalem, 1979), pp. 39-71 (p. 41).
47  *Centralverein (C.V.) Zeitung*, 5 December 1935.
48  Margaliot, op. cit., p. 50.
49  See *Der Angriff*, No. 299 (23 December 1935). Discussion in Margaliot, op. cit.
50  See the important articles by Carl J. Rheins, 'The Schwarzes Fähnlein, Jungenschaft 1932-1934', *LBIYB* (1978), pp. 173-97, and 'The Verband national deutscher Juden 1921-1933', *LBIYB* (1980), pp. 243-68.
51  Robert Wistrich, *Who's Who in Nazi Germany* (London, 1982), pp. 216-17.
52  O. D. Kulka, ' "Public Opinion" in Nazi Germany and The "Jewish Question" ', *Jerusalem Quarterly*, 25 (Autumn 1982), pp. 121-44.
53  *The Times*, 8 November 1935.
54  Helmut Krausnick/Martin Broszat, *Anatomy of the SS State* (Paladin, 1973), pp. 51ff.
55  Ibid, pp. 51-2.
56  'Denkschrift Hitler über die Aufgaben eines Vierjahresplans (1936)', *Vierteljahrshefte für Zeitgeschichte*, Jg. 3 (1955), pp. 204-5.
57  Schleunes, op. cit., p. 165.
58  Ibid, p. 247.
59  Lionel Kochan, *Pogrom: 10 November 1938* (London, 1957), p. 51.
60  Schleunes, op. cit., p. 258, goes too far, however, in stating that Hitler was virtually uninvolved in the actual making of Jewish policy between 1933 and 1938. What is true is that he avoided making any irrevocable decisions in this period and bided his time.
61  Genschel, op. cit., pp. 299-300. See *Reichsgesetzblatt*, Pt. 1, p. 1580, 'Decree

Relating to the Exclusion of Jews from German Economic Life, 12 November 1938'.

62  Dawidowicz, op. cit., pp. 138–40. Also *Documents on Nazism*, pp. 477ff.
63  Stenographic report of meeting on 'the Jewish Question' under Goering's chairmanship, 12 November 1938, in *IMT* (1816-PS).
64  Ibid.
65  *Speeches*, I, pp. 622–3.
66  Ibid.
67  Ian Kershaw, *Popular Opinion and Political Dissent in the Third Reich: Bavaria 1933–1945* (Oxford University Press, 1983), pp. 226, 240.
68  Ibid, p. 231.
69  Kochan, op. cit., p. 61.
70  See Kulka, op. cit., pp. 138–43, who stresses the property-consciousness of German public opinion. He also sees the need to counter the public mood of indifference as a factor in the regime's policy on the 'Jewish question', though the evidence for this assumption is somewhat scanty.
71  See Aronson, op. cit., pp. 44ff. Aronson makes the valid point that Hitler judged the world according to the degree to which it was subject to 'Jewish' influence or not. Similarly he acted as if the Jews really dictated the domestic and foreign policies of other nations. But Aronson's claim that the Nazis believed that everything might collapse in 1937 seems to me doubtful.
72  Domarus, op. cit., I, p. 889, for Hitler's speech on the hypocrisy of the Western democracies with regard to the 'Jewish question'.
73  *DGFP*, D-IV, op. cit., pp. 336–41.
74  Ibid.
75  Ibid, D-V, pp. 921–5 (memo of Schacht, 16 January 1939). Also p. 920 (report to Hitler, 2 January 1939). See also *Documents on British Foreign Policy*, Vol. III, pp. 675–7.
76  *Speeches*, I, pp. 740–1; Domarus, op. cit., II, p. 1058.

## 5 ANTISEMITISM AS A GLOBAL WEAPON

1  *Documents on Nazism*, p. 85.
2  *Hitler aus nächster Nahe. Aufzeichuungen eines Vertrauten 1929–1932* (hrsgb. Henry A. Turner, Jnr, Frankfurt-am-Main, 1978), pp. 153, 180, 290–2. These memoirs of Otto Wagener, SA chief and later head of the NSDAP economic office, were written in British internment after the war and have to be used with great caution. But they help fill a significant gap in our knowledge of Hitler's political thinking in the period between 1928 and 1932.
3  See Norman Cohn, *Warrant for Genocide* (Penguin, 1970), pp. 187–213.
4  Ibid, p. 178.
5  *Mein Kampf*, p. 337 (Munich, 1942, 11th ed.).
6  H. Rauschning, *Hitler Speaks* (London, 1939), pp. 235–6.
7  Ibid.
8  See Alexander Stein, *Adolf Hitler – Schüler der Weisen von Zion* (Karlsbad, 1936); Ruben Blank, *Adolf Hitler – ses aspirations, sa politique, sa propagande, et les Protocoles de Sion* (Paris, 1938); Hannah Arendt, *The Origins of Totalitarianism* (London, 1958), p. 366; and Walter Laqueur, *Russia and Germany* (London, 1965), pp. 9off.
9  The same point is forcefully made by Shlomo Aronson, op. cit. Though I partially

disagree with his heavy emphasis on Hitler as a *Realpolitiker* and with some points of detail in his interpretation, the general drift of his argument seems to me correct.

10 *Berliner Tageblatt*, 15 September 1937. *Speeches*, Vol. I, pp. 694–712.

11 *Speeches*, pp. 699–700.

12 Max Domarus (ed.), *Hitler: Reden und Proklamationen, 1932–1945* (Würzburg, 1962), Vol. I, p. 638 (at the 8th rally of the NSDAP in Nuremberg, 8–14 September 1936).

13 J. Goebbels, 'Der Bolshevismus muss vernichtet werden, wenn Europa wieder gesunden soll!' *Völkischer Beobachter*, 11 September 1936. Also M. Michaelis, op. cit., pp. 108ff., on the Italo-German dimension.

14 Michaelis, op. cit., pp. 109–91.

15 Bela Vago, *The Shadow of the Swastika. The Rise of Fascism and Anti-Semitism in the Danube Basin, 1936–39* (London, 1975), pp. 55–65. Also Emanuel Turczynski, 'The Background of Romanian Fascism', in Peter F. Sugar (ed.), *Native Fascism in the Successor States, 1918–1945* (Santa Barbara, 1971), pp. 101–12.

16 Vago, op. cit., pp. 128–9.

17 György Ránki, 'The Problems of Fascism in Hungary' in Sugar, op. cit., pp. 65ff.

18 For the Polish situation, see Henryk Wereszycki, 'Fascism in Poland', in Sugar, op. cit., pp. 85–91; Celia Heller, *On the Edge of Destruction. Polish Jews between the Two World Wars* (New York, 1976). Also Antony Polonsky and Michael Riff, 'Poles, Czechoslovaks and the "Jewish Question", 1914–1921: A Comparative Study', in Volker R. Berghahn and Martin Kitchen (eds), *Germany in the Age of Total War* (London, 1979), pp. 63–101, on the immediate post-war period.

19 C. A. Macartney, 'Hungarian Foreign Policy during the Inter-War Period, With Special Reference to the Jewish Question', in B. Vago and G. L. Mosse (eds), *Jews and Non-Jews in Eastern Europe* (New York and Jerusalem, 1974), pp. 125–36.

20 Ránki, op. cit., pp. 70–1.

21 Randolph L. Braham, 'The Rightists, Horthy, and the Germans: Factors Underlying the Destruction of Hungarian Jewry', in Vago and Mosse, op. cit., p. 143. See also Miklós Kállay, *Hungarian Premier: A Personal Account of a Nation's Struggle in the Second World War* (New York, 1954), pp. 429–31.

22 Stephen Fischer-Galati: 'Fascism in Romania' in Sugar, op. cit., pp. 112–21. See also the classic account by Eugen Weber, 'Romania', in Hans Rogger and Eugen Weber (eds), *The European Right* (Berkeley, 1966), pp. 501–74, on the Iron Guard and Rumanian fascism in general.

23 On the German dimension, Andreas Hillgruber, *Hitler, Konig Carol and Marshall Antonescu: die deutsch-rumänischen Beziehungen, 1938–1944* (Wiesbaden, 1954), and Hannah Arendt, *Eichmann in Jerusalem* (London, 1963), p. 173.

24 Stephen Fischer-Galati, 'Fascism, Communism, and the Jewish Question in Romania' in: Vago and Mosse, op. cit., pp. 170–1.

25 Th. Lavi, 'The Background to the Rescue of Rumanian Jewry during the Period of the Holocaust', in Vago and Mosse, op. cit., pp. 183–6.

26 Piotr S. Wandycz, 'Fascism in Poland: 1918–1939' in Sugar, op. cit., pp. 92–7.

27 See Lucy S. Dawidowicz, 'The tide of antisemitism', *The Times Literary Supplement*, 22 July 1977.

28 Edward D. Wynot Jnr, ' "A Necessary Cruelty": the Emergence of Official Anti-Semitism in Poland, 1936–39', *American Historical Review*, No. 4 (October 1971), p. 1048. See also the excellent study by Ezra Mendelsohn, *The Jews of East Central Europe Between the Two World Wars* (Indiana University Press, 1983), for concrete

# NOTES

examples of discrimination.

29  See 'Poland and the Jews: An Exchange', *The New York Review of Books*, 18 August, 1983, pp. 51–2.

30  Mordekhai Tennenbaum-Tamaroff, *Pages from the Fires* (Kibbutz Hameuhad, 1947), in Hebrew, pp. 49–50. For examples see Emmanuel Ringelblum, *Polish-Jewish Relations during the Second World War* (Jerusalem, 1974), pp. 42ff.

31  Ringelblum, pp. 50–1.

32  Ibid, p. 198.

33  Ibid, p. 197.

34  Ibid, p. 307.

35  Ibid, p. 280.

36  Ibid, p. 22.

37  S. Ettinger, 'Jews and Non-Jews in Eastern and Central Europe Between the Wars: An Outline', in Vago and Mosse, op. cit., pp. 12–14.

38  *DGFP*, Ser. D, Vol. V, Document No. 664. Schumburg (Referat Deutschland), Circular to all diplomatic representations 25th January 1939, pp. 931–2. See also E. Ben Elissar, *La Diplomatie du III<sup>e</sup> Reich et les Juifs, 1933–1939* (Paris, 1939), pp. 400ff. Also Sidney H. Kessler, 'Fascism under the Cross: The case of Father Coughlin', *WLB* (1980), Vol. XXXIII, New Series, Nos 51/52, pp. 8–12. Coughlin even defended the *Kristallnacht* pogrom and regarded Nazism as a justified 'defence mechanism against Communism'. After 1935 the American Catholic priest's attacks on Jews were often compared by journalists with those of Hitler.

39  See Michael R. Marrus, 'Vichy before Vichy: antisemitic currents in France during the 1930s', *WLB* (1980), pp. 13–19, for an interesting case-study of the impact of the Jewish refugee problem on French antisemitism.

40  Schumberg circular, op. cit.

41  Ibid.

42  Ibid.

43  Ibid.

44  Ibid.

45  Ibid.

46  Ibid.

47  See Herbert A. Strauss, 'Jewish Emigration from Germany – Nazi Policies and Jewish Responses' (1), in *Leo Baeck Institute Yearbook* (1980), pp. 313–62.

48  *Speeches*, I, p. 738 (full text in *Völkischer Beobachter*, 1 February 1939).

49  *Speeches*, I, p. 740.

50  Ibid.

51  Strauss, op. cit., p. 315.

52  *Speeches*, Vol. I, p. 741.

53  *Zweites Buch*, where this is seen as an essential part of the Jewish strategy of survival in the world of nations.

54  *Völkischer Beobachter*, 26 February 1939.

55  Ibid, 3 April 1939.

56  See G. Warburg, *Six Years of Hitler. The Jews under the Nazi Regime* (London, 1939), pp. 269–70.

57  'The Jewish Question as a Factor in German foreign policy. . . .' *DGFP*, D, Vol. V, Doc. 664.

58  *DGFP*, D-V, p. 157.

59  *Völkischer Beobachter*, 8 February 1939.

271

60 *DGFP*, Series D, Vol. IV, Doc. 158.
61 Ibid.
62 *Le Livre Jaune Francais. Documents Diplomatiques* (Paris, 1939), pp. 51–2 (Victor de Lacroix à Bounet, 7 February 1939).
63 Ibid, p. 52.
64 *DGFP*, D–IV, op. cit., pp. 336–341; see also Hitler-Csáky, *DGFP*, D–V, p. 366.
65 E. Ben Elissar, op. cit., p. 403.
66 Rademacher, 3 July 1940, in *Trials of War Criminals before the Nuremberg Military Tribunals* (Washington, 1951–2), pp. 154–6 (Doc. No. NG-2586) *DGFP*, Series D, X (London, 1957) No. 101.
67 Ibid.
68 See Gerald Reitlinger, *The Final Solution* (London, 1968), 2nd revised edn, pp. 79–82. Also Philip Friedman, *Roads to Extinction. Essays on the Holocaust* (New York, 1980), pp. 44–52.
69 Leni Yahil, 'Madagascar – Phantom of a Solution for the Jewish Question' in Vago and Mosse, op. cit., pp. 315–40. Also Klaus Hildebrand, *Vom Reich zum Weltreich. Hitler, NSDAP und Koloniale Frage 1919–1945* (Munich, 1969), pp. 590–1, 649, 651–2.
70 Interestingly enough, Hitler as late as 20 November 1940 had told the Hungarian Minister President, Count Teleki, in Vienna that all states who wished to do so could in a future peace treaty participate in the solution of the Jewish question, 'by forcing France to make some of her possessions available'. Hitler still planned at this date to move all Jews out of Europe after the *end* of the war – a consummation which he apparently believed was already imminent. *DGFP*, D, Vol. XI (London, 1961), Doc. 365, p. 635.
71 Reitlinger, op. cit., pp. 81–2; Leni Yahil, op. cit., p. 328; Hildebrand, op. cit., pp. 718–20.

# 6 HITLER AND THE 'FINAL SOLUTION'

1 Franz Halder, *Kriegstagebuch 1939–1942* (Stuttgart, 1962–4), Vol. I, p. 38.
2 *Zweites Buch*, pp. 153–9.
3 Edouard Calic (ed.), *Secret Conversations with Hitler* (New York, 1971).
4 J. Goebbels, 'Nationalsozialismus und Bolschevismus', *Völkischer Beobachter*, 14 November 1925.
5 Hermann Rauschning, *The Voice of Destruction* (New York, 1940), p. 131.
6 Ibid.
7 Ibid, p. 130.
8 Ibid.
9 Ibid, p. 133.
10 See Meir Michaelis, 'The Third Reich and Russian "National Socialism", 1933', *Soviet Jewish Affairs* (1975), Vol. 5, No. 1, p. 92.
11 Ibid (1974), Vol. 4, No. 1, p. 68.
12 *DGFP*, Series D, Vol. VIII (London, 1954), pp. 604–9. On 21 June 1941 Hitler conceded to Mussolini that the pact with Stalin had indeed been 'a break with my whole origin, my concepts and my former obligations'. *DGFP*, Vol. XII, Doc. 660, p. 1069.
13 Ibid, p. 608. See also Michaelis, op. cit., pp. 279–83, for comment.
14 *DGFP*, Series D, Vol. VIII, pp. 871–80.

15 Ibid, p. 876.
16 Ibid.
17 Ibid, Vol. VIII, pp. 882–93.
18 Ibid, pp. 886–7.
19 Ibid.
20 Ibid, p. 887.
21 Ibid, p. 893.
22 *DGFP*, Series D. Vol. IX (London, 1956), pp. 1–16.
23 Ibid, pp. 8–9.
24 Ibid, p. 7.
25 *Documents of British Foreign Policy*, Third Series, Vol. 7, pp. 258–9.
26 OKW record of Hitler's remarks printed as Doc. No. 134–C *Trial of the Major War Criminals*, Vol. XXXIV, pp. 462–71. See also English translation in *Nazi Conspiracy and Aggression* (Washington, 1946), Vol. VI, pp. 939–46. Also abbreviated version in *DGFP*, Series D, Vol. XI (London, 1961), pp. 1145–51.
27 See Bernd Stegemann, 'Hitlers Ziele im ersten Kriegsjahr 1939/1940', in *Militärgeschichtliche Mitteilungen* (1980), 1, pp. 92–103 (especially, pp. 95ff).
28 *Table Talk*, p. 65.
29 *Testament*, pp. 99–100.
30 See Franz Halder, *Hitler as Warlord* (London, 1950).
31 *DGFP*, D, Vol. XI, pp. 533–70 for the minutes of Molotov's conversations in Berlin.
32 Alan Bullock, *Hitler, A Study in Tyranny* (London, 1962), pp. 620–2.
33 Ibid, pp. 651–2.
34 Ibid, pp. 633–4.
35 General Halder's account in *Nazi Conspiracy and Aggression* (Washington, 1946–8), Vol. VIII, pp. 645–6.
36 Quoted in Dawidowicz, op. cit., p. 159.
37 F. Halder, *Kriegstagebuch 1939–1942* (Stuttgart, 1962–4), Vol. 2, pp. 336–7. For an English translation of relevant passages, see Dawidowicz, op. cit., p. 161.
38 Dawidowicz, op. cit., pp. 162–3.
39 On Heydrich, see Robert Wistrich, *Who's Who in Nazi Germany* (London, 1982), pp. 134–7. On the deportations between 1939 and 1941, see Reitlinger, op. cit., pp. 34–59.
40 Reitlinger, op. cit., p. 37; Friedman, *Roads to Extinction* (New York, 1980), pp. 60–3.
41 Dawidowicz, op. cit., pp. 156–7, argues against this hypothesis. On the Lublin plan, Friedman, op. cit., pp. 34–43.
42 Dawidowicz, op. cit., p. 157. See also A. Hillgruber, 'Die "Endlösung" und das Deutsche Ostimperium als Kernstuck des Rassenideologischen Programms des Nationalsozialismus', *Vierteljahrshefte für Zeitgeschichte*, 20 (1972), pp. 133–55.
43 Quoted in Reitlinger, op. cit., p. 85.
44 Ibid.
45 This is contested *inter alia* by Martin Broszat, 'Hitler und die Genesis der "Endlösung". Aus Anlass der Thesen von David Irving, *Vierteljahrshefte für Zeitgeschichte*, Heft 4 (1977), pp. 739–75. See, however, the elegant refutation in the same journal (January 1981) by Christopher Browning. A revised version in English, 'A Reply to Martin Broszat regarding the origins of the Final Solution', is in *Simon Wiesenthal Center Annual*, Vol. I (New York, 1984), pp. 113–32.
46 Browning, op. cit., p. 117.

47 Rudolf Höss, *Commandant of Auschwitz* (New York, 1959), pp. 135–8, 173–6. Also *Documents on Nazism*, p. 490.
48 'Eichmann Tells His Own Damning Story', *Life Magazine* (28 November 1960).
49 *Eichmann Interrogated. Transcripts from the Archives of the Israeli Police.* Ed. Jochen von Lang in collaboration with Claus Sibyll (New York and London, 1983), p. 75.
50 Ibid, p. 81.
51 Ibid, p. 93.
52 See Browning, op. cit., whose arguments seem to me persuasive in this respect.
53 Ibid, pp. 120–1.
54 Quoted in Dawidowicz, op. cit., p. 163.
55 Ibid, pp. 163–4.
56 Dawidowicz, op. cit., p. 164.
57 Ibid, p. 163.
58 Robert Wistrich, *Who's Who in Nazi Germany* (London, 1982), p. 204.
59 Helmut Krausnick and Martin Broszat, *Anatomy of the SS State* (London, 1973), p. 82.
60 *IMT*, Vol. XXXVIII, pp. 87, 92.
61 Helmut Krausnick and Hans-Heinrich Wilhelm, *Die Truppe des Weltanschauungskrieges* (Stuttgart, 1981).
62 On the parallels between treatment of Soviet POWs and the murder of Jews, see Christian Streit, *Keine Kameraden. Die Wehrmacht und die Sowjetischen Kriegsgefangenen 1941–1945* (Stuttgart, 1978).
63 Raul Hilberg, *The Destruction of the European Jews* (Chicago, 1961) remains the most detailed single account of the machinery of destruction itself. On the role of the bureaucracy in anti-Jewish legislation, see Uwe Dietrich Adam, *Judenpolitik im Dritten Reich* (Düsseldorf, 1972). Also the fine study by Christopher R. Browning, *The Final Solution and The German Foreign Office* (New York, 1978).
64 On the indifference of the German public to the mass murders as reflected in SD reports, see O. D. Kulka, 'Public Opinion in Nazi Germany: the Final Solution', *The Jerusalem Quarterly*, No. 26 (Winter 1983), pp. 34–45.
65 Raul Hilberg, 'German Railroads, Jewish Souls', *Transaction, Social Science and Modern Society* (1976), pp. 60–74.
66 Raul Hilberg, *The Destruction of the European Jews* (Chicago, 1961), p. 640.
67 See Henry Friedlander and Sybil Milton (eds), *The Holocaust: Ideology, Bureaucracy and Genocide* (New York, 1980).
68 Christopher R. Browning, 'The German Bureaucracy and the Holocaust', in Alex Grobman and Daniel Landes (eds), *Genocide. Critical Issues of the Holocaust* (Los Angeles, 1983), pp. 145–8. Also Henry Friedlander, 'The Perpetrators', in ibid, p. 155.
69 Hans Mommsen, 'Die Realisierung des Utopischen: Die "Endlösung der Judenfrage" in "Dritten Reich" ', *Geschichte und Gesellschaft* (Jg. 1983), Heft 3, pp. 381–420, makes this point forcefully but in my view seriously overstates the case when he writes of 'den metaphorisch-propagandistischen Charakter der einschlägigen Hitlerschen Äusserungen'. Extermination (*Ausrottung*) was much more than just a metaphor to Hitler.
70 Martin Broszat, 'Soziale Motivation und Führer-Bindung des Nationalsozialismus', *Vierteljahrshefte für Zeitgeschichte*, 18 (1970), pp. 399–400ff.
71 This is reluctantly conceded by Uwe Adam, op. cit., p. 196. Schleunes, op. cit., p. 131, on the other hand, argued that even when Hitler interfered at crucial moments in Jewish policy, his interventions were usually vacillating and

indecisive. The evidence for this claim, which is accepted by Mommsen, op. cit., pp. 39ff., seems to me unconvincing.

72 Helmut Krausnick, 'The Persecution of the Jews', in Krausnick and Broszat, op. cit., p. 85.

73 Ibid, p. 86 (Himmler files, Institut für Zeitgeschichte, Munich).

74 Ibid.

75 Gerald Fleming, *Hitler und die Endlösung* (Munich, 1982), p. 64.

76 Ibid, pp. 76–7.

77 See H. Trevor-Roper, 'The will to exterminate', *The Times Literary Supplement*, 28 January 1983 (a review of Fleming's book which neatly summarizes the salient points concerning Hitler's personal involvement in the 'Final Solution').

78 Fleming, op. cit., pp. 163–4.

79 Joachim Fest, *Hitler* (London, 1973), pp. 650–1, Hilberg, *The Destruction of the European Jews*, op. cit., pp. 454–6.

80 *Table Talk*, p. 235.

81 See Streit, op. cit., for their fate.

82 *Table Talk*, pp. 235–6.

83 Ibid, p. 260.

84 Quoted in George H. Stein, *Hitler* (Englewood Cliffs, 1968), p. 73.

85 O. D. Kulka, 'Public Opinion in Nazi Germany: The Final Solution', *The Jerusalem Quarterly*, No. 26 (Winter 1983), p. 36.

86 See Reitlinger, op. cit., pp. 98–104 (Nuremberg Document PS 709 for stenographic protocol). Also Hilberg, op. cit., and Helmut Krausnick, 'The Persecution of the Jews', in Krausnick and Broszat, op. cit., pp. 99ff.

87 Walther Hofer (ed.), *Der Nationalsozialismus. Dokumente 1933–1945* (Frankfurt-am-Main, 1957), pp. 303–5.

88 Ibid, p. 304.

89 Ibid.

90 Ibid, pp. 304–5.

91 Hilberg, op. cit., p. 374.

92 Quoted in Krausnick, op. cit., p. 111.

93 Nuremberg Document 365-NO (*Trial of the Major War Criminals before the International Military Tribunal*, 42 vols, Nuremberg, 1947–9).

94 Ibid. Also Krausnick, op. cit., pp. 114–15.

95 H. G. Adler, *Theresienstadt 1941–1945* (Tübingen, 1960), pp. 720–2.

96 Christopher R. Browning, 'A Reply to Martin Broszat', op. cit., pp. 122ff., details the sequence and argues convincingly that it proves that a plan for systematic extermination did exist.

97 Ino Arndt and Wolfgang Scheffler, 'Organisierter Massenmord an Juden in nationalsozialistischen Vernichtungslagern', *Vierteljahrshefte für Zeitgeschichte*, 24, No. 2 (1976), pp. 122–35.

98 Krausnick, op. cit., p. 115; Michael Tregenza, 'Belzec Death Camp', *WLB* (1977), Vol. XXX, New Series, Nos 41/42, pp. 8–24.

99 *IMT*, Vol. XXXIII, p. 435; Krausnick, op. cit., p. 88.

100 Krausnick, op. cit., p. 120.

101 *Goebbels Diaries*, p. 86.

102 Ibid, p. 114.

103 Ibid, p. 138.

104 Ibid, p. 148.

105 Ibid.

106 Ibid, p. 344. On 1 May 1943 Goebbels wrote of 'exceedingly serious fights' in the
    Warsaw ghetto. It showed 'what is to be expected of the Jews when they are in
    possession of arms' (p. 351).
107 Ibid, p. 359.
108 Ibid.
109 Ibid, p. 366.
110 Ibid, p. 377.
111 Ibid (13 May 1943).
112 Ibid, pp. 357ff.
113 Ibid, p. 357.
114 Minutes of the interpreter, Dr Paul Otto Schmidt, 17 April 1943, *IMT* Blaue
    Serie, Bd. X, pp. 463ff. See also the comments of Gerald Reitlinger, *The Final
    Solution* (2nd ed., London, 1968), pp. 451–3.
115 *IMT*, ibid.
116 Mario D. Fenyo, *Hitler, Horthy and Hungary. German-Hungarian Relations* (New
    Haven and London, 1972), p. 129.
117 Ibid, p. 201.
118 Aufzeichnung über die Unterredung zwischen dem Führer und Marschall
    Antonescu in Schloss Klessheim am 13. April 1943, *IMT*, Bd. XXXV,
    Nürnberg-Dok. 9–736, pp. 426ff.
119 See George L. Mosse, *Nazism* (New Brunswick, 1978), p. 119, to whom I owe
    this insight.
120 *Table Talk* (1953 ed.), p. 332.
121 See the postscript by Nathan Rotenstreich in Yehuda Bauer and Nathan
    Rotenstreich (eds), *The Holocaust as Historical Experience* (New York, 1981),
    pp. 278–9.
122 Yoash Meisler, 'Himmler's Doctrine of the SS Leadership', *Jahrbuch des Instituts
    für deutsche Geschichte* (Tel Aviv, 1979), Vol. VIII, pp. 389–432.
123 For Himmler's original plan which did not yet envisage mass extermination, see
    'Einige Gedanken über die Behandlung der Fremdvölkischen im Osten (Mai
    1940)', *Vierteljahrshefte für Zeitgeschichte*, Vol. V (1957), pp. 192–8.
124 Meisler, op. cit., pp. 428–32. The SS man is neatly defined here as 'a pure ethos
    existing in a pure ethical vacuum'.
125 Josef Ackermann, *Heinrich Himmler als Ideologe* (Göttingen, 1970), p. 158.
126 *Documents on Nazism*, pp. 492–3.
127 *Nuremberg Document* PS 1918.
128 Ibid.
129 Ibid.
130 Ackermann, op. cit., p. 163. Also *Documents on Nazism*, p. 493.
131 Nuremberg Document No. 5574, quoted in Krausnick, op. cit., p. 122.
132 Ibid, p. 138.
133 Ibid, p. 139.
134 Jacques Delarue, *The History of the Gestapo* (London, 1964), pp. 368–70; Gerald
    Reitlinger, *The Final Solution* (London, 1968), 2nd rev. edn, pp. 466ff. Also
    Yehuda Bauer, *The Holocaust – Some Historical Aspects* (in Hebrew) (Tel Aviv,
    1982), pp. 196–208, on the negotiations between Sally Mayer and the SS in
    1944/5.
135 Uwe Adam, op. cit., pp. 331f.
136 Ibid, p. 315f.
137 Bormann to Lammers, 2 November 1944, in Adam, op. cit., p. 332.

138 Ibid, pp. 320ff.
139 See E. Goldhagen, 'Weltanschauung und Erlösung', *Vierteljahrshefte für Zeitgeschichte* (1976), p. 124.
140 Bullock, op. cit., p. 40.
141 Ibid, p. 407.
142 Lucy S. Dawidowicz, *The War against the Jews 1933–45* (Pelican Books, 1983), p. xxii.
143 *Le Testament Politique de Hitler* (Paris, 1959), p. 79.
144 Ibid, p. 89.
145 *Nazi Conspiracy and Aggression*, Vol. VI, op. cit., pp. 260–3.
146 Ibid.
147 Ibid.
148 Ibid.
149 Ibid.

## 7 THE NEMESIS OF CHRISTIANITY

1 Franklin H. Littell, 'Christian Antisemitism and the Holocaust', in *Judaism and Christianity under the Impact of National-Socialism (1919–1945)*, International Symposium (The Historical Society of Israel, June 1982), p. 462.
2 Ibid.
3 Ibid, p. 471.
4 Emil L. Fackenheim, *The Jewish Return into History. Reflections in the Age of Auschwitz and a New Jerusalem* (New York, 1978), p. 76.
5 Ibid, p. 221. See also Rosemary R. Ruether, *Faith and Fratricide: The Theological Roots of Anti-Semitism* (New York, 1974).
6 J. S. Conway, *The Nazi Persecution of the Churches under Hitler* (London, 1968); E. Helmreich, *The German Churches under Hitler* (Detroit 1979).
7 *Mein Kampf*, p. 65.
8 *Table Talk* pp. 314–15 (17 February 1942).
9 See Uriel Tal, *Christians and Jews in Germany. Religion, Politics and Ideology in the Second Reich 1870–1914* (New York, 1975), especially the final chapter.
10 Uriel Tal, 'Aspects of Consecration of Politics in the Nazi era', in *Judaism and Christianity*, op. cit., p. 50.
11 Ibid, p. 58. See also J. P. Stern, *Hitler: The Führer and the People* (Fontana, 1975), pp. 85–91.
12 See Jules Isaac, *Genèse de l'antisémitisme* (Paris, 1956) and Joshua Trachtenberg, *The Devil and the Jews* (New Haven, 1943).
13 Richard Grunberger, *A Social History of the Third Reich* (London, 1977, Penguin Books), pp. 560–3.
14 Speech in Munich, 17 December 1922, in Jäckel/Kuhn, op. cit., p. 770: 'Schon von 1900 Jahren war die Welt von den Juden und dem jüdischen Geiste genau wie heute durchseucht, und als Christus sich gegen den Krämergeist, aufbäumte, schlugen sie ihn ans Kreuz.'
15 *Speeches*, I, p. 20.
16 Speech of 12 April 1922 in Jäckel/Kuhn, op. cit., p. 623.
17 *Mein Kampf*, p. 336.
18 Jäckel/Kuhn, op. cit., pp. 718, 867 (2 November 1922, 6 April, 1923).
19 Ibid, pp. 769, 877 (17 December 1922, 10 April 1923).

20 G. Pridham, *Hitler's Rise to Power: The Nazi Movement in Bavaria 1923–33* (London, 1973).
21 *Speeches*, Vol. I, p. 20 (12 August 1922).
22 Kurt G. W. Ludecke, *I Knew Hitler* (London, 1938), pp. 465–6.
23 *Table Talk*, p. 76.
24 Ibid, p. 143.
25 Ibid, p. 721 (29–30 November 1944).
26 See Friedrich Heer, *Gottes erste Liebe* (Munich, 1968), p. 388. Also *Der Glaube des Adolf Hitler*, op. cit. Heer among the few writers to have fully grasped the importance of Hitler's Austrian background, while perhaps overstating the Catholic influences.
27 Grunberger, op. cit., p. 101.
28 *Mein Kampf*, pp. 108–9.
29 Ibid, p. 114.
30 Ibid, p. 115.
31 Ibid.
32 Ernst Nolte, *Three Faces of Fascism* (New York, 1966), p. 333.
33 H. Rauschning, *The Voice of Destruction* (New York, 1940), p. 54.
34 Ibid, p. 52.
35 Ibid, p. 53.
36 *Mein Kampf*, p. 561.
37 Ibid, p. 562.
38 Ibid, p. 564.
39 Ibid, p. 565.
40 Ibid, p. 306.
41 Ibid.
42 Ibid, p. 307.
43 Ibid.
44 The best study of Eckart, to date, is by Margarete Plewnia, *Auf dem Weg zu Hitler. Der 'völkische' Publizist Dietrich Eckart* (Bremen, 1970).
45 *Auf Gut Deutsch*, 1 (1919), p. 18.
46 See *Mein Kampf*, p. 687, for a tribute to Eckart. Also E. Calic (ed.), *Conversations with Hitler* (New York, 1971), p. 51.
47 See D. Eckart, 'Das Judentum in und ausser uns', *Auf Gut Deutsch* (Jan.-April 1919). Translation in Barbara Miller Lane and Leila J. Rupp, *Nazi Ideology before 1933. A Documentation* (Manchester University Press, 1978), pp. 18–26.
48 Ibid, p. 22.
49 *Auf Gut Deutsch*, 2 (1919), p. 554.
50 Plewnia, op. cit., p. 53.
51 See E. Nolte, 'Eine Frühe Quelle zu Hitlers Antisemitismus', *Historische Zeitschrift*, Vol. 92 (1961), pp. 584–606. Nolte was the first to see the importance of this source, but in my opinion overstated its importance for Hitler's development. For a more balanced view see Margarete Plewnia, op. cit., pp. 101–11, and the earlier critique by Shaul Esh, 'Eine neue literarische Quelle Hitlers? Eine methodologische Überlegung', *Geschichte in Wissenschaft und Unterricht*, 15 (1964), No. 8, pp. 487–93.
52 *Der Bolschevismus von Moses bis Lenin. Zwiegespräch zwischen Adolf Hitler und mir* (Bolshevism from Moses to Lenin – A Dialogue between Adolf Hitler and Me), by Dietrich Eckart (Munich, 1924) pp. 6–7.
53 Ibid, p. 28.

54 Ibid, pp. 35–6.
55 Ibid, p. 36.
56 Ibid, p. 39.
57 On Luther's antisemitism, see the important study by Heiko A. Oberman, *Wurzeln des Antisemitismus. Christenangst und Judenplage im Zeitalter von Humanismus und Reformation* (Berlin, 1981). Also Richard Gutteridge, *Open thy Mouth for the Dumb. The German Evangelical Church and the Jews 1879–1950* (London, 1976), pp. 316–25. Gutteridge deals extensively with the subservience of the Lutheran Church to the Hitler regime and its lack of resistance to anti-Jewish policies.
58 *Der Bolschevismus von Moses*, op. cit., p. 46.
59 Conway, op. cit., p. 5.
60 Ian Kershaw, *Der Hitler-Mythos* (Stuttgart, 1980), p. 37.
61 Ibid, pp. 90–2.
62 See Franz von Papen, *Memoirs* (London, 1952), p. 261.
63 *Table Talk*, p. 422. For the contemptuous reactions of rival Nazi leaders like Goering and Goebbels to Rosenberg's *magnum opus*, see 'The Story of Rosenberg's Mythus', in *WLB* (1953), Vol. VII, Nos 5–6, pp. 33–4.
64 Rauschning, op. cit., p. 49.
65 Ibid.
66 Grunberger, op. cit., pp. 557–8.
67 Rauschning, op. cit., p. 51.
68 Ibid, p. 55.
69 See Uriel Tal, 'Nazism as a "Political Faith" ', *The Jerusalem Quarterly* (Spring 1980), No. 15, pp. 70–90.
70 Klaus Scholder, 'Judentum und Christentum in der Ideologie und Politik des Nationalsozialismus 1919–1945', in *Judaism and Christianity*, op. cit., pp. 190–1.
71 Ibid, p. 191.
72 Ibid, p. 193.
73 Ibid, pp. 196–7.
74 *Table Talk*, pp. 6–7.
75 Ibid, p. 7.
76 Ibid.
77 Ibid, p. 78.
78 Ibid, p. 79.
79 Ibid.
80 Ibid, p. 78.
81 Ibid.
82 Ibid, p. 77.
83 Ibid, p. 143.
84 Ibid, p. 314.
85 Ibid.
86 Ibid, pp. 314–15.
87 Ibid, p. 323.
88 Ibid, p. 322.
89 Ibid, p. 323.
90 Ibid, p. 142.
91 Ibid, p. 89.
92 Ibid, p. 288.
93 Ibid.
94 Ibid, p. 513.

95 Ibid, p. 206.
96 See Norman Cohn, *The Pursuit of the Millennium: Revolutionary Messianism in Medieval and Reformation Europe and its Bearing on Modern Totalitarian Movements* (New York, 1961), 2nd edn, p. 4.
97 James J. Rhodes, *The Hitler Movement. A Modern Millenarian Revolution* (Stanford, 1980).
98 *Table Talk*, pp. 142–3 (13 December 1941).
99 See Milton Himmelfarb, 'No Hitler. No Holocaust', *Commentary* (March 1984), pp. 37–43.
100 *Table Talk*, p. 722.
101 Ibid.

## 8 SWASTIKA, CRESCENT AND STAR OF DAVID

1 Robert S. Wistrich, 'Karl Lueger and the Ambiguities of Viennese anti-semitism', *Jewish Social Studies* (Summer–Autumn 1983), Vol XIV, Nos. 3–4, for an analysis of the social background.
2 See, for example, Frederick Busi, 'Anti-Semites on Zionism – The Case of Herzl and Drumont', *Midstream* (February 1979), pp. 18–27.
3 On the issue of 'collaboration' in its earlier nineteenth-century phase, see Jacob Katz, 'Zionism vs. antisemitism', *Commentary* (April 1979).
4 Robert Wistrich, 'Antisemitism and Jewish Nationalism', *Midstream* (November 1982), pp. 10–15.
5 Ibid, p. 11.
6 *Mein Kampf*, pp. 324–5.
7 Ibid, pp. 56–7.
8 Ibid, p. 57.
9 Ibid.
10 Alfred Rosenberg, *Der staatsfeindliche Zionismus* (Munich, 1938), 2nd ed.
11 Ibid, pp. 9–19.
12 Ibid, pp. 52–3.
13 Ibid, p. 28.
14 Ibid, pp. 54–5.
15 Ibid, pp. 73ff.
16 Ibid, pp. 81–3.
17 Ibid, p. 86, 'Zionismus ist, bestenfalls, der ohnmächtige Versuch eines unfähigen Volkes zu produktiver Leistung, meistens ein Mittel für ehrgeizige Spekulanten, sich ein neues Aufmarschgebiet für Weltbewucherung zu schaffen.'
18 *Mein Kampf*, p. 302.
19 Ibid, p. 303.
20 Ibid, p. 305.
21 'Parteipolitik und Judenfrage' (Munich, 8 December 1920), Dok. 172 in Jäckel/Kuhn, op.cit., p. 225.
22 *Speeches*, I, pp. 30ff. (speech of 28 July 1922).
23 'Warum sind wir Antisemiten?' Rede auf einer NSDAP Versammlung, in Jäckel/Kuhn, pp. 184–203.
24 Ibid, pp. 190–2.
25 See Otto Wagener's *Hitler aus nächster Nahe* . . . op. cit., pp. 319–20.
26 *Der Bolschevismus von Moses bis Lenin*, op.cit., pp. 16–17.

27 Ibid, p. 17. Hitler, in terms very reminiscent of Otto Weininger's *Geschlecht und Charakter* (Vienna, 1903), describes the organic connection between Zionism and the parasitic essence of Diaspora Jewry.

28 Edwin Black, *The Transfer Agreement. The Untold Story of the Secret Pact between the Third Reich and Jewish Palestine* (New York, 1984).

29 Werner E. Braatz, 'German Commercial Interests in Palestine: Zionism and the Boycott of German Goods 1933–1934', *European Studies Review*, IX (1979), pp. 485–7.

30 See *DGFP*, op.cit., Series C, 1: pp. 256–62 for the way the Nazis perceived the boycott danger.

31 Black, op.cit., p. 79.

32 Ibid, p. 97.

33 *Speeches*, Vol. I, p. 729 (speech of 24 October 1933).

34 Braatz, op.cit.

35 Black, op.cit., p. 166.

36 The 'Revisionist' right-wing of the Zionist movement, on the other hand, was strongly opposed to the *Ha'avara* agreement as a sell-out of the Jewish people. It became an important issue in the internecine conflicts between Mapai (the dominant socialist sector of the Zionist movement which had engineered the détente with the Third Reich) and the Revisionists. The murder in 1933 of Chaim Arlosoroff, the labour leader who had devised the transfer plan, occurred against this background. See Walter Laqueur, *A History of Zionism* (New York, 1976) and Black, op. cit., pp. 146–53.

37 Jacob Boas, 'A Nazi Travels to Palestine', *History Today*, 30 (January 1980), pp. 34–8. See also the interesting thesis by the same author, *The Jews of Germany: Self-Perception in the Nazi Era as Reflected in the German Jewish Press 1933–1938* (University of California, Riverside, 1977).

38 Boas, op.cit., p. 37.

39 Kurt Grossmann, 'Zionists and non-Zionists under Nazi Rule in the 1930s,' *Herzl Yearbook*, Vol. VI, p. 340.

40 Karl Schleunes, *The Twisted Road to Auschwitz, Nazi Policy toward German Jews 1933–1939* (Urbana, Chicago and London, 1970), pp. 193–4.

41 *Eichmann Interrogated*, op.cit., pp. 23–3.

42 Ibid, pp. 23–5.

43 Ibid, p. 31.

44 Ibid, p. 45.

45 Hannah Arendt, *Eichmann in Jerusalem* (London, 1963), pp. 36–7, tends to exaggerate Eichmann's fascination with the 'idealism' of the Zionists. On the practical co-operation between Eichmann and the Zionists, see ibid, pp. 55–6. For a more detailed account, Jon and David Kimche, *The Secret Roads: the 'illegal' Migration of a People, 1938–1948* (London, 1954).

46 Ernest Marcus, 'The German Foreign Office and the Palestine Question in the Period 1933–39', *Yad Vashem Studies*, II (Jerusalem, 1958), pp. 187–91.

47 Ibid, p. 191.

48 Ibid.

49 *DGFP*, Series D, Vol. V (Washington, 1953), Doc. No. 567, pp. 73–5.

50 David Yisraeli, *Ha-Reich Ha-Germani ve Erez-Israel* (The Third Reich and Palestine) (Ramat-Gan, 1974), pp. 114–21, 152ff.

51 E. Ben-Elissar, *La Diplomatie du IIIᵉ Reich et Les Juifs, 1933–39* (Paris, 1969), pp. 189ff.

52 Schleunes, op.cit., p. 209.

53 *DGFP*, D, Vol. V, pp. 746–7.

54 Ibid.

55 Alexander Schölch, 'Das Dritte Reich, Die Zionistische Bewegung und der Palästina-Konflikt', *Vierteljahrshefte für Zeitgeschichte*, 30 (1982), pp. 662–3.

56 See Milan Hauner, *India in Axis strategy: Germany, Japan and the Indian nationalists in the Second World War* (Stuttgart, 1981).

57 Fritz Grobba, *Männer und Mächte im Orient* (Göttingen, 1967), p. 317.

58 *Table Talk*, p. 547 (1 July 1942).

59 For a Communist interpretation which is not without interest, see Heinz Tillmann, *Deutschlands Araberpolitik im Zweiten Weltkrieg* (East Berlin, 1965). The best general account of relations between Germans and Arabs is still by Lukasz Hirszowicz, *The Third Reich and the Arab East* (London, 1966).

60 David Yisraeli, op.cit., pp. 103ff.

61 Hirszowicz, op.cit., p. 263. Hitler once described the Arabs as belonging to the lower races (coloured peoples), as lacquered half-apes who ought to be whipped. *Akten zur deutschen Auswärtigen Politik*, Series D, Vol. 7, p. 172.

62 In a few speeches in 1938, Hitler did, in passing, criticize British policy in Palestine. Thus on 20 February 1938 he mentioned the draconian justice dished out by British courts martial in Jerusalem. See Max Domarus (ed.), *Hitler: Reden und Proklamationen, 1932–1945* (Würzburg, 1962), I, p. 800. Speaking of the Sudeten crisis on 12 September 1938, he stated that he had no intention of creating a 'second Palestine' in Germany (ibid, p. 904). On 8 November 1938 in a speech at the Bürgerbräukeller in Munich, the Führer sarcastically suggested that British MPs would do better to concern themselves with Palestine than with German policy in Central Europe (ibid, p. 969). In other words, Palestine was at best a useful stick with which to beat the British, especially as Anglo-German relations deteriorated. The fate of Arabs and Jews in the country was a secondary matter.

63 See Tillmann, op. cit., pp. 247ff. Also Walther Hubatsch (hrsgb.) *Hitlers Weisungen für die Kriegführung 1939–1945: Dokumente des Oberkommandos der Wehrmacht* (Frankfurt-am-Main, 1962), pp. 120ff.

64 Hirszowicz, op.cit., pp. 143ff.; Hubatsch, op.cit., pp. 120–2.

65 See the important article by Daniel Carpi, 'The Mufti of Jerusalem, Amin el-Husseini, and His Diplomatic Activity during World War II (October 1941–July 1943)', *Zionism* (1984), pp. 101–31.

66 Carpi (ibid, p. 109) points out that in addition to Grobba's record, the Arabic minutes which the Mufti entered in his diary have survived. But they contain only Hitler's answers. The German minutes appear in Yisraeli, op.cit., pp. 308–11.

67 *DGFP*, D, Vol. XIII, op.cit., pp. 201–4 (all quotations from this source). See also Joseph Schechtman, *The Mufti and the Führer. The Rise and Fall of Haj Amin el-Husseini* (New York, 1965), pp. 306–8.

68 Ibid, p. 201 (*DGFP*).

69 Ibid, p. 202. See also Weizsäcker's reply to the Mufti's letter on behalf of the Führer, dated 8 April 1941. In this note the Arabs were described as 'a people with an old civilisation, who have demonstrated their competence for administrative activity and their military virtues'. The letter also stated that 'Germans and Arabs have common enemies in the English and the Jews and are united in the struggle against them.' *DGFP*, Series D, Vol. XII (London, 1962), p. 489.

70  *DGFP*, Vol. XIII, p. 202.
71  Ibid, pp. 202–3.
72  Ibid, p. 204.
73  Ibid, p. 203.
74  Ibid.
75  Ibid.
76  Ibid.
77  Ibid, p. 204.
78  Ibid.
79  Ibid, p. 203.
80  Ibid, pp. 203–4.
81  Ibid.
82  Carpi, op. cit., pp. 110–12.
83  Ibid, pp. 117ff.
84  D. Carpi, 'The Diplomatic Negotiations over the Transfer of Jewish Children from Croatia to Turkey and Palestine in 1943', *Yad Vashem Studies* (1977), Vol. XII, pp. 109–24. Also J. Schechtman, op. cit., pp. 154–9, 310.
85  Schölch, op. cit., pp. 669–70.
86  Ibid, p. 670; Schechtman, op. cit., pp. 139ff.
87  Schechtman, op. cit., pp. 147–52.
88  Ibid, also Schölch, op.cit., p. 671.
89  Schechtman, ibid, p. 160. The claim appears in Simon Wiesenthal, *Grossmufti – Grossagent der Achse* (Salzburg and Vienna, 1947), p. 37.
90  Schechtman, op.cit., pp. 139–40.
91  Ibid. For an earlier example of the ideological similarity between the Mufti's antisemitism and that of the Nazis, see Haj Amin el-Husseini's letter to Hitler of 20 January 1941, where he describes the 'Jews of the entire world' as dangerous enemies, 'whose secret arms are money, corruption and intrigues' which were being exploited by the British against the cause of Arab unity. The Mufti in this letter also told Hitler: 'Arab nationalism owes Your Excellency a debt of gratitude and of recognition for having again and again brought up in ringing tones the question of Palestine.' *DGFP*, Vol. XI (London, 1961), pp. 1153–4.
92  Francis Nicosia, 'Arab Nationalism and National Socialist Germany, 1933–1939: Ideological and Strategic Incompatibility', *International Journal of Middle East Studies*, 12 (1980), pp. 351–72. This interesting article, in my view, somewhat overstates the ideological 'incompatibility'.
93  Ibid, p. 353.
94  Haim Shamir, 'The Middle East in the Nazi Conception', in *Germany and the Middle East 1835–1939* (International Symposium, Tel-Aviv University, April 1975), ed. Jehuda L. Wallach, pp. 167–74.
95  Itamar Rabinovich, 'Germany and the Syrian Political Scene in the late 1930s', in ibid, pp. 194–5.
96  Ibid, p. 197.
97  Ibid, p. 198.
98  See Harold P. Luks, 'Iraqi Jews during World War II', *WLB* (1977), Vol. XXX, New Series, Nos 43/44, pp. 30–9.
99  Elie Kedourie, *Arabic Political Memoirs* (London, 1974), pp. 283–314, describes in detail the *Farhud* in Baghdad.
100 Luks, op. cit., p. 36. See also Sylvia Haim, *Arab Nationalism* (Berkeley, 1962), pp. 67–8.

101 See Richard P. Mitchell, *The Society of the Muslim Brothers* (London, 1969).
102 Shimon Shamir, 'The Influence of German National-Socialism on Radical Movements in Egypt', *Germany and the Middle East*, op. cit., pp. 200–208.
103 James P. Jankowski, 'Egyptian Responses to the Palestine Problem in the Interwar Period', *International Journal of Middle East Studies*, 12 (1980), pp. 1–38 (the quotation is from footnote 118 on page 33).

## 9 MILITANT ISLAM AND ARAB NATIONALISM

1 Majid Khadduri, *War and Peace in the Law of Islam* (Oxford University Press, 1955), pp. 49–137. Khadduri points out that 'the jihad may be regarded as Islam's instrument for carrying out its ultimate objective by turning all people into believers' (p. 64). It is a 'permanent obligation upon the entire Muslim community'. In Muslim law there is a sharp division between the *dār al-Islām* (abode of Islam) and the *dār al-harb* (abode of war). The latter consists of all the states and communities outside the world of Islam – the infidels or unbelievers. They must ultimately be reduced to non-existence. In the short term non-Islamic communities in the *dār al-Islām* may exist as tolerated religious groups accepting certain disabilities as long as they submit to Muslim rule.
2 For a pioneering discussion and documentation, see Bat Ye'or, *Le Dhimmi. Profil de l'opprimé en Orient et en Afrique du nord depuis la conquête arabe* (Paris, 1980). On the legal status, see Khadduri, op. cit., pp. 175–201.
3 Bat Ye'or, op. cit., pp. 176–275. Also Albert Memmi, *Juifs et Arabes* (Paris, 1974), pp. 49–75, for a personal account.
4 See the texts in Anouar Abdel-Malek, *La pensée politique arabe contemporaine* (Paris, 1970), and Sylvia G. Haim, *Arab Nationalism* (Berkeley, 1962).
5 Ronald L. Nettler, 'Fundamentalist Waves. The Reality of Islamic Revivalism', *Scopus* (Hebrew University, Jerusalem), Vol. 34 (1984), pp. 10–13, 16–18.
6 Bernard Lewis, *The Middle East and the West* (London, 1964), p. 114. See also his important article, 'The Return of Islam', in *The Middle East Review* (Autumn 1979), Vol. XII, No. 1.
7 Emil Fackenheim, *The Jewish Return Into History* (New York, 1978), p. 212.
8 Quoted in Dafna Alon, *Arab Racialism* (Jerusalem, 1969), p. 5.
9 *Al Musawar*, 18 September 1953. Quoted in D. F. Green (ed.), *Arab Theologians on Jews and Israel* (Geneva, 1976), p. 87.
10 Dafna Alon, op. cit., pp. 22ff.
11 *WLB* (1957), 1–2, p. 4.
12 *Manchester Guardian*, 5 February 1957.
13 Alon, op.cit., pp. 25–6.
14 A full Arabic version of *Mein Kampf* had been available in Baghdad since 1936 and two years later appeared in Cairo. See 'Mein Kampf among Arabs', *WLB*, Vol. X, Nos 3–4 (1956), p. 37.
15 *Die Welt* (Hamburg), 12 October 1956.
16 Abdel-Moneim Shemeis, *Asrar al-Sahyuniya* (Secrets of Zionism) (Cairo, 1957). Also Muhammad Khalifa al-Tunisi, *Al-Khatr al-Yahudi, Brutakalat Hukama Sahyn* (The Jewish Danger. The Protocol of the Elders of Zion) (Cairo, 1961). For a comprehensive account of the role played by the Protocols in modern Arabic antisemitism, see the classic work by Y. Harkabi, *Arab Attitudes to Israel* (paperback edn, Jerusalem, 1976), pp. 220–37, which forms the basis of this chapter.

17 Harkabi, op. cit., pp. 230–1.
18 Ibid, p. 233.
19 R. K. Karanjia, *Arab Dawn* (Bombay, 1958), quoted in ibid, p. 235, and in Alon, op. cit., p. 30.
20 See Norman Cohn, *Warrant for Genocide* (Harmondsworth, 1970), pp. 156–62.
21 Muhammad Ali Aluba, *Filastin wa-al-Damir al-Insani* (Cairo, 1964). See Alon, op. cit., p. 30.
22 See C. C. Aronsfeld, 'Arab antisemites' Nazi model', *Patterns of Prejudice*, Vol. 16, No. 3 (May-June 1972), pp. 13ff. Also Harkabi, op. cit., p. 237.
23 For the unabridged translation of Salih Jawdat's article, 'Israel Dreams', *Al Musawar* ( 6 October 1967), see 'The "Satanic Plot". Arab-Know-Your Protocols Campaign', *WLB* (Winter 1967/68), Vol. XXII, No. 1, new series, No. 10, pp. 25–7.
24 Misbahul Islam Faruqi (ed.) *Jewish Conspiracy and the Muslim World: With the Complete text of the Protocols of the Learned Elders of Zion of the 33rd Degree* (Karachi, 1967). See Sylvia G. Haim, 'A Muslim View of the "Protocols", *WLB* (Summer 1967), Vol. XXI, No. 3, new series, No. 8, pp. 48–9.
25 Sylvia Haim, ibid.
26 'Khomeini's Holy War', *Newsweek* (26 July 1982), pp. 10ff.
27 'Khomeiny à la conquête du monde', *L'Express* (6–12 July 1984), pp. 11ff.
28 Michael Curtis, 'Khomeini's Thoughts on Jews and Israel', *Middle East Review* (Spring 1979), Vol. XI, No. 3, pp. 59–60. See also Ayatollah Khomeiny, *Pour un gouvernement islamique* (Paris, 1979).
29 Curtis, op.cit., p. 60.
30 Ibid. From interview with *Der Spiegel Magazine* (Hamburg), 22 January 1979.
31 *France Soir* (Beirut), 13 February 1979. Quoted in David Littman, 'Jews under Muslim Rule: the Case of Persia', *WLB* (1979), Vol. XXXII, New Series, Nos 49/50, p. 15. See also Bat Ye'or, op.cit., pp. 289–90, for Arafat's message and the charges against the honorary president of the Iranian Jewish community, summarily shot on 8 May 1979 by an Islamic revolutionary tribunal for 'contacts' with Israel and Zionism, defined by his executioners as 'les plus cruels ennemis de Dieu et de la Nation palestinienne'.
32 *Jewish Echo* (Glasgow), 30 March 1984, reported, for instance, that the Board of Deputies of British Jews called on the British Foreign Secretary, Sir Geoffrey Howe, to take 'prompt action' to stop the Iranian Embassy in London from propagating race hatred literature.
33 *Imam* (February 1984), pp. 14–15. My thanks to Laurence Green of the Board of Deputies Research Unit, London, for drawing my attention to this material.
34 Ibid.
35 Ibid.
36 Ibid, p. 15.
37 *Imam* (March 1984), p. 21.
38 Ibid, p. 22.
39 *Imam* (April 1984), pp. 14–15.
40 Ibid, p. 15.
41 *Imam* (May 1984), p. 12.
42 Ibid, p. 21.
43 Ibid.
44 Ibid, p. 12.
45 Ibid.

46  D. F. Green (ed.) *Arab Theologians on Jews and Israel*, 3rd. edn (Geneva, 1976). The conference enjoyed Nasser's sponsorship and was convened to discuss the fundamentals of the Middle East conflict. Seventy-seven Muslim *ulemas* and invited guests attended.

47  D. F. Green in his introduction (ibid, p. 8) correctly emphasizes that the Jews' evilness is seen as having been genetically transmitted through history. It is part of their religion and cultural inheritance and has, in Arab eyes, *deservedly* called forth antisemitism and hatred throughout the ages.

48  Ibid, pp. 22–3. 'Evil, wickedness, breach of vows and money worship are inherent qualities in them.'

49  Ibid, p. 44.

50  Ibid, p. 65.

51  Ibid.

52  Ibid, p. 19.

53  Ibid, p. 22.

54  Ibid, p. 24.

55  Ibid, pp. 69–70.

56  Ibid, p. 38.

57  Ibid, p. 41.

58  Ibid, p. 8.

59  Dafna Alon, op. cit., p. 93.

60  *Tahrir Al Aktar al Muhtala Alkifah Dhid Al Instiinar Almubashar* (The Liberation of the Occupied Lands and the Struggle against Direct Imperialism), No. 8 in a Fatah pamphlet series called *Dirasat Watajarib Thawriya* (Revolutionary Studies and Experiments). See pp. 16–17 for the text in question.

61  Ibid.

62  See Bruno Frei, 'Progressive Auschwitz', in Robert S. Wistrich (ed.), *The Left Against Zion* (London, 1979), pp. 260–371. Frei was for many years a member of the Austrian Communist Party.

63  *Al Anwar*, 8 and 15 March 1970. See Y. Harkabi, 'The Meaning of a Democratic Palestinian State', *Ma'ariv* (3 and 17 April 1970), in Hebrew. Also *WLB* (1970), Vol. 24, pp. 1–6, for a revised English version.

64  Phil Baum, 'The Unchanging Goal of the PLO', *Congress Bi-Weekly*, 6 December 1974. Y. Harkabi, 'The Palestinian National Covenant', in *Palestinians and Israel* (Jerusalem, 1974), pp. 49–68, including the full text of the 33 articles.

65  Y. Harkabi, *The Palestinian Covenant and its Meaning* (London, 1980).

66  Y. Harkabi, *Palestinians and Israel*, op. cit., p. 127.

67  'Paz Para Nosotros Significa la Destrucción de Israel', *El Mundo* (Caracas), 11 February 1980.

68  *Jewish Chronicle*, 6 June 1980.

69  Harkabi, op. cit., p. 9.

70  *Al Akhbar* (mid-February 1972) and *Akhir Sa'ah* (10 April 1974). Quoted in D. F. Green, op. cit., pp. 92–3.

71  Ibid, p. 93.

72  Ibid, pp. 90–1.

73  Ibid, p. 90.

74  Ibid, p. 94.

75  Ibid, p. 95.

76  Ibid, quoted from *Al Jihad wa al-Nasr* (Cairo, 1974), pp. 148–50.

77  Ronald L. Nettler, 'The Ambivalence of Camp David Rhetoric. The Arab Idea

of 'Peace with Israel', *Encounter* (June–July 1982), pp. 100–108.

78 I am grateful to Dr Rivka Yadlin, senior researcher of the Truman Institute at the Hebrew University, for pointing out to me in conversation the extent of contemporary Egyptian antisemitism, as it is manifested in the press.

79 Bernard Lewis, 'Semites and Anti-Semites: Race in the Arab–Israel Conflict', *Survey* (Spring 1971), Vol. 17, No. 2, pp. 169–84. Also Maxime Rodinson, 'Quelques idées simples sur l'antisémitisme', *Revue d'Études Palestiniennes*, No. 1 (Autumn 1981), pp. 13ff., for a useful corrective to this view.

80 Lewis, op. cit., p. 175.

81 Hannah Arendt, op. cit., p. 17.

82 Harkabi, *Arab Attitudes to Israel* (Jerusalem, 1976), op. cit., p. 279.

83 Ibid, p. 276. Abdallah al-Tall, *Khattr al-Yahūdiyya al-'Alamiyya 'Ala al-Islām wa-al-Masihiyya* (The Danger of World Jewry to Islam and Christianity) (Cairo, 1964), pp. 115–17.

84 Harkabi, op. cit., p. 277.

85 Ibid.

86 Ibid.

87 *Almnamara wa Ma'arakat al Masir* (The Conspiracy and the Battle of Destiny) (Beirut, 1968), pp. 20–2. See *Holocaust* (Jerusalem, 1974), p. 182, for the brief note by Harkabi.

88 *Al-Akhbar*, 19 August 1973. See the commentary in *Le Monde*, 21 August 1973.

89 *Jewish Currents* (November 1975), p. 21.

90 Ibid. Also *New York Amsterdam News* (15 October 1975).

91 Robert Weisbord, 'Islam, Black Nationalism and the Jews', *Congress Monthly* (June 1977), pp. 13–15.

92 *New York Times*, 16 April 1984.

93 Ibid, 29 June 1984, for excerpts from the transcript.

94 Ibid.

95 Raphael Israeli, 'Anti-Jewish Attitudes in the Arabic Media, 1975–1981', *IJA Research Report* (September 1983), No. 15, pp. 1–18.

96 Quoted in Daniel Pipes, 'The Politics of Muslim Antisemitism', *Commentary* (August 1981), p. 39.

97 Ibid.

98 (United Nations General Assembly) Thirty-Ninth Session. 24 January 1984, No. A 39/79. Report of the Economic and Social Council. Letter dated 16 January 1984 from the Permanent Representative of Israel to the United Nations, addressed to the Secretary-General, p. 4.

99 (A/38/PV.13, p. 41).

100 (A/38/PV.42, pp. 53–55) ibid, p. 2.

101 (A/38/PV.102, p. 47) ibid.

102 (A/38/PV.88, pp. 19–20) ibid. Blum refers here to his earlier letter to the Secretary-General of the UN of 8 December 1983 which drew attention to the racist incitement of the Libyan representative.

103 See Olivier Carré, 'Juifs et chrétiens dans la société islamique idéale d'après Sayyid Qutb (M. 1966). Le maître à penser des Frères musulmans radicaux d'aujourd'hui', *Revue des Sciences Philosophiques et Théologiques* (Jan 1984), No. 1, Tome 68, pp. 50–72. Ronald Nettler also discusses Qutb in his fine article 'Islam vs. Israel', *Commentary* (December 1984), pp. 26–30, which deals with the Muslim Brotherhood in the context of contemporary Egypt. My thanks to him, to Emmanuel Sivan, Moshe Sharon, Bat Ye'or and to David Littman for helping

me to crystallize my thoughts on this issue.

## 10 THE SOVIET PROTOCOLS

1 See Hannah Arendt, *Origins of Totalitarianism* (New York, 1951); Carl J. Friedrich and Zbigniew K. Brzezinski, *Totalitarian Dictatorship and Autocracy* (Cambridge, Mass., 1956).

2 Robert Conquest, *The Great Terror* (London, 1971), who estimates at least 20 million victims of the Stalin regime.

3 See Robert C. Tucker, 'The Stalin Heritage in Soviet Policy', in *The Soviet Political Mind* (London, 1972), pp. 87–102.

4 Trotsky claimed with some justification that Stalin had instigated a clandestine antisemitic campaign against him as early as 1926. See his *My Life* (London, 1975), p. 376. Also Leon Trotsky, *On the Jewish Question* (New York, 1970), pp. 21ff. Robert S. Wistrich, *Revolutionary Jews from Marx to Trotsky* (London, 1976), pp. 201ff. Also my *Trotsky, Fate of a Revolutionary* (London, 1979).

5 Robert Wistrich, *Trotsky, Fate of a Revolutionary* (London, 1979), pp. 176–94.

6 Theodore Draper, 'The Ghost of Social-Fascism', *Commentary* (February 1969), pp. 29–42.

7 For further documentation see Hermann Weber (ed.), *Der Deutsche Kommunismus. Dokumente* (Köln, 1964). See especially the 'Offener Brief der KPD an die Werktätigen Wähler der NSDAP und die Mitglieder der Sturmabteilungen', published in *Die Rote Fahne*, 1 November 1931, and reproduced in Weber, ibid, pp. 155–7.

8 For a devastating critique of this blind Stalinist policy made in January 1932, see 'What Next? Vital Questions for the German Proletariat', in Leon Trotsky, *The Struggle Against Fascism in Germany* (London, 1975), p. 148.

9 See Thomas Weingartner, *Stalin und der Aufstieg Hitlers. Die Deutschlandpolitik der Sowjetunion und der Kommunistischen Internationale 1929–1934* (Berlin, 1970), and the critique by Evelyn Anderson, 'Soviet Policies and the Rise of Hitler', *WLB* (1970/71), Vol. XXIV, No. 4, new series, No. 21, pp. 29–35.

10 *XVII S'ezd vsesoiuznoi Kommunisticheskoii partii (b). Stenograficheskii otchet* (Moscow, 1934), pp. 13–14. Also in J. V. Stalin, *Sochineniya*, Vol. 13 (July 1930–January 1934) (Moscow, 1951), p. 302.

11 See Robert C. Tucker, 'Stalin, Bukharin, and History as Conspiracy', *The Soviet Political Mind* (London, 1972), pp. 49–86, for a very illuminating interpretation with which I largely agree.

12 Ibid, p. 77.

13 Roy A. Medvedev, *On Stalin and Stalinism* (Oxford University Press, 1979), pp. 120ff. Above all Nikita Khrushchev's 'Secret Speech' to the 20th Congress of the CPSU, reproduced in *Khruschev Remembers* (London, 1971), Appendix 4, pp. 503ff. (especially pp. 532–3).

14 Svetlana Alliluyeva, *20 Letters to a Friend* (Penguin Books, 1968), p. 171. See also her remark: 'He never liked Jews, though he wasn't yet as blatant about expressing his hatred for them in those days as he was after the war' (p. 140). Also Milovan Djilas, *Conversations with Stalin* (Penguin, 1963), p. 120, for further confirmation of Stalin's antisemitism.

15 Reuben Ainsztein, 'Soviet Jewry in the Second World War', in Lionel Kochan (ed.), *The Jews in Soviet Russia since 1917* (Oxford University Press, 1970), pp. 269ff.

16 Leonard Schapiro, 'The Jewish Anti-Fascist Committee and Phases of Soviet Anti-Semitic Policy During and After World War II', in B. Vago and G. L. Mosse (eds.), *Jews and non-Jews in Eastern Europe* (New York and Jerusalem, 1974), pp. 291ff.

17 Benjamin Pinkus, 'Soviet Campaigns against "Jewish Nationalism" and "Cosmopolitanism", 1946–1953', in *Soviet Jewish Affairs* (1974), Vol. 4, No. 2, pp. 53–69.

18 Schapiro, op. cit., pp. 295ff., sees the Doctors' Plot as directed primarily at Beria, the overlord of the Security Services. Nevertheless, he calls the Soviet anti-semitism of this last phase 'an open policy aimed at the extermination of, at any rate, the articulate sections of the Jewish population; and the encouragement of a wave of popular anti-Jewish violence'.

19 See Peter Brod, 'Soviet-Israeli Relations 1948–1956' and Arnold Krammer, 'Prisoners in Prague: Israelis in the Slansky Trial', in Robert Wistrich (ed.), *The Left against Zion. Communism, Israel and the Middle East* (London, 1979), pp. 57–64, 72–85. Also Eugene Loebl, *Sentenced and Tried: The Stalinist Purges in Czechoslovakia* (London, 1969).

20 See Artur London, *L'Aveu* (Paris, 1968). English translation quoted from W. Oschlies, 'Neo-Stalinist Antisemitism in Czechoslovakia', in Robert S. Wistrich, *The Left against Zion*, op. cit., pp. 156–7.

21 Wistrich, op. cit., p. 157.

22 Ibid, p. 159.

23 Ibid, p. 160.

24 See Paul Lendvai, *Antisemitismus ohne Juden. Entwicklungen und Tendenzen in Osteuropa* (Vienna, 1972).

25 *Staline contre Israël* (Supplément du Bulletin D'Études et D'Informations Politiques Internationales), Bi-mensuel, No. 16/28, Février 1953. Also François Fejtö, *Les Juifs et l'antisémitisme dans les pays communistes* (Paris, 1960) for a systematic survey of the problem.

26 Michel Mirsky, 'Zionism – instrument of American Imperialism' (in Polish), in *Nowe Drogi*, No. 1 (43), January 1953.

27 Ibid.

28 See François Fejtö, op. cit., on the violently antisemitic *feuilletons* which appeared in the Polish press in 1957 to encourage the emigration of Polish Jews. By the end of 1958 only 27,000 Jews remained in the country.

29 See Anonymous (Michael Checinski), 'USSR and the Politics of Polish Anti-semitism 1956–68', *Soviet Jewish Affairs*, No. 1 (June 1971), pp. 19–38, for a first-hand eyewitness account.

30 Ibid, p. 21.

31 Ibid, p. 23.

32 Adam Ciolkosz, ' "Anti-Zionism" in Polish Communist Party Politics', in Robert S. Wistrich (ed.), *The Left against Zion*, op. cit., pp. 137–51 (especially p. 142).

33 Andrzej Werblan, 'Przyczynek do genezy Konfliktu', *Miesiecznik Literacki* (June 1968). Quoted in Ciolkosz, op. cit., p. 145.

34 Ibid, p. 146.

35 Ciolkosz, op. cit., pp. 146–7.

36 See Checinski (anon.), op. cit., pp. 30–3.

37 Ibid, pp. 35–6.

38 George Garai, 'Hungary's Liberal Policy and the Jewish Question, with a Note on Rakosi', *Soviet Jewish Affairs*, No. 1 (June 1971), pp. 101–7.

39 See Paul Lendvai, op. cit., for respective chapters on post-war Hungary and Rumania under Communist rule, viewed from the Jewish angle.

40 Robert S. Wistrich, 'Anti-Zionism in the USSR: from Lenin to the Soviet Black Hundreds', in *The Left against Zion*, op. cit., pp. 272–300.

41 Uri Ra'anan, 'Moscow and the "Third World" ', *Problems of Communism*, XIV (January–February 1965).

42 Yaacov Roi, *From Encroachment to Involvement. A Documentary Study of Soviet Policy in the Middle East 1945–1973* (Jerusalem, 1974), pp. 190ff.

43 K. Ivanov and Z. Sheinis, *The State of Israel. Its Position and Policies* (Moscow, 1958).

44 *L'Humanité*, 24 March 1964, quoted in Jacques Hermone, *La Gauche, Israel et les Juifs* (Paris, 1970), p. 89.

45 See Shmuel Ettinger, 'Anti-Zionism and Anti-Semitism', *Insight*, Vol. 2, No. 5 (May 1976).

46 Robert S. Wistrich, *The Left against Zion*, op. cit., pp. 288ff.

47 See the imaginative, if somewhat overblown, theses of Reuben Ainsztein 'The Roots of Russian Antisemitism', *The Jewish Quarterly*, Vol. 20, No. 3 (75) (Autumn 1972), pp. 4–20. Also the thought-provoking article by Mikhail Agursky, 'Russian Neo-Nazism – A Growing Threat', *Midstream* (February 1976), pp.35–42.

48 Robert S. Wistrich, 'From Lenin to the Soviet Black Hundreds', *Midstream* (March 1978), pp. 4–12.

49 *Pravda*, 6 July 1967. See also my article on 'Anti-Zionism in the USSR', *The Left against Zion*, op. cit., pp. 288ff.

50 Y. Ivanov, *Ostrozhno! Sionizm!* (Moscow, 1969). For fuller extracts in English see *Bulletin on Soviet and East European Jewish Affairs* (London), No. 3, January 1969. Robert S. Wistrich, 'Anti-Zionism in the USSR', op. cit., p. 288.

51 V. I. Kiselev, 'Sionizm v sisteme imperializma', in *Mezhdunarodny Sionism – istoriya i politika* (Moscow, 1977), pp. 5–28.

52 L. Korneyev, 'Sionizm kak on yest', *Moskovskaya Pravda*, 16 February 1977.

53 L. Korneyev, 'Samy sionistskii byznes', *Ogonyok*, 8 July 1978.

54 L. Korneyev, 'Otravlennoye oruzhiye sionizma', *Krasnaya Zvezda*, 16 November 1977.

55 See Vladimir Begun, *Polzuchaya Kontrrevolutysiya* (Creeping Counter-Revolution) (Minsk, 1974). Extensive extracts translated from the Russian by Dr Howard Spier for the Institute of Jewish Affairs, London, 1975. See also M. A. Goldenberg, 'Iudaizm na sluzhbe sionizma', in *Mezhdunarodny sionizm*, op. cit., pp. 88–98.

56 Robert Wistrich, 'Anti-Zionism in the USSR', op. cit., p. 290.

57 Begun, op. cit., p. 151.

58 Ibid.

59 V. Begun, *Creeping Counter-Revolution* (Spier version), p. 29.

60 Dmitri Zhukov, 'The Ideology and Practice of Violence', *Ogonyok* (12 October 1974). The parallel text in Russian and English is available in *Israel At Peace* (organ of the Communist Party of Israel, MAKI), January 1975, No. 1. See the sharp protest by Yair Tsaban at Zhukov's reviling of the Talmud in the style of medieval Jew-baiting. 'Not just fifty years divide Lenin from Zhukov, but an ethical and philosophical abyss divides them, and no use of any Marxist vocabulary and no adornment with Lenin-quotations will manage to bridge the gap.'

NOTES

61 The article was first put out by the semi-official Novosty Press on 22 September 1972. It gave rise to legal proceedings because of its appearance in a French-language journal. See Emmanuel Litvinoff, *Soviet Antisemitism: The Paris Trial* (London, 1974).

62 *Jews in Eastern Europe*, Vol. V, No. 3 (August 1973), p. 51.

63 For a revealing collection of quotations showing the close parallels between Russian Black Hundred, Nazi and contemporary Soviet antisemitism, see R. Okuneva, 'Anti-Semitic Notions: Strange Analogies', in *Anti-Semitism in the Soviet Union. Its Roots and Consequences*, Vol. 2 (The Hebrew University of Jerusalem, 1980), pp. 198–323. Also her letter to Leonid Brezhnev, pointing out the 'very pronounced anti-Semitic nature' of current Soviet anti-Zionist literature (ibid, pp. 189ff.).

64 'Selling Anti-Semitism in Moscow' (Michael Agursky), *New York Review of Books*, 16 November 1972.

65 Emanuel Litvinoff, 'Return of the Slavophiles', *Insight*, Vol. 4, No. 12 (December 1978), pp. 1–5.

66 Ibid, pp. 5–6. See also Zeev Ben-Shlomo, 'Soviet Jews a fifth column', *Jewish Chronicle*, 24 March 1978.

67 Howard Spier, 'Zionists and Freemasons in Soviet Propaganda', *Patterns of Prejudice*, Vol. 13, No. 1 (January–February 1979), pp. 1–5.

68 Ibid, p. 2.

69 Ben-Shlomo, op. cit.

70 Spier, op. cit., pp. 4–5.

71 Reuben Ainsztein, 'The fall of an anti-semite', *New Statesman* (11 July 1980), p. 45. Emelianov killed his wife in a domestic quarrel, but shortly after her remains were discovered in Moscow on 7 April 1980 he was arrested.

72 Reuben Ainsztein, 'Antisemitism: Official Soviet Ideology?', *Congress Monthly* (January 1979), Vol. 46, No. 7, pp. 6–10.

73 Ibid, p. 8.

74 See William Korey, 'The Smell of Pogrom', *Jewish Chronicle*, 18 March 1977.

75 K. Ivanov, 'Israel, Zionism and International Imperialism', *International Affairs* (June 1968), pp. 13–19.

76 V. Bolshakov, 'Antisovetism – professiya sionistov', *Pravda*, 18–19 February 1971.

77 William Korey, 'Soviet Anti-Semitism Since the Six-Day War', *Insight*, Vol. 3, No. 11 (November 1977), p. 4.

78 V. Skurlatov, *Sionizm i aparteid* (Kiev, 1975), p. 14.

79 Ibid, p. 12.

80 Ibid, p. 11.

81 V. Kudryavtsev, 'The Criminal Handwriting of Zionism', *Izvestia*, 2 December 1975. V. Misik, 'Zionism – A form of Racism, *Aziya i Afrika Segodnya*, No. 4, 1976.

82 *Soviet Antisemitic Propaganda*. Evidence from books, press and radio (Institute of Jewish Affairs, 1978), pp. 56–8. This excellent collection of quotations amplifies the points made here.

83 'Looking Back: The Brezhnev Era. Part One – The Anti-Zionist "Crusade" ', *Insight* (ed. Emanuel Litvinoff), Vol. 9, No. 1 (January 1983), p. 6.

84 *Soviet Antisemitic Propaganda*, op. cit., p. 81.

85 Ibid.

86 D. Pavlov, 'An Ominous Conspiracy', *Asia and Africa Today*, No. 1, 1978, in ibid, p. 43.

87 G. Afanasyev, *Za Rubezhom*, 10–16 February 1978.

88  *Soviet Antisemitic Propaganda*, op. cit., p. 44.
89  *New Times*, No. 44 (1972), p. 26.
90  V. Sidenko, 'Israel's African Ambitions', ibid, No. 3, (1971), p. 25.
91  Ibid.
92  S. Komarov, 'The Tentacles of Zionism in Africa', *Moscow News*, No. 25 (1971), p. 7.
93  Quoted in Kalman Sultanik, 'Antisemitism: An Overview', *Forum* (Fall/Winter 1979), No. 36, p. 89.
94  *International Herald Tribune*, 17 November 1975.
95  L. Korneyev, 'The Sinister Secrets of Zionism' (Part Two), *Ogonyok*, No. 35 (1977).
96  V. A. Semenyuk, *Natsionalisticheskoe bezumie* (Minsk, 1976), p. 47.
97  Ruvim Groyer, 'Why We Condemn Zionism', *Soviet Weekly*, 1 November 1977.
98  See Theodore H. Friedgut, 'Soviet Anti-Zionism and Anti-Semitism: Another Cycle' (The Hebrew University, Research Paper No. 54, Soviet and East European Research Centre), January 1984.

## 11 INVERSIONS OF HISTORY

1  See Robert Wistrich, 'The Anti-Zionist Masquerade', *Midstream* (August/September 1983), pp. 8–19.
2  R. Scholom, 'Telltale Trial', *New Times*, No. 23 (1955), pp. 20–2.
3  *Izvestia*, 3 September 1961; *Trud*, 28 July 1961; *Pravda*, 28 April 1961.
4  L. Korneyev, 'The Sinister Secrets of Zionism' (Part 2), *Ogonyok*, No. 35 (1977).
5  Ibid.
6  L. Korneyev, 'Sekretnye Sluzhby mezhdunarodnogo sionizma i gosurdarstva Izrail', *Narody Azii i Afriki*, No. 1 (1976).
7  L. Korneyev, 'Shpionsky sprut sionizma' (The Zionist Espionage Octopus), *Ogonyok*, 29 January 1977.
8  See *Soviet Antisemitic Propaganda*, op. cit., pp. 73–4.
9  Ibid, p. 72.
10  Ts. Solodar, *Dikaya polyn* (Wild Wormwood) (Moscow, 1977), p. 34.
11  Ibid. Also his 'The Hunt for Youth', *Komsomolskaya Pravda*, 3 August 1983.
12  V. A. Semenyuk, *Natsionalisticheskoe bezumie* (Nationalistic Madness) (Minsk, 1976), p. 47.
13  D. I. Soyfer, *Sionizm – orudie antikommunizma* (Dnepropetrovsk, 1976), p. 50.
14  Semenyuk, op. cit., p. 94.
15  Y. Ivanov, *Ostrozhno! Sionizm!* (Moscow, 1969).
16  *Pravda Ukrainy*, 13 March 1970.
17  See Israel Klejner, 'The Soviet Ukrainian Press on Zionism and Israel', *Soviet Jewish Affairs*, Vol. 4, No. 2 (1974), pp. 46–52.
18  Ibid, p. 49.
19  *Pravda*, 17 January 1984. See also the report by Richard Owen from Moscow, 'Israel savaged by Pravda', *The Times*, 18 January 1984.
20  For such cartoons and for an excellent demonstration of how the Zionist–Nazi amalgam is used in Soviet visual propaganda, see Judith Vogt, 'Old Images in Soviet Anti-Zionist Cartoons', *Soviet Jewish Affairs*, Vol. 5, No. 1 (1975), pp. 20–35.

21 Ze'ev Ben-Shlomo, 'Soviets and Zionism', *WLB* (Winter 1965–66), Vol. XX, No. 1, new series, No. 2, pp. 7–9.

22 N. T. Fedorenko, 'Perfidy and Aggression', *New Times*, 28 June 1967. Also reprinted in Walter Laqueur (ed.), *The Israel-Arab Reader. A Documentary History of the Middle East Conflict* (Bantam Books, 1969) pp. 300–308. For an eloquent reply, see the pamphlet published by the Anglo–Israel Association entitled *The Diplomatic History of the Six Day War*, a lecture by Gideon Rafael delivered on 25 September 1975 at the Royal Society of Arts. Mr Rafael was Israeli Ambassador to the United Nations in June 1967.

23 See Vogt, op. cit., p. 26.

24 Y. Yevseyev, 'Lackeys at Beck and Call', *Komsomolskaya Pravda*, 4 October 1967.

25 Y. Yevseyev, 'Fashizm pod goluboy zvezdoy' (Fascism under Blue Star), *Komsomolskaya Pravda*, 17 May 1970.

26 B. M. Fikh, 'Sionizm i fashizm', *Sovetskaya Belorussia*, 2 April 1970. Quoted in Jonathan Frankel, 'The Anti-Zionist Press Campaigns in the USSR 1969–1971: An Internal Dialogue?'', *Soviet Jewish Affairs*, No. 3 (May 1972), p. 22.

27 Vogt, op. cit., p. 27.

28 E.g. 'The Well-Known Assortment', *Sovetskaya Rossiya* (11 August 1967), in Vogt, op. cit., p. 25.

29 Ibid, pp. 26–7.

30 See, for example, V. Ladeikin, 'Criminal Policy of the Israeli Extremists', *International Affairs*, No. 1 (1972), p. 43. *Za Rubezhom*, 3 October 1973, carried an article on the 'Zionist Heirs of the Gestapo'. These are merely two among thousands of similar articles.

31 'The Pharisees from Tel Aviv', *Krasnaya Zvezda*, 3 March 1970.

32 For a representative example see K. Ivanov, 'Israel, Zionism and International Imperialism', *International Affairs* (June 1968), p. 20.

33 G. Kuznetsov, 'Zionism in the Pillory', *Za Rubezhom*, 21 November 1975; Y. Valakh in *Pravda Ukrainy*, 15 November 1975; V. Korotev, 'The Zionist Witches' Sabbath', *Gudok*, 15 November 1975. Lydia Madzhoryan, 'The Criminal Policy of Zionism and International Law', *Moscow News* (English-language daily), 22 September 1973, typically insisted on the organic link between the 'man-hating racial conception of Jewish superiority' and the so-called Israeli *praxis* of genocide.

34 See Nicolas Spulber, 'Israel's War in Lebanon through the Soviet Looking Glass', *Middle East Review* (Spring/Summer 1983), pp. 18–27.

35 'Tragedy without an Epilogue', *Novoe Vremiya*, 27 August 1982.

36 Quoted in Spulber, op. cit., p. 21.

37 'Crusade by Washington and Tel Aviv', *Selskaya Zhizn*, 26 June 1982.

38 Spulber, op. cit., p. 22.

39 Ibid, p. 20.

40 'In the Footsteps of the Nazis', Tass, broadcast quoted in Nicolas Spulber, ibid, p. 21.

41 V. Bolshakov, 'Fascism and Zionism: the roots of kinship', *Pravda*, 17 January 1984. See also *IJA Research Report*, '*Pravda* Equates Zionism with Fascism' (March 1984), and 'Israel Savaged by *Pravda*', *The Times*, 18 January 1984.

42 Fredelle Z. Spiegel, 'The Emperor's Clothes: The New Look in Arab Public Relations', *Middle East Review* (Spring/Summer 1983), pp. 25ff.

43 Robert Wistrich, 'The Anti-Zionist Masquerade', op. cit.

44 See Sultanik, op. cit., pp. 83ff.

45 W. D. Rubinstein, *The Right, The Left and the Jews* (London, 1982), for a stimulating analysis of this phenomenon.

46 See 'New Vision at the Vatican', *WLB* (Winter 1965–66), Vol. XX, No. 1, new series, No. 2, pp. 1–5, including the Document on the Jews promulgated by Pope Paul VI on 28 October 1965.

47 For a global survey of the situation, see *WLB* (Spring 1966), Vol. XX, No. 2, new series, No. 3, especially 'Warnings from Germany' and 'Antisemitism in Britain'.

48 The Italian neo-fascist *Movimento Soziale Italiano* received 35 seats in the House of Representatives and 15 in the Senate in 1976. Three years later it still had 30 seats in the House and 13 in the Senate. On West Germany see Gitta Sereny, 'Facing up to the new "Hitlerwave" in Germany', *New Statesman*, 19 May 1978, who points out: 'Neo-Nazism as a political force is negligible in Germany.' Also Milton Ellerin and Samuel Rabinove, 'Does Neo-Nazism Have a Future?', *Midstream* (October 1983), pp. 1–6.

49 Christopher T. Husbands, 'The Decline of the National Front', *WLB* (1979), Vol. XXXII, new series, Nos 49/50, pp. 60–6.

50 See 'Harwood's distortion of Holocaust facts', *Patterns of Prejudice*, Vol. 9, No. 3 (May/June 1975), pp. 25ff. Georges Wellers 'La "solution finale de la question juive" et la mythomanie néo-nazie' (Paris, 1977) supplement to No. 86 (April–June 1977) of the review *Le Monde Juif*. C. C. Aronsfeld, 'Whitewashing Hitler: "Revisionist" History Distorters at Work', *Patterns of Prejudice* (January 1980), pp. 16–23.

51 Paul Rose, 'An Obsession with Jews. Antisemitism and the Extreme Right', *Jewish Chronicle*, 3 February 1978, p. 21.

52 For an exhaustive analysis of the 'revisionist' phenomenon, see Pierre Vidal-Naquet, 'Un Eichmann de Papier' in his *Les Juifs, la mémoire et le présent* (Paris, 1981), pp. 195–289.

53 Y. Bauer, *The Holocaust in Historical Perspective* (Seattle, 1978), pp. 38–41.

54 The Holocaust 'revisionists' generally deny any connection with neo-Nazism, but the thematic and historical connection is clearly evident in their publications and the background of many of their leading figures. See Yisrael Gutman, *Denying the Holocaust* (Study Circle on World Jewry in the Home of the President of Israel, Jerusalem, 1985).

55 'Mr. Toynbee and the Jews', *Jewish Frontier* (December 1954), reprinted in the January/February 1983 issue, pp. 30–2. For a perceptive critique of Toynbee's philosophy of history, see Pieter Geyl, *Debates with Historians* (Fontana, 1962), pp. 112–210. Geyl characterized Toynbee's outburst against the Jews as 'amazing' and completely lacking in balance or proportion (p. 190). He attributed it to Toynbee's 'hatred against nationalism in every shape and form'. But this antipathy did not extend to Arab nationalism'.

56 A. Toynbee, *A Study of History* (London, 1954), Vol. X, p. 94.

57 Ibid, Vol. VIII, p. 289.

58 See, for example, Abba Eban, 'The Toynbee Heresy', in M. F. Ashley Montagu (ed.), *Toynbee and History* (Boston, 1956), p. 333.

59 Peter Kaupp, 'Toynbee and the Jews', *WLB* (Winter 1966–67), Vol. XXI, No. 1, new series, No. 6, pp. 21–9.

60 Toynbee, op. cit., Vol. VIII, p. 289.

61 Ibid, Vol. XII (London, 1961), p. 627ff.

62 H. R. Trevor-Roper, 'Arnold Toynbee's Millennium', *Encounter* (London, 1957) Vol. 8, No. 45, p. 17.

63 Toynbee, op. cit., Vol. VIII, p. 290.
64 See Yaacov Herzog, *A People that Dwells Alone* (London, 1975), pp. 21–47. In 1961 Herzog debated with Toynbee at MacGill University, Montreal on the comparison he had made between Israeli behaviour towards Arabs and that of the Nazis towards the Jews. This debate is reproduced in the collection of his speeches and writings listed above.
65 On reactions in France to De Gaulle's remarks, made at a press conference on 27 November 1967, see François Bondy, 'Communist Attitudes in France and Italy to the Six-Day War', in Wistrich (ed.), *The Left against Zion*, op. cit., pp. 180ff.
66 See Henryk M. Broder, 'Antizionismus – Antisemitismus von links?', *Aus Politik und Zeitgeschichte* (supplement to the weekly *Das Parlament*) B 24/76 (12 June 1976) pp. 31–46.
67 Ibid.
68 Rudolf Krämer-Badoni, 'Zionism and the New Left', in Wistrich (ed.), *The Left against Zion*, op. cit., pp. 226–35.
69 Ibid, p. 234.
70 Ibid, p. 250.
71 Gerd Langguth, 'Anti-Israel Extremism in West Germany', in ibid, p. 257.
72 For an account of the proceedings see *Frankfurter Allgemeine Zeitung*, 15 December 1972.
73 Jillian Becker, *Hitler's Children. The story of the Baader–Meinhof Gang* (London, 1977), p. 234.
74 Jillian Becker, 'Another Final Battle on the Stage of History', *Terrorism: An International Journal*, Vol. 5, Nos 1–2 (1981).
75 Ibid.
76 Becker, *Hitler's Children*, op. cit., pp. 17–18.
77 Heinrich Broder, 'You Are No Less Anti-Semites than Your Nazi Parents', *Forum* (Winter 1981), Nos 42/3, pp. 109–17. This is the English translation of Broder's open farewell letter to his former left-wing comrades, originally published in the Hamburg weekly, *Die Zeit*.
78 Ibid, p. 112.
79 Ibid, p. 113.
80 Ibid, p. 117.
81 Jacques Givet, *Israël et le génocide inachevé* (Paris, 1979).
82 Yohanan Manor, 'L'Antisionisme', *Revue française de science politique* (April 1984), Vol. 34, No. 2, pp. 295–322.
83 See Annie Kriegel, *Israël est-il coupable?* (Paris, 1982), p. 41. 'Ce qu'avait été l'antisémitisme au nazisme des années 1930 et 1940, la révélation de l'essence même du projet hitlérien, l'antisionisme l'est désormais au communisme des années 1980.'
84 See Dennis Prager and Joseph Telushkin, 'Why anti-Zionism equals anti-semitism', *Jewish Chronicle*, 30 March 1984, p. 24.
85 Henryk Broder, 'Behind German masks', *Jerusalem Post Magazine*, 10 December 1982, pp. 8–9.
86 C. Aronsfeld, 'Antizionism and the extreme right', *IJA Research Report*, 14 (September 1980).
87 Manor, op. cit., pp. 320ff.
88 Ruth R. Wisse, 'The Delegitimation of Israel', *Commentary* (July 1982), pp. 29–36.
89 Alain Finkielkraut, *Le Juif Imaginaire* (Paris, 1980), pp. 184–5.
90 Ibid, p. 193.

91 See the perceptive diagnosis by Alain Finkielkraut, *L'Avenir d'une négation. Réflexion sur la question du génocide* (Paris, 1982) which touches on some of the points raised here.

92 Kriegel, op. cit., for a detailed analysis of the role of the Communist movement and the PLO in the diffusion, especially in France, of anti-Zionist stereotypes which were then absorbed by the mass media.

## 12 FROM BERLIN TO BEIRUT

1 Interview with the American magazine, *Rolling Stone*, 3 November 1977. Also quoted in Eric Silver, *Begin. A Biography* (London, 1984), p. 8.

2 Silver, op. cit., p. 117.

3 See Jacobo Timerman, *The Longest War. Israel in Lebanon* (New York, 1982), p. 154.

4 Ibid, p. 155.

5 Silver, op. cit., p. 8.

6 Timerman, op. cit., p. 73. Though I share many of Timerman's criticisms of the political abuse of Holocaust imagery in Israel, his own account of the Lebanon war leaves a lot to be desired on empirical grounds. See Robert. S. Wistrich, 'Timerman's Hall of Mirrors', *Partisan Review* (1983), 3, pp. 475–80. Also my 'Israeli Letter', ibid (1983), I, pp. 122–7.

7 Michael R. Marrus, 'Is there a New Antisemitism?', *Middle East Focus* (November 1983), Vol. 6, No. 4, pp. 13–16.

8 Ibid.

9 Edward Alexander, 'The Journalists' War against Israel. Techniques of Distortion, Disorientation and Disinformation', *Encounter* (September–October 1982), pp. 87–97.

10 Ibid, p. 91.

11 See Kriegel, op. cit., and Leon Poliakov, *De Moscou à Beyrouth. Essai sur la désinformation* (Paris, 1983).

12 See Robert Wistrich, 'Between Vienna and Jerusalem. The Strange Case of Bruno Kreisky', *Encounter* (May 1979), pp. 78–84, for an analysis of 'Nazi' and 'Jewish' complexes in Kreisky's view of Israel and Zionism.

13 Ibid, pp. 81–2.

14 See Alexander, op. cit., p. 91, who quotes the Malaysian *New Straits Times'* prognosis (29 June 1982), that 'just as Adolf Hitler's diabolical plan for a "final solution to the Jewish problem" failed to drive the Jews out of Europe, so will Israel's savage efforts to uproot the Palestinians'.

15 Timerman, op. cit., p. 41.

16 Ibid.

17 See Norman Podhoretz, 'J'Accuse', *Commentary* (September 1982) for an incisive critique of the double standards employed by some American liberals and 'progressives' like von Hoffmann, Anthony Lewis and George Ball in writing about Israel.

18 Quoted by Conor Cruise O'Brien, *The Observer*, 26 June 1984.

19 Ibid.

20 Ibid.

21 Ibid.

22 Robert Wistrich, 'The Anti-Zionist Masquerade', op. cit.

23 See John Laffin, *The PLO Connections* (Corgi, 1982).
24 *The Economist*, 7 August 1982.
25 Ibid, 21 August 1982. The letters column contained a number of interesting responses, including that of the fanatically anti-Zionist Professor Israel Shahak from Jerusalem, who grudgingly admitted that 'the Old Testament is not a homogeneous work'.
26 Peter Reading, 'Cub', *Times Literary Supplement*, 23 March 1984.
27 Roger Scruton, 'Race hatred the antis ignore', *The Times*, 3 April 1984.
28 Ibid.
29 See, for example, Tony Greenstein's *Antisemitism's twin in Jewish garb* (Brighton Labour Briefing discussion document, n.d.).
30 *The News Line*, 11 June 1982, p. 2.
31 Ibid, 18 June, 30 June, 10 July 1982.
32 *Young Socialist*, 21 August 1982.
33 *Socialist Worker*, 3 July 1982, Tony Cliff, 'The road from Zionism to Genocide'.
34 'From Malvinas to Lebanon', *Labour Review* (July 1982).
35 Ibid.
36 *The News Line*, 12 July 1982.
37 Sean Matgamna, 'Gerry Healy discovers World Jewish Conspiracy', *Socialist Organiser*, 14 April 1983.
38 Ibid.
39 *Sussex Front* (January 1983).
40 D. Holland, *Israel – the Hate State* (produced as part of *Nationalism Today*, a 20-page magazine which supports the National Front), p. 9. The capitalized last words of the article read: 'ISRAEL MUST BE DESTROYED!'
41 *Caribbean Times*, 2 July 1982.
42 *Labour Herald*, 25 June 1982, p. 7.
43 'London meeting condemns genocide', ibid, 2 July 1982.
44 *Morning Star*, 7 July 1982.
45 H. C. Mullin, 'Zionism and the Holocaust', *Labour Herald*, 19 March 1982.
46 See *Israel – A Racist State* (Socialist Worker Pamphlet No. 3). Also Tony Greenstein, op. cit.
47 Lenni Brenner, *Zionism in the Age of the Dictators* (London, 1983), pp. 267–8.
48 See David Yisraeli, *Ha-Reich Ha-Germani ve Erez Israel* (Ramat-Gan, 1974), pp. 315–17.
49 Brenner, op. cit., p. 269.
50 'The pro-Nazi past of Israel's prime minister', *Socialist Action*, 6 January 1984.
51 'Nazi links catch up with Shamir', *Morning Star*, 2 April 1984.
52 'Shamir and the Nazis', *Labour Herald*, 6 January 1984.
53 Brian Cheyette, 'Revisionism of the Left', *Patterns of Prejudice*, Vol. 17, No. 3 (July 1983), pp. 49–51.
54 Roald Dahl, *Literary Review* (August 1983). This article was reprinted in the mass circulation *Time Out* (18–24 August 1983).
55 Ibid.
56 *New Statesman*, 26 August 1983. It should be pointed out that the *New Statesman* certainly did not sympathize with this outburst.
57 Robert Wistrich, 'The Appeal of Anti-Zionism in Western Europe Today', in *Antisemitism/Anti-Zionism. The Link* (Centre for Contemporary Studies, 1984), pp. 16–20.
58 P. J. Franceschini, 'Une guerre à outrances', *Le Monde*, 30 June 1982.

59  Roger Garaudy, *L'affaire Israel: le sionisme politique* (Paris, 1982), p. 155.
60  *Libération* (Paris), 20 September 1982.
61  *Le Nouvel Observateur* (14/20 August 1982).
62  A. Finkielkraut, *L'Avenir d'une négation*, op. cit., pp. 140–1.
63  Leon Poliakov, op. cit., pp. 163ff.
64  Kriegel, op. cit., pp. 230–2.
65  Ibid, pp. 66–7, for examples of the Nazi–Zionist equation in the fortnightly journal *Afrique-Asie* published in Paris.
66  See Alain Finkielkraut, *La Réprobation d'Israël* (Paris, 1983), pp. 18ff.
67  Ibid, p. 57.
68  Rudolf Pfisterer, 'Le cas allemand', in Poliakov, op. cit., pp. 181–94.
69  Ibid, p. 187.
70  Ibid, p. 188.
71  Finkielkraut, op. cit., pp. 60–1.
72  For a representative if typically one-sided attempt to substantiate the thesis advocated by, among others, Israel Shahak, Chairman of the Israeli League for Human and Civil Rights, that Israel is 'in a process of Nazification', see Patrick Marnham, 'Is Israel racist?', *Spectator*, 6 March 1976. See Robert S. Wistrich, *The Myth of Zionist Racism* (London, 1976, W.U.J.S. publications) for the other side of the coin.
73  See Janet O'Dea, 'Gush Emunim: Roots and Ambiguities', *Forum* (1976), No. 2 (25), pp. 39–50. Also Yigal Elam, '*Gush Emunim* – A False Messianism', *The Jerusalem Quarterly*, No. 1 (Autumn 1976), pp. 60–9.
74  Uriel Tal, 'The Nationalism of Gush Emunim in Historical Perspective', *Forum* (Autumn/Winter 1979), No. 36, pp. 11–14.
75  Ibid, p. 12.
76  See Robert Wistrich, 'Vladimir Jabotinsky – a reassessment', *WLB* (1981), Vol. XXXIV, new series, Nos. 53/54, pp. 41–8.
77  Ibid, pp. 42–3.
78  Shlomo Avineri, *Varieties of Zionist Thought* (Tel Aviv, 1980), in Hebrew, pp. 182–215. Also 'The Political Thought of Vladimir Jabotinsky', *The Jerusalem Quarterly*, No. 16 (Summer 1980), pp. 3–26. In his illuminating article, Avineri rather overstates the 'fascist' component in Jabotinsky.
79  Wistrich, op. cit., p. 46. Avineri, op. cit., *The Jerusalem Quarterly*, pp. 14–16.
80  Avineri, p. 22.
81  Vl. Jabotinsky, 'A Jewish State Now: Evidence submitted to the Palestine Royal Commission by V. Jabotinsky, 11 February 1937'. See Walter Laqueur, *A History of Zionism* (New York, 1976), p. 370.
82  Ibid, p. 61.
83  Avineri, op. cit., pp. 20–1.
84  Yaakov Shavit, 'Revisionism's View of the Arab National Movement', in Shmuel Almog (ed.), *Zionism and the Arabs* (Jerusalem, 1983), pp. 73–94.
85  Ibid, pp. 80–2.
86  Ibid, pp. 86–7.
87  Ibid, pp. 88–9.
88  Avishai Ehrlich, 'The crisis in Israel – danger of Fascism?', *Khamsin*, 5 (1978), pp. 81–108.
89  Ibid, pp. 104–7.
90  Amos Oz, *In the Land of Israel* (Fontana, 1984), p. 87.
91  Ibid, p. 94.

92 See the excellent article by Yehuda Bauer, 'The Place of the Holocaust in Contemporary History', *Studies in Contemporary Jewry*, I, edited by Jonathan Frankel (Bloomington, 1984), pp. 201–24.

93 Dan Diner, 'Israel and the Trauma of the Mass Extermination', *Telos*, No. 57, (Autumn 1983), pp. 41–52.

94 Emil Fackenheim, 'Post-Holocaust Anti-Jewishness, Jewish Identity and Israel', *The Jewish Return into History* (New York, 1978), p. 213.

# Index